Anglo-Saxon Studies 13

TREES IN ANGLO-SAXON ENGLAND
LITERATURE, LORE AND LANDSCAPE

Trees played a particularly important part in the rural economy of Anglo-Saxon England, both for wood and timber and as a wood-pasture resource, with hunting gaining a growing cultural role. But they are also powerful icons in many pre-Christian religions, with a degree of tree symbolism found in Christian scripture too. This wide-ranging book explores both the 'real', historical and archaeological evidence of trees and woodland, and as they are depicted in Anglo-Saxon literature and legend. Place-name and charter references cast light upon the distribution of particular tree species (mapped here in detail for the first time) and also reflect upon regional character in a period that was fundamental for the evolution of the present landscape.

DELLA HOOKE is Honorary Fellow of the Institute for Advanced Research in Arts and Social Sciences at the University of Birmingham.

Anglo-Saxon Studies

ISSN 1475–2468

GENERAL EDITORS
John Hines and Catherine Cubitt

'Anglo-Saxon Studies' aims to provide a forum for the best scholarship on the Anglo-Saxon peoples in the period from the end of Roman Britain to the Norman Conquest, including comparative studies involving adjacent populations and periods; both new research and major re-assessments of central topics are welcomed.

Books in the series may be based in any one of the principal disciplines of archaeology, art history, history, language and literature, and inter- or multi-disciplinary studies are encouraged.

Proposals or enquiries may be sent directly to the editors or the publisher at the addresses given below; all submissions will receive prompt and informed consideration.

Professor John Hines, School of History and Archaeology, Cardiff University, Colum Drive, Cardiff, Wales, UK CF10 3EU

Dr Catherine Cubitt, Centre for Medieval Studies, University of York, The King's Manor, York, England, UK YO1 7EP

Boydell & Brewer, PO Box 9, Woodbridge, Suffolk, England, UK IP12 3DF

Previously published volumes in the series are listed at the back of this book

Trees in Anglo-Saxon England

LITERATURE, LORE AND LANDSCAPE

Della Hooke

THE BOYDELL PRESS

First published 2010
The Boydell Press, Woodbridge
Reprinted 2011
Reprinted in paperback 2013

ISBN 978 1 84383 565 3 hardback
ISBN 978 1 84383 829 6 paperback

The Boydell Press is an imprint of Boydell & Brewer Ltd
PO Box 9, Woodbridge, Suffolk IP12 3DF, UK
and of Boydell & Brewer Inc.
668 Mt Hope Avenue, Rochester, NY 14620–2731, USA
website: www.boydellandbrewer.com

The publisher has no responsibility for the continued existence or accuracy
of URLs for external or third-party internet websites referred to in this book,
and does not guarantee that any content on such websites is,
or will remain, accurate or appropriate.

A catalogue record of this publication is available
from the British Library

Papers used by Boydell & Brewer Ltd are natural, recyclable products
made from wood grown in sustainable forests

Printed and bound in Great Britain by
CPI Group (UK) Ltd, Croydon CR0 4YY

CONTENTS

ILLUSTRATIONS AND TABLES

PREFACE AND ACKNOWLEDGEMENTS

This book developed out of two loves – those of literature and of landscape. In literature and lore, tree symbolism has played a major role throughout history, often attaining a spiritual significance. These sources are explored in the first part of this book, including the role of trees in pre-Christian religion. The second part concentrates upon trees within the actual landscape. Trees are some of the most significant features of our countryside: of undoubted practical value for their produce and timber, they are also a valuable habitat for wildlife, while the distribution of individual species helps to give rise to the varied countryside we cherish. Archaeological evidence is gradually increasing our knowledge of the landscape of Anglo-Saxon England and the presence of particular tree species within it but the vegetation data (mostly derived from pollen sampling) is still sporadic and is only briefly touched upon here. Nevertheless, there is abundant data to be found within charter boundary clauses and early recorded place-names, and the evidence for the distribution of individual species are presented in the third and final part of the book, which also reviews again their symbolism and attributes.

My thanks go to all those who have inspired this work: the late Professor Harry Thorpe, who first introduced me, as an undergraduate, to the richness of pre-Conquest charters, to the late Dr Margaret Gelling, who took me under her wing, and the ecologists I have worked with over many years as a landscape consultant. Grateful thanks, too, are extended to all those colleagues who have made other helpful suggestions, especially Professor Oliver Rackham. I am grateful, too, to the officers of the National Tree Register, especially David Alderman, who have allowed me to include the latest statistical information from the Tree Register, and Jill Butler of the Woodland Trust for her help and encouragement. This publication has been made possible by a grant from the Scouloudi Foundation in association with the Institute of Historical Research. I should like to thank the Revd Tim Sledge for permission to reproduce Plate I, which remains the copyright of Romsey Abbey, and Phoebe Merrick for drawing this sculpture to my attention.

ABBREVIATIONS

*	a postulated form
B	W. de Gray Birch, *Cartularium Saxonicum*, 3 vols (London, 1885–99)
Brit.	British
CBDC	D. Hooke, *Pre-Conquest Charter-Bounds of Devon and Cornwall* (Woodbridge, 1994)
CDEPN	Watts, V. ed., *The Cambridge Dictionary of English Place-Names* (Cambridge, 2004)
EETS	Early EnglishText Society
K	J. M. Kemble, *Codex diplomaticus aevi Saxonici*, 6 vols (London, 1839–48)
ODan	Old Danish
OE	Old English
OHG	Old High German
ON	Old Norse
OSax	Old Saxon
PrW	Primitive Welsh
S	P. H. Sawyer, ed., *Anglo-Saxon Charters. An Annotated List and Bibliography* (London, 1968)
sp	spurious
WaASCB	D. Hooke, *Warwickshire Anglo-Saxon Charter-Bounds* (Woodbridge, 1999)
WoASCB	D. Hooke, *Worcestershire Anglo-Saxon Charter-Bounds* (Woodbridge, 1990)

PART I

Tree Symbolism

1

Trees and Groves in Pre-Christian Belief

Life, death and rebirth – these are all aspects of the symbolism attached to the tree, and are united in much mythological tradition. 'The symbolism of trees is complex: their roots and branches evoked an image of a link between sky and Underworld; their longevity represented continuity and wisdom; the seasonal behaviour of decid-uous trees gave rise to a cyclical symbolism, an allegory of life, death and rebirth.'[1] Some early European traditions envisaged a World Tree, called in Norse mythology *askr Yggdrasill*, 'the ash-tree Yggdrasill', a steed (*drasill*) on which the god Óðinn (also called Yggr) was thought to have hung in voluntary sacrifice in order to acquire hidden knowledge and wisdom: by undergoing ritualistic death he learned the secret of the runes. Christianity substituted a wooden cross for the living tree, but through death Christians believe that Christ suffered for all and gained redemption for all. The World Tree linked the underworld to the heavens and the gods to mankind, the dead to the living – it was, indeed, the backbone of all worlds, an idea met with in a number of ancient religions from across the world. Such ideas must be very ancient. Only a few years ago, coastal erosion on the east coast of Norfolk near Holme-next-the-Sea uncovered a great upturned tree which had been deliberately set with its roots upwards some 4,000 years ago – an oak-tree uprooted in the spring of 2049 BC, just as it would have been bursting into life. This Bronze Age upturned oak in Norfolk may have been a mortuary table to hold the dead but it was enclosed within an oval-shaped stockade of split poles that still carried their bark on the outer side, producing the image of yet another great tree some 6.7 metres (22ft) in diameter and perhaps 3½ metres (12ft) high. Was the central upturned tree reaching down into a perceived underworld, perhaps attempting to unite the world of men with a hidden realm? Was it, as Francis Pryor, an archaeologist closely linked to the lifting operation carried out by English Heritage, believes, an attempt to transfer life from this plane to a parallel, upside-down universe: 'a living organism of this world . . . being offered to the world below the ground, which was possibly seen as the source of all life'?[2] One is also reminded of the *Katha Upanishad*, one of the Hindu Veda texts written between 600 and 300 BC.[3] 'The Tree of Eternity has its roots in heaven above and its branches reach down to the earth. It is Brahman, pure Spirit, who in truth is called Immortal. All the worlds rest in that Spirit and beyond him no one can go.'[4] The Indian Cosmic Tree seems to have been unlike most other trees in this respect but it may not have been alone (the idea re-emerges in the twelfth-century Jewish *Kabbala*).[5]

The tree of life is probably the most ancient and seemingly universal symbol. Symbols in southern European caves that have been interpreted as the Tree of Life appear to date from the palaeolithic period.[6] It appears, too, in Sumerian art from *c.*3000 BC and permeated most sophisticated religions of the Near East. It is met with in the writings of ancient Egypt and in Ottoman poetry, perpetuated in the woven designs of many Near Eastern cultures. At the time that Christianity was establishing itself (for the trees of the Garden of Eden see Chapter 2) the Persians also recognised a World Tree that stood at the centre of Paradise as 'the oldest living thing, and the nourisher of all', and in Islam 'a magnificent and gigantic tree called Tooba' provided shade and fruit to mortals.[7] The tree might be regarded 'as a symbol of divine beings or as the locus of numinous powers'.[8] The deciduous tree with its annually replaced leaves might become a symbol of the rebirth of life while the evergreen might become a symbol of immortality.

Why should particular trees be regarded as sacred? The tree spreads downwards and upwards; like Yggdrassill its roots and branches may unite several different mythological 'worlds' in the minds of early peoples – the underworld, the earth and the heavens. This is surely also the concept expressed in the 'upside-down' tree of Bronze Age Norfolk. Pryor notes the beliefs of the Saami (Lapps), who also see the world as a three-part cosmos. This would envisage the tree as a means of drawing the different worlds together, 'a way of communicating between our world and the world below ground'.[9]

The tree is also bountiful – the forest was one of the earliest life-support systems known to early man, and the tree of especial bounty is a feature of many early cultures, whether real or imaginary. The tree, the most prominent feature of the forest, was a natural feature to be protected. Vulnerable and fragile ecosystems were frequently regarded as sacred in traditional law and customs. 'On land, trees and forests are as important as earth and water';[10] they are part of *Rita*, the cosmic law and order which regulates the universe and is probably best interpreted in present-day language as the laws of nature, something to be respected for man's survival: 'He who waters the seed of the Forest, has flowers and fruits in abundance.'[11] Trees are not only of importance for their fruit and other properties but play an unprecedented role in conserving soil fertility and moisture, their role in the dynamics of the ecosystem only now admitted in many 'modern' societies. Moreover, to earlier peoples, the tree was 'god-given' – not the result of man's early agricultural enterprises. Unlike a man, it could rise again from death: 'A tree when it is felled springs up from its root in a newer form; from what root does man spring forth when he is cut off by death?'[12] At a very early date, particular trees received special reverence: *Ficus religiosa* was noted for its bountifulness in India and worshipped even before the arrival of Indo-European culture; elsewhere it was *Cedrus deodara* that was regarded as 'God's tree'. The reason for selecting particular species may not always be immediately apparent: in Bali, Indonesia, the *rudraksha* tree (*Eleocarpus ganeti*) has, among other species, been conserved in temple complexes because it symbolises worship and divinity as possessing the aspect of Shiva's third eye, food for the spirit.[13] To the Celts, it seems that it was the oak-tree which they held most sacred, the reasons for which will be discussed in later chapters.

Some consider that the veneration of trees was part of an animistic belief that the trees themselves were embodiments of the spirits of dead ancestors.[14] However, it seems more likely that it was not the trees themselves that were magical, but the fact that they were the dwelling places of deities whose 'hidden presence . . . is seen only by the eye of reverence'.[15] Within the Hindu religion, however, a supreme being can be worshipped in innumerable forms, which might vary from a majestic or handsome human being to a featureless stone (or, presumably, a tree) and, indeed, every tree and river has a divine being associated with it.[16] The tree and its god could not be separated.

It was not, however, only individual living trees that were singled out, for the veneration of trees, either as individual specimens or as groups within sacred groves, was once widespread across Europe and found in many other parts of the world, especially in those regions sharing a common Indo-European ancestry. However, tree cults go back far into antiquity, way before they emerge among the Germanic races, and permeate many ancient cultures world-wide. They may have very early origins. Many hunter-gatherer societies had sacred groves and it is not unlikely that the practice goes back into palaeolithic times. The tree symbols in the caves of southern Europe, if this is what they are, have also been interpreted as a ladder to the cosmos, connecting light and darkness, and such symbols are traced later throughout Europe, Asia and North America.[17] Most early societies seem to have envisaged a world populated by spirit beings, with animals and plants seen as sentient entities to be approached with awe and respect, even when hunted or felled. Like the Celtic druids, pre-Christian Siberian shamans went on spirit journeys in sacred groves and forests and were ultimately, at death, placed upon a tree platform in order for their spirits to return to the other world: 'the tree with its roots in the ground, its trunk on the earth and the branches in the sky, was a model of the cosmos'.[18] Deities dwelt in particular places, and groves were but one example of such a place – wondrous, hidden and secretive, especially as, in time, more and more land was cleared for agriculture. Man was but a part of nature.

Some early peoples practised divination and/or blood sacrifice in sacred groves. The link between trees and divination is exemplified in literary references to 'the tree of knowledge' (see Chapter 2); in part, this is further associated with the tree's perceived connection to the underworld, where the spirits of the ancestors remained a source of knowledge and past learning, and to that of the gods in the heavens above. To keep the practice of sacrifice in perspective it must be realised that it was seldom carried out as simple blood lust: sacrificial victims might act as 'messengers'. In some societies it is even possible that eminent members of that society may have volunteered to act as intermediaries to the gods and to the ancestors, uniting with them in the 'otherworld'. Some of the bodies found deposited in bogs have had an almost serene expression upon their faces at death, as if aware and in acceptance of their destined role (although most appear to have been brutally murdered); sometimes special victims may have been chosen – children and virgins were deemed most pure. If gods had to be thanked for victory then prisoners taken in battle might be sacrificed, but eventually it was more usual to propitiate the gods with animal sacrifice. Sheep and goats are still sacrificed in sacred groves among the Kikuyu tribe of Africa.[19] In at least one instance, the sacrifice of sheep within a grove was perpetuated by the Christian Church: Christians in Armenia still carry out this practice.[20]

Along the northern fringes of the Roman Empire in Europe, in what is now north Germany and the Jutland peninsula, lived Germanic tribes, which were emerging as expansionist tribal kingdoms by the third century AD, and again it is from Roman historians, especially Tacitus, that we hear of their spiritual beliefs. He noted how they also practised divination and human sacrifice in holy groves, in some of which they kept sacred white horses (see below).[21] Here, in such a liminal locality, 'was the gateway to the underworld of spirits that was unlocked by ritual'.[22] The druid priests of the Celtic peoples, too, practised divination by blood sacrifice within oak groves. Established in the west of the British Isles (see below), the 'Celts' were part of an assemblage of peoples sharing a common family of languages rather than a blood relationship. While Classical writers spoke of the *Keltoi* having once been present in central Europe during the Iron Age, expanding westwards into Gaul and the western littoral, others have been less certain of large-scale migration having taken place, at least into Britain.[23] In Caesar's time the language appears to have been spoken in southern Gaul but it was to 'Albion' that students turned for training in the druid religion (see below).

In all this, then, the British Isles were something of a melting pot. Successive cultures were introduced by trade, cultural contact and/or warfare, to be assimilated and adapted. Much new cultural contact came directly from Western Europe, carried first to eastern and south-eastern England across the shortest sea-ways, but other influences followed a more westerly route. With the so-called 'Anglo-Saxon conquest', additional folk entered the country, largely from the Low Countries and the North Sea coastlands. Ireland retained its 'Celtic' culture when the Romans dominated England, Wales and southern Scotland; the Anglo-Saxons failed to reach it, although the Vikings became strongly established along its eastern coasts. Eventually it was to be Christianity that would be the unifying factor, but in Ireland ancient traditions were absorbed rather than totally eradicated. Christianity was to eradicate tree *worship* for ever but tree *symbolism* would not be lost, especially in Ireland and within the Christian Orthodox Church elsewhere in Europe.

THE EVIDENCE OF ARCHAEOLOGY

Early beliefs were undoubtedly heavily embroidered in medieval literary sources and it is difficult to disentangle those that genuinely stem from a purely pagan past. Archaeological evidence, such as that from Holme-next-the-Sea, offers unequivocal proof of ritual involving tree symbolism, and there are other instances of this in the archaeological record, although the interpretation of such data is bound to be little more than guesswork. Wooden posts have been found in Neolithic long barrows, occasionally deliberately broken after the interment. Deliberate damage to ritual objects and worldly goods is a common feature of early burial and of votive offerings in watery locations, and appears to involve the conveyance of such objects into the spirit world. Such votive offerings have often been found in locations close to the sea – in estuaries or intertidal zones, liminal areas on the fringe of human occupation. In some cases, wooden figures have been found, sometimes in association with trackways, such as those found buried with the wooden trackways which were laid down across the wetlands of the Somerset Levels in the prehistoric period. On the Somerset trackways the figures may have been ancestor figures guarding the route and perhaps preventing the passage of evil spirits or unwanted persons.

Even the species of wood used to make the prehistoric wooden figures used as votive offerings in Britain and Ireland from the Neolithic to the Iron Age seems to have been significant. (Many seem to show affinities with Scandinavian rock art.) Two oak figures from Lagore in eastern Ireland (2135–1944 cal BC) and from Kingsteignton in Devon (426–352 cal BC) have unambiguously male genitals, while a figure from Ballachulish, western Scotland (728–524 cal BC), carved from alder wood, is obviously female. (The small wooden figure from Ballachulish appears to have been associated with a wicker structure and was apparently 'pinned down' with hurdles, as if it was a substitute for earlier offerings of humans as 'bog bodies' in similar locations.)[24] Other figures are of ash (including those found buried with the wooden trackways of the Somerset Levels), or of evergreen pine or yew.[25] The latter are distinguished by a hole in the pubic region and often show damage to the left side of the face. Coles notes the later literary associations of the oak with Jupiter or Þórr; and of the ash with the ancestor figure of the first man, Askr, who was allegedly brought to life from an ash log found by Óðinn on the seashore, and, perhaps, with the Scandinavian World Tree Yggdrasill (although the yew has also been suggested, because Yggdrasill was evergreen).[26] She further discusses the role of wooden figures in shamanistic rites associated with Óðinn, and the sexual ambiguity of this god who was to sacrifice an eye to gain the knowledge of the runes when he hung upon Yggdrasill: obvious connotations with the figures in evergreen yew or pine which show damage to the left eye together with sexual ambiguity. These have been dated to 2351–2139 cal BC (Dagenham, Greater London), 1096–906 cal BC (Ralaghan, Ireland), and 606–509 cal BC (Roos Carr assemblage from East Yorkshire). Þórr was to replace Óðinn in popularity by the first millennium AD and mark a move away from shamanism.

Many of the early timbered henges must also have resembled a forest of tall trees, although the raising and subsequent removal of posts appears to have been an essential part of the ritual, and it is unlikely that excavated postholes signify posts that were all in existence at the same time. At the Neolithic Sanctuary on Overton Hill, Avebury, in Wiltshire, two of the seven circles seem to have consisted of repeatedly renewed posts, tall oak posts (possibly carved or painted) set into pits in the chalk but removed before they had time to rot;[27] their erection was obviously part of a recurrent ceremony, albeit it at a permanent site. On the Continent, too, an enormous wooden post, perhaps as high as 12 metres, stood at the centre of an enclosure known as the Goloring in Germany, built in the sixth century BC.[28] Large posts were present at other ceremonial sites. In Ireland, five circles of oak posts with a massive oak pillar in the centre, visible for miles, represented a ceremonial Celtic centre in about 100 BC at Navan Fort in Armagh, the site of the legendary court of Eamhain Mhacha, an entirely ceremonial centre.[29] Ó hÓgáin sees this as an example of 'a sort of "world-tree", at the sacred centre of the community's territory with a ceremonial function of linking the earth with the skies. As such it would have been a symbol of the prosperity of the tribe or sept, and important ceremonies would have centred on it'.[30] There were great timber posts, too, set in a circle within the Iron Age enclosure of Aillind at Knockaulin, Co. Kildare, one of the largest hillforts in Ireland. As at Navan Fort, no sign of settlement has been found, and the centre appears to have been entirely one for ritual usage. Such traditions were incorporated into 'historical' narrative. Aillind is situated in what was the heart of the territory of the Leinstermen, who in the sixth and seventh century claimed that their own great king, Find File, had ruled 'round Aillin'.[31]

In England, too, Iron Age sites have produced evidence of ritual trees or pillars set within enclosures. In the West Midland region, a single tree seems to have stood within an enclosure some 20 metres across, situated within a Middle Iron Age settlement at Bubbenhall in Warwickshire, almost certainly a ceremonial site, and similar evidence has been found at Longford, Gloucestershire.[32] At Uley, in the Gloucestershire Cotswolds, a tree or post may have marked another such centre on West Hill, perhaps one associated with an ancestral cult, and the tradition of the presence of a sacred tree may have been transferred to the yew, which gave rise to the place-name here.[33] Although the sacredness of tree symbolism was dispelled by Christianity (see Chapter 2) a tree cult might be absorbed or linger on in folk tradition (see Chapter 4). In Northumbria, a large posthole feature had stood before the royal palace and assembly place of *Ad Gefrin*, Yeavering, perhaps a symbol of royal power and place of judgement at a major centre of assembly for an early-seventh-century Anglian kingdom that had inherited strong British traditions.[34]

It has been suggested that the use of timber, as opposed to stone, in early monuments may not have been entirely fortuitous. Stone, with its non-changing nature, may have been the symbol of the dead and of the ancestors, while wood may have been the symbol of the living, just as it was itself living – the amount of occupation debris at the timber henges of southern England has long been a source of puzzlement. Even with votive deposits, stone objects have been found in different locations from those made from wood.[35]

> Like humans, trees are polyvalent and 'imaginatively provocative', and may become embedded in the identity of places. But the essential ambiguity of trees is perhaps the most powerful source of their metaphoric vibrance: they are alive and yet seemingly not alive; they have a celestial and a chthonic dimension; they are vulnerable and powerful; they seem to embrace nature and structure; even when dead, they may still stand and remain part of the forest for many years. The forest is a beneficial life-force, a world in microcosm providing an entire ecosystem for woodland creatures, but it can also be dark, mysterious and full of risk. Cyclicity, seasonality and apparent death in winter are all woven into the symbolic currency of trees; they are changeful (particularly if deciduous) but enduring elements in the landscape.[36]

The columns of Greek temples, surmounted by their wreaths of foliage, also seem to have symbolised tree trunks. In Classical cultures, the tree might be depicted by a stone column, often dedicated to an important personage but one who stood on a pillar that was decorated to suggest a tree. In Gaulish iconography the column might represent 'a cosmic pillar which at once divides and unites sky and earth . . . The cosmic pillar would therefore represent the joining together of the high sky and the underground depths'[37] (a recurrent theme noted in this chapter). Such an image seems to be portrayed by the Norse Yggdrasill, although Ó hÓgáin argues that the original cosmic pillar would have stood in the sea.[38]

LITERARY EVIDENCE

Classical writers in the Greek and Roman world have left a great deal of information about the role of trees and groves in their spiritual culture. The twenty-second *Idyll* attributed to Theocritus (third century BC) notes how the divine twins Castor and Pollux wandered into a kind of paradise untouched by man 'where trees of all sorts grew wild on the hillside . . . Tall pines grew beside [a brimming spring], and poplars, plane trees, and cypresses'.[39] Many Greek and Roman gods were associated with individual trees and groves. The chief god of Rome, Jupiter Feretrius, was worshipped in the form of a sacred tree, probably an oak. According to Pausanias, writing in the second century AD in Greece, images were carved on selected trees and dedicated to divinities – a wooden image of Dionysus in ancient Corinth, trees dedicated to Helen of Troy at Rhodes, a myrtle tree at Boeae held sacred to Artemis, and so on.[40] Many of the religious rites associated with priestly and kingly power had taken place in sacred groves; that of Zeus at Dodona in Epirus, at the foot of Mount Tomarus in north-western Greece, was a grove of oaks which had flourished for over two thousand years. Here oracles were delivered through the rustling of the oak leaves, interpreted by priests and priestesses (but in some versions, such as that of Herodotus, the most holy tree is described not as an oak but as a beech). In mythological tradition, the sacred grove of Nemi at Aricia near Rome was the home of 'the priest-king who served the oak goddess Diana. He bore the name *Rex Nemorensis*, the "King of the Wood"'. He was the personification of the god Jupiter, and Frazer recounts how he remained there until his power was challenged (by one who had first plucked a branch – the 'Golden Bough' – from a certain sacred tree in the temple grove) and how he was killed in personal battle.[41] There are also Classical allusions to trees that offered the right to asylum, such as the holy tree at Ephesus, where the Amazons sought refuge, or Apollo's laurel, where Orestes, fleeing from the Furies, sought sanctuary.[42] In the garden of the Hesperides, the daughters of Atlas guarded the 'rich, golden apples' (symbols of immortality) given by Hera to Zeus at their wedding. Like the paradisal woods conjured up by Theocritus, a 'grove exceedingly beautiful and well supplied with flowing streams' sheltered the place or shrine of Amaltheia, the goat-nymph and goddess of fertility, in the *Deipnosophists* of Athanaeus.[43] Nature's sacred groves provided the setting for such gods and goddesses.

Early Classical writers are also the main sources of knowledge of the tribal groups of Gaul and the regions beyond the Roman Empire, as noted above. They are also one of our main sources of knowledge of pagan tree worship beyond their own homelands. The names of several tribal groups imply tree veneration: the Eburones (among Caesar's left-bank Germani in what is now part of Belgium and Germany, invaded by him in 55 BC) were the 'Yew Tribe' and the Lemovices the 'People of the Elm'.[44] In many cases, trees stood in sacred groves, dark, mysterious and secret places. Writing of the Celtic priests, the druids, Pliny claims 'They choose groves formed of oaks for the sake of the tree alone, and they never perform any of their rites except in the presence of a branch of it; so that it seems probable that the priests themselves may derive their name from the Greek word for that tree'.[45] Ó hÓgáin believes that this is based on the supposition that the initial element in *drui(d)s* was the word for the oak-tree (Gaulish *dervo-*, Irish *dair*) compounded in *dervo-wid-es* to give 'oak-wisdom possessor' when the element for wisdom (*wid-*) had become confused with the term for a wood (*vidu-*), the oak in particular thus becoming associated with druids. The oak had, however, been regarded as a sacred life-giving tree since palaeolithic times.[46] For the druids, the mistletoe growing upon the oak (not commonly found on this tree) was especially sacred, the combination of the two more potent species. The mistletoe was believed to possess the power of both healing and fertility. It may be significant that Lindow Man, whose body was found, apparently sacrificed, in a bog known as Lindow Moss in Cheshire, had mistletoe pollen in his gut. This was probably part of a ritual meal eaten before he succumbed to the 'threefold' death by strangulation, pole-axing and throat-cutting, in the mid-first century AD.[47]

The sacrifice of victims in sacred groves was common throughout Europe. Tacitus notes how, among the Suebi tribes of Germany, the Semnones considered their sacred grove to be *tamquam inde initia gentis, ibi regnator omnium deus, cetera subiecta atque parentia* ('the cradle of the race and the dwelling-place of the supreme god to whom all things are subject and obedient').[48] Thus they met in 'a certain forest' at fixed times where they publicly offered up a human life: *in silvam auguriis patrum et prisca formidine sacram* ('in a grove hallowed by the auguries of their ancestors and by immemorial awe').[49] Elsewhere, traitors and deserters were tried at an assembly and those found guilty were hung upon trees.[50] Germanicus felled the sacred groves across the Rhine in his campaigns of AD 15–17, and Tacitus describes the gruesome sights which met the Roman armies as they entered the forests of Westphalia: skulls nailed to tree trunks (probably offered in sacrifice), and woodland altars where captives had been slain.[51] But other practices were less blood-thirsty: he also notes how German kings might be chosen by the interpretation of auguries proclaimed by the neighing of sacred white horses, 'undefiled by any toil in the service of man' and pastured in such sacred woods and groves.[52] Animals were often considered to act as meaningful links, able to mediate in intellectual exchange between the worlds of men, gods and animals.

The goddess of a group of tribes including the Anglii, Nerthus, also inhabited 'an inviolate grove' which was located on an island in the sea. She was attended only by a priest who was able to sense her presence. From time to time she would visit the countryside in her chariot drawn by cows and during her stay wars would cease, every iron object would be locked away and the country would enjoy peace. When she grew weary of the company of men she would retire to her sacred precinct and the chariot would be cleansed in a secluded lake by slaves, who would then be drowned immediately afterwards in the lake. 'Thus mystery begets terror and a pious reluctance to ask what that sight can be which is seen only by men doomed to die'.[53]

It has been noted above that the Celtic priests, the druids, also worshiped in sacred oak groves, and the Roman historians again wrote with horror of the supposed activities of the druids in such places. Caesar felled a sacred Celtic grove near Marseilles in the first century BC, which was described by Lucan:

The axe-men came on an ancient and sacred grove. Its interlacing branches
enclosed a cool central space into which the sun never shone, but where
an abundance of water sprouted from dark springs . . . the barbaric gods
worshipped here had their altars heaped with hideous offerings, and every
tree was sprinkled with human blood . . . Nobody dared enter this grove
except the priest; and even he kept out at midday, and between dawn and
dusk – for fear that the gods might be abroad at such hours.[54]

Within the grove, Lucan refers to several different kinds of tree – yew, oak, ash,
alder and cypress – but the grove remained a place apart from the earthly world.[55]
Human sacrifice appears to have been as much a part of this religion as it was of
Germanic cultures. The Romans thought that the druidic religion had been intro-
duced into Gaul from Britain. Indeed, in the Irish tale of the *Táin Bó Cuailgne*,
Fedelm, a woman poet of Connacht, claims to have learnt her 'verse and vision' in
'Alba', although this name was not always restricted to England.[56] In narrating the
Roman campaigns in Britain, Tacitus describes the attack upon Anglesey and its
druidic stronghold in AD 60 by Suetonius Paulinus:

On the shore stood the opposing army with its dense array of armed warriors,
while between the ranks dashed women in black attire like the Furies, with
hair dishevelled, waving brands. All around, the druids, lifting up their hands
to heaven and pouring forth dreadful imprecations, scared our soldiers by
the unfamiliar sight, so that, as if their limbs were paralysed, they stood
motionless and exposed to wounds. Then urged by their general's appeal and
mutual encouragements not to quail before a troop of frenzied women, they
bore the standards onwards, smote all resistance, and wrapped the foe in the
flames of their own brands. A force was next set over the conquered; and
their groves, devoted to inhuman superstitions, were destroyed.[57]

It is difficult to know the truth behind such writings. It was not tree worship that
worried the Romans, and before accepting Christianity this was as much part of their
culture as it was of the 'barbarian' tribes. Neither could they have argued that it was
the abhorrent rites that were carried out in the groves that appalled them for some
of their own 'sports' and events that had taken place in amphitheatres throughout
the Roman world had been equally blood-thirsty. It is more likely that they were
determined to exterminate druidism because it focused and united native resistance
against Rome.[58]

IRISH TRADITION

It is in Ireland that 'Celtic' tradition survived longest. The earliest literary sources
appear to incorporate much from earlier beliefs. In addition to the druidical groves,

the Irish tradition also had a legendary Otherworld tree, one that bore 'blossoms and fruit of gold and silver, making music when shaken and healing sickness and despair. It is usually pictured as an apple tree, although the great trees of the past are sometimes described as bearing mixed fruit of apples, acorns and nuts.[59] Sometimes branches bearing such gold and silver fruit were brought by visitants from the Otherworld, as in the *Echtrae Cormaic* when a warrior bearing a branch with three golden apples visits Cormac at Tara. This may be a very ancient tradition: a golden 'tree' with hanging golden fruit or leaves was found in the Iron Age *oppidum* of Manching near Ingelstadt in Bavaria, dating from the third century BC.[60] In a seventh- to eighth-century text, *Immrain Brain*, from east Ulster, there is an hint of the tree which upheld the world, apparently supporting the Isle of Man, then known as Eumania or, later, Eamhain: this had 'four legs of white silver', but was perhaps a confused echo of the great tree-trunk and timber stakes which had stood within the structure of the Eamhain Mhacha, the assembly place of the Ulster kingship (Navan hillfort, a few miles west of Armagh city; the name may have been a play on the word *emuin*, 'twin', regarding otherworld islands as the doubles of the mound).[61]

Particular trees also occupy a prominent place in later Celtic mythology, a sacred tree being referred to as a *bile*. The five great legendary trees of Ireland included an oak (here the term *eó* can be used for other species than the more usual 'yew'[62]), a yew, and three ashes which stood at the centre of five provinces and were of such a size that they spread over the entire province, able to shelter the whole population of the tribe (see Chapter 4).[63] These trees were regarded as the source of sacred wisdom and were closely associated with the druid priests as the men of learning responsible for maintaining forms of sacred wisdom, the poet replacing the priest as the last vestige of the old religious order.[64] (It is interesting that five is also a cardinal number in Indian belief, standing for entirety, as expressed in the five great trees of Sanskrit tradition, although the species included might differ regionally.)[65] There were additional sacred trees in Irish legends, about which rather less is known.[66] The yew occupied a special position as the symbol of both death and immortality. Such a view was apparently widespread: in Roman literature the yew was frequently associated with poison, death and the underworld, a concept taken at an early stage into the beliefs of continental tribes, while 'at the same time its evergreen nature made it a symbol of immortality'.[67] Elliott argues that it was in Britain that reverence for the yew flourished. Wands of yew were used for divination, and ogham characters were often inscribed upon them, thus doubling their efficacy (see further Chapter 3); these are mentioned in early folklore.[68] King Conchobar of Ulster's palace was also built of yew wood.

One of the oldest legends, however, concerns the hazel. The area of the River Boyne, in the Iron Age in the 'middle' province of Midhe, was particularly sacred, and legends associated with it may incorporate pre-Celtic ritual and belief. At Newgrange stands a great megalithic tomb that seems to have been regarded as a sacred centre of ancestral power, which had links with the world of the dead and, through them, with the other world. It is at this tomb that the rays of the sun at the midwinter solstice briefly penetrate into the inner chamber, presaging the end of dark winter and the rebirth of the sun.[69] To the Celts, the sun-god Daghdha became resident in the tumulus. But another ancient goddess, possibly of pre-Celtic origin, dwelt at the source of the Boyne, the name of whom was *Bou-vinda (known to Ptolemy in the early second century AD as 'Buvinda') 'the white lady with bovine attributes', in later form *Bóinn*. At her residence was a well surrounded by nine hazel-trees, from which nuts fell into the water (again described in the *Echtrae Cormaic* 'The Adventure of Cormac'). These nuts contained *imbas*, the all-encompassing knowledge claimed by the druidic seers, and the river became pregnant with this wisdom, so that anyone drinking its water in June would become a poet. Much has been surmised about the 'white goddess'[70] and the ancient 'earth mother', but several stories describe an illicit union between Bóinn and the Daghdha that resulted in the birth of a son, Aonghus, thus representing the new sun replacing the old one at midwinter in the tumulus, perhaps a very ancient belief indeed.[71] The similarities between such a belief and the Sanskrit *Rig Veda*, in which the cow is repeatedly used as a metaphor for the river goddess, suggest an ancient Indo-European origin for the myth and show how closely ancient beliefs of widely distributed cultural traditions were interlinked.

The role of sacred springs is also manifest in pre-Christian European cultures. A pagan silent, sacred well is noted on the island of Fosikeland (Heligoland) in Alcuin's *Life of St Willibrord*, written in the eighth to early ninth century; early Irish sources, drawing upon ancient Celtic beliefs, also refer to sacred springs, often associated with healing.[72] In later legend, the presence of a certain tree might augment the power of such a spring (see Chapter 4).

NORSE TRADITION

The Celtic druid religion had been finally vanquished by the Romans in the first century AD, but it was the Germanic tribes, including the Vandals and Visigoths from east of the Danube, who were to gradually break the might of the Roman Empire and its Classical culture in the late fourth and early fifth centuries AD. Eventually most Germanic kingdoms were, in turn, to accept Christianity, but again another heathen group was to emerge, who would trade, invade and settle along the coastal regions of Europe – the Vikings, from what is now Scandinavia. Details of their tree rituals survive in considerable detail because they were described in medieval literature when they were still well known.

The Norse Yggdrasill was a giant ash-tree which extended from the underworld (sometimes seen as Niflheimr, the realm of Hel and the abode of the dead) to the

Figure 1. Yggdrasill, an image based upon a
seventeenth-century Icelandic manuscript

heavens, linking the cosmos (Fig. 1). Beneath its roots was the well of Urðr or
destiny, a realm denied and unknown to man.[73] Waters from the well kept the tree
alive despite constant attack from gnawing animals. From its branches fell the dews
that would, in turn, replenish the well: all power coming from beneath the tree
but constantly folded back into its base in a continuous cycle of activity. Within
Urðr were thus enfolded the actions of all beings who existed within the enclosing
branches of Yggdrasill, drawn into a past which remains the driving power of the
present: 'Urth, whose well it is and whose name brings the active power of all
accomplished action to bear upon the cosmic self-generating activity . . . expressive
of all that animates the realms of both tree and well'.[74]

The Yggdrasill legend is a relatively late form of tree symbolism but embodies
many older beliefs – no other Germanic literature of the Middle Ages has the same

quantity of pre-Christian material.[75] It is described in the *Edda* of Snorri Sturluson (d. 1241) and in the *Poetic Edda* (consisting of traditional poems recorded in the thirteenth century), for example in *Völuspá* st. 19.

> Asc veit ec standa,   heitir Yggdrasill,
> hár baðmr, ausinn   hvítaauri;
> þaðan koma dǫggvar,   þærs í dala falla,
> stendr æ yfir, grœnn,   Urðar brunni.

> 'I know that an ash-tree stands called Yggdrasill,
> a high tree, soaked with shining loam;
> from there come the dews which fall in the valley,
> ever green, it stands over the well of fate.'[76]

Snorri Sturluson's works reveal that Yggdrasill grew in the middle of Ásgarðr, the world of the gods, itself part of middle earth. Its three roots encompassed the world – that of humans, giants, and the Otherworld; its top reached the sky. At the root of the tree, usually described as an ash, was the serpent, Níðhöggr. To some this represented ancient earth (female) energies while the eagle at the top of the tree was associated with the energies of the sky (male);[77] within its branches lived the four deer from whose antlers fell the dew to water the earth. The tree itself was not eternal but underwent constant regeneration. Three maids, known as the Norns, who were said to live in a nearby hall, sprinkled water daily from the spring of Urðr over the ash to prevent its limbs from withering (i.e. keep it 'evergreen'), but the tree constantly suffered more than men can know, its limbs, according to *Grímnismál*, eaten by a goat and a hart, its roots gnawed by the serpent Níðhöggr.

Individual real trees could partake of this sanctity and might symbolise the World Tree. In the eleventh-century writings of Adam of Bremen the author describes what he has learnt of the temple at Uppsala in central Sweden, the ancient burial place of kings. Gamla Uppsala is said to have been the political, religious and economic centre of the Svear and, into the eleventh century, of the Yngling dynasty whose kings were also leaders in the cult of Freyr, the Norse god of fertility. Recent archaeological excavations have identified the site of a major timbered hall on a plateau at the end of a ridge behind the church, with a hall *c*.30m in length and 12m in width, which was used from the early seventh century to the late eighth century, when it was burned down and never rebuilt.[78] Later tradition claims that the church stands on the site of a 'most splendid temple' in which were the gold-coloured statues of Þórr, Óðinn and Freyr (Fricco), and next to it a grove in which, according to Adam, sacrifices would be made every ninth year: 'of every living thing that is male, they offer nine heads, and with the blood of which it is customary to placate gods of this sort. The bodies they hang in the sacred grove that adjoins the temple. Now this grove is so sacred in the eyes of the heathen that each and every tree in it is believed divine because of the death or putrifaction of the victims. Even dogs and horses hang there with men.'[79] But Adam refers also to an enormous tree which stood beside the temple:

> Prope illud templum est arbor maxima late ramos extendens, semper viridis in hieme et aestate; cuius illa generis sit, nemo scit. Ibi etiam est fons, ubi sacrificia paganorum solent exerceri et homo vivus inmergi. Qui dum non invenitur, ratum erit votum populi.

> 'Near this temple stands a very large tree with wide-spreading branches, always green winter and summer. What kind it is nobody knows. There is also a spring at which the pagans are accustomed to make their sacrifices, and into it to plunge a live man. And if he is not found, the people's wish will be granted.'[80]

This is not the description of an eyewitness and neither the temple nor the grove have ever been identified archaeologically, but this tradition may encapsulate the mythological Yggdrasill and the well of Urðr; the sacrifices may have been genuine, the disappearance of the body in the well signifying that the gift had found acceptance below, the present carried into the past.[81]

Adam of Bremen also reveals something about pre-Christian Slavic religion, for he notes how a sacred forest protected the tribal and cult centre of the Redars at Radogosc, the seat of assembly for a powerful tribe that controlled a vast territory stretching from the Oder to the Elbe and from the Havel to the Baltic. Here the temple of the deity stood alone 'within a triangular stronghold, adjacent to a lake and surrounded by a forest untrodden by the natives'. Through this secrecy the leaders were able to control worship of the deity, this power helping to maintain their political as well as spiritual leadership over other tribes, from whom they drew tribute to maintain the sanctuary.[82]

The golden apples of ancient Greek, continental and Celtic mythology also resurface in Nordic tales, still regarded as the apples of perpetual youth. The precious tree which bore them was in this tradition guarded by the goddess Iðunn. She was, however, lured away by Loki and the loss of the apples caused the gods to become weak and old and to be faced with the fear of death. Óðinn, however, the chief god of Norse and Germanic mythology, was able to gather his remaining strength and, by threatening Loki with the forces of magic, force him to return Iðunn and the magic apples. This story shows again how closely intertwined were the ancient mythologies of European and Near Eastern culture, some of them still circulating in the early medieval period.

ENDNOTES

[1] M. J. Green, *Celtic Myths* (London, 1993), p. 50.

[2] F. Pryor, *Seahenge, New Discoveries in Prehistoric Britain* (London, 2001), p. 277.

[3] G. Flood, *An Introduction to Hinduism* (Cambridge, 1996), pp. 37–9.

[4] *Katha Upanishad* VI: *The Upanishads. Translation from the Sanskrit with an Introduction by Juan Mascaró* (London/Harmondsworth, 1965), p. 65.

[5] S. K. Prem, *The Yoga of the Kathopanishad* (Ahmedabad, 1982); F. Hagender, *The Heritage of Trees. History, Culture and Symbolism* (Edinburgh, 2001), pp. 162–5.

[6] Hagender, *The Heritage of Trees*, p. 31.

[7] Ibid., pp. 66, 81.

[8] U. Becker, *The Continuum Encyclopedia of Symbols* (New York and London, 1992), pp. 305–8.

[9] Pryor, *Seahenge*, p. 278.

[10] M. Vannucci, 'Sacredness and sacred forests', in *Conserving the Sacred for Biodiversity Management*, ed. P. S. Ramakrishnan, K. G. Saxena and U. M. Chandrashekara (Enfield, New Hampshire, 1998), pp. 18–19.

[11] B. Saraswati, 'The logos and the mythos of the sacred grove', in *Conserving the Sacred*, p. 45.

[12] *Brhad-āranyaka Upaniṣad* III.9.28: *The Principal Upanishads, edited with introduction, text and notes by S. Radhakrishnan* (Atlantic Highlands, NJ, 1992), p. 244.

[13] Vannucci, 'Sacredness and sacred forests', p. 26.

[14] P. Marshall, *Nature's Web, Rethinking our Place on Earth* (London, 1992).

[15] Tacitus, *Germania* 9: H. Mattingley, trans., revised trans. S. A. Hanford, *Tacitus. The Agricola and the Germania* (London, 1970), p. 109.

[16] Flood, *An Introduction to Hinduism*, pp. 10, 44.

[17] Hagender, *The Heritage of Trees*, pp. 26–33, figs 2–7, citing the work of the German scholar, Herman Wirth, *Die heilige Urschift der Menscheot* (Faruenberg, 1979). E. Reichel-Dolmatoff discusses the sacred tree or palm that was the sacred centre of the earths, skies and under-worlds of several Amazonian tribes: 'The landscape in the cosmoscape, and sacred sites and species among the Tanumuka and Yukuna Indians (North-West Amazon)', in *Sacred Species and Sites, Advances in Biocultural Conservation*, ed. G. Pungetti, G. Oviedo and D. Hooke (Cambridge, forthcoming).

[18] R. Smith, 'The Russian bear, and others', unpublished paper, University of Birmingham Institute for Advanced Research in Arts and Social Sciences (2001). For a recent overview of the role of trees in shamanism, see C. Tolley, *Shamanism in Norse Myth and Magic*, 2 vols (Helsinki, 2009), especially pp. 304–68.

[19] J. D. Hughes and M. D. S. Chandran, 'Sacred groves around the earth: an overview', in *Conserving the Sacred*, p. 70.

[20] Ibid., p. 72.

[21] Tacitus, *Germania* 10: trans. Mattingly and Handford, pp. 109–10.

[22] R. Hayman, *Trees, Woodlands and Western Civilization* (London and New York, 2003), p. 11.

[23] For fairly recent views, see B. Cunliffe, *The Celts* (Oxford, 2003), pp. 94–6; S. Oppenheimer, *The Origins of the British. A Genetic Detective Story* (London, 2006); http://www.channel4.com/history.

[24] M. Aldhouse-Green, *Seeing the Wood for the Trees: The Symbolism of Trees and Wood in Ancient Gaul and Britain* (Aberystwyth, 2000), p. 18.

[25] B. Coles, 'Wood species for wooden figures: a glimpse of a pattern', in *Prehistoric Ritual and Religion*, ed. A., Gibson and D. Simpson (Stroud, 1998), pp. 163–73.

[26] R. Simek, *Dictionary of Northern Mythology* (English edn of *Lexicon der germanischen Mythologie*, 1984) (Cambridge, 1993); but see C. Tolley, *Shamanism in Norse Myth and Magic* (Helsinki, 2009), vol. I, p. 357.

[27] M. Pitts, 'Excavating the Sanctuary: new investigations on Overton Hill, Avebury', *Wiltshire Archaeological and Natural History Magazine* 94 (2001), pp. 1–23.

[28] Green, *Celtic Myths*, p. 66.

[29] Ibid., p. 26.

[30] D. Ó hÓgáin, *The Sacred Isle. Belief and Religion in Pre-Christian Ireland* (Woodbridge, 1999), p. 172; M. Eliade, *The Sacred and the Profane: The Nature of Religion*, trans. W. R. Trask (New York, 1959), pp. 39–44.

[31] Ó hÓgáin, *The Sacred Isle*, pp. 179–80.

[32] S. J. Yeates, *Religion, Community and Territory. Defining Religion in the Severn Valley and Adjacent Hills from the Iron Age to the Early Medieval Period, Vol. I*, British Archaeological Reports, British Series 411(i) (Oxford, 2006), p. 68, citing *Birmingham and Warwickshire Archaeological Society Newsletter*, June 2005; and M. Atkin, 'Excavations in Gloucester 1989: an interim report', *Glevensis* 24 (1990), pp. 2–13.

[33] Yeates, *Religion*, p. 68; A. Woodward and P. Leach, *The Uley Shrines: Excavation of a Ritual Complex on West Hill, Uley, Gloucestershire* (London, 1993), pp. 13–32; A. H. Smith, *The Place-Names of Gloucestershire, Part II*, English Place-Name Society 39 (Cambridge, 1964), pp. 253–4.

[34] B. Hope-Taylor, *Yeavering: An Anglo-British Centre of Early Northumbria* (London, 1977), pp. 244–5, 258–60, fig. 55; P. S. Barnwell, 'Anglian Yeavering: a continental perspective', in *Yeavering. People, Power and Place*, ed. P. Frodsham and C. O'Brien (Stroud, 2005), pp. 174–84.

[35] Aldhouse-Green, *Seeing the Wood for the Trees*, pp. 1–2.

[36] Ibid., p. 23.

[37] Ó hÓgáin, *The Sacred Isle*, pp. 144–5.

[38] Ibid.; Tolley, *Shamanism*, I, pp. 327–9.

[39] C. Thacker, *The History of Gardens* (London, 1985), p. 10.

[40] Hayman, *Trees, Woodlands and Western Civilization*, p. 13.

[41] Sir J. G. Frazer, *The Golden Bough*, 13 vols; *The Illustrated Golden Bough* (1890 ff.), illustrated abridgement by S. MacCormack (London, 1978), p. 18.

[42] A. Morton, *The Trees of Shropshire* (Shrewsbury, 1986), p. 21.

[43] *Deipnosophists Book XII*: Thacker, *The History of Gardens*, p. 11; (probably written after AD 228).

[44] Green, *Celtic Myths*, p. 50.

[45] Pliny, *Historia naturalis* XVI.249, after Ó hÓgain, *The Sacred Isle*, p. 92.

[46] Ó hÓgáin, *The Sacred Isle*, p. 93.

[47] Aldhouse-Green, *Seeing the Wood for the Trees*, p. 8, citing I. M. Stead, J. B. Bourke and D. Brothwell, eds, *Lindow Man: The Body in the Bog* (Ithaca, New York and London, 1986).

[48] Tacitus, *Dialogus, Agricola, Germania*: Loeb Classical Library (London, 1914), *Germania* 39, p. 318; trans. here Mattingly and Handford, p. 134.

[49] Ibid.

[50] Tacitus, *Germania* 12: trans. Mattingley and Handford, p. 111.

[51] Tacitus, *Annales* I.61, ed. N. P. Miller, *Annals, Book I* (London, 1959), pp. 84–5.

[52] Tacitus, *Germania* 10: trans. Mattingley and Handford, pp. 109–10.

[53] Tacitus, *Germania* 40: trans. Mattingly and Handford, p. 135.

[54] Lucan, *Pharsalia*, trans. R. Graves (Harmondsworth, 1957), cited by Green, *Celtic Myths*, p. 66.

[55] Aldhouse-Green, *Seeing the Wood for the Trees*, pp. 4–5.

[56] T. Kinsella, *The Tain* (Oxford, 1970), p. 61.

[57] Tacitus, *Annales* XIV.30, after Ó hÓgáin, *The Sacred Isle*, p. 95.

[58] P. Salway, *Roman Britain* (London, 1981), p. 677.

[59] H. E. Davidson, *The Lost Beliefs of Northern Europe* (London, 1993), p. 69.

[60] F. Maier, 'Das Kultbäumchen von Manching', *Germania* 68 (1990), pp. 129–65.

[61] Ó hÓgáin, *The Sacred Isle*, pp. 151–2, 171–3.

[62] A. T. Lucas, 'The sacred trees of Ireland', *Journal of the Cork Historical and Archaeological Society* 68 (1963), pp. 17–18.

[63] A. Watson, 'The king, the poet and the sacred tree', *Études celtiques* 18 (1981), pp. 175–6.

[64] Ibid., p. 167.

[65] Saraswati, 'The logos and the mythos of the sacred grove'.

[66] Lucas, 'The sacred trees of Ireland'.

[67] R. W. V. Elliott, 'Runes, yews, and magic', *Speculum* 32 (1957), p. 252.

[68] Ibid., p. 254, citing E. O'Curry, *On the Manners and Customs of the Ancient Irish: A Series of Lectures Delivered by the Late Eugene O'Curry*, ed. W. K. Sullivan (London and Dublin, 1873), vol. II.

[69] Ó hÓgáin, *The Sacred Isle*, p. 11; M. J. O'Kelly, *Newgrange* (London, 1982).

[70] R. Graves, *The White Goddess, a Historical Grammar of Poetic Myth*, ed. G. Lindop (Manchester, 1997).

[71] Ó hÓgáin, *The Sacred Isle*, pp. 110–11.

[72] Ibid., p. 214.

[73] P. C. Bauschatz, *The Well and the Tree* (Ann Arbor, 1982), pp. 3–29, 125.

[74] Ibid., pp. 27–8.

[75] R. North, *Pagan Words and Christian Meanings* (Amsterdam and Atlanta, 1991), p. 1.

[76] *Vǫluspá*: G. Neckel, *Edda: Die Lieder des Codex Regius nebst verwandten Denkmälern*, 4th edn (Heidelberg, 1962), cited in Bauschatz, *The Well and the Tree*, pp. 3–4; trans. C. Larrington, *The Poetic Edda* (Oxford, 1996), p. 6.

[77] J. M. Paterson, *Tree Wisdom* (London and San Francisco, 1996), p. 149; see, too, Tolley, *Shamanism*, I, pp. 338–44.

[78] W. Duczko, ed., *Arkeologi och miljöarkeologi i Gamla Uppsala*, vol. II (1993).

[79] Adam of Bremen, *Hamburgische Kirchengeschichte*, ed. B. Schmeidler (Hanover, 1917), IV, scholia 140–1 [136–7]: trans. F. J. Tschan, *Adam of Bremen: History of the Archbishops of Hamburg-Bremen*, Records of Civilization 53 (New York, 1959), p. 208.

[80] Adam of Bremen, IV, scholium 138 [134]: Tschan, p. 207 n. a; Bauschatz, *The Well and the Tree*, p. 60.

[81] Bauschatz, *The Well and the Tree*, pp. 60–1. See also O. Sundqvist, *Freyr's Offspring. Rulers and Religion in Ancient Svea Society*, Historia Religionum 21 (Uppsala, 2002).

[82] Adam of Bremen quoted in R. Loveday, *Inscribed across the Landscape. The Cursus Enigma* (Stroud, 2006), p. 171.

2

Christianity and the Sacred Tree

It has been shown how Roman historians confirm that tree worship was a potent force in Europe at the beginning of the first millennium AD and that, in common with other world-wide beliefs, it was often thought that trees themselves had souls or, at the very least, were inhabited by spirits. Christianity abhorred such beliefs. While the Church was probably genuinely disgusted by some of the pagan practices associated with trees and sacred groves, it is likely to be the fear of a powerful competitive belief which led to such forcible attempts to expunge tree worship. The conflict was an ancient one: in the Old Testament, the Bible recounts how the Israel-ites, when they were promised, through Moses, the land of Canaan, were instructed to cut down and burn the 'groves', perhaps referring to a large sacred pole of wood which was an emblem of old tree-worship and the instruction is in Deuteronomy 12.2: 'Ye shall utterly destroy all the places wherein the nations which ye shall possess served their gods, upon the high mountains, and upon the hills, and under every green tree.'[1] The association of trees with prophecy, or even with healing power, had to be reinterpreted as evil. The story of John Cassian, composed in the late fourth century, tells how the virtuous children of Seth (the third son of Adam and Eve) allied themselves with the daughters of Cain and turned their learning to profane uses, thus showing such magic to be a malefic art assisted by demons.[2]

> I exhort you, and before God and His angels I proclaim, that you should not come to those devilish banquets which are held at a shrine, or fountains or trees.[3]

Beliefs in sacred trees had to be extinguished, and trees figure in the *Lives* of many Christian saints. In the late fourth century, according to a later *Life*, Martin, bishop of Tours, destroyed a heathen temple in the region that was associated with a sacred tree: 'destruction of the first caused little protest, attack on the tree an uproar'.[4] Ælfric's *Lives of the Saints* notes:

> Se halga martinus to-wearp sum hæðen-gild.
> on sumere tide. on sumere stowe.
> þa wæs an pin-treow wið þæt templ ge-friðed
> swiðe halig ge-teald on þa hæþenan wisan.

þa wolde he for-ceorfan eac swilce þæt treow.
ac ða hæðen-gildan þam halgan wið-cwædon.
sædon þæt hi ne mihton on heora mode findan.
þæt he þæt treow for-curfe. þeah ðe he heora templ towurpe.

The holy Martin overthrew an idol
on a certain occasion, in a certain place;
and there was a pine-tree close to the temple, protected
and accounted very holy in heathen wise.
Then desired he also to cut down the tree;
but the idolaters opposed the saint,
saying that they could not find it in their mind
that he should cut down the tree, although he had overthrown their temple.[5]

The story recounts how those forced to cut down the tree intended it to fall upon Martin but how, as Martin made the sign of the cross, it fell in another direction, thereby converting them to a belief in Christianity. Rattue notes how some time around 452 the Second Council of Arles declared that 'if in the territory of a bishop infidels light torches or venerate trees, fountains or stones, and he neglects to abolish this usage, he must know that he is guilty of sacrilege'.[6] This was only to be one of a continuing series of edicts banning or deprecating worship of pre-Christian 'sacred' sites: in 561 x 605 the Third Canon of the Council of Auxerre states 'it is forbidden to discharge vows among woods, or at sacred trees or springs'.[7] St Eligius, bishop of Noyon-Tornai, presided over a diocese whose inhabitants were largely pagan and also undertook the conversion of the Flemings, Antwerpians, Frisians, Suevi and the barbarian tribes along the coast. His sermon of c.640 attempted to combat the pagan practices of the time in forbidding Christians to place lights at temples, stones, springs or trees (see below).[8]

There was a further, more deeply significant change expressed in Christian belief. Man was no longer merely a part of nature but, through his special level of consciousness, was placed higher than all other creatures:

When paganism prevailed, the link between people and Nature was closer and more accommodating. There was no Christian mythology concerning a God-given dominion over natural resources. Instead, people considered themselves to be within Nature and to be inhabiting a world where everything was permeated by spirituality. . . . Pagan beliefs were characterised by the indivisibility of the natural world, the subsuming of individuality into the stream of life, a low-profile regard for property rights and the existence of meaningful relationships between humans and the trees, beasts, water bodies and landforms that constituted the context of their lives . . . Christianity, however, came to be associated with control, hierarchies, and a code of values that elevated humans far above the contents of their context and saw all other creations as being subservient and provided merely for human use.[9]

This may represent an idealised view of paganism, and Christians will argue that man thus became the protector and steward of the world and nature, but there is remarkably little in the Bible that explicitly advocates such a function, and it is, sadly, a task man is sorely failing to fulfil. However, Christianity was itself to make use of tree symbolism in a more positive way (see below and Chapter 3).

It is not straightforward to try to distinguish between pre-Christian beliefs and continuing superstition, something that has remained strong throughout the Christian era but which may not necessarily always have ancient roots. Certainly, tree worship or superstitions which recognised a power of trees remained difficult to eliminate, and in the eighth century (c.722) Boniface also felt compelled to chop down a particularly large sacred oak at Geismar near Frankfurt, which may have served as an assembly point for diviners and enchanters.[10] The *Life* of Saint Barbatus of Benevento (d. 682), a ninth-century compilation, 'tells how this saint, in his struggle against pagan practice, destroyed both a great sacred tree (hung with the skin of a sacrificed wild beast and shot at by riders in the horse-games) and a golden image of a viper' (the latter melted down to make a chalice and paten for the greatest sacrifice of all, the sacrifice of the Mass).[11] The Irminsul destroyed by Charlemagne, which probably stood on or near the Externsteine close to the present-day town of Obermarsberg in Westphalia, seems also to have been a huge tree or pillar that was regarded as a sanctuary for the Germanic tribes.[12]

In addition to the destruction of such powerful national images, therefore, some such 'holy' trees had to be removed as the symbols of another religion that had to be vanquished and replaced. Trees regarded as in some way sacred, like other places of pagan worship, had to be rendered subordinate to new ways of invoking the supernatural.[13] On occasions, the wood of the pagan sanctuary might rightfully be used for a Christian temple. In pre-Christian times the wood from sacred trees, although rarely taken, was believed to retain its magical powers when fashioned into other objects, whether idols, insignia, divining rods, lot-tokens or so forth.[14] In what is probably the oldest literary reference to the destruction of a sacred grove, the *Epic of Gilgamesh* (originating from Sumeria in the fourth millennium BC), the wood of the cedar forest was used to build a palace. The wood of the Geismar oak was used by Boniface to construct an oratory. Despite the stigma attached to pagan sacred groves, Abraham built an altar among the holy oaks of Mamre and planted a grove in Beersheba.[15] 'Holy' trees, subsequently sanctioned by the Christian Church, usually by associating them with a particular saint, have remained a feature in many European countries, especially those following the teachings of the Orthodox Church. Trees have also retained an affinity with spirituality. As late as 1696, a chapel dedicated to the Virgin Mary was built by the priest of Allouville-Bellefosse, a village near Rouen in Normandy, France, within the hollow trunk of an ancient oak-tree, one of the largest and oldest in France, perhaps as much as 800 years old, with a girth of over 10 metres. Later a second chapel was added above which may have been occupied for a time by a hermit.[16]

It may seem strange that in a book that is mainly about Anglo-Saxon England, this country has figured very little in the discussion so far, but Christianity (at least Roman Christianity) was to expunge the tree regarded as 'sacred' in pre-Christian belief from virtually every Old English written record. In keeping with Pope Gregory's suggestion, in his letter to Mellitus, bishop of London, in 601, that centres of pagan worship should be adapted to Christian usage, efforts were made to offer an acceptable Christian alternative to the tree on many occasions, replacing it with the cross. The pope's instructions are well known:

> However, when Almighty God has brought you to our most reverent brother Bishop Augustine, tell him what I have decided after long deliberation about the English people, namely that the idol temples of that race should by no means be destroyed, but only the idols in them. Take holy water and sprinkle it in these shrines, build altars and place relics in them. For if the shrines are well built, it is essential that they should be changed from the worship of devils to the service of the true God. When this people see that their shrines are not destroyed they will be able to banish error from their hearts and be more ready to come to the places they are familiar with, but now recognizing and worshipping the true God.[17]

By adapting pagan buildings, festivals and sacrifices for Christian use, the pope hoped that people might ascend 'gradually step by step, and not in one leap'.[18] In the case of the sacred spring, Christians were more inclined to exorcise pagan belief by purifying the waters: Rattue quotes a blessing, which he ascribes to c.725, enjoining the Deity to 'drive hence the occult ghosts and demons lying in wait so that purified and faultless this well will remain'.[19] However, sacred trees in some societies had been too powerful as foci of pre-Christian belief and had to be removed and replaced by Christian symbols. In others, tree symbolism could more easily be accommodated in a different form.

Tree worship was not, however, easily eradicated. On the Continent, the need for heathen practices to be eradicated by the Christian Church continued. There is a sermon attributed to St Eligius, who attempted to combat the pagan practices of his time and who became consecrated bishop of Noyon-Tournai in the mid-seventh century. In this he exhorts believers to call upon Christ before setting out on a journey or beginning any other work rather than having recourse to pagan superstition or magic arts: 'Let no Christian place lights at the temples, or the stones, or at fountains, or at trees, . . . or at places where three ways meet . . . Let no one presume to make lustrations, nor to enchant herbs, nor to make flocks pass through a hollow tree, or an aperture in the earth; for by so doing he seems to consecrate them to the Devil.'[20] The Frankish kings were anxious to wipe out the worship of springs, trees and sacred groves, and set fines in the later eighth century for those who thus made vows at such places or squandered praise on pagan gods, and ordered that such trees, stones and springs where foolish lights or other observances were used or carried out should be removed and destroyed.[21] The Council of Nantes in 895 specifically ordered the destruction of trees consecrated to 'demons' or local gods.[22] The worship of trees continued among the Hessians in the eighth century, for when St Boniface travelled to their territory as a missionary he noted how many had failed to accept the teachings of the Christian Church in their entirety: 'Moreover, some continued secretly, others openly, to offer sacrifices to trees and springs, to inspect the entrails of victims; some practised divination, legerdemain and incantations; some turned their attention to auguries, auspices and other sacrificial rites.'[23]

Bede tells of the more conciliatory approach adopted by Pope Gregory, who advised that the pagan temples should not be destroyed but should be sanctified with holy water (see above). Christian saints, too, might replace sprites, especially those associated with water. However, as on the Continent, heathen practices were not easily eliminated in England. In the early days, especially, conversion was not to make steady progress. Bede notes how the East Saxons drove out Bishop Mellitus but accepted Christianity again in the mid-650s under the influence of King Oswy of Northumbria, who would reason with Sigbert of the East Saxons:

> Erat enim rex euisdem gentis Sigberct, qui post Sigberctum cognomento Paruum regnauit, amicus eiusdem Osuiu regis, qui cum frequenter ad eum in prouinciam Nordanhymbrorum ueniret, solebat eum hortari ad intellegendum deos esse non posse, qui hominum manibus facti essent; dei creandi materiam lignum uel lapidem esse non posse, quorum recisurae uel igni absumerentur uel in uasa quaelibet humani usus formarentur uel certe dispectui habita foras proicerentur et pedibus / conculcata in terram uerterentur.

> 'The latter [King Oswiu] used to urge Sigeberht, on his frequent visits to the kingdom of Northumbria, to realize that objects made by the hands of men could not be gods. Neither wood nor stone were materials from which gods could be created, the remnants of which were either burned in the fire or made into vessels for men's use or else cast out as refuse, trodden underfoot and reduced to dust.'[24]

Tree worship was to virtually disappear in England but lingering beliefs continued elsewhere in more remote parts of Europe. Stephen of Perm, the first bishop of Perm in Russia in the fourteenth century, confronted the Permian shaman, Pam, when he cut down the fir grove which was the site of many deities and destroyed the sacred groves of the heathens.[25] Even as late as the nineteenth century, Christian missionaries were destroying monuments sacred to the Nenets people that were kept in the copses of the Russian Siberian tundra.[26]

CHRISTIAN TREE SYMBOLISM

Christianity itself was able to absorb a great deal of tree symbolism, as will be shown in Chapter 3. Much of this is obviously ancient, drawing upon pre-existing traditions, some of it similar to that of Indo-European myth: 'It is impossible to draw a line between sacred Myths and sacred Scriptures; they flow into each other, and they obviously have the same kind of origin'.[27] Gaskell views the scriptures as manifestations of 'Omniscient Wisdom . . . teaching universally the great truths of the nature of man, of the soul-process, and of the cosmos',[28] transferred through inspiration to those able to convey it. Others will see it as a way in which man has attempted to understand this spiritual plane ever since his own origins as a thinking creature – no less impressive in its own right.

In the Bible, the tree is also used to express the kingdom of God:

> as a diagram of the evolution of the Divine life, the growth from the seed, the sprout, roots, trunk, branches, leaves, flowers and fruit, typify the entire cosmic process, and serve to show how gloriously and wonderfully the Great Spiritual Universe, the archetype of the phenomenal cosmos, is contrived, envisaged, and sustained by the Master Builder – its Source and Centre. The 'birds of the heaven' are symbolic of those individualities who have 'gone before', having aspired to the things which are above. They are the Elder Brethren of humanity.[29]

In the New Testament, Christ likens the kingdom of heaven to a tree: in Luke 13:19 'It is like a grain of mustard seed, which a man took, and cast into his garden; and it grew, and waxed a great tree; and the fowls of the air lodged in the branches of it' (*ongelic is corne senepes þætte genummen wæs monn sende in Lehtune his & awox & aworden wæs on treo miclum & flegendo heofnes gehræston on telgum his*).[30] Some of the earliest tree symbolism in the Bible is found in the Old Testament. In particular, among the trees standing in the Garden of Eden, planted there by God, there were two (or the tree in a two-fold form) in the midst of the garden that were of special significance: the Tree of Life and the Tree of Knowledge of good and evil: in Genesis 2:9 'the tree of life also in the midst of the garden [Paradise], and the tree of knowledge of good and evil' (*treow on middan neorxnawange and treow ingehydes godes & yfeles*).[31] It was the fruit of the latter that Adam and Eve were forbidden to eat but which they tasted, after Eve had been lured to do so by the serpent. They thus lost their innocence by gaining the ability to distinguish between good and evil (betrayed by their perception of their own nakedness). Is there a hint here that Adam had partaken of a forbidden faith, represented by the ancient symbol of the serpent and encouraged by woman (perhaps the embodiment of an earlier matriarchal faith)? Humanity was thus destined, as punishment, to a life of sorrow and travail followed by death. Because they had succumbed to the temptation of

Eve and the serpent and had eaten of the fruit of 'the tree . . . in the midst of the garden', Adam and Eve had to be cast out of Eden. The other tree, however, held the power of eternal life; it had to be guarded, therefore, with seraphim, armed with a flaming sword: Genesis 3:22: 'And the Lord God said, Behold, the man is become as one of us, to know good and evil: and now, lest he put forth his hand, and take also of the tree of life, and eat, and live for ever', and 3:23–4: 'Therefore the Lord God sent him forth from the garden of Eden . . . and he placed at the east of the garden of Eden Cherubims, and a flaming sword which turned every way, to keep the way of the tree of life.' As the Old English poem *Elene* states (X, lines 755–7):

> He sceal neorxnawang
> ond lifes treo   legene sweorde
> halig healdan.

'They must keep paradise and the tree of life sacred with flaming sword.'[32]

In the Old English poem, *Genesis B*, a ninth-century work of German origin inserted into an earlier eighth-century version written by a monk in one of the northern English monasteries, the tree of the Garden of Eden is also described as two separate trees:

> Oðer wæs swa wynlic,   wlitig and scene.
> liðe and lofsum,   þæt wæs lifes beam;
> . . .
> Þonne wæs se oðer   eallenga sweart,
> dim and þystre;   þæt wæs deaðes beam,
> se bær bitres fela.

'One was so pleasant, beauteous and bright, gentle and praiseworthy; that was the tree of life. . . . Then the other was all black, gloomy, and dark; that was the tree of death; it bore much bitterness.'[33]

The fruit of the first granted eternal life and guaranteed glorious honours eventually in high heaven; the fruit of the second ensured misery in this world, 'torment with toil and sorrows', an old age deprived of 'mighty deeds, delights, and power' with death the final destiny before a descent to the darkest realms of the fire. It was the fruit of this tree that was offered by the serpent, but rejected by Adam until persuaded to eat it by Eve. Although the trees in the Garden of Eden may have been associated with the fall of man, within the new Jerusalem would also be the tree of life, continuously bearing fruit, with leaves for the healing of the nations (Revelation 22:2; see below).

Illustrations in 'The Cædmon Manuscript', compiled *c.*1000 and containing part of the *Genesis* poem, frequently depict three separate trees in the Adam and Eve

Eden scene with one in the centre (shown on one occasion bearing a cross) perhaps 'prefiguring the redemption of mankind by the sacrifice of God'.[34] The Tree of Jesse, too, represented in Christian art from the eleventh century, depicted the descent of the Messiah. The angel of the Lord appeared before Moses as a flame in a burning bush (Exodus 3:2).

As an extension of the symbolism of the tree, the cross of crucifixion itself became the *hālig trēo*, 'holy tree', and Christ's death the means by which men could obtain eternal life in the 'hereafter'.

> Þurh treow us com deað, þa ða adam geæt þone forbodenan æppel. and ðurh treow us com eft lif. and alysednyss. ða ða crist hangode on rode for ure alysednysse.[35]

> 'Through the tree death came to us, as Adam took the forbidden fruit, and through the tree came again life to us, and redemption, for Christ hung on the cross for our redemption.'

Christian writings from a very early date, therefore, incorporate features of World-Tree symbolism but convert this into the Christian cross. One of the trees of the Garden of Eden, the Tree of Knowledge, became *deaðes beam* 'the death-bringing tree', for it had been Adam's transgression that had brought death to the children of men. The living tree as a feature of delight was thus to be replaced by the dead tree in the form of the cross. This was no longer the *wulfheafedtreo* 'wolfshead tree, gallows' (*Riddle 55*) but became the *wuldres beam/treo* 'tree of glory', the *æðelan beam* 'noble tree', the *wuldres wynbeam* 'glorious tree of gladness/delight', the *sige-beam* or *lifes treo, selest sigebeama* 'triumphant tree, tree of victory', 'tree of life, the most excellent triumphant cross', *rodorcyninges beam* 'the King of Heaven's tree' (*Elene*), *beama beorhtost* 'the brightest of trees' (*The Dream of the Rood*) or the *ful blacne beam* 'very (full) bright tree/most glorious tree' (*Day of Judgement*). Thus the cross, *sio halige rod . . . mærost beama* 'the sacred cross, most famous of trees' (*Elene*) became the new tree of life.[36]

The replacement of the tree by the cross in the New Testament was to continue both in reality and in a literary context. The replacement of real sacred trees by a Christian cross seems to have been a deliberate way of replacing the old non-Christian beliefs. Blair notes how the Old English word for 'cross' was drawn not from any loan-word based upon the Latin *crux*, but was *rōd*, *trēow* or *bēam*, all meaning 'tree'.[37] Whereas a large posthole feature had stood before the royal palace and assembly place of Yeavering, tall crosses were now to be erected beside monasteries in Northumbria in the pre-Viking period.[38] Crosses were also raised before battles, as when Saint Oswald erected a cross as an omen of victory before his last battle at Heavenfield against the heathen Penda, 'a procedure not too greatly removed from the seeking of omens before battle at a sacred oak'.[39] They also replaced trees at the sides of roads or crossroads, especially in Northumbria, although the ornamented stone crosses of eighth-century Northumbria continued to be decked with foliage, jewels and hung with garments like pagan trees.[40] Some were even soaked with blood, a familiar association with necromancy but changed here to represent the blood of Christ. Others remained associated with healing and the archers depicted on the Ruthwell cross or at Hexham may represent Ishmael or elfshot. The Ruthwell Cross has carved upon it a few lines from a poem known as *The Dream of the Rood*. Here the conversion of the tree to the holy cross is portrayed in verse:

> Þæt wæs geara iu, ic þæt gyta geman,
> þæt ic wæs aheawen holtes on ende,
> astyred of stefne minum. Genaman me ðær strange feondas,
> geworhton him þær to wæfersyne, heton me heora wergas hebban.
> Bæron me þær beornas on eaxlum oð ðæt hie me on beorg asetton,
> gefæstnodon me þær feondas genoge. Geseah ic þa Frean mancynnes
> efstan elne micle þæt He me wolde on gestigan.
> Þær ic þa ne dorste ofer Dryhtnes word
> bugan oððe berstan þa ic bifian geseah
> eorðan sceatas. Ealle ic mihte
> feondas gefyllan, hwæðre ic fæste stod.

'Long ago was it – I still remember it – that I was cut down at the edge of the forest, moved from my trunk. Strong foes took me there, fashioned me to be a spectacle for them, bade me raise up their felons. Men bore me on their shoulders there, till they set me on a hill; many foes made me fast there. I saw then the Lord of mankind hasten with great zeal that He might be raised upon me. Then I durst not there bow or break against the Lord's behest, when I saw the surface of the earth shake; I could have felled all the foes, yet I stood firm . . .'

Thus transformed,

> Is nu sæl cumen
> þæt me weorðiað wide and side
> menn ofer moldan and eall þeos mære gesceaft,
> gebiddaþ him to þyssum beacne. On me Bearn Godes
> þrowode hwile; for þan ic þrymfæst nu
> hlifige under heofenum, and ic hælan mæg
> æghwylcne anra þara þe him bið egesa to me.

'Now the time has come when far and wide over the earth and all this splendid creation, men do me honour; they worship this sign. On me the Son of God suffered for a space; wherefore now I rise glorious beneath the heavens, and I can heal all who fear me'.[41]

To some Christians of the third century, such as the poet Pseudo-Cyprian, the tree of life which embraced the world, with the spring of baptism at its roots affording everlasting life, stood at the place regarded by Christians as the centre of the world, a place which was called by the Jews Golgotha.[42]

> This tree, wide as the heavens itself, has grown up into heaven from the earth. It is an immortal growth, it is the fulcrum of all things, it is the foundation of the round world, the centre of the cosmos. In it all the diversities in our human nature are formed into a unity. It is held together by invisible nails of the Spirit so that it may not break loose from the divine. It touches the highest summit of heaven and makes the earth firm beneath its foot and it grasps the middle regions between them with immeasurable arms. O crucified one, thou leader of the mystical dances. O joy of the universe by which dark death is destroyed and life returns to all and the gates of heaven are opened.[43]

The borders of Israel, promised in the Bible, were to be watered with rivers rich in fish:

> Along the river, on either bank, will grow every kind of fruit tree with leaves that never wither and fruit that never fails; they will bear new fruit every month, because this water comes from the sanctuary. And their fruit will be good to eat and their leaves medicinal.[44]

This imagery is repeated in Revelation where the messianic Jerusalem of the last days of earth will have the same 'trees of life' bearing twelve crops of fruits a year. Because paganism will still not have been eradicated, the leaves of the trees will offer a last chance of conversion. But the trees will not be lost, for this foreshadows the heavenly Jerusalem that will develop after the Apocalypse, Revelation 22:1–2: 'And he shewed me a pure river of water of life, clear as crystal, proceeding out of the throne of God and of the Lamb. In the midst of the street of it, and on either side of the river, was there the tree of life, which bare twelve manner of fruits, and yielded her fruit every month: and the leaves of the tree were for the healing of the nations.'

A rather more mournful picture of tree iconography emerges in a homily preserved in a twelfth-century manuscript describing the events leading up to the final Day of Doom:

> On þan fiften dæige, ealle wyrte ⁊ ealle treowwes ageafeð read swat swa blodes dropen. Þæt doð þa wyrtan, for þy þ þa synfulle mæn heo træden, ⁊ þa treowwen, for þan þe þa synfulle hæfden freome of heom ⁊ of heora wæstmen.[45]

> 'On the fifth day, all plants and all trees will give out a red exudation like drops of blood. The plants will do that because sinful people have been used

to trample on them, and the trees because sinful people had benefit of them and their produce'.

CONTINUING HEATHENISM

Although Christianity became accepted across the country by the later seventh century, heathen customs still did not entirely cease. The need to wipe out heathen practices and superstitions is a recurrent theme in Christian writings right through to the eleventh century and beyond, with a flurry of warnings to churchmen and people emanating from both the king and leading churchmen. However, not all are as early as alleged, and most follow the eleventh-century reformation of the Catholic Church. The Penitentials ascribed to Archbishop Theodore of York (d. 669) (allegedly written c.690) or those ascribed to Ecgberht, archbishop of York (eighth century), were greatly embellished when compiled 'around 1000', when attacks on the veneration of wells, trees and stones reached full blast (Bethurum suggests that pagan practices may have been 'resurgent under Danish influence').[46]

> Siquis ad arbores vel ad fontes vel ad lapides sive ad cancellos . . . votum voverit . . . poeniteat
>
> 'Punish those who dedicate votive offerings . . . to trees, or to springs, or to stones, or to enclosures'.[47]

> Gif hwylc man his ælmessan gehate oððe bringe to hwylcon wylle. oððe to stane. oððe to treowe. oððe to ænigum oðrum gesceaftum. butan on Godes naman to Godes cyrican. fæste. III. gear on hlafe ⁊ on wætere.[48]
>
> 'If any man alms vows or brings to any spring or to a stone or a tree or to any other element/thing /creature except in God's name to God's church, let him fast for 3 years on bread and water.'

The Penitentials attributed to Ecgberht were one of the sources used in the so-called *Canons of Edgar* that probably hark back to the early eleventh century. The *Canons of Edgar* survive in several slightly different versions: that in Corpus Christi College, Cambridge, manuscript 201 (D), dates from the mid-eleventh century, and that in Bodleian, manuscript Junius 121 (X) from the third quarter of the eleventh century, copied from a manuscript written by a Worcester scribe, with X frequently giving better readings than D, not the product of a Worcester scribe. Many of the regulations are aimed at correcting evils in the life of churchmen, and their context seems to fit in with the period of the Benedictine reforms of Dunstan and Edgar. Moreover, they appear to have been compiled by Wulfstan after he attained the see of Worcester in 1002; Fowler dates the *Canons* to 1005–7.[49] Wulfstan held

Worcester in plurality with the archbishopric of York until he appointed Leofsige as his suffragen in Worcester. Even if the content of the section given here borrows from earlier sources collected by Wulfstan, it is obvious that he still felt the need to violently condemn heathen practices; these particularly stressed the need for holy baptism to rescue infants from 'paganism'.

> And riht is þæt preosta gehwylc cristendom geornlice lære and ælcne hæþendom mid ealle adwæsce;
> [And we lærað þæt preosta gehwilc cristendom geornlice arære and ælcne hæþendom mid ealle adwæsce;]
> and forbeode wyllweorðunga, and licwigelunga, and hwata, and galdra, and treowwurðunga, and stanwurðunga,
> [and forbeode wilweorþunga, and licwiglunge, and hwata, and galdra, and manweorðunga,]
> and ðone deofles cræft þe man dryhð þær man þa cild þurh þa eorðan tihð, and ða gemearr þe man drihð on geares niht on mislicum wigelungum and on friðsplottum and on ellenum,
> [and þa gemearr ðe man drifð on mistlicum gewiglungum and on friðsplottum and on ellenum,]
> and on manegum mislicum gedwimerum þe men on dreogað fela þæs þe hi ne sceoldan. (fol. 27)
> [and eac on oðrum mistlicum treowum and on stanum, and on manegum mistlicum gedwimerum þe men on dreogað fela þæs þe hi na ne scoldan.][50]

> 'And it is right that every priest zealously teach the Christian faith and entirely extinguish every heathen practice; and forbid worship of wells, and necromancy, and auguries and incantations, and worship of trees and worship of stones, and that the devil's craft which is performed when children are drawn through the earth, and the nonsense which is performed on New Year's day in various kinds of sorcery, and in sanctuaries (*on friðsplottum*) and at elder-trees, and in many various delusions in which men carry on much that they should not'.[51]

This content is found in Wulfstan's other works, directed not at formal organised paganism but with witchcraft and superstition, especially the worship of natural objects, such as the offerings of gifts or making vows, at trees, wells or rocks.

> and ne gyman ge galdra ne idelra hwata, ne wigelunga ne wiccecræfta; ꝺ ne weorðian ge wyllas ne ænige wudutreowu, forðam æghwylce idele syndon deofles gedwimeru.[52]

> 'and regard neither enchanters nor augeries, nor divinations nor witchcraft; and worship neither springs nor any woodland tree, because all idols are the delusions of the devil'.

The penitential falsely attributed to Theodore explains the purpose of drawing children through a hole in the earth, for the sickness is transferred to the pit or trench which is then filled in. Whitelock considers this a late insertion into the Junius manuscript, noting *Poenitentiale Pseudo-Egberti* IV.16 which says that 'it is great heathenism if a woman draws her child through the earth at cross-roads', replaced in the Cambridge manuscript by the word *manweorðunga*, which Whitelock interprets as 'evil forms of worship not specifically mentioned'.[53] A passage from St Eligius refers to a similar practice: 'Let no one presume . . . to make flocks pass through a hollow tree, or an aperture in the earth . . .'[54] Is it possible that the *þyrlan æsc* 'pierced ash-tree' of a charter of Manworthy in Milverton, Somerset, concerning a small one-hide estate granted in 963, hints at such a feature?[55] For some of these practices, again condemned in Christian writings, Fowler notes the frequency with which the laws of Æthelred II reiterate the necessity to *ælcne hæþendom georne ascunian* 'zealously shun all heathen practices',[56] continuing:

> ˥ gif wiccan oððe wigeleras, scincræftcan oððe horcwenan, morðwyrhtan oððe mánsworan ahwar on earde wurðan agytene, fyse hy man georne ut of þysan earde ˥ clæ[n]sige þas þeode, oþþe on earde forfare hy mid ealle, butan hy geswican ˥ þe deoppor gebetan

> 'And if wizards or sorcerers, magicians or prostitutes, those who secretly compass death or perjurers be met with anywhere in the land, they shall be zealously driven from this land and the nation shall be purified; otherwise they shall be utterly destroyed in the land, unless they cease from their wickedness and make amends to the utmost of their ability'[57]

Ælfric, a monk at the monastery of Cerne Abbas in Dorset and later abbot of a new monastery founded at Eynsham (1005–*c*.1010), was equally vehement at this time. Indeed, the diatribes of Wulfstan and Ælfric extended to other deplorable activities such as lot-casting or the possession of 'lucky' objects, the selection of 'propitious days', anything connected with wizardry or witchcraft, or even 'heathen songs' and drunken festivities at wakes or feast-days.[58] Wulfstan's preamble to the Laws of Edward and Guthrum written in the early eleventh century reminded bishops of their duty to most diligently suppress heathenism, and in 1020/1 he drafted the law against idol-worship, the first in England for three centuries.[59] This became part of Cnut's laws of *c*.1020–3, which note the heathen practices (*hæðenscipe*) he felt bound to forbid:

> idol weorðige, hæþne godas ˥ sunnan oððe monan, fyr oððe flod, wæterwyllas oððe stanas oððe æniges cynnes wudutreowa, oððe wiccecræft lufie, oððe morðweorc gefremme on ænige wisan, oððe on blote oððe on fyrhte, oððe swylcra gedwimera ænig ðing dreoge.

'the worship of idols, heathen gods, and the sun or the moon, fire or water, springs or stones or any kind of forest trees, or indulgence in witchcraft, or the compassing of death in any way, either by sacrifice or by divination or by the practice of any such delusions.'[60]

Whitelock believed that a new surge of heathen belief may have been brought in after the conquest of England under Cnut, reinforcing 'superstitious practices', especially by Norse invaders from Ireland: 'Wulfstan may have been speaking from personal knowledge of conditions in the north when, in his *Sermo ad Anglos* (decrying 'wizards and witches') he speaks of the way *gedwolgoda* and sanctuaries are honoured "among heathen people"';[61] however, Mitchell points out that in this he was also following a tradition of blame already instigated by Gildas much earlier.[62] Such themes recur with some frequency in Christian teachings and some are more explicit:

> Sume men synd swa ablende. þæt hi bringað heora lac
> to eorðfæstum stane. and eac to treowum.
> and to wylspringum. swa swa wiccan tæcað.
> and nellað under-standan. hu stuntlice hi doð.
> oððe hu se deade stan. oððe þæt dumbe treo
> him mæge gehelpan. oððe hæle forgifan.
> þone hi sylfe ne astyriað. of ðære stowe næfre.

> 'Some men are so blinded, that they bring their offerings to an earth-fast stone, and also to trees, and to well-springs, just as wizards teach, and refuse to understand how foolishly they act, or how the dead stone or the dumb tree might help them, or grant healing, when they never stir themselves from the place'.[63]

The 'Northumbrian Priests' Law', possibly composed by Archbishop Ælfric Puttoc (1023–51),[64] appears to recognise that ancient sacred places had not been entirely eradicated in the mid-eleventh century:

> Gif friðgeard sy on hwæs lande abuton stan oððe treow oððe wille oððe swilces ænigge fleard, þonne gilde se ðe hit worhte lahsliht, healf Criste healf landrican. ⁊ gif se landrica nelle to steore filstan, þonne habbe Crist ⁊ cyningc þa bote.

> 'If there is on anyone's land a sanctuary round a stone or a tree or a well or any such nonsense, he who made it is then to pay *lahslit* [Danish, i.e. a fine], half to Christ and half to the lord of the estate. And if the lord of the estate will not help in the punishment [i.e. assist to levy the fine], then Christ and the kings are to have the *bōt* (compensation)'.[65]

The *friðgeard* is the *friðsplottum* of the *Canons of Edgar*. Heathen practices were not restricted to the peasantry for this same law orders a fine for *ænige hæðenscipe . . . oððe on blot on firhte* 'any heathen practice, either by sacrifice or divination', or the practice of *ænig [wisan] wiccecræft lufige oððe idola wurðinge* 'witchcraft by any means or worship of idols': if the perpetrator is a king's thegn he should pay '10 half-marks, half to Christ, half to the king'.[66]

While Christianity appears, therefore, to have been successful with the higher levels of society by the seventh century (the heathen king Penda who died in 655 was one of the last Anglo-Saxon kings to cling on to his pagan beliefs), there can be little doubt that tree and well 'worship' continued at a local level, and was a constant thorn in the side of the Christian Church. Such an instance is illustrated when Wulfstan effectively removed 'a nut tree with wide shady leafage, which by the unpruned spread of its branches darkened the church' at Longney-on-Severn in Gloucestershire. Ailsi, a servant of King Edward, had had the church consecrated but, before this, had been wont to 'sit under that tree, especially in summer, dicing and drinking, and amusing himself with other games'. Not unnaturally, he refused Wulfstan's directive to cut down the tree, which the bishop claimed had been used for 'wantonness', and Wulfstan thereupon 'hurled his curse at the tree'. Stricken, it gradually 'became barren and bare no fruit and withered from the roots' until its owner, who 'had jealously possessed it and loved it dearly', cut it down himself.[67]

ASSIMILATION

In Ireland, Christian churches seem to have been established near the sites of sacred trees on several occasions. Lucas refers to the founding by St Patrick of a church near the *Bile Tortan* recorded in the eighth-century Book of Armagh, but at Armagh the sacred wood was burned.[68] Killeshin in Co. Carlow was the site of an early monastery which may have replaced a sacred grove, for a notice of 1077 runs: '*Gleann Uiseann*, with its yews, was burned'.[69] Another legend relates how St Brigid exorcised a pagan sacred wood at Ross na Ferta in Kildare.[70] Kildare itself, where St Brigid established her monastery in the sixth century, means 'the church/cell [Latin *cella*] of the oak tree', perhaps another sacred tree. The name of Moville, where Finnian (d. *c.*530) founded his monastery, comes from *maigh bhile* 'plain of the ancient holy tree'.[71] There are numerous place-name examples of names combining the word for 'church' and the name of a tree, such as *Iubhar Arnun*, 'Arnun's yew', recorded in 1015 and tentatively identified as *Cell iubhair*, 'church of the yew' now anglicised as Killure. As Lucas comments, 'At first, in brief, the church came to the tree, not the tree to the church'.[72] In Irish literary tradition, what may represent a Celtic island of the otherworld or dead is named in a ninth-century text as the 'Island of Fedach', which means 'tree-man'. In the story, a king called Diarmaid mac Aodha Sláine meets a beautiful woman, Beagfhola, who is taken to the island when attempting to make a tryst with the king's foster-son; here she meets and falls in love with a handsome warrior called Flann who forbids her, however, to stay with him. Flann belongs to the otherworld but a year later is wounded in a fight on the monastic island of Damh-Inis, Devenish on Lough Erne, the only survivor of a group of eight warriors. Beagfhola is left to go to him but the king uses the armour of the other seven to make a shrine and crozier for the monastery. This story shows the Christian world replacing the earlier pagan one where the living and the dead intermingle.[73]

There are instances of pagan sites in England being used for later churches and monastic foundations, as in the case of the *wēoh* 'pagan shrine' sites of the Weedons of Northamptonshire, including the seventh-century monastery founded by St Werburgh at Weedon Bec, but at present it is not clear what previously marked the pagan shrine. Tribal minsters in some cases may have replaced tribal sanctuaries.[74] There is little direct evidence of the replacement of a sacred tree or grove at these locations, but the letter of Pope Gregory to Mellitus clearly stated that the English should be encouraged to make huts 'from the branches of trees around the churches which have been converted out of shrines'. This implies that some pagan temples stood within groves.[75] Indeed, Gallic bishops since the fourth century had been ready to consecrate healing springs and associate trees with the graves of saints.[76] Again, the reluctance of Ailsi to accept Bishop Wulfstan's orders to cut down the large nut-tree which overshadowed the church of Longney-in-Severn in Gloucestershire in the eleventh century may refer to the destruction of a sacred tree, especially as nuts, particularly those of the hazel, had long played a significant role in religious ceremonies and ritual deposits. Some of these can be traced back to the Neolithic period.[77] Few instances of earlier sacred tree sites, however, can be identified. John Blair has drawn attention to the place-name Bampton in Oxfordshire, where a site known as 'The Beam' (OE *bēam* 'tree, post, pillar') is that of a chapel surrounded by burials, one at least of seventh-century date, close to an earlier Roman settlement, strongly suggesting a pre-Christian cult site. At Ketton in Rutland two groups of graves have been found, one around a small church but the other clustered around a large tree.[78]

The sacred tree, therefore, was not entirely expunged by the early Church in Gaul or Ireland. Indeed, there are medieval Irish accounts of 'the wondrous tree of St Ruadhán at Lorrha, the sap of which gave full sustenance to all the monks of the monastery and to their guests'.[79] The attributes of the ancient Celtic goddess Brighid – 'the woman of poetry, the goddess whom the seer-poets adored' and who sustained men with corn and milk – were in part transferred to the Christian saint of the same name, regarded as a patroness of milk-cows and with the dew and herbs sacred to her, and this St Brighid is said to have Christianised a pagan sanctuary located near an oak tree, thus giving rise to the place-name *Cill Dara*, 'the oak-cell'.[80]

As Christian symbols had to change the focus of pre-Christian sites, so Christianity in Ireland had also to be grafted onto earlier belief. In the case of the five sacred trees of Celtic mythology, the poet seems to have been in a contest with the tree, responsible for the fall of three of them, but the poet himself is, apparently, felled in turn. The symbolism of this may be complicated but it is relevant here that in the case of *Eó Rossa* it is not an unfit poet that is stricken down but a Christian saint, St Moling, the final representative of the druid priest and the Celtic poet. His *Life* tells how he was blinded by a chip of wood when felling a tree, not directly from *Eó Rossa*, but that particular tree figures prominently in the story.[81] This blinding tests his sainthood just as the other contests tested the poets. In seeking a cure he is offered one by a student who represents the native school of learning (here described as the devil in disguise), or one through the wisdom of the Church. The latter proves to be the effective cure and Moling is thus seen fit to become a saint, incidentally also proving the might of the new teaching.[82] Some Anglo-Saxon charms prescribe the cutting of Christian formulae into sticks of wood, adopting the earlier use of rune and ogham characters, even involving the pagan idea of shedding blood (see Chapter 3).[83]

There has also been a tendency to associate trees with particular saints. In the case of the Glastonbury thorn, an ancient tree cult is placed within a Christian setting, probably in the sixteenth century. This thorn is said to have bloomed on Christmas Day in honour of the divine birth of Christ. The legend claims that the thorn originated from Joseph of Arimathea's staff after he had thrust it into the ground on Wearyall Hill near Glastonbury after his arrival in Britain in AD 63. Similar tales were not uncommon in early saints' *Lives*: Gregory of Tours's late-sixth-century *Life of the Fathers*, mostly concerning sixth-century ecclesiastics, recounts how St Friardus, a recluse in the territory of Nantes, made a stick from a wind-fallen branch, which he subsequently planted in the ground and which, after having been watered frequently, 'grew into a tall tree'. Alarmed by the renown of this tree he was forced to cut it down but he later 'rescued' another tree that had been blown down while in full blossom. He sharpened the trunk like a stake and planted it without roots 'and the withered flowers took again their earlier freshness, and that same year the tree bore fruits for its cultivator'. The miracle shows that by the mercy of God the saint could 'well raise men from death by his prayers just as he obtained [*sic*] that withered trees should burst into leaf with renewed greenness'.[84] This type of legend is also found elsewhere in Britain, as at St Newlyn East in Cornwall. Here a fig growing against the south wall of the church is said to have sprouted from the staff of St Newlina, a virgin martyr. Again there is a tradition that anyone harming the tree will suffer (and apparently after pruning this has occurred!).[85] Another thorn reputed to have grown from a saint's staff is that of St Mullen's Well at Listerling, Co. Kilkenny.[86] The conversion of a saint's staff to a growing tree is something of a stock miracle in hagiographical literature, occurring in the lives of the saints Ninian (sixth-century bishop of Whithorn), Æthelthryth (Ethelreda, late-seventh-century abbess of Ely), Aldhelm (early-eighth-century bishop of Sherborne), and many others. The tradition was probably based upon the biblical story of Aaron's rod (Numbers 17:8), the rod that was passed on to Moses and the children of Israel. The staffs driven into the ground by Aldhelm, Cynehelm and Eadwold sprouted miraculously into ash-trees.[87] The legend of St Kenelm (Cynehelm) will be discussed in Chapter 3. In Ireland, St Senan dug a well for his community with a hazel stake which he set beside the well and which grew into a hazel *bile* (see next section).[88] Some saints' lives contain tree miracles – thus, as previously noted, St Martin was able to avert disaster by a falling tree collapsing onto a group of people by making the sign of the cross and making it fall in a different direction, as if it had been struck by a sudden whirlwind.[89]

In much of the Middle and Near East, nature represented as much a threat as a blessing. The flooding of Mesopotamian cities by the Tigris and Euphrates, the occasional outbursts of volcanic activity in the region, and other such natural events, led some early civilisations to see nature as something with which man had to undertake a constant battle. Hughes notes the literary references from early Sumerian times down through Akkadian and Assyrian writings, which represent nature as 'a female monster of chaos who was confronted and overcome by a hero-god'. What is perhaps the oldest extant long poem, the Mesopotamian *Epic of Gilgamesh*, also expresses an attitude of hostility to untamed nature, the conflict between civilisation and wilderness. Here, in a sacred cedar wood in the far mountains, the giant Humbaba was killed by Enkidu and King Gilgamesh and the wood was to be cut down as a symbol of the subjugation of the wilderness by the city, its timber used to build the palace of Gilgamesh at Uruk.[90] The wilderness in Hebrew scripture remained a place of thorny plants and danger, a place to test man's commitment to God. This allegory is copied in much Old English literature and Christian hermits are frequently said to have sought out forests and wildernesses (Greek *eremos* 'desolate', Latin *deserta*, *solitudo* or *vastitas* 'waste, wilderness'). Thus the saintly Guthlac heard of such a wilderness in eastern England:

> There is in Britain a fen of immense size, which begins from the River Granta not far from the city of the same name, called Grantchester. There are immense swamps, sometimes dark stagnant water, sometimes foul rivulets running; and also many islands and reeds and tummocks and thickets. And it extends to the North Sea with numerous wide and lengthy meanderings.

Here he chose to confront the 'various horrors and fears . . . because of the loneliness of the broad wilderness', the place where no man could ever live because of the dwelling-place there of the accursed spirits[91] (see, further, Chapter 3). The *Visio Sancti Pauli* presents an even more forbidding image of a northern hellish 'wilderness': in part a chilling, icy, wood where black souls hanging from trees are tormented by monsters seizing them like greedy wolves.[92] This is also reflected in the Christianised tale of *Beowulf* in discussing the location of the monsters' lair (see Chapter 3).

Plant-life is not well represented in Anglo-Saxon art, and where it does occur is most likely to represent the influence of a pre-existing 'Celtic' artistic tradition (that of the Iron Age peoples of Britain and Ireland) or the art of the late imperial, early Christian Roman world.[93] Plants had often become mere highly stylised scrolls, sometimes copied onto shield bosses and so forth, but were less favoured than representations of birds and animals in the Christian manuscripts of the time. Nevertheless a simple foliate motif is found on eighth-century cross-heads from Yorkshire and almost hidden within a carpet page of the Lindisfarne Gospel book, representing the cross of the Son of God. Other manuscripts, such as the eighth-century *Codex Amiatinus* produced in the Jarrow-Wearmouth scriptorium, drew directly on sixth-century Italian models, perhaps in an attempt to recreate an 'authentic' early Christian Mediterranean product, and are much more naturalistic in style. These show that plants had, indeed, been adopted into Christian iconography: there are even landscapes with trees in the eleventh-century Harley Psalter (based upon a continental manuscript) and other wooded settings when the stories being depicted required them (such as the dense vegetation in the scene of Romulus and Remus on the Franks casket, a whalebone casket probably produced in Northumbria in the first half of the eighth century, Fig. 2). The trees are seldom naturalistic, however, the 'Tree of Knowledge' becoming a single trunk on the tenth- or eleventh-century carving at Dacre in Cumbria, and even those shown in the Anglo-Saxon calendar pictures are rarely identifiable. It is clear that the iconographic symbolism was all-important in these examples of Anglo-Saxon art, with the vine a common motif taken from Classical sources. On early Christian monuments, the vine, as the source of the wine used for the Eucharist, served as a symbol of Christ's blood but the tree was the source for Christ's crucifix, often also identified as the 'Tree of Life' from the Garden of Eden (for reference to the Cædmon Manuscript, see above). The way these are depicted, Hawkes has argued, 'may suggest that stylization was deliberately cultivated by those responsible for the design of the stone monuments, at the expense of naturalistic representation, in order to fully exploit and exhibit the symbolic potential of the motif'.[94]

The 'Tree of Life' remained a not uncommon symbol on medieval grave slabs, observed, for instance, in the north of England at Durham Cathedral and Lanecost Priory, Cumbria. They are particularly numerous, and probably much earlier, however, in Scandinavia: over 350 are known from the west Swedish region of Västergötland alone, where, rather than being influenced by the English Romanesque style, they may represent a Byzantine style from the early eleventh century, brought to Sweden in an Orthodox Christian period prior to the Catholic mission (the Roman Catholic and Greek Orthodox Churches separated officially in 1054).

Figure 2. The left panel of the Franks Casket as displayed in the British Museum

Here archaeology may be offering a date earlier than the written sources and the evidence for such contact is mirrored in some rune stones.[95] Orthodox Christianity, like the 'Celtic' Church, appears to have assimilated tree symbolism rather more easily, although it clearly played a part in most early Christian art.

Christianity, of any sect, also could not fail to recognise the value of trees as valuable building timber, and the *Life and Miracles of Saint Modwenna*, compiled by Geoffrey of Burton in the twelfth century, records how those attempting to restore the church and monastery eventually found a suitable tree to complete the roof growing in a rough and inaccessible spot, entirely surrounded by huge rocks. Although they were able to fell it and trim it they were unable to move it away. However, after the abbess had prayed to Modwenna the timber was miraculously found near to the churchyard, 'skilfully trimmed, as if by design, and hollowed out and carefully made ready for this work, as if by human craft, to the measure of the church'. Returning to check out the original location, the workmen could find only broken branches among the tops of the trees showing that it had been moved by 'angelic power' and transported through the air to the monastery. Thereupon they raised the timber to complete the building, blessing both Modwenna and the abbess.[96]

Even in the austere world of Roman Christianity, all was not lost for the living tree in iconographic representation. A sculpture preserved in Romsey Abbey, originally gilded and though to date from c.960, shows living tendrils emerging from Christ's crucifix, as the rood took on new life perhaps signifying the forthcoming resurrection (Plate I).

There remained a deep reluctance to destroy old sacred trees entirely: on occasions penances were given to Christians unwilling to destroy the wood of ancient shrines, as noted above. 'Theodore's Penitential' notes that wood used for churches was only to be used for other churches, so as not to fall into lay hands.[97]

A tree that found a niche in Christian iconography relatively early was the yew (OE īw, ēoh; OHG īwa), which was perhaps even adopted by late Roman Christians. An evergreen, this may have been the nearest substitute available for the Christian palm. Later found in many Christian churchyards, perhaps as a symbol of death and resurrection, the date at which it attained this role remains debatable as ancient yews can seldom, if ever, be dated, despite claims that some may pre-date the churches beside which they stand. Romano-British burials have been found close to an ancient yew at Claverley in Shropshire, and early British memorial stones, probably marking a grave, beneath the yew (or yews) at Llanerfyl in Gwynedd; many more examples could be cited but no direct association proved. Neither is there any English documentary source confirming this but Bevan-Jones[98] claims that a charter of 684 (source not referenced) gives instructions to the builders of a church at Peronne in Picardy that a particular yew already growing on the site there should be preserved and, commenting upon the prevalence of ancient yews in the churchyards of the Welsh Borderland, argues that some of the oldest yews may have been planted by the very first Christians at a site, marking early saints' cells.[99] He argues that such trees may be as much as 1500 to 2000 years old. Indeed, in this area Christianity may even have survived from late Roman times. Even the present size of some of these venerable churchyard yews can be deceptive: Bevan-Jones notes that the present state of the yew at Church Preen in Shropshire (Plate II), now tightly bound, belies its true antiquity, for the rotting fragments of the base of the old trunk are now barely visible at ground level, and it may have had a girth of 12m (40ft) or more in the past, making it 'the largest ever recorded girth in Shropshire'.[100] Indeed, numerous ancient churchyard yews in this county and that of adjacent Herefordshire could conceivably represent examples of a yew cult absorbed or adopted by the British Church. At Hope Bagot, beneath Brown Clee in Shropshire, an enormous yew overshadows a 'holy' well.

Unfortunately, there is no reliable documentary evidence to cast light on this problem: pre-Conquest (i.e. early medieval) charters in England which might confirm the antiquity of some of the landmarks noted in any associated boundary clause

Plate I. The Romsey Saxon rood, a (?)tenth-century crucifix
showing the rood taking on new life, perhaps as
a symbol of the resurrection.

Plate II. The Church Preen yew, Shropshire, in the churchyard of St John the Baptist, is perhaps the oldest yew tree in the county. Its current girth of 6.8m – the tree is hollow – is held together with an iron band.

normally concern whole estates, describing features that lay along their boundaries. Even where a grant or lease concerned only part of an estate the boundary is most unlikely to have cut through a churchyard, so that any existing churchyard yew would not have been noted in such a document. Yews do occur in the boundary clauses but not in such a location, one near Chepstow being noted as growing upon a mound (or perhaps barrow), allegedly c.625.[101] The churchyard yews themselves are now often hollow, such as that at Much Marcle in Herefordshire (with a seat inside able to accommodate seven people). Such trees would be difficult to date by scientific means even if this were permitted (dendrochronological dating methods might carry disease into the tree). Only in medieval times – in the twelfth century – did Giraldus Cambrensis write of the yews found in Ireland 'in old cemeteries and sacred places, where they were planted in ancient times by the hands of holy men, to give them what ornament and beauty they could'.[102] However, even if the actual date of these trees remains debatable – and Rackham concedes that some surviving today may be over a thousand years old – the strength of their legendary association with churchyards was obviously established very early and was strong, especially in western England and Wales.[103]

The idea of the yew being a symbol of death and regeneration (the yew is renowned not only for its extreme longevity but it is one of the few conifers which will regrow even if severely cut back) is common throughout Europe. As a symbol of the resurrection, shoots were sometimes put into the shrouds of the dead to protect their spirits in the life to come.[104] The yew (éo) was one of the five magical trees of Ireland but it appears to have been accepted by the Church. 'Yew trees, so familiar a feature of early churchyards, may similarly have been quite intentionally allowed to live on from the pre-Christian grove', a place of earlier ritual, perhaps because this tree was thought to offer protection against supernatural and elemental forces,[105] or because it had long been associated with rebirth. Burials within yew charcoal have been noted in a Bronze Age barrow by Donald Graham in Yorkshire.[106] As a native evergreen, the yew may also have represented the biblical cedar or palm: in the Near East, it was the palm that became the symbol of heavenly paradise, to be incorporated into ecclesiastical architecture with the spread of Christianity.

The sacred well was probably the other most potent feature of pre-Christian belief among both the Germanic and Celtic tribes and many, like the springs beneath the Norse Yggdrasill, were associated with trees. This remained true in Ireland, long after the acceptance of Christianity had led to the adoption of such wells as 'holy'. The clergy would often dedicate a tree by placing a statue in its branches, and a statue of the Virgin and Child is said to have appeared miraculously in the branches of an oak near Ffynnon Fair Penrhys in Glamorgan, Wales.[107] Even today, there may be as many as 3,000 holy wells in Ireland, many of which Lucas found to be associated with trees. In a random sample of some 210 he found that these were most commonly the hawthorn (103) and the ash (75). The frequency of the latter, he comments, is in itself 'a testimony to the sacred character of the trees growing there for nothing else could have saved them from use as fuel or timber in a country as starved of wood as was the greater part of Ireland during the 18th and 19th centuries, when the dearth of timber erected the winning of the semi-fossil timber from the bogs into a major rural industry'.[108] At Aughagrun, a holy well recorded in the mid-nineteenth century was associated with a megalith called St Patrick's Bed and two ancient trees, all of which were included in the ritual.[109] The association seems weaker in Wales, for fewer such associations have been noted, but Jones notes some thirty examples and comments: 'the traditions and ritual concerning them are so much in sympathy with the tree-well association of other Celtic lands, as well as in Celtic antiquity, that it is not difficult to recognise in them a ragged remnant of what was formerly a widespread custom'.[110] Some long-lived yews are still associated with 'holy wells', as at Ffynnon Bedr near Conwy in Gwynedd or at Hope Bagot in Shropshire. A Holywell place-name is recorded by 1086 in Cambridgeshire and other 'holy' springs are occasionally referred to in Anglo-Saxon charters, confirming an early context for at least some of them: in Somerset one such spring is recorded as a landmark in the bounds of Ruishton in a document kept in the archives of Winchester Old Minster, and in Northamptonshire *þam halgan wylles forda* 'the ford of the holy well' is noted on the boundary of Church Stowe in 956, a spring close to the Watling Street.[111]

Certain trees dedicated to saints were recognised in the medieval Welsh Laws attributed to Hywel Dda as being of higher value than other trees: *ywen sant punt atal*, 'a yew of a saint is a pound in value', while a yew in wood was only worth fifteen pence.[112] The trees included the yew, the hazel, the oak, the hawthorn and the ash, and Bord and Bord note that the tree-well cult represented one of the seven kinds of 'vegetation cult' identified by Eliade, here the tree as 'symbol of life, of inexhaustible fertility, of absolute reality; as related to the Great Goddess or the symbolism of water; as identified with the fount of immortality'.[113]

An Irish poem from about the seventh century states a prohibition against cutting down sacred trees.[114] The value of particular species of trees in the later medieval laws is also not just a reflection of their practical value and trees continued to occupy a special place in the Irish medieval laws. Graves describes *quert*, the wild apple, and the *coll*, the hazel, as two of the most sacred of trees in mythology, in the early Irish tradition of *The Triads of Ireland* the only two sacred trees 'for the wanton felling of which death is exacted'.[115] 'Three unbreathing things paid for only with breathing things: An apple tree, a hazel bush, a sacred grove.'[116]

The sequence of trees indeed varied over time: under later Brehon Law the seven chieftain trees were the oak, hazel, holly, yew, ash, pine and apple (upgrading the ash over the alder as in the *Câd Goddeu*); the seven peasant trees the alder, willow, hawthorn, rowan, birch, elm and *idha*; the seven shrub trees the blackthorn, elder, white hazel, white poplar, arbutus, *feorus* and *crann-fir*; the eight bramble trees the fern, bog-myrtle, furze, briar, heath, ivy, broom and gooseberry. Earlier, however, in a seventh-century poem appended to the ancient Irish Law *Crith Gablach*, the seven chieftain trees included the alder, willow and birch instead of the ash, yew and pine (with the others as the oak, holly, hazel and apple). However, the *Triads*, giving precedence to the hazel and apple, appear to represent the earliest tradition.[117] Graves associates the seven trees of the sacred grove in the *Crith Gablach* with the seven days of the week.[118]

SACRED TREES IN PLACE-NAMES

The sacred grove seems to be remembered in certain British place-names. *Nemet*, *nemeton* derives from a Celtic source based on an assumed **nem-os* 'heaven' (**nem-* 'sky') and Old Irish *nemhta* 'holy', becoming in primitive Welsh **nïved*. In Ireland the term *fidnemedh/fiodhneimhidh* was given to sacred groves (*fiodh* 'tree'), such as the one burned at Armagh; in Gaul, too, *nemeton* was 'holy place' and in Latin, *nemus* was 'sacred wood'. A goddess Nemetona appears on an altar at Bath and another goddess is represented in the name *Aquae Arnemetiae*, meaning 'waters of Arnemetia' which was the Roman name for Buxton in Derbyshire.[119] *Vernemetum*, 'very sacred grove', perhaps implying a grove with a shrine or temple, was the name of the Roman settlement near Willoughby on the Wolds in Nottinghamshire; *Medionemetum* 'middle grove', was perhaps the shrine of Arthur's O'on, Larbert, Stirlingshire; while a dedication slab to *Mars Rigonemetos*, 'king of the sanctuary', was found at Nettleham in Lincolnshire.[120] Lydney in the Forest of Dean has been suggested as the site of Roman *Metambala*, and this name may rightly have been **Nemetobala* 'walls of the sacred grove, sanctuary walls' (**nemeto-* with *gwawl* from Irish *fala* 'rampart'), a site perhaps to be identified as Lydney Park hillfort, a sanctuary subsequently to be rededicated to the Roman god Nodens-Mercury when a temple complex was built within the ramparts.[121]

Some groups of names of this kind survived, especially in the south-west of England. On the northern flanks of Dartmoor, in Devon, an area of deep wooded ravines drained by the River Yeo and its tributaries, the River Troney, a headwater stream of the *Eowan*, the Yeo (on this occasion derived from OE *īw* 'yew' or a British equivalent[122]), appears in an early medieval boundary clause of Crediton estates as the *Nymet*. The name occurs again further along this boundary, applied to a headwater stream of the River Taw, also known today as the Yeo, which forms part of the western boundary of Morchard Bishop.[123] This river gave its name to the settlements of Nymet Tracy, Nymet Rowland, Nichols Nymet, Broad-nymet and several other *nymed/nymet* names. (At Nymet Rowland the church dedication is, tellingly, to St Bartholomew, 'the caster out of demons',[124] and the building contains Norman fabric.) An estate at Down St Mary was also known as *Nymed* in the tenth century and, within this estate, the single-virgate holding of Wolfin was named as *Nimet* in 1086 and the single-hide manor of Zeal Monachorum as *Limet* (for *Nymet*), indicating that the name had become associated with a considerable area around the headwaters of the Taw and Yeo rivers. North Tawton, beside the Taw, may have been the site of the Roman fort known as *Nemeto Statio*, a name possibly derived from *Nemeto-totatio* referring to a Celtic deity whose name meant 'ruler of the people', hence 'sacred grove of Teutatis', a war god equated with Mars.[125] North Tawton lies on the flanks of a low ridge overlooking the valley of the Taw where it is crossed by a major east–west highway. However, Todd suggests a preferred location for *Nemeto Statio* at Bury Barton near Lapford a few miles to the north-east, where two rectangular enclosures lie on a flat spur above the west bank of the River Yeo (here the *Nymed*), the smaller one probably a fort of first-century date, the larger one perhaps the late Roman *statio*.[126] Further north in the same county, another river, the Mole, was also called the *Nymet* and here another group of settlements, Bishop's, King's and George Nympton, and the (?later) parish name Queen's Nympton, preserve the earlier name of the river. All the *nymet* names noted here lie within the area of rolling countryside between the Taw and the Crediton Yeo (Fig. 3). No specific *nemeton* 'sacred grove' has yet been identified. Only small scattered woods survive here today, mostly in the valley heads, but there are numerous 'leigh' (OE *lēah*) names – often compounded with tree names such as birch, oak and ash – indicative of once more extensive woodland in the area, much of it in the valleys radiating out from the higher land. Both these regions form part of the Culm Measures belt where infertile cold, clay soils supported only sparse settlement in this early period and where numerous areas of rough moorland remained to be reclaimed only at a much later date.

The *nymet* stream name is also found in Somerset in a mid-eighth-century boundary clause of Baltonsborough and *Scobbanwirth*, places which lie to the south-east of Glastonbury;[127] here *Nimet* perhaps refers to the River Brue. The name usually seems to survive as a stream name rather than as a woodland name yet, in Gloucestershire, Nympsfield is 'tract of open country (*feld*) belonging to a place called *Nymed*'. The *feld* term is normally found close to wooded areas and *lēah* place-names indeed surround Nypmsfield, suggesting ample woodland along the Cotswold scarp. The reason for the Nympsfield place-name is not known but, interestingly, this was also a place where the medieval church was to be dedicated to St Bartholomew. Within the vicinity of Nympsfield are several Neolithic long barrows, several Iron Age or Roman settlements, and, perhaps significantly, a fortified Iron Age site at Uley which contained a Celtic shrine that was to be replaced by a Christian church.[128] The most westerly occurrences of the *nymet* term are found in Cornwall in the names Lanivet, Old Cornish *neved* 'pagan sacred place, sacred grove' with *lann* 'enclosed cemetery'; Carnevas in St Merryn with *cruc* 'barrow, hillock'; as an adjective in Trenovissick in St Blazey with *tre* 'estate, farmstead';

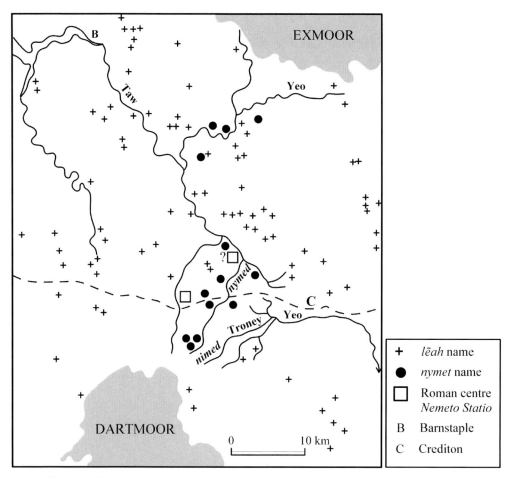

Figure 3. Devon *nymet* names. The possible sites of *Nemetio Statio* are shown.
Lēah names are indicative of former woodland. B = Barnstaple, C = Crediton

and Trewarnevas in St Anthony in Meneage with *tre* and **gor* 'very, over', possibly
'high'.[129]

Smith notes that the Old Norwegian word for a wood, *lundr*, was sometimes
used in Scandinavia to denote 'a sacred grove, one offering sanctuary', sometimes
combined with the name of a heathen god.[130] Gelling and Cole[131] find little reason to
expect such an implication in the use of this term in early medieval England, but a
religious association is found in Plumbland, Cumberland, in which, according to the
twelfth-century writings of Reginald of Durham, a *lund* was *nemus paci donatum* 'a
grove given to peace'. This situation is mirrored in an inscription on a rune-stone
at Eklunda near Lundby in Sweden, which states that an outlaw settled there in
such a grove.[132] The term is best represented in place-names in northern England in

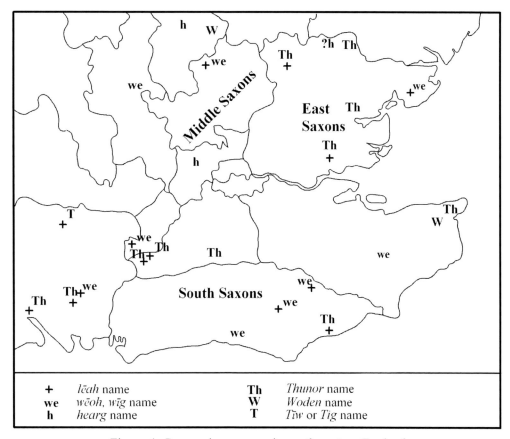

Figure 4. Pagan place-names in south-eastern England

areas of Scandinavian settlement. Some woods noted as *lēah* features may also have
had pagan connotations, although the place-name interpretations are rarely secure.
Although scattered across the country, they may, however, occur in groups, perhaps
suggesting enclaves of pagan belief. Weoley in Northfield, Birmingham, may incorporate OE *wēoh* (unbroken form *wīg*) 'idol, ?temple' with *lēah*, but there are doubts
about the origin of this name; however, there are other names which may refer to the
Anglo-Saxon gods Wōden and Tīw in the vicinity (but a derivation of one name in
this area, Arrowfield in Alvechurch, from *hearg* 'temple' is disputed by Gelling).[133]

   In the area shown on Fig. 4, south-eastern England, Willey in Surrey, *weo leage*
in a charter of Farnham, Surrey, has the same derivation, perhaps associated with a
pagan temple (*wīg*, *wēoh*) recorded as *Cusanweoh* in another charter (both charters
are spurious), and only a few kilometres distant Thursley may be a wood dedicated
to the god Þunor, while Peper Harow in the vicinity incorporates OE *hearg* 'heathen

temple'. Tisley, to the north-west in Hampshire, may be another reference in the bounds of Hannington to the god Tīw/Tig.[134] Three other names in the south-eastern region associate Þunor with *lēah*: *thunreslea* near Southampton, in the bounds of Millbrook, Hampshire; *thunresleg* in the bounds of Droxford, Hampshire, close to Wheely, *weoleage* in the bounds of Hinton Ampner; *thunorslege* in the bounds of Barnhorne, near Bexhill in Sussex; and both Thunderley and Thundersley in Essex, while other names which incorporate *wēoh* or *wīg* with *lēah* include Whiligh in Ticehurst and Whyly in East Hoathly, both in East Sussex, and, less certainly, Weeley in Essex (Fig. 4).[135] Thurstable Hundred in Essex, recorded in 1066–7, appears to be *Þunres-stapol*, 'pillar of the god Þunor' which presumably lay at the centre of the hundred; it may have stood upon a tumulus close to the church of Tolleshunt Major.[136] On these occasions, however, the references seem to indicate Anglo-Saxon paganism rather than any surviving Celtic belief. Neither were woods the only features associated with such names, for they are also found compounded with other natural features such as hills, meres or OE *feld* 'open land'.

Other pagan names in the south-east region, unassociated directly with woodland, include, with Þunor, Thunderfield, 'open space of Þunor' in Horley, Surrey, and, with *hlǣw* 'tumulus', *Thunoreshlǣw* near Manston in Kent and *Thunreslau* in Bulmer, Essex, both 'tumulus of Þunor', while names associated with Wōden include Woodensborough near Sandwich in Kent and *Wodneslawe* near Biggleswade, Bedfordshire, both 'Wōden's tumulus (*beorg*)', and *Wodnesfeld* in Widdington, Essex. Harrow in Middlesex, Harrowden, Bedfordshire, and possibly Harrowdown in Birdbrook, Essex, are other *hearg* names referring to a pagan shrine (the latter two with *dūn* 'hill') while other *wēoh* names include Wye in Kent and Patchway in Stanmer Park, East Sussex, 'Pæccel's pagan shrine', and Weedon, Buckinghamshire, here again with *dūn* 'hill'. It seems that while woods were often noted as the site of pagan shrines, more frequently referred to in the south-east than any other feature, other favoured sites included hills or mounds.

Successive admonitions from the Church point to the continuance of pagan practices in the countryside, and this is borne out by occasional references which have slipped through into the literature in pre-Conquest charter bounds. One charter, in particular, containing a boundary clause of the estates of Taunton, Somerset, allegedly in 854, notes as a landmark *ðan halgan æsce*, 'the holy ash', although the reference is in a spurious charter surviving in a twelfth-century manuscript.[137] It is this second copy which refers to this as *quendam fraxinum quem imperiti sacrum vocant*, 'an ash-tree which the ignorant call holy' which indicates how this should be interpreted. Further research needs to be carried out, but the tree may have stood at Cat's Ash in Fitzhead parish close to the Quantock hills. This site is a crossroads, itself a significant location in pagan belief. Another 'holy' tree, a 'holy oak', stood on the boundary of Chetwode in Buckinghamshire, standing at the northern tip of a possible British estate[138] on the fringe of a wooded area in the northern claylands.

Some such trees may indeed have been associated with a pagan tradition for it has been suggested that the place-name Holyoaks in Stockerston, Leicestershire (*Haliach* 1086), in a region of Danish influence, may take its name from a tree once sacred to Þunor (a *þureslege* or 'grove sacred to the god Þunor' is recorded in the nearby parish of Ayston in Rutland). It is highly likely that this was an attempt to Christianise the feature, standing on an estate held by the bishop of Lincoln in 1086 – and a medieval hermitage was also to be established close by.[139]

It is unclear whether the other charter oaks described as 'holy' had any pagan antecedents. It is possible that these may have been merely boundary oaks which carried a Christian cross or bore the sign of a cross. (A 'holy stone' may also have been of this nature, found as a boundary landmark of Wilton Abbey's estate of Watchingwell, Isle of Wight.)[140] 'Gospel oaks' were not uncommon as markers on later parish boundaries, places where those perambulating the bounds at Rogation-tide might pause and outline their parish boundary, perhaps also seeking a blessing for the land. Crucifixes on boundaries are not, however, common features in Anglo-Saxon charters and may have represented an attempt to Christianise a place with pagan connections. In north Worcestershire, two 'crucifix oaks', one on the parish boundary, together with one later-recorded 'holy oak', stood beside roads leading towards the present-day church of Tardebigge,[141] another church again dedicated in Norman times to St Bartholomew. It is not known whether other crucifixes named on boundaries had replaced once sacred trees – a tall crucifix, *þam langan cyrstel mæle æt hafuc þorne*, stood beside a 'hawk thorn' on the boundary of Aston Tirrold near Blewbury (Berkshire) beside an east–west routeway known as the 'stone way' (Chapter 7; Fig. 13b).[142] In Worcestershire a crucifix that stood beside 'the folk highway' along the western side of the River Severn became associated with later field-names 'Big Willhee' and 'Willtree', possibly 'Wilheard's tree'.[143] It stood, interestingly, on the boundary of Grimley, the name which means 'Grim's *lēah* (wood)', Grim being a nick-name for the god Wōden. Unexplained earthworks which attracted superstition may have given rise to such a name and the remains of a rectangular enclosure, likely to be prehistoric or Roman, have been identified in the vicinity. Blair considers, however, in discussing the fourteen instances of *crīstelmǣl* in charter-bounds from the 940s onwards, that these represented a traditional way of marking important locations beside routeways, like crossroads, fords or high points, whether by stones, trees, cairns or some other distinguishing feature.[144] He also notes the illicit rites that continued at such locations in early medieval Europe despite the condemnation of the Church.

ENDNOTES

1   Deuteronomy 12:2; see also Exodus 34:13; Hughes and Chandran, 'Sacred groves around the earth', p. 81. All biblical references follow the Authorized King James Version of the Bible unless otherwise stated.
2   V. I. J. Flint, *The Rise of Magic in Early Medieval Europe* (Princeton, 1991), pp. 334–5.
3   Caesarius, Sermon 54, i.270, *c*.506: *Saint Caesarius of Arles. Sermons. Vol. I (1–80)*, trans. M. M. Mueller (Washington, 1956), I, p. 270.
4   E. M. Wightman, *Gallia Belgica* (London, 1985), p. 283.
5   *Vita S. Martini episcopi*, 'St Martin, Bishop and Confessor', XXXI.X, lines 388–95: W. W. Skeat, ed., *Ælfric's Lives of the Saints, Vol. II*, EETS, OS 94, 114 (London, 1890), pp. 244–5.
6   J. Rattue, *The Living Stream. Holy Wells in Historical Context* (Woodbridge, 1995), 78, citing J. Bord and C. Bord, *Sacred Waters* (London, 1985), p. 19.
7   Rattue, op. cit., citing J. N. Hillgarth, ed., *Christianity and Paganism* (Philadelphia, 1986), p. 103.
8   Rattue, op. cit., citing A. L. Meaney, *Anglo-Saxon Amulets, Charms and Curing Stones* (Banbury, 1981), p. 11.
9   R. Muir, *Ancient Trees, Living Landscapes* (Stroud, 2005), pp. 55, 230.
10 *Life of Boniface* by Willibald VI: C. H. Talbot, ed. and trans., *The Anglo-Saxon Missionaries in Germany* (London and New York, 1954), pp. 45–6.
11 Flint, *The Rise of Magic*, p. 266.
12 *Annals of the Kingdom of the Franks*, p. 75, cited by Flint, *The Rise of Magic*, p. 209.
13 Flint, *The Rise of Magic*.
14 J. D. Hughes, 'Sacred groves of the ancient Mediterranean area: early conservation of biological diversity', in *Conserving the Sacred*, p. 115.
15 N. K. Sandars, trans., *The Epic of Gilgamesh* (Harmondsworth, 1960), cited by Hughes and Chandran, 'Sacred groves around the earth', pp. 71–2.
16 English14, http://82.24.219/~jpa/english14.htm.
17 Bede, *Historia gentis Anglorum ecclesiastica*; *A History of the English Church and People* I.30: *Bede's Ecclesiastical History of the English People*, edited by B. Colgrave and R. A. B. Mynors (Oxford, 1969), pp. 106–7; Flint, *The Rise of Magic*, p. 76.
18 Bede, loc. cit.
19 Rattue, *The Living Stream*, p. 78, citing R. C. Hope, *Legendary Lore of the Holy Wells of England Including Rivers, Lakes, Fountains and Springs* (London, 1893), p. 211, after Jean Mabillon's *Museum Italicum* (Paris, 1724).
20 F. Grendon, *Anglo-Saxon Charms* (New York, 1909), p. 39.
21 *Capitularia regum Francorum*, 'Capitulatio de partibus Saxoniae', no. 21: A. Boretius, ed., *Capitularia regum Francorum*, Monumenta Germaniae Historica 77 (Hanover, 1883), p. 69; *Capitularia regum Francorum*, Admonitio generalis, no. 22: Boretius, p. 59.
22 23 Council of Nantes, cited by J. H. Philpot, *The Sacred Tree in Religion and Myth* (London, 1897; Mineola, New York, 2004), p. 20.
23 *Life of St Boniface* by Willibald: Talbot, *The Anglo-Saxon Missionaries*, p. 45.
24 Bede, *Historia ecclesiastica* III.22: Colgrave and Mynors, pp. 280–3.
25 Hughes and Chandran, 'Sacred groves around the earth', p. 82, citing P. Weiss, *Kandinsky and Old Russia: The Artist as Ethnographer and Shaman* (New Haven and London, 1995).
26 Ibid., p. 82.
27 G. A. Gaskell, *Dictionary of Scripture and Myth* (New York, 1988), p. 12.
28 Ibid., p. 13.

29 Ibid., p. 766.

30 Lindisfarne Gospels: W. W. Skeat, ed., *The Holy Gospels in Anglo-Saxon, Northumbrian and Old Mercian Versions* (Cambridge, 1871–87), p. 87. An Old English translation of the Latin version of the *Lindisfarne Gospels* had been added by the priest Aldred in the mid-tenth century: J. Backhouse. The *Lindisfarne Gospels* (London, 1981), pp. 12–16.

31 S. J. Crawford, ed., *The Old English Version of the Heptateuch*, EETS, OS 160 (London, 1922; repr. with addition by N. R. Ker 1969), p. 86.

32 G. P. Krapp, ed., *The Vercelli Book*, Anglo-Saxon Poetic Records II (New York, 1932), p. 87; trans. R. K. Gordon, *Anglo-Saxon Poetry* (London: 1954), p. 224.

33 *Genesis*, lines 467–8: G. P. Krapp, ed., *The Junius Manuscript*, Anglo-Saxon Poetic Records I (New York, 1931), pp. 17–18, trans. Gordon, *Anglo-Saxon Poetry*, p. 104.

34 Oxford Bodleian Library, manuscript Junius 11, e.g. pp. 11, 13, 20, 24, 34 and 39; M. Bintley, 'The south Sandbach Cross "Ancestors of Christ" panel in its cultural contexts', paper presented at University College of London conference 'Woodlands, Trees, and Timber in the Anglo-Saxon World', 13–15 November, 2009.

35 Ælfric, *Homilies*, II.13 'Dominica V, Quadragesima': M. Godden, ed., *Ælfric's Catholic Homilies. The Second Series*, EETS, SS 5 (Oxford, 1979), p. 136.

36 For *deaðes beam* see *Genesis B*, lines 492, 646: *The Junius Manuscript*, pp. 18, 23; for the *wulfheafedtreo* see Riddle 55, *Exeter Book*: G. P. Krapp and E. van K. Dobbie, eds, *The Exeter Book* (New York, 1936), p. 208; for *wuldres beam* and *wuldres treo*, see *Elene*, lines 217, 827 and 1251: Krapp, *The Vercelli Book*, pp. 71, 89, 100; for *æðelan beam*, see *Elene*, line 1073: Krapp, p. 95; for *wuldres wynbeam* see *Elene* line 843: Krapp, p. 89; for *sigebeam(e)/selest sigebeama* see *Elene*, lines 444, 665, 964, 1027: Krapp, pp. 78, 84, 92, 94; for *rodorcyninges beam*, see *Elene* line 886: Krapp, p. 90; for *beama beorhtost*, see *Dream of the Rood*, line 6: Krapp, p. 61, trans. Gordon, *Anglo-Saxon Poetry*, p. 235; for *ful blacne beam* see *The Day of Judgement*, line 66: W. S. Mackie, ed., *The Exeter Book, Part II*, poems IX–XXXII, EETS, OS 194 (London, 1934), pp. 160–1; for the last ref. see *Elene*, lines 1111–12: Krapp, p. 94; trans. Gordon, p. 229.

37 J. Blair, *The Church in Anglo-Saxon Society* (Oxford, 2005), p. 227.

38 R. Cramp and R. N. Bailey, *Corpus of Anglo-Saxon Stone Sculpture* (Oxford, 1984–), I.2–3, fig. 2; cited in Flint, *The Rise of Magic*, p. 258.

39 Flint, *The Rise of Magic*, pp. 257–8.

40 Ibid.

41 *Dream of the Rood*, lines 29–38, 80–6: R. Hamer, *A Choice of Anglo-Saxon Verse* (London, 1970), pp. 160–71; trans. Gordon, *Anglo-Saxon Poetry*, p. 237.

42 D. Davies, 'The evocative symbolism of trees', in *The Iconography of Landscape*, ed. D. Cosgrove and S. Daniels (Cambridge, 1988), p. 39.

43 Hippolytus of Rome, third century, cited by Davies, 'The evocative symbolism of trees', p. 40.

44 Ezekiel 47:12, cited from the Jerusalem Bible here (as is the citation from Revelation following).

45 *Early English Homilies* XXXIII, 'Sign of the Last Judgement': R. D-N. Warner, *Early English Homilies from the Twelfth-Century MS. Vespasian D.xiv*, EETS, OS 152 (London, 1917), p. 90.

46 Blair, *The Church in Anglo-Saxon Society*, p. 481; D. Bethurum, ed., *The Homilies of Wulfstan* (Oxford, 1957), p. 319, n. 165–8 (see also below).

47 *Peon. pseudo-Theodore* XXVII, 18; *Liber poenitentialis Theodori archiepiscopi Cantuariensis ecclesiae*: B. Thorpe, ed., *Ancient Laws and Institutes of England, Monumenta ecclesiastica*

(London, 1840), II.1–86; Grendon, *Anglo-Saxon Charms*, p. 37; see Bethurum, *The Homilies of Wulfstan*, pp. 319–20, for discussion.

[48] *Poenitentiale pseudo-Egberti* ii.22: Thorpe, *Ancient Laws and Institutes*, II.xxii.371.

[49] N. R. Ker, *A Catalogue of Manuscripts Containing Anglo-Saxon* (Oxford, 1957), pp. 82–91, xviii, 5, 412: R. Fowler, ed., *Wulfstan's Canons of Edgar*, EETS, OS 266 (London, 1972), pp. xvi–xxix.

[50] *Canons of Edgar*, XX.16, Bodleian manuscript Junius 121, pp. 97–8, with alternative readings from Corpus Christi manuscript 201, bracketed: Fowler, *Wulfstan's Canons of Edgar*, pp. 4–5.

[51] Trans. Blair, *The Church in Anglo-Saxon Society*, pp. 481–2.

[52] VIIIc: 'Sermo de Baptismate', lines 165–8: Bethurum, *Homilies of Wulfstan*, p. 184.

[53] D. Whitelock, M. Brett and C. N. L. Brooke, eds, *Councils and Synods with Other Documents Relating to the English Church, A.D. 871–1204, Part I, 871–1066* (Oxford, 1981), p. 320, n. 2.

[54] Fowler, *Wulfstan's Canons of Edgar*, p. 27.

[55] S 709, B 1116, S. E. Kelly, ed., *Charters of Bath and Wells*, Anglo-Saxon Charters XIII (Oxford, 2007), no. 32, pp. 220–4.

[56] Æthelred VI.6: A. J. Robertson, ed. and trans., *The Laws of the Kings of England from Edmund to Henry I* (Cambridge, 1925), pp. 92–3, *cf.* Æthelred V.34; VIII.44; IX.1; Fowler, *Wulfstan's Canons of Edgar*, pp. 26–7.

[57] Æthelred VI.7: Robertson, *The Laws of the Kings of England*, pp. 92–3.

[58] Blair, *The Church in Anglo-Saxon Society*, p. 483, citing A. L. Meaney, 'Ælfric and idolatry', *Journal of Religious History* 13 (1984), p. 135; Whitelock, Brett and Brooke, *Councils and Synods I*, p. 321.

[59] Blair, *The Church in Anglo-Saxon Society*, p. 482.

[60] Canute II.5.1: Robertson, *The Laws of the Kings of England*, pp. 176–7.

[61] D. Whitelock, 'Wulfstan at York', in *Franciplegius, Medieval and Linguistic Studies in Honor of Francis Peabody Magoun, Jr*, ed. J. B. Bessinger Jr and R. P. Creed (New York, 1965), p. 226; Bethurum, *Homilies of Wulfstan*, pp. 267–75.

[62] B. Mitchell, *An Invitation to Old English and Anglo-Saxon England* (Oxford, 1995), p. 285.

[63] Ælfric's translation of Augustine's homily 'On Auguries' (early eleventh century), lines 129–36: W. W. Skeat, ed., *Ælfric's Lives of Saints*, vol. I, EETS, OS 76 (London, 1881), pp. 372–4 [990–4]; trans. Blair, *The Church in Anglo-Saxon Society*, p. 482.

[64] P. Wormald, *The Making of English Law: King Alfred to the Twelfth Century, I: Legislation and its Limits* (Oxford, 1999), pp. 208–10, 396–7; Blair, *The Church in Anglo-Saxon Society*, p. 490, n. 286.

[65] *Northumbrian Priests' Law* 54, 54.1, Corpus Christi College, manuscript 201: F. Liebermann, ed., *Die Gesetze der Angelsächsen*, vol. I (Halle, 1903), I.383; Fowler, *Wulfstan's Canons of Edgar*, pp. 26–7; trans. D. Whitelock, *English Historical Documents, Vol. 1, c. 500–1042* (London, 1955), p. 471, assigning a date of 1020–3.

[66] Ibid., see Whitelock, *English Historical Documents*, I, p. 474.

[67] *Vita Wulfstani*, II.27, cited by J. H. F. Peile, ed., *William of Malmesbury's Life of St. Wulfstan, Bishop of Worcester* (Oxford, 1934), pp. 60–1.

[68] Lucas, 'The sacred trees of Ireland', p. 27, citing J. O'Donovan, ed., *The Annals of the Kingdom of Ireland by the Four Masters*, 2nd edn (Dublin, 1856), 2.735, and W. M. Hennessy, ed., *The Annals of Ulster* (Dublin, 1887), p. 503.

[69] *The Annals of the Kingdom of Ireland*, 2.913.

[70] Lucas, 'The sacred trees of Ireland', p. 30.

[71] M. Rees, *Celtic Saints. Passionate Wanderers* (London, 2000), p. 27.

[72] Ibid., pp. 32–4.

73 *Ériu* 35, 72–6, cited by Ó hÓgáin, *The Sacred Isle*, pp. 100–3.

74 R. Morris, *Churches in the Landscape* (London, 1989), pp. 67–9.

75 Ibid., p. 76.

76 Blair, *The Church in Anglo-Saxon Society*, p. 226; Flint, *The Rise of Magic*, pp. 254–73.

77 Morris, *Churches in the Landscape*, pp. 79–81.

78 Blair, *The Church in Anglo-Saxon Society*, pp. 186, 381, fig. 44. There is, as yet, little substance for the claims made by Yeates, *Religion, Community and Territory*, pp. 71–2.

79 Ó hÓgáin, *The Sacred Isle*, p. 215, citing W. W. Heist, ed., *Vitae sanctorum Hiberniae ex codice olim Salmanticensi nunc Bruxellensi* (Brussels, 1965), p. 163.

80 Ó hÓgáin, *The Sacred Isle*, pp. 112, 202.

81 W. Stokes, ed and trans., 'The birth and life of St. Moling', *Revue celtique* 27 (1906).

82 Watson, 'The king', pp. 168–9.

83 G. Storms, *Anglo-Saxon Magic* (The Hague, 1948), pp. 46, 52, 237, 255, 287.

84 Gregory of Tours, *Life of the Fathers*, ed. E. James (Liverpool, 1985), p. 86, St Friardus, X.3.

85 J. E. Milner, *The Tree Book: The Indispensible Guide to Tree Facts, Crafts and Lore* (London, 1992), pp. 141, 143.

86 Bord and Bord, *Sacred Waters*, p. 99.

87 C. G. Loomis, *White Magic: An Introduction to the Folklore of Christian Legend* (Cambridge, Mass., 1948), pp. 94–5, 205 n. 1, notes the many saints whose *Lives* absorbed this tradition. Most are noted by J. Bolandus, *Acta sanctorum quotquot toto orbe coluntur etc.* (Antwerp, 1643–). For the early saints of Brittany, see J. M. H. Smith, 'Oral and written; saints, miracles and relics in Brittany *c.*850–1250', *Speculum* 65 (1990), pp. 326, 335, 342–3. For the named second three, see Blair, *The Church in Anglo-Saxon Society*, p. 476. The basis of the story is noted in R. Love, ed. and trans., *Three Eleventh-Century Anglo-Latin Saints' Lives* (Oxford, 1996), p. 59, n. 7.

88 Lucas, 'The sacred trees of Ireland', p. 35.

89 *Vita sancti Martini* 13: J. Fontaine, ed. and trans., *Sulpice Sévère, Vie de Saint Martin i* (Paris, 1967), pp. 280–3; and see reference no. 5.

90 J. D. Hughes, *Pan's Travail. Environmental Problems of the Ancient Greeks and Romans* (Baltimore and London, 1994), pp. 33–4.

91 Felix *c.*713–49, *Life of St Guthlac*: M. Swanton, ed., *Anglo-Saxon Prose* (Letchworth, 1975), p. 44.

92 R. Morris, ed., *The Blickling Homilies*, EETS, OS 63 (1967), no. 17, pp. 208–11.

93 J. Hawkes, 'The plant-life of early Christian Anglo-Saxon art', in *From Earth to Art*, ed. C. P. Biggam (Amsterdam and New York, 2003).

94 Ibid., p. 283.

95 A. L. Rhodin, L. Gren and V. Lindblom, 'Liljestenarna och Sveriges kristnande från Bysans', *Forvännen* 95 (2000).

96 Geoffrey of Burton, *Life and Miracles of St Modwenna*, ed. and trans. R. Bartlett (Oxford, 2002), pp. 177–8.

97 Flint, *The Rise of Magic*, p. 262.

98 R. Bevan-Jones, *The Ancient Yew* (Bollington, Macclesfield, 2002), pp. 45–6.

99 Ibid., p. 51.

100 Ibid., pp. 33–5.

101 J. Gwenogvryn Evans, with J. Rhys, *The Text of the Book of Llan Dâv reproduced from the Gwysaney Manuscript* (Oxford, 1893/1979), p. 166. W. Davies, *An Early Welsh Microcosm. Studies in the Llandaff Charters* (London, 1978), p. 171, notes this as a 'dubious' charter.

[102] T. Forester, trans. and ed., revised T. Wright, *The Historical Works of Giraldus Cambrensis* (London, 1891), p. 125.

[103] O. Rackham, *Ancient Woodland, its History, Vegetation and Uses in England*, new edn (Dalbeattie, Kirkcudbrightshire, 2003), p. 524; see too Morris, *Churches in the Landscape*, pp. 78–9.

[104] Paterson, *Tree Wisdom*, pp. 22–3, 25.

[105] Flint, *The Rise of Magic*, p. 262, citing E. A. Philippson, *Germanisches Heidentum bei den Angelsachsen* (Leipzig, 1929), p. 184.

[106] Donald Graham, pers. comm.

[107] F. Jones, *The Holy Wells of Wales*, 2nd edn (Cardiff: 1992), p. 19.

[108] Lucas, 'The sacred trees of Ireland', pp. 40–2.

[109] P. D. Hardy, *The Holy Wells of Ireland* (Dublin, 1836), pp. 15, 18.

[110] Jones, *The Holy Wells of Wales*, p. 18.

[111] S 352; B 549. A possibly suspicious charter probably likely to date from 878 (where a charter has been judged spurious this will be indicated in the references): Electronic Sawyer, Revised catalogue of Anglo-Saxon Charters, http://www.esawyer.org.uk/content/charter/199.html. S 615, B 986; S. E. Kelly, *The Charters of Abingdon Abbey, Part 2*. Anglo-Saxon Charters VIII (Oxford, 2001), no. 62, pp. 264, 266. References to boundary clauses in print are normally to Birch (B) when available in this source (for convenience), then to Kemble (K), with the more recent British Academy editions also noted. The preferred primary sources are given in the revised edition of the Electronic Sawyer.

[112] A. W. Wade-Evans, *Welsh Medieval Law* (Oxford, 1909), British Library, Cleopatra A, xiv, W fol. 85b, line 8, pp. 104, 248.

[113] J. Bord and C. Bord, *Earth Rites* (St Albans, 1982), pp. 103–5, citing M. Eliade, *Patterns in Comparative Religion* (London, 1958), pp. 266–7.

[114] Ó hÓgáin, *The Sacred Isle*, p. 71, citing *Celtica* 9, pp. 157–8.

[115] Graves, *The White Goddess*, p. 246.

[116] Ibid., p. 198.

[117] Ibid., pp. 197–8.

[118] Ibid., p. 246.

[119] A. L. F. Rivet and C. Smith, *The Place-Names of Roman Britain* (London, 1979), p. 254.

[120] Ibid., pp. 495, 416–17, 255, citing *Journal of the Royal Society* 52 (1962), p. 192.

[121] Rivet and Smith, *Place-Names of Roman Britain*, p. 424; A. Breeze, 'Plastered walls at Rudchester? The Roman place-names Vindovalva and Nemetovala', *Archaeologia Aeliana* (5th series), 30 (2002), pp. 49–51; P. J. Casey and B. Hoffman, 'Excavations at the Roman temple in Lydney Park, Gloucestershire in 1980 and 1981', *Antiquaries Journal* 79 (1999), pp. 81–143; A. Ross, *Pagan Celtic Britain: Studies in Iconography and Tradition* (London, 1974), pp. 69, 230–3; Yeates, *Religion, Community and Territory*, p. 24.

[122] B. O. E. Ekwall, *English River-Names* (Oxford, 1928), pp. 480–1.

[123] S 255, B 549 (bounds added, possibly in eleventh century), M. A. O'Donovan, ed., *The Charters of Sherborne*, Anglo-Saxon Charters III (Oxford, 1988), pp. liv, 2. *CBDC*, pp. 86–99.

[124] G. Jones, 'Ghostly mentor, teacher of mysteries: Batholomew, Guthlac and the Apostle's cult in early medieval England', in *Medieval Monastic Education*, ed. G. Ferzoco and C. Muessig (Leicester, 2000), pp. 126–52.

[125] Rivet and Smith, *Place-Names of Roman Britain*, pp. 424–5.

[126] M. Todd, *The South-West to AD 1000* (London, 1987), pp. 197–9, 203.

[127] S 1410; B 168.

[128] Woodward and Leach, *The Uley Shrines*.

129 O. J. Padel, *Cornish Place-Name Elements*, English Place-Name Society 56/57 (Cambridge, 1985), pp. 109, 172.

130 A. H. Smith, *English Place-Name Elements, Part II*, English Place-Name Society 26 (Cambridge, 1956), pp. 27–8.

131 M. Gelling and A. Cole, *The Landscape of Place-Names* (Stamford, 2000), p. 242.

132 Smith, *English Place-Name Elements*, II, p. 28.

133 M. Gelling, *Signposts to the Past. Place-Names and the History of England* (London, 1978), p. 160, fig. 11; M. Gelling, 'Further thoughts on pagan place-names', *Otium et Negotium. Studies in Onomatology and Library Science Presented to Olof von Feilitzen*, Acta Bibliothecae Regiae Stockholmiensis 16 (Stockholm, 1973), pp. 109–28.

134 S 382, B 627 (sp); S 235, B 72; S 960, K 739; J. E. B. Gover, A. Mawer and F. M. Stenton, with A. Bonner, *The Place-Names of Surrey*, English Place-Name Society 11 (Cambridge, 1969), pp. xii, 175, 211, 207. For a gazetteer of such names see Gelling, 'Further thoughts', pp. 120–7; Gelling rejects Tuesley in Surrey as a reference to the Anglo-Saxon god Tīw.

135 S 636, B 926; S 446, B 742; S 1007, K 780; S 108, B 208 (bounds are an addition: S. E. Kelly, ed., *The Charters of Selsey*, Anglo-Saxon Charters VI (Oxford, 1998), pp. xxx, lxxx–lxxxiii, 107–10; Gelling, 'Further thoughts', pp. 124–5).

136 P. H. Reaney, *The Place-Names of Essex*, English Place-Name Society 12 (Cambridge, 1969), p. 302.

137 A. G. C. Turner, 'Some Old English passages relating to the episcopal manor of Taunton', *Proceedings of the Somerset and Natural History Society* 98 (1953), p. 120, *ex* manuscript 2, British Library, Add. 15350, fols 27v–28; B 476 *ex* manuscript 1, British Library, Add. 15350, fol. 59rv; S 311, B 476 (sp).

138 M. Reed, *The Buckinghamshire Landscape* (London, 1979), p. 63.

139 B. Cox, *The Place-Names of Leicestershire, Part IV: Gartree Hundred*, English Place-Name Society 84 (Nottingham, 2009), p. 251. Holyoaks Liberty was part of the manor of the adjacent Stoke Dry in Rutland until 1885.

140 S 766, Sir W. Dugdale, *Monasticon Anglicanum*, ed. B. J. Bandinel, Caley and H. Ellis, vol. II (London, 1846), pp. 323–4, no. 6.

141 S 60, B 204 (sp); *WoASCB*, pp. 65–9; S 1598, B 361; *WoASCB*, pp. 403–7.

142 S 496, B 801, S. E. Kelly, ed., *The Charters of Abingdon Abbey, Part 1*, Anglo-Saxon Charters VII (Oxford, 2000), no. 36; M. Gelling, *The Place-Names of Berkshire, Part III*, English Place-Name Society 51 (Cambridge, 1976), pp. 758–9.

143 S 201, B 462, *WoASCB*, pp. 116–17 (sp).

144 Blair, *The Church in Anglo-Saxon Society*, pp. 480–1.

3

Trees in Literature

RUNES, RIDDLES AND REMEDIES

Some literary sources referring to magical or religious belief were discussed in Chapter 1 and there are other forms of literature in Anglo-Saxon England which provide a bridge between the two, in particular runes, riddles and leechdoms. Runes were a form of writing used by Germanic peoples that involved incised letters, at first on wood, deliberately conceived as a series of easily made vertical or slanting strokes. The series of twenty-four letters is known as the *futhark* and can be archaeologically dated as far back as the second century AD, although it is likely to have its origin a century or so earlier. Scholars are divided over whether the runes stemmed from an adaptation of the Roman alphabet or began amongst the German tribes of Denmark.[1] Certainly, runes could be used for magical scripts, but scholars such as Page and Bæksted[2] argue that there is no evidence that this was their prime usage, despite the Eddic poems which note how Óðinn learned the wisdom of the runes during his nine-day ordeal hanging upon Yggdrasill. Elliott presents the evidence for the opposite view, arguing that the runes were essentially closely connected with 'magical or ritualistic practices'; Page also notes how OE *rūn* 'mystery, secrecy' has been 'held to connect the script with the occult, with magic'.[3] Each rune had a name that was also a meaningful word, sometimes that of a tree.[4] Some characters were lost in the Scandinavian *futhark* but in England others were added, among them the runes for 'oak' and 'ash', while þ, the thorn, may be an adaptation from a original *þorisaz*, meaning 'giant, monster'; a number of new runes were restricted to the north and north-west of Anglo-Saxon England. The ash and oak runes appear in Riddle 42: *se torhta æsc . . . acas twegen* 'the bright Ash . . . two Oaks',[5] as letters spelling out, with others, HANA and HÆN for 'cock and hen'.[6] The Old English runes are interpreted in the *Rune Poem*, a West Saxon poem perhaps composed in the latter half of the tenth century.[7]

The yew-tree and the birch-twig already appeared among the *futhark*:

> (eoh) byþ utan   unsmeþe treow,
> heard hrusan fæst,   hyrde fyres,
> wyrtruman underwreþyd,   wynan on eþle.

'The yew is a tree with a rough bark,
hard and firm in the earth, a keeper of flame,
well-supported by its roots, a pleasure to have on one's land.'[8]

The yew had a prized status in many early cultures, and in both the Germanic and Celtic worlds was considered to have protective qualities – its use here as firewood must mean something more than everyday usage and Schneider amends the phrase *hyrde fyres* to *hyrde feres* 'guardian of life' in keeping with the yew's association with eternal life.[9] Elliott argues that the special role of the yew in Celtic lore and in ogham inscriptions (accepting Jackson's view that ogham dates from the late fourth century) was to influence the Anglo-Saxons and Frisians who were influential in runic cryptography.[10]

(beorc) byþ bleda leas;   bereþ efne swa ðeah
tanas butan tudder;   biþ on telgum wlitig,
heah on helme,   hrysted fægere;
gelodan leafum,   lyfte getenge.

'The birch has no fruit; nonetheless it bears
shoots without seed; it is beautiful in its branches,
high of crown, fairly adorned;
tall and leafy, it reaches up to touch the sky.'[11]

Halsall notes how the birch was 'the pre-eminent deciduous tree in northern forests and the first to turn green in the spring' and also played an important part in Germanic fertility rights, while Schneider discusses the birch-tree goddess as manifestation of Mother Earth.[12] Because of the allusion to the lack of (edible) fruit and seed, it has been suggested, however, that this stanza might rightly describe the grey poplar, *Populus canescens*, rather than the birch with its catkins.[13]

The runes seem to have been brought to England from the North Sea littoral, from Frisia/Friesland, and these runes had added the oak and the ash, as noted previously, both trees that were common features in the English landscape (see further Chapter 8).

(ac) byþ on eorþan   elda bearnum
flæsces fodor;   fereþ gelome
ofer ganotes bæþ;   – garsecg fandaþ
hwæþer ac hæbbe   æþele treowe.

'The oak nourishes meat on the land
for the children of men; often it travels
over the gannet's bath – the stormy sea tests
whether the oak keeps faith nobly.'[14]

This is a riddling format, for the oak produced acorns that fed the pigs that became food for men; it was used to build the stoutest ships. This may foreshadow the association of the oak with steadfastness and strength – a popular concept in later English folklore. There is little here to indicate any magical aspect but it has to be remembered that the poem was produced in a by now Christianised country.

> (æsc) biþ oferheah,   eldum dyre,
> stiþ on staþule;   stede rihte hylt,
> ðeah him feohtan on   firas monige.
>
> 'The ash is extremely tall, precious to mankind,
> strong on its base; it holds its ground as it should,
> although many men attack it.'[15]

The ash rune had been present in the original German *futhark* but as the name **ansuz* 'god' which became OE *ōs* and acquired an altered rune, due to sound-change.[16] It is here seen in a battle situation for ash-wood was widely used for weapons, especially spears, again hinting at an association with bravery in battle.

In England, the runes are first found inscribed on portable pre-Christian objects, mainly in the south and east of the country. These include the mouthpiece of a scabbard from a sixth-century grave at Chessell Down, Isle of Wight, and those cut into a burial urn found in the cemetery of Loveden Hill, Lincolnshire, but by the mid-eighth century were being produced on coins in East Anglia and Mercia.[17] Although in south-eastern Europe and central Germany the use of runes seems to disappear with the acceptance of Christianity after the end of the seventh century, in England they seem to have been absorbed into Christian usage and Anglo-Saxon runes lingered on in use into the ninth century. They are found on memorial stones and on the eighth-century Ruthwell Cross in Dumfries and Galloway, where they reproduce an early version of a poem called *The Dream of the Rood*. In Scandinavia a new *futhark* also survived into Christian times and was used in conjunction with Christian symbols: for instance, a runic text accompanies a carving of Christ crucified on a stone from Jelling in Denmark and runestones were commonly used to commemorate the dead, sometimes set beside major routeways or at meeting-places. The Scandinavians brought with them to England their runes but Viking runes are few here and not found after the eleventh century.[18]

Ogham was another early script much used in Ireland after the fourth century AD. It was a Classical system of writing used on memorial stones until about the eighth century. The words are in Celtic form but are conveyed by a series of notches and grooves which probably represent the letters of the Latin alphabet. Certainly primitive forms of writing were in use in prehistoric Europe but it is unclear how reliable medieval writers were in ascribing the use of this script to druidic priests, said to have cut ogham characters into yew rods for purposes of divination (see later in this chapter).

Riddles were particularly popular with the Anglo-Saxons and several (but a small minority) contain runes, one of which refers to the oak, its first letter part of the name *higera*, 'jay or magpie', others with runes also referring to birds and animals (horse and dog are mentioned).[19] Most riddles are chiefly Christian and were indeed composed or collected by churchmen. Several refer to the symbolism of tree and cross. The conversion of trees to the sacred cross was noted in *The Dream of the Rood* in Chapter 2. This may appear again in a riddle where the cross (part of a composite image alluding to a scabbard, sword, cross, Holy Rood and the gallows) is made up of four different woods:

> IC þæs beames mæg
> eaþe for eorlum   æþelu secgan.
> þær wæs hlin ond acc.   ond se hearda iw.
> ond se fealwa holen

> 'I can readily report   on the excellence of the wood:
> there was maple and oak   and tough yew
> and the dark holly.'[20]

The cross is also given the name 'Wolf-Head Tree', that is the tree of an outlaw, a gallows, here the cross upon which Jesus was crucified. Another riddle also begins with a description of the tree as a 'free and fanciful' object before changing to the cross (see below):

> IC eom legbysig   lace mid winde
> Bewunden mid wuldre   wedre gesomnad
> Fus forðweges   fyre gebysgad
> Bearu blowende   byrnende gled

> 'I am an active flame;   'I sport with the wind
> enwound with wonder,   enwrapped by the storm,
> eager on my way,   troubled by fire,
> a blooming grove.'   a burning flame.'[21]

Not all tree riddles refer to the cross for there is another which first describes the living tree:

> IC seah on bearwe   beam hlifian
> tanum torhtne   þæt treow wæs on wynne
> wudu weaxende   wæter hine ond eorþe
> feddan fægre   oþþæt he frod dagum

> on oþrum wearð   aglachade
> deope gedolgod   dumb in bendum
> wriþen ofer wunda   wonnum hyrstum
> foran gefrætwed

> 'I saw a tree   'with bright branches
> stand high in a grove.   The tree was happy,
> the growing wood.   Water and earth
> fed it well,   till wise with time
> it met with a change: it was deeply hurt,
> dumb with bonds,   covered with wounds,
> but adorned in front'   with dark ornaments.'[22]

This tree had become a battering-ram; another which gew up in a field, fed by the earth and sky, was to become a lance or spear.[23] In another riddle the tree 'hung with bright leaves' appears to represent the distaff with flax on it, part of the weaving process.[24]

The third type of literature that sometimes includes runes are healing charms, part of a wide variety of cures which preserve much superstition and folklore but also show how this was being overlaid by the new Christian faith. They are preserved in tenth-century manuscripts 'but the passages in them untouched by Christian beliefs are probably among the oldest lines in the English language'.[25] The Old English *Nine Herbs Charm* contains reference to the runes in a combination of heathen and Christian symbolism and seems to be 'an old heathen thing which has been subjected to Christian censorship':[26]

> ða genam woden   VIIII wuldortanas,
> sloh ða þa næddran,   þæt heo on VIIII tofleah.

> 'Then took Wōden nine twigs of glory
> Smote then that adder that in nine bits she flew apart'[27]

This is explained by Storms:

> He takes nine glory-twigs, by which are meant nine runes, that is nine twigs with the initial letters in runes of the plants representing the power inherent in them, and using them as weapons he smites the serpent with them. Thanks to their magical power they pierce its skin and cut it into nine pieces.[28]

The charm is found within the leechdom known as the *Lacnunga* (*c*.1000), considered to be one of the earliest of the leechdoms and one which may have been influenced by Celtic belief but with many cures based upon Graeco-Roman material, 'modified by barbarian interpretation and mishandling'.[29] Talbot is in some agreement with this view, noting the *Lacnunga*'s use of material derived from Greek,

Roman, Byzantine, Celtic and Teutonic sources.[30] These were often in garbled form before being used by the Anglo-Saxons, but he has been able to demonstrate that much of the Old English medical literature contained in *Bald's Leechbook* was derived from Greek and Roman sources that were often intelligently rewritten and selected with attention to the local needs of the compiler's society.[31] Although the leechdoms embody much of a magical bent, in so far as they depend to a great extent upon the receptiveness and faith they invoke in the receiver, many of the suggested cures are indeed now known to be medically efficacious.[32] Ælfric shows how the oldest substratum of pre-Christian belief had been overlaid by Christian culture and absorbed into Christian practice:

> Nis nanum cristenum men alyfed þæt he his hæle gefecce æt nanum stane: ne æt nanum treowe buton hit sy halig rodetacen. ne æt nanre stowe buton hit sy hali godes hus. se þe elles deð he begæð untwylice hæþengyld;

> Se wisa augustinus cwæð þæt unpleolic sy þeah hwa læcewyrte þicge: ac þæt he tælð to unalyfedlicere wigelunge. gif hwa þa wyrt on him becnytte buton he hi to þam dolge gelecge. ðeahhwæðere ne sceole we urne hiht on læccewyrtum besettan ac on þam ælmihtigum scyppende þe ðam wyrtum þone cræft fergeaf; Ne sceal nan man mid galdre wyrte besingan ac mid godes wordum hi gebletsian ך swa þicgan.

> 'No Christian man is allowed to fetch his health from any stone, nor from any tree, unless it is the holy cross-sign [*rode-tacen*], nor from any place, unless it is the holy house of God. The one who does otherwise undoubtedly falls into heathenworship [*hæthengild*].

> The wise Augustine said that it is not dangerous if any one eat a medicinal herb [*læce-wyrte*]; but he censures it as unlawful sorcery [*wiglung*] if any one tyes those herbs on himself, unless he lays them on a sore. Nevertheless we must not set our hope in medicinal herbs, but in the Almighty Creator who gave that virtue [*cræft*] to those herbs. Nor must any man shall enchant [*besingan*] an herb with charms [*galdre*], but with God's words must bless [*gebletsian*] it, and so eat.'[33]

Although the majority of cures were based upon the use of herbs, trees do find a place. As a 'bone salve' for 'a headache and for infirmity of all organs', the bark of the ash, oak, *wīr* (?myrtle), crab-apple and sallow, together with twigs of willow, were to be 'boiled in holy water' to soften them and added to hazel, ivy-berries and certain herbs to be pounded in a mortar, mixed with grease and old butter, reboiled and filtered several times, mixed with other ingredients which included garlic that had been blessed and 'font-holy wax', all stirred together with a 'quick-beam' [stick] while psalms and prayers were sung over them; this was frst applied to the head wherever the sore might be – this sounds very much like the Christianisation of a more ancient remedy.[34] Quickbeam (interpreted by Grattan and Singer as the aspen but possibly rowan, juniper or gorse – see Chapter 12) and ash bark and so forth could also be boiled in water for *theor* (?bronchial trouble); holly bark taken in goat's milk for a tight chest; sloethorn bark boiled and added to wheat grains and honey as a bath for a finger that has lost a nail; hazel, too, amongst other ingredients for a lung salve.[35] The leaves of trees seem to be less used but, along with herbs, those of the hazel and nut-tree with herbs could be used for a green salve; peach and red sallow leaves in a draught for 'any evil'.[36]

The leechdoms collected by Cockayne also seem to use the bark or 'rind' of trees rather than their leaves in many 'cures', although it is the juice of sloe that is used for a spot on the eye and alder juice for a deaf ear. Ingredients were usually mixed together within the recipes. The following, for instance, gives the recipe for the production of a salve 'for every wound':

> collect cow dung, cow stale, work up a large kettle full into a batter as a man worketh soap, then take appletree rind, and ash rind, sloethorn rind, and myrtle rind, and elm rind, and holly rind, and withy rind, and the rind of a young oak, sallow rind, put them all in a mickle kettle, pour the batter upon them, boil very long, then remove the rinds, boil the batter so that it be thick, put it ever into a less kettle as it groweth less, pour it, when it is thick enough, into a vessel, heat then a calcareous stone thoroughly, and collect some soot, and sift it through a cloth with the quicklime also into the batter, smear the wound therewith.[37]

The bark of the nut tree and thorn, or burnt elm rind, was a cure for tooth ache; that of alder for white spot of the eye; that of quickbeam, elder, ash, elm and so forth, or ash, quickbeam, holly, black alder and spindle were used in a bath for a leper. The bark of quickbeam, aspen, apple, maple, elder, withy, sallow, myrtle, wych-elm, oak, sloethorn, birch, olive and lotus (?hornbeam) but mainly ash, and no hawthorn or alder, were used against shingles; dust of the rinds of oak, ash, elder and so forth used for 'a worm-eaten body'. Oak rind or, alternatively, oak, apple and sloethorn, formed a good wound salve, as did apple, ash, sloethorn, myrtle, elm, holly, withy, young oak and sallow rinds boiled with cow dung. Oak and sloethorn rind was used to ease 'secretion of the joints'. Holly rind or alder rind was mixed in a drink for 'a dry lung'. Elder, hazel or alder and other ingredients were used as an emetic. Aspen, *wīr*, quickbeam, sloethorn and birch were boiled in cheese whey as 'a smearing for a penetrating worm'. Elm, ash, sloethorn and apple rinds were boiled with other ingredients for palsy. Occasionally twigs are specified, as in the case of the elder and oak twigs boiled with other herbs and used for bathing against the effects of leprosy. Leaves figure less frequently but 'an old holly leaf' formed one of the constituents of a recipe for tooth ache. The leaves of the elder could be used to alleviate foot ache, the blossoms boiled in butter as a salve or mixed with honey and wine for the 'half dead' disease, the rind of the roots mixed with other herbs as a weak emetic. The fruits of the apple, pear and medlar eased a distended stomach. The lichen from certain trees was also used: that from the hazel, sloethorn and birch specified – *hæsles ragu* (hazel lichen) with holly rind in a wound salve, *slahþorn rage* (blackthorn/sloe lichen) against the bite of the weaving spider, *berc rago* with other herbs for lung disease.[38] The ability of certain lichens to alleviate ailments later became an accepted form of medicine.[39]

Thus, runes riddles and remedies, all forms of literature that developed in a pre-Christian environment, were adapted to allow them to take their place in the early medieval Christian world.

NATURE IN OLD ENGLISH LITERATURE

The Anglo-Saxon poet was not unaware of the beauty of natural surroundings. A poem known as *The Phoenix*, the first part of which drew upon a late Latin poem *De ave phoenice*, describes the Earthly Paradise in which the bird lived as consisting of delightful woodlands (two translations are given):

> smylte is se sige-wong   sun-bearo lixeð
> wudu-holt wynlic   wæstmas ne dreosað
> beorhte blede   ac þa beamas a.
> grene stondað   swa him god bibead.

> 'Serene is all that glorious plain; sunny groves shine there,
> and winsome woody holts; fruits fall not there,
> nor bright blossoms, but the trees abide
> for ever green, as God commanded them.'[40]

> 'Serene that country, sunny groves gleaming;
> Winsome the woodlands; fruits never fail
> Or shining blossoms. As god gave bidding.'[41]

or further:

> sindon þa bearwas   bledum gehongene
> wlitigum wæstmum   þær no waniað .o.
> halge under heofonum   holtes frætwe
> ne feallað þær on foldan   fealwe blostman
> wudu-beama wlite   ac þær wrætlice
> on þam treowum symle   telgan gehladene
> ofett edniwe   in ealle tid

'The groves are all be-hung with blossoms,
with beauteous growths; the holt's adornments,
holy 'neath heaven, fade never there,
nor do fallow blossoms, the beauty of the forest-trees,
fall there to earth; but there, in wondrous wise,
the boughs upon the trees are ever laden,
the fruit is aye renewed, through all eternity.'[42]

But this is an ideal and unearthly world and the Latin poem is given a thoroughly Christian overtone in which the phoenix becomes a symbol of Christian life in this world and the next, even if not a symbol of Christ himself.[43] The tree demoted by the sins of Adam and Eve is undone by the tree of obedience, bearing Christ at his crucifixion (also in the Tree of Jesse, the genealogical tree):

Crux fidelis, inter omnes arbor una nobilis,
Nullamtalem silua profert, flore, fronde, germine.

'Faithful cross, noblest tree of all,
The forest boasts no peer in blossom, leaf or shoot.'[44]

ðæt is se hea beam   in þam halge nu
wic weardiað

'That is the lofty tree, where His holy ones
hold now their habitation.'[45]

The poem also presents the imagery of the tree upon which the bird dies before its rebirth, an obvious symbol of the resurrection of Christ after his crucifixion on the cross but also invoking shadows of the other legendary Otherworld tree:

on wudu-bearwe   weste stowe
biholene and bihydde   hæleþa monegum.
ðær he heanne beam   on holt-wuda
wunað and weardað   wyrtum fæstne
under heofun-hrofe   þone hatað men
fenix on foldan   of þæs fugles noman.
hafað þam treowe forgiefen   tir-meahtig cyning
meotud mon-cynnes   mine gefræge
þæt se ana is   ealra beama
on eorð-wege   up-lædendra
beorhtast geblowen   ne mæg him bitres wiht
scyldum sceððan   ac gescylded a.
wunað ungewyrded   þenden woruld stondeð.

'a lone spot in the shadow of some woody grove,
concealed and hidden from the crowd of men.

In that holt-wood it keepeth and inhabiteth
a lofty tree, full firmly rooted
'neath heaven's roof; men call the tree
"Phoenix" on earth, from this bird's name.
The gloriously mighty King, Lord of all mankind,
hath granted to that tree, as I have learned,
that of all the trees upon earth's tract
that rear on high their branches,
this one tree blossometh brightest; naught bitter
may cruelly scathe it, but shielded ever
it shall continue unimpaired, while the world standeth.'[46]

'In a woodland covert,   a secret spot
Sequestered and hidden   from the hosts of men.
There he takes lodging   in a lofty tree
Fast by its roots   in the forest-wood
Under heaven's roof.   The race of men
Call the tree Phoenix   from the name of the fowl.'[47]

Carol Heffernan discusses the relevance of the tree symbolism in the poem to Christian belief but relates this to wider feminine symbolism. It is clear that the poem reflects 'humanity's immemorial desire to escape the limits of time, to win second chance, to begin anew', but it also questions the meaning of our existence here on the earth.[48] Briefly, the phoenix lives in a grove on a high Eastern plateau which is remote from man and blessed with temperate weather; at the centre of the grove is a fountain, overflowing once each month of the year, where the bird bathes daily, flying up afterwards to its perch on a tall tree to sing as the sun rises:

wæter wynsumu   of þæs wuda midle.
þa monþa gehwam   of þære moldan tyrf
brim-cald brecað   bearo ealne geond-farað
þragum þrymlice
. . .
þær se tir-eadga   twelf siþum hine.
bibaþað in þam burnan
. . .
Siþþan hine sylfne   æfter sund-plegan
heah mod hefeð   on heanne beam.

'From the midst of the wood a winsome water
Each month breaks out from the turf of earth,
Cold as the sea-stream, coursing sweetly
Through all the grove.
. . .
twelve times the glorious creature there

batheth in the brook.

. . .

Thereafter the proud one   after his watery play,
Takes his flight   to a lofty tree'[49]

The fountain and the tree bear strong similarities to the imagery of the Apocalypse,
noted in the previous chapter.

After a thousand years the old phoenix needs to renew itself and flies to Syria to
seek out another tree in an equally lonely spot for its rebirth, a palm tree in which to
die and recreate itself. There it dies in flames ignited by the sun but the young bird
arises from the amassed ashes of its predecessor. When the young bird grows it takes
the remaining ashes and places them upon the altar in Heliopolis, the Egyptian city
of the sun. The Old English version Christianises the Latin one by likening the tree
in which the bird makes its nest to Christ; the bird is said to be the sign of Christ
as well as of the resurrection of the body on Judgement Day.

Heffernan adds a further interpretation to the imagery of the poem, envisaging
a rich female dimension connected with menstruation, conception and birth, and
also draws upon an Egyptian creation myth. Although this book must be used with
caution, Heffernan has interesting views. She argues that the overflowing fountain
represents the menstrual cycle; the well is the womb; the rites followed by the bird
in seclusion mirror female initiation rites at the onset of puberty, essential signs of
fecundity. Moreover she likens the flight of the bird to the lofty tree to the ascent of
the shaman's ritualistic climb of a pole or tree to re-establish contact with Heaven.[50]
Conception is equated with the flight of the bird towards the sun. Space precludes
a full discussion of this imagery here and readers are advised to read Heffernen's
book for themselves.

The symbolism of a living tree being replaced by the cross, as represented in the
Rood poem, recurs in one of the Riddles, as noted above (although earlier solutions
have proposed a cup and harp for some of the middle lines):

IC eom legbysig   lace mid winde
bewunden mid wuldre   wedre gesomnad
fus forðweges   fyre gebysgad
bearu blowende   byrnende gled
ful oft mec gesiþas   sendað æfter hondum
þæt mec weras ond wif   wlonce cyssað
þonne ic mec onhæbbe   ond hi onhnigaþ to me
monige mid miltse   þær ic monnum sceal
ycan upcyme   eadignesse

'I am an active flame;   I sport with the wind,
enwound with wonder,   enwraped by the storm,
eager on my way,   troubled by fire,

a blooming grove,   a burning flame.
Friends often pass me   from hand to hand
so that men and women   proudly kiss me.
When I rise up   they bow down to me,
many joyfully,   where I shall add
to the oncoming   of blessedness to men.'[51]

Outside Christian symbolism, the Church was implemental in suppressing an interest in wordly surroundings, *mid ðære unnyttan lufe þisse middan geardes* 'with the vain love of this middle-earth'[52] and warned of *þone frecnan wlite þises midda-neardes* 'the dangerous splendour of this middle-earth'.[53] Nature for its own sake finds little place in Old English literature; tree magic, even the enjoyment of trees for the sake of their own beauty, was effectively expunged from the literature.

Jennifer Neville, in her study of *Representations of the Natural World in Old English Poetry*, argues that 'the absence of pagan cosmology can be attributed to a particularly successful campaign by Christian writers, with the result that the continuing worship of trees and stones made no impression on the texts eventually preserved'.[54]

In England, writers like Aldhelm, Bede and Alcuin refused to condone any interaction between Christian and pagan ideas and this remained the case until the twelfth century. In addition, most early medieval literature stems from the Church. The power of Christinianity to permeate every cultural literary expression renders it impossible to differentiate between the secular and the religious.

There are, however, other reasons for the poor representation of nature in literature, both prose and poetry, for this was constrained by the requirement to fulfil particular roles, roles in which the natural surroundings of landscape and wildlife played very little part except in a stylised format. The 'wilderness', often exaggerated, was the place to test the virtue of saints or to be tamed for the better observance of Christ, as Guthlac in his remote fenland restreat states:

Wid is þes westen,   wræcsetla fela,
eardas onhæle   earmra gæsta.
Sindon wærlogan   þe þa wic bugað.

'This wilderness is wide – [there are] many places of exile and secret dwelling places of wretched spirits. They are devils who dwell in this place.'[55]

The grand new cathedral built at Durham, where Cuthbert's body was at last to be interred in 1104, led to the composition of a poem in which the countryside around Durham, perhaps in contrast to the 'noble city', is descibed thus:

And ðær gewexen is wudafæstern micel;
wuniad in ðem wycum wilda deor monige,
in deope dalum deora ungerim.

'A sprawling, tangled thicket has sprung up
there; those deep dales are the haunt
of many animals, countless wild beasts.'[56]

Woodland, especially, is usually portrayed as a wild place with its own inhabitants, especially the wolf:

wulf sceal on bearowe,
earm anhaga;   eofor sceal on holte,
toðmægenes trum.

'the wolf must live in wood
Wretched and lonely; boar must dwell in grove
Strong with his mighty tusks;'[57]

References to the *wulf on wealde* 'wolf in the wood' are common in Old English
poetry, being found in *Elene*, *Judith* and the *Battle of Brunanburh*. The latter
describes the scenes of slaughter after battle:

Letan him behindan   hræw bryttian
saluwigpadan,   þone sweartan hræfn,
hyrnednebban,   and þane hasewanpadan,
earn æftan hwit,   æses brucan,
grædigne guðhafoc   and þæt græge deor,
wulf on wealde.

'They [Æthelstan and his brother Prince Eadmund] left behind them the
dark-coated, swart raven, horny-beaked, to enjoy the carrion, and the dark
grey-coated eagle, white-tailed, to have his will of the corpses, the greedy
war-hawk, and that grey beast, the wolf in the wood.'[58]

Neville notes the roles that the natural world was required to fill. Firstly, the
natural world was depicted in such a way that it stressed the danger and insecurity
of worldly life. Even Bede's description of the sparrow flying through the house
stresses how it must, 'after the briefest space of calm', fly out to meet the winter
storm, likening this to the brief span of man's life upon earth:

cume an spearwa ⁊ hærædlice þæt hus þurhfleo, cume þurh oþre duru in,
þurh oþre ut gewite. Hwæt he on þa tid, þe he inne bið, ne bið hrinen mid
þy storme þæs wintres; ac þæt bið an eagan bryhtm ⁊ þæt læsste fæc, ac
he sona of wintra on þone winter eft cymeð. Swa þonne þis monna lif to

medmiclum fæce ætyweð; hwæt þær foregange, oððe hwæt þær æfterfylige
we ne cunnun.

'and there came a sparrow and swiftly flew through the house, entering at
one door and passing out through the other. Now as long as he is inside,
he is not pelted with winter's storm; but that is the twinkling of an eye and
a moment of time, and at once he passes back from winter into winter. So
then this life of man appears for but a little while; what goes before, or what
comes after, we know not.'[59]

The natural world inescapably and overwhelmingly overshadowed the human
race and the poems use it to indicate danger, peril, powerlessness and uncertainty in
contrast to the afterlife offered by Christianity. The natural world was unmastered
and threatening, a place frequented by those exiled from their kinsfolk and tribe. To
achieve this aim nature is often depicted in periods of storm, as in *The Wanderer*:

> þas stanhleoþu   stormas cnyssað,
> hrið hreosende   hrusan bindeð,
> wintres woma,   þonne won cymeð,
> nipeð nihtscua,   norþan onsendeð
> hreo hæglfare   hæleþum on andan.
> Eall is earfoðlic   eorþan rice
> onwendeð wyrda gesceaft   weoruld under heofonum.

'The storms strike against the rocky cliffs, the attacking snowstorm binds
the earth, the howling of winter. Then the darkness comes: the night-shade
grows dark [and] sends a fierce hailstorm from the north in enmity againt
men. All is full of hardship in the kingdom of the earth; the decree of fate
changes the world for the worse under the heavens.'[60]

If nature is presented, it is shown as an untamed wilderness of devils and dangers.
In *Beowulf*, Grendel and his mother lived in a horrid wilderness:

> Hie dygel lond
> warigeað, wulf-hleoþu,   windige næssas,
> frecne fengelad,   ðær fyrgen-stream
> under næssa genipu   niþer gewiteð,
> flod under foldan.   Nis þæt feor heonon
> milgemearces,   þæt se mere standeð;
> ofer þæm hongiað   hrinde bearwas;
> wudu wytrum fæst   wæter oferhelmað.

'They occupy a secret land, wolf-haunted slopes, windswept crags,
dangerous swamp tracks where the mountain stream passes downwards
under the darkness of the crags, water under the earth. It is not far from

here, measured in miles, that the lake stands; over it hang frost-covered
groves, trees held fast by their roots overshadow the water.'[61]

When Hrothgar followed Grendel's mother to the lake where she bore the bodies
of those she had killed, he

> fyrgenbeamas
> ofer harne stan   hleonian funde,
> wynleasne wudu

'found mountain-trees leaning out over a grey rock, a cheerless wood'.[62]

The vulnerability of man in this world is expressed in a biblical setting in religious poetry but it is nature that provides the evidence for this. In *Judgement Day
II* there are ominous signs of future havoc:

> Hwæt! Ic ana sæt   innan bearwe,
> mid helme bepeht,   holte tomiddes,
> þær þa wæterburnan   swegdon and urnon
> on middan gehæge,   eal swa ic secge.
> Eac þær wynwyrta   weoxon and bleowon
> innon þam gemonge   on ænlicum wonge,
> and þa wudubeamas   wagedon and swegdon
> þurh winda gryre;   wolcen wæs gehrered,
> and min earme mod   eal wæs gedrefed.

> 'Listen! I sat alone in a grove, sheltered by the covering [of the trees],
> in the midst of a wood, where a stream resounded and ran through a
> meadow – all just as I say. Also pleasant plants grew and bloomed there
> in a multitude on the splendid field. And then the trees swayed and
> resounded from the terror of the winds; the cloud[s were] disturbed, and
> my miserable mind was troubled.'[63]

This expresses the 'speaker's precarious and powerless position before the Apocalypse'[64] but it is interesting to find a relationhip between man and nature that has
been used by novelists and poets ever since, vividly more developed than Bede's
original Latin version in his *De die iudicii*:

> Inter florigeras fecundi cespitis herbas,
> Flamine ventorum resonantibus undique ramis,
> Arboris umbriferae maestus sub tegmine solus,
> Dum sedi, subito planctu turbatus amaro.

> 'Among the flowering plants of the fruitful grassy field, with the branches
> rustling everywhere from the gusts of the winds, under the cover of a

shady tree, I, while I sat troubled and alone, [was] suddenly disturbed by a bitter lament.'[65]

Very few images are unique in Old English literature, and there is almost a direct evocation of these passages in the tenth-century manuscripts collected in the *Blickling Homilies*, contained in the section 'The dedication of St Michael's church'.[66] Here, woods again formed part of the horrendous and desolate background:

> Swa Sanctus Paulus wæs geseonde on norðanweardne þisne middangeard, þær ealle wætero niðergewítað, & he þær geseah ofer ðæm wætere sumne harne stán; & wæron norð of ðæm stane awexene swiðe hrimige bearwas, & ðær wæron þystro-genipo, & under þæm stane wæs niccra eardung & wearga. & he geseah þæt on ðæm clife hangodan on ðæm ísigean bearwum manige swearte saula be heora handum gebundne; & þa fynd þara on nicra onlicnesse heora gripende wæron, swa swa grædig wulf; & þæt wæter wæs sweart under þæm clife neoðan. & betuh þæm clife on ðæm wætre wæron swylce twelf míla, & ðonne ða twigo forburston þonne gewitan þa saula niðer þa þe on ðæm twigum hangodan, & him onfengon ða nicras. Ðis ðonne wæron ða saula þa ðe her on worlde mid unrihte gefyrenode wæron, & ðæs noldan geswican ær heora lifes ende.

> 'As St. Paul was looking towards the northern region of the earth, from whence all waters pass down, he saw above the water a hoary stone; and north of the stone had grown woods very rimy. And there were dark mists; and under the stone was the dwelling place of monsters and execrable creatures. And he saw hanging on the cliff on the icy woods, many black souls with their hands bound; and the devils in likeness of monsters were seizing them like greedy wolves; and the water under the cliff beneath was black. And between the cliff and the water there were about twelve miles, and when the twigs brake, then down went the souls who hung on the twigs and the monsters seized them. These were the souls of those who in this world wickedly sinned and would not cease from it before their life's end.'[67]

At best, natural surroundings were a place of little concern until worked by the hand of man. While their bounty at times has to be acknowledged, this cannot be trusted. Neville summarises the Christian attitude thus revealed: 'Through the depiction of the natural world, the state of the human race on earth reveals itself to be a state of perpetual siege. Passive endurance against the natural world is thus transformed into, and interpreted as, active performance of heroism against the devil'.[68]

The natural world is also used to symbolise the fundamental insecurity of the earthly world. Nowhere is this better expressed, using natural symbolism, than in a later manuscript of the twelfth century, Bodley 343, where, in *Homily XII* – 'A message from the tomb' – listeners are reminded that the highest dignitaries and the wealthiest people were open to the greatest dangers and had the furthest to fall, hence, presumably, the folly of desiring high office or earthly riches, but also stressing the transitory nature of any earthly beauty:

> þ treow þe weaxeð on þam wude be ar up ofer alle þa oðre treon, Ᵹ hit þenne feringæ strang wind wiðstont, þenne bið hit swiðor iwæȝed Ᵹ iswenced þene þe oðer wudæ. Eac þa heahȝæ torraes Ᵹ clifæs þe heaȝæ stondæþ ofer alle oþre eorðæ, heo eac þe mare rune nimæð, ȝyf heo feringæ to eorðe fællæþ. Swy[l]ce eac þa heaȝæ muntæs Ᵹ dunæ þa ðe heaȝe stondæþ Ᵹ torriæð ofer alne middæneard; þeahhwæðere heo habbæð wite þæs ealderdomes, þ heo beoð mid heofenlice fure iþread Ᵹ iþreste, Ᵹ mid liȝe toslaȝene. Swa eac þa heaȝæ mihtæ her on worlde fællæð Ᵹ drosæð Ᵹ to lure wurðæþ. Ᵹ þisre weorlde welæ wurðæþ to soreȝæ. . . . For þam nis þissere weorlde wlite noht, ne þisses middaneardes feȝernes, ac he is hwilendlic, Ᵹ feallendlic, Ᵹ brosnodlic, Ᵹ drosendlic, Ᵹ brocenlic, Ᵹ yfellic, Ᵹ forwordenlic.

> 'When suddenly a strong wind arises against it, the tree which grows in the wood up above all other trees in dignity is accordingly more harassed and more lashed than the other trees. So too lofty towers and cliffs, which stand high above all other regions, have likewise the greater ruin, if they suddenly fall to earth. So also, the high mountains and hills which stand lofty and tower above all the world; they nevertheless pay the penalty of their pre-eminence, because they are struck and damaged by fire from heaven and shattered by its flame. So, too, the high powers in this world fall and perish and come to destruction, and the riches of this world turn to sorrow. . . . Then are the riches and the ornaments destroyed, and the splendour annihilated and the gems melted and the gold poured away. And the body is crumbled to pieces and turned to dust. Therefore the beauty of this world is nothing, nor is the loveliness of this earth anything, but it is transitory, and perishable, and crumbling, and decaying, and fragile, and mean, and perishing.'[69]

This is drawn from an earlier tenth-century homily found in the Vercelli manuscript and a homily of Wulfstan:

> Swa ge magon bi ðan þa bysene oncnawan Ᵹ ongitan: þæt treow, þonne hit geweaxeð on ðam wudubearwe Ᵹ hit hlifað up ofer ða oðre ealle Ᵹ brædeþ. Ᵹ hine se strangra wind þonne gestandeð, hit bið swiðlicor geweged Ᵹ geswenced þonne se oðer wuda.

> 'So that we may by that understand and perceive the example: that tree, when it grows in the forest and towers up over all the others and spreads out, and when the strong wind assails it, it is more violently moved and troubled than that other (tree) of the forest.'[70]

Earthly life was transient:

sceawige . . . hwylc se deadlica lichama biþ, þonne seo saul of bið, & seo fægernes þe he her on worlde lufade, swylc þes blowenda wudu & þas blowendan wyrta. We witon þæt Crist sylfa cwæþ þurh his sylfes muþ, 'Þonne ge geseoþ growende & blowende ealle eorþan wæstmas, & þa swetan stencas gestincað þara wuduwyrta, þa sona eft adrugiaþ & forþ gewitaþ for þaes sumores hæton.' Swa þonne gelice bið þære menniscan gecynde þæs lichoman . . .

'contemplate . . . what the mortal body is like when the soul is gone, and the beauty which he loved here in this world – like to the flowering tree and blooming flowers. We know that Christ himself said by his own mouth, "When ye see growing and blowing all the fruits of the earth, and the fragrant odours exhaling from plants, then soon afterwards they shall dry up and dwindle away on account of the summer's heat." So is it like to the nature of man's body . . .'[71]

Even worse, Christianity believed in progressive deterioration:

> þes middangeard
> ealra dogra gehwam   dreoseð and fealleþ

> 'every day this world fails and decays'

(probably because of the sin of mankind).[72] Neville notes how Wulfstan refers to this belief in his explanation of the Vikings' successful attacks against the English.[73]

Trees form a dismal part of this world:

For þan gif hwylc man bið on helle ane niht, þonne bið him leofre, gif he þanon mot, þæt he hangie siofon þusend wintra on þam lengestan treowe ufeweardum þe ofer sæ standað on þam hyhstan sæclife, and syn þa fet gebundene to ðam hehstan telgan and þæt heafod hangige ofdunrihte and þa fet uprihte, and him sige þæt blod ut þurh þone muð, and hine þonne gesece ælc þæra yfela þe æfre on helle sy, and hine ælc yð gesece mid þam hehstan þe seo sæ forðbringð, and þeah hine ælc tor gesece þe on eallum clyfum syndon, þonne wile he eall þis luflice þrowian wið ðan þe he næfre eft helle ne gesece.

'Therefore if any man should be in hell for one night, then he would rather, if he might [depart] from there, that he hang for seven thousand winters at the top of the tallest tree which stands over the sea on the highest seacliff, and that his feet be bound to the highest branch and that his head hang downwards and his feet upwards, and that it appear to him that blood [go] out through his mouth, and that each of the evils which are in hell afflict him then, and that each wave afflict him with the highest which the sea brings forth, and though all the rocks which are on all the cliffs afflict him, he will then endure all this so long as he never seek hell again.'[74]

The association with Óðinn and Christ is obvious but the tree hardly appears here as an image of hope. Similarly, in *The Wife's Lament*, she must live beneath the bole of an oak, rejected by her kin and deprived of the society of friends:

> Heht mec mon wunian   on wudu bearwe,
> under actreo   in þam eorðscræfe.
> Eald is þes eorðsele,   eal ic eom oflongad,
> sindon dena dimme,   duna uphea,
> bitte burgtunas,   brerum beweaxne,
> wic wynna leas.

> 'One commanded me to dwell in the forest's grove, under an oak tree in
> a cave. This earth-hall is old, [and] I am completely seized with longing;
> the hills, the tall mountains, are dark, the fortified towns painfully grown
> over with briars, this dwelling absent of joys.'[75]

A further reference to trees without hope is of course to the gallows tree, so aptly decribed in *The Fates of Men*:

> sum sceal on geapum   galgan ridan
> seomian æt swylte   oþþæt sawlhord
> bancofa blodig   abrocen weorpeð
> þær him hrefn nimeþ   heafodsyne
> sliteð salwigpad   sawelleasne.
> noþer he þy facne mæg   folmum biwergan
> laþum lyftsceaþan   biþ his lif scæcen
> ond he feleleas   feopres orwena
> blac on beame   bideð wyrde
> bewegen wælmiste   bið him werig noma.

> 'Another shall swing on the wide gallows,
> hang dead, until the casket of his soul,
> his bleeding body, is rent to pieces.
> There the raven takes the eyes from his head,
> the dark-coated bird tears at the corpse;
> nor can he ward off with his hands the outrage
> of the hateful flying foe; his life is gone,
> and he, without feeling, and past hope of life,
> pale on the gallows-tree endures his fate,
> enveloped in the midst of death: his name is accursed.'[76]

In tree symbolism there is often an inferred association between the inevitable death of a tree and the fate of man:

> beam sceal on eorðan
> leafum liþan   leomu gnornian

fus sceal feran   fæge sweltan
ond dogra gehwam   ymb gedal sacan
middangeardes

'The tree shall suffer
the loss of its leaves upon the earth, and lament its branches,
The dying man shall depart, the doomed man die,
and every day shall struggle
at his parting from the world.'[77]

Se wlite þæs lichoman is swiþe flionde. ꝺ swiþe tedre. and swiþe anlic
eorþan blostmum. Ðeah nu hwa seo swa fæer.

'The beauty of the body is very fugitive and very frail, and truly like the
flowers of the earth.'[78]

Sometimes the fall of leaf is a gnomic simile for the downfall of the wicked:

Lytle hwile   leaf beoð grene;
ðonne hie eft fealewiað,   feallað an eorðan
and forweorniað,   weorðað to duste.
Swa ðonne gefeallað   ða ðe fyrna ær
lange læstað,

'For a little while the leaves are green, then afterwards they turn yellow
and fall to earth and pass away and become dust; such then is the fall of
those who for a long while commit evil deeds'.[79]

The association between the tree and fate is picked up again in the *Life of St
Kenelm* (Cynehelm), in a legend apparently composed in the middle of the eleventh century (probably between 1066 and 1075) but perhaps incorporating material already in circulation.[80] Two versions of the *Life* are known, one the *Vita brevior* and a fuller *Vita et miracula*, both written in Latin. The first was probably written at Worcester in the third quarter of the eleventh century but with twelfth-century additions while the second is found in an early-thirteenth-century collection of saints' lives. Kenelm is described as a young child, allegedly the rightful successor to his father Cœnwulf, the king of Mercia, when he is said to have been murdered by his foster-father Askebert at the instigation of his jealous sister, Quendrith. The murder took place in the wood of Clent (in northern Worcestershire). The youthfulness of Kenelm cannot be historically true but it was not uncommon in late Anglo-Saxon England for martyrdom to be seen as a strong prerequisite for sainthood. Kenelm was already venerated as a saint in the late tenth century so the oral tradition may well be older than the written *Life*. The manuscript recounts how the child saw, in a dream, a tree standing before his bed, 'so high that it reached right up to the

stars' with himself standing 'in its lofty top, from where I could see everything for
miles around'. Moreover, *arbor pulcherrima et late effusis ramis spatiosa ab imo ad
summum omnibus floribus refertissima*, 'the tree was very beautiful and spreading,
with wide-stretched branches, filled from bottom to top with all kinds of flowers'.
He could see that *innumeris luminaribus et lampadibus totam ardere* 'the whole
thing blazed with countless lights and lamps' and that three parts of this land were
bending low in devotion to him.[81] This is eloquently described in verse in an Early
Middle English version:

> Þis treo was fair and noble inovȝ and schon wel briȝte and wide,
> Ful of blostmene and of fruyt and mani a riche bouȝ biside,
> Berninde wex and laumpes also picke brenninde and liȝte;
> Se noble treo nas neuere iseiȝe, ne non þat schon so briȝte.[82]

However, he saw a trusted friend smite the tree so that it fell, he himself changing
into a white bird that soared into the sky. His nurse interpreted this dream as fore-
telling his future fate and the story continues that when he is led into the forest
('the wood of Clent') by his foster-father Askebert, supposedly on a hunting expedi-
tion, he awakes from sleep to find the latter digging his grave. However, the child
claims that this is not the right spot and that his staff will indicate a different place
'which God has provided'. He planted his staff in the ground and *radicata uirga
cepit frondescere, unde adhuc ingens fraxinus ostenditur*, 'immediately the staff
took root and began to grow leaves, and from it grew a huge ash-tree'. This would
remain a memorial to the murder which swiftly followed in 'a deep valley hidden
between two mountains in that wood called Clent', a tree, the *Vita* claims, *que in
memoriam beati Kelenelm celebris habetur*, 'which is honoured in memory of St
Kenelm'.[83] Tree imagery does not cease here for Askebert cuts off Kenelm's head
beneath a hawthorn tree, his soul rising as a milk-white dove which made its way to
Rome to tell of his martyrdom. The body was buried but the place was indicated by
a white cow which always chose to browse there (in what became known as *uacce
uallis*, 'Cow-valley' – *Kovbache* in the Early Middle English poem), and when, after
disclosure by the dove, the body was exhumed, a spring was to burst forth on the
spot 'which to this day flows into the stream and gives healing to the many who
drink from it'.[84] This medieval story, a fable of no known provenance but perhaps
incorporating elements of truth, combines two of the potent icons of pre-Christian
belief, the tree and the spring, in a Christian martyrdom and miracle story. A church
was built above the spring but the latter was diverted when the building was restored
in the nineteenth century; today the water flows a little to the east but the source is
still reputed to be a healing well.

The ash-tree, the very tree described as that which 'the ignorant call holy/sacred',
in the twelfth-century Taunton charter, figures in other saints' lives: the staffs driven

into the ground by Aldhelm, Cynehelm and Eadwold sprouted miraculously into ash-trees (see Chapter 2).[85] Disaster awaited anyone who felled the ashes at St Nectan's grove at Hartland in Devon; several ashes were associated with 'holy' springs, as at Ilam in Staffordshire; and in twelfth-century legend the site of King Oswald's martyrdom at *Maserfelð* near Oswestry in Shropshire was marked by both a spring and a health-giving ash-tree. As Blair comments, 'The ash was in fact the archetypal sacred tree of northern pagans, and the recurrent choice of it in hagiographies shows beyond doubt that these associations were a veneer on a pre-Christian substratum'.[86] The thorn too was adversely regarded by Christians. While its thorny nature readily identified it with the troubles that beset mankind it may also have been a symbol of profanity and untamed wilderness. Blair notes how, in Æthelwulf's poem *De abbatibus*, an early-eighth-century Northumbriam nobleman called Eadmund is instructed by Ecgberht in Ireland to clear a certain hillside of thorn bushes to create 'a fair church for God', for which he is willing to provide an altar. Æthelwulf twice identifies thorn-bushes with haunts of wickedness and comments that Christ's suffering 'took away the thorny thickets of evil from the world'.[87]

Gnomic verses are a kind of literature found in the early stages of many cultures. They embody a mixture of literary styles with much proverbial material but are yet indisputedly of a Christian nature. It would be unfair, however, to state that, except for the holy cross, the tree was always presented as an image of doom. The Old English *Gnomic Verses* use the tree as the symbol of an expanding Christian faith:

> treo sceolon brædan   ond treo weaxan
> sio geond bilwitra   breost ariseð.

> 'Trees shall spread out and the faith increase
> that arises in the breast of the innocent.'[88]

Much Old English literature was, of course, translated from older texts in other languages, much of it contained in translations of the Gospels or translations of Latin sources. Among Anglo-Saxon reworkings of earlier Classical texts is *De consolatione philosophiae* which was originally composed *c.*475–525 by the consul Boethius after his wrongful imprisonment by Theoderic, king of the Ostrogoths and ruler of Rome. This was translated and re-presented in King Alfred's time, perhaps even by Alfred himself. Works such as the *Paris Psalter* or the *Meters of Boethius* are reworkings of the Latin psalms; King Alfred's West Saxon version of Gregory's *Pastoral Care* draws upon the Gospels, as do the various collections of Old English homilies. This natural symbolism did not necessarily arise, therefore, from Anglo-Saxon thought. Nevertheless, it was accepted and perhaps, indeed, embellished: King Alfred's Anglo-Saxon version of *Boethius*, for instance, adds much that is new to the original and deliberately alters the fatalism and stoical idealism that Boethius drew from the much older writings of the Greeks to a conception of the universe that envisaged freedom of choice. The natural world, instead of symbolising the order of the cosmos, illustrated the power of God to control 'the chaos of the struggling elements'.[89] Recurrent themes, such as that of the tallest tree in the wood being the most vulnerable to the wind, noted above, can be detected, especially in the homilies. In the translated biblical works it is acknowledged that God himself made the natural world which included all fruitful trees: the Cedars of Lebanon (OE *cederbēam*, singular) are especially named (Psalm 104:16). In translations of biblical texts, believers and unbelievers are also likened to barren or fruitful trees: 'the tree is known by his fruit' (Matthew 12:33) and, according to King Alfred's version of Gregory's *Pastoral Care*, the unbeliever must expect to be treated accordingly: *Ælc triow man sceal ceorfan, þe gode wæstmas ne birð, & weorpan on fyr, & forbærnan*, 'Every tree that does not bear fruit shall be cut down and cast into the fire and burnt'.[90] The *Pastoral Care* also repeats Solomon's comparison of the barren fig-tree with a useless and foolish man:

> Swæ se fiicbeam ofersceadoð ðæt land ðæt hit under him ne mæg gegrowan, forðon hit sio sunne ne mot gescinan, ne he self nanne wæstm ðærofer ne bireð, ac ðæt land bið eall unnyt swæ he hit oferbræt, swæ bið ðæm unnytwyrðan & ðæm unwisan men, ðonne he mid ðære sceade his slæwðe oferbræt ða scire þe he ðonne hæfð, & ðonne nauðer ne ðone folgoð self nytne gedon nyle, ne ðone tolætan þe hiene ðurh ða sunnan godes weorces geondscinan wille, & nytwyrðne & wæstmbærne gedon wile.

> 'As the fig-tree overshadows the land, so that nothing grows under it, because the sun's rays cannot reach it, and it does not bear any fruit above it itself, but the land is all useless, it spreads over it so; so it is with the useless and foolish man, when with his disgraceful sloth he covers the district he possesses, and will neither himself make his authority beneficial, nor admit him who is ready to shine over it with the sun of good works, and make it useful and fruitful.'[91]

St Eustace, exiled, and believing that his sons had been eaten by predators, lamented that he had previously grown *swa þæt treow þe mid wæstmum bið fægre gefrætwod*, 'like the tree which is beautifully adorned with fruits' but was then *swa þæt twig. þæt bið acorfen of þam treowe. and aworpen on micclum ystum. and eg-hwanon gecnissed*, 'like the twig that is cut off the tree and cast away in a great storm, and buffeted on all sides'.[92]

More positively, the stronger growth of trees in protected and well-watered places is likened to the word of God. The word can grow from a very small seed just as the tree can grow from the kernal of a nut: *of anum lytlum cyrnele. cymð micel treow.*[93] The *geblowen treow wæstm-berende*, 'full-blown tree bearing fruit', that appeared before St Andrew (from his hair and flesh mixed in the earth after he had been dragged through the streets of Marmadonia) was seen as a sign of God's presence.[94] (Does this share a property of the pre-Christian sacred tree?) A man listening to the word of God

> bið swa swa treow þæt geplantud ys neh ryne wætera þæt wæstm hys sylyð on tide his & leaf his ne gefeallað & eall swa hwæt swa deð beoð gesundfullude.[95]

> Psalm 1:3: 'shall be like a tree planted by the rivers of water, that bringeth forth his fruit in his season; his leaf also shall not wither; and whatsoever he doeth shall prosper'.

The righteous were to flourish like the palm tree, grow like 'a cedar in Lebanon' (Psalm 92). The seasons of man's life are likened to those of trees and herbs:

> Ac cumað oðre for hy, swa swa leaf on treowum; and æpla, and gears/ and wyrtan, and treoweu foraldiað and forseriað; and cumað oððer grenu: wexað, and gearwað, and ripað, for þat hy eft onginnað searian; and swa eall nytenu and fugelas, swelces ðe nu ys lang æall to ar imanne.[96]

> 'Moreover others come instead of them, just as leaves on trees, and apples [fruit] and blades [shoots], and herbs, and trees age and wither; and others come green, grow and are clothed, and ripen, so that they again begin to wither; and thus all beasts and fowl, in like manner it is long all to recount.'

But (Job 14:7–10, 12) 'there is hope of a tree, if it be cut down, that it will sprout again, and that the tender branch thereof will not cease. Though the root thereof wax old in the earth, and the stock thereof die in the ground; yet through the scent of water it will bud, and bring forth boughs like a plant. But man dieth, and wasteth away . . . So man lieth down, and riseth not: till the heavens be no more, they shall not awake, nor be raised out of their sleep.'

The resurrection of man at *domes dæg* 'doomsday' is also likened to the quickening of *ealle treowa . . . on lenctenes timan. þe ær þurh wyntres cyle wurdon adydde*, 'all trees . . . in the Lenten time, which before had been deadened by the winter's chill'.[97]

Paul's well-known words to the Corinthians about a man casting aside childish things as he grows older (1 Corinthians 13:11) are embellished in Ælfric's *Homilies* by reference to the natural process of the development of the tree, likened to the virtuous man turning away from frivolity to virtue and wisdom as he ages: *Ælc treow blewð ær þan þe hit wæstmas bere, and ælc corn bið ærest gærs*, 'Every tree blossoms before it bears fruit, and every corn is first a blade'.[98]

Gregory also uses the tree as an analogy for the way that St Paul, 'the great husbandmen', undertook the care of the holy assembly:

Sumu treowu he watrade, to ðæm ðæt hie ðe swiður sceolden weaxan. Sumu he cearf ðonne him ðuhte ðæt hie to swiðe weoxen, ðylæs hie to ðæm forweoxen ðæt hie forsearoden, & ðy unwæstmbærran wæren. Sumu twigu he leahte mid wætre, ðonne hie to hwon weoxon, ðæt hie ðy swiðor weaxan sceolden.

'Some trees he watered, to make them grow better; some he pruned, when they seemed to grow too luxuriantly, to prevent them growing so much as to wither away and become unfruitful; some twigs he irrigated with water, when they were slow of growth, to make them grow the better.'[99]

Chapter 4 of Alfred's *Boethius* praises the hand of God in the natural cycles of the world:

þu þe þam winterdaʒum selest scorte tida ⁊ þæs sumeres dahum lanʒran. þu þe þa treowa þurh þone stearcan wind norþan ⁊ eastan on hærfest tid heora leafa bereafast. ⁊ eft on lencten oþru leaf sellest. þurh þone smyltan suþan westernan wind.

'Thou, who, to the winter days, givest short times, and to the days of summer, longer! Thou, who, the trees, by the sharp north-east wind, in harvest time, of their leaves bereavest; and again in spring, other leaves givest, through the mild south-west wind!'.[100]

In this natural cycle, wild things preferred their own habitats, as the wild fowls preferred the woods (*weald*), with their own kind, even when tamed. So, also, the trees grew upwards:

Swa bið eac þam treowum ðe him ʒecynde bið up heah to standanne. þeah ðu teo hwelcne boh of dune to þære eorþan. swelce þu beʒan mæge. swa þu hine alætst. swa sprincþ he up. ⁊ wriʒað wiþ his ʒecyndes.

'So it is also with the trees, whose nature it is to stand up high. Though thou pull any bough down to the earth, such as thou mayest bend; as soon as thou lettest it go, so soon springs it up and moves towards its kind.'[101]

Or

Swa bið eallum treowum þe him on æðele bið
þæt hit on holte hyhst geweaxe;
þeah ðu hwilcne boh byge wið eorðan,
he bið upweardes, swa ðu an forlætst
widu on willan, went on gecynde[102]

In his mental endeavours to understand the wisdom of Christ, Boethius wrestles with the meaning of the natural world. Expressed in Alfred's translation, he states that he cannot comment upon the compulsion to live of trees or herbs or other 'creatures as have no souls'. He is instructed not to doubt God's will:

> Hu ne miht þu gesion þ ælc wyrt ⁊ ælc wuda wile weaxan on þæm lande
> selost. ðe him betst gerist. ⁊ him gecynde biþ ⁊ gewunelic. and þær þær
> hit gefret þ hit hraþort weaxan mæg. latost wealowigan. Sumra wyrta oððe
> sumes wuda eard biþ on dunum. sumra on merscum. sumra on morum.
> sumra on cludum. sumre on barum sondum. Nim þonne swa wuda. swa
> wyrt. swa hweþer swa ðu wille. of þære stowe þe his eard ⁊ æþelo biþ on to
> weaxanne. ⁊ sette on uncynde stowe him. ðonne ne gegrewþ hit ðær nauht.
> ac forsearaþ. forþam ælces landes gecynd is. þ hit him gelice wyrta ⁊ gelicne
> wudu tydrige. and hit swa deþ. friþaþ ⁊ fyrþraþ swiþe georne. swa longe
> swa heora gecynd biþ. þ hi growan moton. Hwæt wenst þu forhwi ælc sæd
> growe innon ða eorþan. ⁊ to ciþum ⁊ to wyrtrumum weorþe on ðære eorþan.
> buton for þy þe hi tiohhiaþ þ se stemn ⁊ se helm mote þy fæstor ⁊ þy leng
> standon. Hwi ne miht þu ongitan. ðeah þu hit geseon ne mæge. þ eall se
> dæl. se þe þæs treowes on twelf monþum geweaxeþ. þ he onginþ of ðam
> wyrtrumum. and swa upweardes grewþ oþ þone stemn. ⁊ siððan andlang
> ðæs piþan. ⁊ andlang þære rinde oþ ðone helm. and siððan æfter ðam bogum
> oððe þ hit ut aspringþ. on leafum. ⁊ on blostmum. ⁊ on bledum. Hwi ne
> miht þu ongitan þ te ælc wuht cwices biþ innanweard hnescost. ⁊ unbroc
> heardost. Hwæt þu miht geseon hu þ treow biþ uton gescyrped ⁊ bewæfed
> mid þære rinde wiþ ðone winter. ⁊ wiþ þa stearcan stormas. ⁊ eac wiþ þære
> sunnan hæto on sumere. Hwa mæg þ he ne wundrige swylcra gesceafta
> ures sceoppendes. ⁊ huru þaes sceoppendes. and ðeah we his nu wundrien.
> hwelc ure mæg areccan medemlice ures sceppendes willan ⁊ anweald. hu
> his gesceafta weaxaþ ⁊ eft waniaþ. ðonne ðæs tima cymþ. ⁊ of heora sæde
> weorþaþ eft geedniwade. swylce hi þonne weordon to edsceafte. hwæt hi
> ðonne eft bioþ. ⁊ eac hwæt hwegu anlice bioð. swilce he a beon. forþam hi
> ælce geare weorþaþ to ædsceafte.

'Canst thou not see, that every herb and every tree will grow best in that land which best agrees with it, and it is natural and habitual to it; and where it perceives that it may soonest grow, and latest fall to decay? Of some herbs or of some wood, the native soil is on hills, of some in marshes, of some in moors, of some on rocks, of some on bare sands. Take therefore tree or herb, whichsoever thou wilt, from the place which is its native soil and country to grow in, and set it in a place unnatural to it; then will it not grow there, but will wither. For the nature of every land is, that it should nourish herbs suitable to it, and wood suitable. And it so does; protecting and supporting them very carefully, as long as it is their nature that they should grow. What thinkest thou? Why should every seed grow in the earth; and turn to shoots and to roots in the earth; except because they endeavour that the trunk and the head may the more firmly and the longer stand? Why canst thou not understand, though thou art not able to see it, that all that part of the tree which grows in twelve months, begins from the roots, and so grows upwards into the trunk, and afterwards along the pith, and along the bark, to the head; and afterwards through the boughs, until it springs out in leaves, and in blossoms, and in fruits? Why canst thou not understand, that every living thing, is inwardly softest, and unbroken hardest? Moreover thou mayest observe, how trees are outwardly clothed and covered round with bark, against the winter, and against the sharp storms, and also against the heat of the sun in summer. Who can refrain from admiring such works of our Creator, and still more the Creator? And, though we admire him, which of us can declare worthily our Creator's will and power? how his creatures grow, and again decay, when the time thereof comes; and from their seed become again restored, as if they were then newly created? What they then again are, and also in some measure unchangedly are; such they ever shall be, because they are every year newly created.'[103]

This passage has been reproduced here in full because it combines so much of the biblical imagery into one theme: that God has ordained the world in a particular way, and because it shows tree symbolism in Christian literature at its strongest. Many of these themes are also met in Christian homilies, especially those of Ælfric, abbot of Eynsham (990–2) and of Wulfstan, archbishop of York (d. 1023), which continue to draw upon the earlier biblical imagery but interpret it afresh for the general populace. Within Christian writings there is, therefore, a considerable amount of tree imagery. Admittedly, however, this imagery seems only to be permissable within a thoroughly Christian concept.

As noted above and in Chapter 2, the wilderness is often represented as a fitting place to test the steadfastness of saints; many, like Guthlac, sought remote surroundings as a test of their faith, imitating, no doubt, Christ's trials as he wandered for forty days and forty nights in the wilderness before his decision to ride into Jerusalem (Luke 4:2), but perhaps they are also following Athanasius' *Life of St Antony*, known in Western Europe through the translation of Evagrius.[104] There is, however, a kinder view of the wilderness, apparently sanctioned by the Church, for the Exeter Book, given by the city's first bishop, Leofric, to Exeter Cathedral, notes how Guthlac came to love the remote spot within a wood revealed to him by God, despite its location upon an island in the desolate fens. Here he dwelt close to *beorg on bearwe*, 'the hill/mound within the grove'.[105] The Exeter Book, copied out *c*.965–75, is perhaps the oldest surviving book of vernacular poetry from Anglo-Saxon England and was probably written either at Crediton or Exeter.[106] Might it have drawn some of its sympathy for natural surroundings from its westerly origins, where Christianity seems to have sat more easily within nature? An earlier work, the *Confessions* of St Patrick (*c*.390–*c*.461), relates how this saint, too, found God through his long hours of prayer in the woods and mountains of Ireland, probably in the forest of Foclut, near the western sea, as he grew up there, tending the stock, after his capture by Irish raiders. In his *Confessions*, he wrote how he 'stayed in the forest and on the mountainside, and awoke to pray before dawn, whatever the weather, snow, frost or rain'. It was the natural world, in a Celtic setting, that led him to a perception of God.[107] For, although hermits chose remote locations, these were not entirely unpleasant. God revealed to Guthlac a secret place within a wood where he is said to have dwelt upon an island in the desolate fens, a location he learned to love (according to the A version in the Exeter Book):

> to þam leofestan
> earde on eorðan   þæt he eft gestag
> beorg on bearwe
>
> 'to that dearest home
> on earth, so that he reached again
> the hill/[mound] within the grove.'[108]

A subsequent passage tells of God's love for his creation[109] and how, upon Guthlac's return to his favourite spot before his death, he was greeted by *treo-fugla tuddor* 'the bird-brood of the woods' who he had been used to feeding:

> Smolt wæs se sige-wong   and sele niwe
> fæger fugla reord   folde geblowan
> geacas gear budon
>
> 'Bright was the glorious plain and his new home;
> sweet the birds' song; earth blossomed forth;
> cuckoos heralded the year.'[110]

Some hermitages became the sites of minsters (or, at least, it was became appropriate to claim that a monastery had begun in such a place) and several minsters stood within woods. Thus, Bede notes that a 'fair timbered minster' stood 'in woods' at *Cnofereburg*, Burgh Castle, near Yarmouth, that Bosham near Chichester was set within woods, and Beverley minster was built within *Dera Wuda* 'the wood of the Deiri'. Chad was granted fifty hides of land for a new monastery in Lindsey *At Barwe* 'in the grove', probably Barrow.[111] William of Malmesbury claims that the Benedictine priory at Great Malvern was established *c.*1085 upon the site of a hermitage at the foot of the Malvern Hills in Worcestershire (another version of the foundation myth places the hermitage in a small cave on the hill) and a similar claim is made for the Benedictine priory founded at Little Malvern nearby in the twelfth century.[112] According to Geoffrey of Burton's twelfth-century *Life of St Modwenna*, this Irish saint had also chosen to found a hermitage upon an island in the River Trent in Mercia. This location she 'loved . . . very much . . . For at that time all these places were a complete wilderness, full of woods but empty of people, the dwelling place of wild animals and a desolate solitude'.[113]

In narrative literature, forests may be seen as refuges: the British are said to have fled to them in the face of Anglo-Saxon invasion, as did the warriors of the *Gododdin* or the cowardly followers of Beowulf when attacked by the dragon. The *Anglo-Saxon Chronicle* claims that the fortress at Appledore was a *wudufæstenne* 'fortress protected by wood', i.e. the Weald, in which King Alfred might if necessary seek safety from the Danes.[114] In biblical literature, it was also into *þone grenan weald* 'the green wood' that Adam and Eve went seeking to hide in *þisses holtes hleo* 'this copse's covering/shelter' after their transgression in Eden.[115]

In Irish literature, the natural world continued to play a significant role in early literature and pagan associations seem to have been absorbed successfully after the adoption of Christianity. The strong role of the sacred tree has been discussed earlier but this does not seem to have diminished the obvious joy of depicting trees in their natural surroundings, especially in the *A Marbáin, a díthrubaig*, the tales of King Gúaire, king of Cannacht, and his hermit brother Marbán who preferred to dwell alone in his 'bothy in the wood'.[116] Jackson ascribes this work to the tenth century;[117] the poem is, however, set in the seventh century and describes the ideal of solitude encouraged by the Culdees (*Céli Dé*: 'Servants of God').[118]

> I have a bothy in the wood;
> none but my Lord knows it;
> from here an ash, from there a hazel,
> a great tree of a fort closes it.
>
> Mane with twists
> of the yew of gray trunk
> (famous omen),
> beautiful the place,
> the great green oak,
> besides that augury.
>
> An apple tree, apples
> (great the good fortune)
> big, fit for a hostel;
> a fine crop by fistfuls
> of the green branching hazel
> with small nuts.
>
> Choice wells,
> falls of water
> excellent for drinking –
> they gush forth in abundance;

berries of yew,
bird-cherry, privet.

Produce of rowan,
black sloes
of dusky blackthorn,
food of acorns,
bare fruits
of bare slopes.[119]

There is no Germanic fear of woodlands in the *Dom-farcai fidbaide fál*, which Jackson ascribes to the eighth or ninth century, and where the poet found inspiration:

The woodland thicket overtops me,
the blackbird sings me a lay, praise I will not conceal:
above my lined little booklet
the trilling of birds sings to me.

The clear cuckoo sings to me, lovely discourse,
in its grey cloak from the crest of the bushes;
truly – may the Lord protect me! –
well do I write under the forest wood.[120]

This love of woodland retreats was a constant feature in the *Lives* of the Celtic saints, and the woods depicted here were not always cruel places to test their worth. St Deglan built himself a cell between a hill and the sea hidden away with 'trees close about it in lovely wise'.[121] Nature, including both plant and animal life, seems to be more overtly appreciated for its own sake, and several poems note the beauty of the changing seasons, nature harmonising with the moods of man:

Green bursts out on every plant,
wooded is the copse of the green oak-grove;
summer has come, winter has gone,
tangled hollies wound the hound.
The hardy blackbird sings a strain,
to whom the thorny wood is a heritage.[122]

Or, in the words of Amhairghen to his foster-son Athairne: 'A good season is summer for long journeys; quiet is the tall fine wood, which the whistle of the wind will not stir; green is the plumage of the sheltering wood; eddies swirl in the stream; good is the warmth in the turf'.[123]

Medieval Irish legends abound with tree symbolism, much of it drawn from an earlier age. In the story of Diarmaid ua Duibhne in the Fionn (Fenian) Cycle, the couple elope and in their wanderings enter the forest of Duvnos, wherein is a Tree of Immortality (translated by Dillon as 'the quicken tree'), guarded by the giant Sharvan. After killing the giant, Diarmaid and Gráinne eat the berries (at Gráinne's request), thereby gaining near-immortality. Diarmaid is, however, bound to die by means of enchantment.[124] A version of this story existed as early as the tenth century, referred to in a document of that time, although the earliest manuscript belongs to the seventeenth century.[125] It is in the *Immram Curaig Maíle Dúin*, a story surviving in a tenth-century manuscript, but perhaps emanating from the eighth century, describing a voyage to the Other World, that one hears of one island with apple trees that bear golden apples and another half covered with yews and oaks. On the second island, a huge bird is rejuvenated by washing itself in a lake that is reddened by the fruit from a branch it carries in its claws.[126] This is the tree of immortality again. In the legend of *Scél Baili Binnbérlaig*, ascribed by Dillon from its language to the eleventh century, two trees, a yew and an apple, grew from the graves of two lovers, Baile of the Clear Voice from Ulster and Ailinn from Leinster, who had been separated by death. Each tree, after seven years, carried the likeness of the departed sweetheart but was cut down to make poets' tablets with the wooings of the Ulster or Leinster written on each. When poets congregated to celebrate Samain the two tablets sprang together in the hands of Art, son of Conn of the Hundred Battles, thus uniting the lovers in death.[127]

In the district of Bruing na Bóinne, clearly related here to the Otherworld, as recorded in the *De Babáil int Sída*, 'The Taking of the Fairy Mound', which is preserved in the twelfth-century Book of Leinster but is one of the earliest in its extant form, three fruit trees are always in fruit.[128] Golden apples are a not uncommon theme in earlier tales: as a symbol of authority, Conchobar of Ulster kept 'a rod of silver with apples of gold' above his head in his private room 'for keeping order over the throng. If it shook, or he raised his voice, everyone fell into such a respectful silence you would hear a needle drop to the floor'.[129] It was a branch of three golden apples, too (brought to King Cormac by a warrior from the Otherworld), that gave forth delightful music when shaken 'so that wounded men or those in sickness would fall asleep when they heard it'.[130] Apples figure, too, in the feats that had to be mastered by Cúchulainn in his training with Scáthach in the craft of arms: the 'applefeat' – 'juggling nine apples with never more than one in his palm' – and the 'breath-feat' – 'with gold apples blown up into the air'.[131]

The idea of trees at places of assembly (see Chapter 4) reappears in medieval literature, as in the *Serglige con Culainn inso sís ⁊ Óenét Emire*, 'The Wasting Sickness of Cúchulainn and the Only Jealousy of Emer' (alternatively now entitled *Serglige conCulainn ocus aenét Emire*, 'CúChulainn's Sickbed and Emer's One Jealousy'). This is an adventure story telling how the goddess Fann fell in love with Cuchulainn and lured him to the underworld. It is contained in a twelfth-century manuscript but uses eleventh-century language; again it refers to a *síd* 'fairy mound' in the Other World:

> Before the entrance to the east three trees of purple crystal, in which birds sing softly without ceasing to the children from the royal fort. There is a tree at the entrance of the inclosure – it were well to match its music – a silver tree on which the sun shines, brilliant as gold.[132]

Trees are used in obscure ways in the Ulster Cycle, especially in the *Táin Bó Cuailnge* 'The Cattle-Raid of Cooley', traditionally set in the century before Christ, and related stories. These are probably eighth- or ninth-century material contained in a twelfth-century manuscript, the Book of Leinster, heavily overwritten, and a later fourteenth-century version. In the raid, the armies of Connacht raid Ulster to capture a renowned brown bull, Donn Cuailnge, for Medb, queen of Connacht, so that she might have one to equal the white-horned bull, Finnbennach Ai, which had left her to join the herds of her husband Ailill. Ulster is defended against the Connacht armies by Cúchulainn, the 'Hound of Ulster', in almost single combat. At Ard Cuillenn (Crossakel, Co. Westmeath), he takes an oak sapling, cut in a single stroke, to make a hoop bearing warnings in ogham script for the Connacht army, whom he threatens to destroy.[133] Furthermore, he cuts off the fork of a tree next morning, again with a single stroke, and casts it into the middle of a stream to block the route at the ford of Ath Gabla, 'the ford of the forked branch' (a ford across a tributary of the River Boyne above Drogheda close to the boundary between Ulster and Leinster). He then kills two Connacht warriors and their charioteers, hanging their heads upon the tree-fork to deter the rest of the Connachtmen.[134] Later he carves another ogham message on an oak cut down to bar the way at Mag Muceda, the Pig-keeper's Plain.[135]

Much tree symbolism was drawn from druidic lore. Druidic teachings, however, were all passed on orally and deliberately kept secret. All poetic rhetoric in early Irish literature belongs to the historic period and contains no original Celtic word-forms, which became obsolete in Ireland in about the fourth century AD, although poets might invent arcane ways of expression to stress the antiquity of their profession.[136] Any attempt, therefore, to relate Irish literary tradition to pre-Christian belief must be fraught with doubt and uncertainty. One script in use in early Ireland (as well as parts of Scotland and Wales), probably between the third and sixth century AD, was ogham, a rudimentary system of symbolic writing involving linear marks. This was used for talismanic and memorial inscriptions, which were carved on stones, wood or metal. Some see it as a deliberately secret alphabet created by Irish scholars or druids during the late Iron Age/Roman period, perhaps as early as the first century BC; others as a unique alphabet invented by the first Christian communities, probably modelled on another script (Latin appears to be the likeliest source).[137] Some inscriptions appear to have been cut on aspen, yew and oak logs, but it is a late-fourteenth/early-fifteenth-century text, *The Book of Ballymote* (*Leabhar Bhaile an Mhóta*), that ascribes each letter to a tree name; the 'Tree Alphabet' idea may only go back to around the tenth century.[138] The letters are known collectivly as the *Beith-luis-nin*, an alphabet of originally twenty distinct characters.

Robert Graves, in his treatise *The White Goddess*, first published in 1948, which might be best described as a personal literary quest, believes that a tree symbolism can be traced in Celtic literature which harks back to extremely ancient traditions. He examines an early Welsh poem, *Câd Goddeu*, the mysterious 'Battle of Trees', which is found in the thirteenth-century *Book of Taliesin* but which may draw upon a sixth-century poem.[139] Set during an imaginary war between Gwydion and Arawn, the god of the underworld, the former is said to have called upon the trees of the forest to fight for him. Graves's argument is that the word for 'trees' means 'learning' in all the Celtic languages, and that the alphabet forms the basis of all learning. He claims that each letter was represented by a tree-name, for the druidic alphabet was a jealously guarded secret, and he interprets the poem as a struggle between wits and scholarship: a battle of alphabets which took place between different druid sects, at the same time concealing druidic secrets from Christian authorities.[140] Graves's interpretation of this tale has been contested and, indeed, rejected by many Welsh scholars.[141]

Câd Goddeu 'The Battle of the Trees'

The tops of the beech tree
Have sprouted of late,
Are changed and renewed
From their withered state.
When the beech prospers,
Though spells and litanies
The oak tops entangle,
There is hope for the trees.
The alders in the front line
Began the affray.
Willow and rowan-tree
Were tardy in array.
The holly, dark green,
Made a resolute stand;
He is armed with many spear-points
Wounding the hand.[142]

These are just four of many verses which refer to a number of trees and shrubs, among them the 'swift oak', 'savage fir', 'cruel ash', 'late-coming birch', the 'unbe-loved whitethorn', the 'dower-scattering yew' and the 'blessed wild apple'. Graves examines the symbolism of each tree in complex detail: the seven trees of the Irish grove all belong to the summer months of the Irish tree alphabet, except for the birch, but this has taken the place of the hawthorn. Whatever reliability can or cannot be placed on Graves's deductions, there is little doubt that tree symbolism was a fundamental part of much spiritual belief in many European societies.

ENDNOTES

[1] R. I. Page, *Runes* (London, 1987), pp. 6–9.

[2] Ibid.; A. Bæksted, *Målruner og Troldruner: Runemagiske Studier*, Nationalmuseets skrifter 4 (Copenhagen, 1952).

[3] Elliott, 'Runes, yews, and magic', p. 250; Page, *Runes*, p. 11.

[4] Page, *Runes*, p. 14.

[5] Riddle 42, *Exeter Book II*: Mackie, *Exeter Book*, II, p. 138.

[6] Riddle 69: P. F. Baum, trans., *Anglo-Saxon Riddles of the Exeter Book* (Durham, N. Carolina, 1963), pp. 53–4.

[7] M. Halsall, *The Old English Rune Poem: A Critical Edition* (Toronto, 1981), p. 32.

[8] Ibid., st. 13, pp. 88–9.

[9] Ibid., p. 127; K. Schneider, *Die germanischen Runennamen: Versuch einer Gesamtdeutung* (Meisenheim am Glan, 1956), p. 28.

[10] Elliott, 'Runes, yews, and magic', p. 255; J. K. H. Jackson, *Language and History in Early Britain* (Edinburgh, 1953), p. 152.

[11] Halsall, *The Old English Rune Poem*, st. 18, pp. 90–1.

[12] Ibid., p. 138; R. W. V. Elliott, *Runes, an Introduction* (New York and Manchester, 1959), pp. 47–50; Schneider, *Die germanischen Runennamen*, pp. 262–7.

[13] B. Dickins, *Runic and Heroic Poems of the Old Teutonic Peoples* (Cambridge, 1915), p. 19.

[14] Halsall, *The Old English Rune Poem*, st. 25, pp. 92–3.

[15] Ibid., st. 26.

[16] Ibid., p. 154.

[17] Page, *Runes*, pp. 32–4.

[18] Ibid., p. 53.

[19] *Exeter Book II*, Riddle 24: Krapp and Dobbie, *The Exeter Book*, pp. 192–3; trans. Baum, *Anglo-Saxon Riddles*, no. 68, pp. 53–6.

[20] Riddle 55: (Krapp and Dobbie, *Exeter Book*, p. 208); Mackie, *Exeter Book*, II, p. 146; trans. Baum, *Anglo-Saxon Riddles*, no. 13, p. 17.

[21] Riddle 30: (Krapp and Dobbie, *Exeter Book*, p. 195); Mackie *Exeter Book*, II, p. 120; trans. Baum, *Anglo-Saxon Riddles*, no. 14, p. 17.

[22] Riddle 53: (Krapp and Dobbie, *Exeter Book*, p. 207); Mackie *Exeter Book*, II, p. 144; trans. Baum, *Anglo-Saxon Riddles*, no. 47, p. 39.

[23] Riddle 73: (Krapp and Dobbie, *Exeter Book*, pp. 233–4); trans. Baum, *Anglo-Saxon Riddles*, no. 48, pp. 39–40.

[24] Riddle 56: (Krapp and Dobbie, *Exeter Book*, p. 208); Baum, *Anglo-Saxon Riddles*, no. 37, p. 31 changes the translation to read 'bright leaves'.

[25] Gordon, *Anglo-Saxon Poetry*, p. 85.

[26] Ibid., p. 92.

[27] *The Lacnunga*, LXXXb, fol. 161b (British Library, Harley 585): J. H. G. Grattan and

C. Singer, *Anglo-Saxon Magic and Medicine, Illustrated Especially from the Semi-Pagan Text 'Lacnunga' by J. H. G. Grattan and Charles Singer* (London, 1952), pp. 152–3.

28 Storms, *Anglo-Saxon Magic*, p. 195.

29 Grattan and Singer, *Anglo-Saxon Magic and Medicine*, pp. 65–6.

30 C. H. Talbot, *Medicine in Medieval England* (London, 1967), p. 23.

31 C. H. Talbot, 'Some notes on Anglo-Saxon medicine', *Medical History* 9 (1965); T. O. Cockayne, ed., *Leechdoms, Wortcunning and Starcraft of Early England, Vol. II*, Rolls Series (London, 1865).

32 M. L. Cameron, 1988. 'Anglo-Saxon medicine and magic', *Anglo-Saxon England* 17, ed. P. Clemoes pp. 191–215; M. Grieve, *A Modern Herbal* (Darien, Conn., 1970).

33 *Ælfric's Homilies*, I, 31: Kalendas Septembris. Passio Sancti Bartholomei Apostoli. 'Bartholomew', line 312: P. Clemoes, ed., *Ælfric's Catholic Homilies. The First Series, Text*, EETS, SS 17 (Oxford, 1997), p. 450; trans. K. L. Jolly, *Popular Religion in Late Saxon England, Elf Charms in Context* (London and Chapel Hill, 1996, pp. 92–3.

34 *Lacnunga* XXXIa: Grattan and Singer, *Anglo-Saxon Magic*, pp. 110–13.

35 Ibid. LXXIa: pp. 146–9; CXXIa: pp. 168–9; CXLIXa: pp. 180–1; XXXIIIa: pp. 114–15.

36 Ibid., XVa: pp. 100–3; CLVa: pp. 180–1.

37 *Leechdoms* I.xxxviii.11, fols 37a, b: Cockayne, II, pp. 98–9.

38 *Leechdoms* I.xxxviii.8, fol. 36b; I.lxviii, 1.4, fol. 54a; II.li, fol. 99b: Cockayne, II, pp. 96–7, 142–5, 266–7 (3).

39 Cameron, 'Anglo-Saxon medicine and magic', pp. 206–7.

40 *The Phoenix*, lines 33–6, *Exeter Book I*: I. Gollancz, ed. and trans., *The Exeter Book, an Anthology of Anglo-Saxon Poetry, Part I, Poems I–VIII*, EETS, OS 104 (London, 1895), pp. 202–3.

41 Trans. C. F. Heffernan, *The Phoenix at the Fountain* (Newark and London, 1988), p. 52.

42 *The Phoenix*, lines 71–7: Gollancz, *Exeter Book*, I, pp. 204–5.

43 Gordan, *Anglo-Saxon Poetry*, p. 239.

44 Early-sixth-century hymn: Heffernan, *The Phoenix at the Fountain*, p. 118.

45 *The Phoenix*, lines 447–8: Gollancz, *Exeter Book*, I, pp. 226–9; discussed Heffernan, *The Phoenix at the Fountain*, p. 63.

46 *The Phoenix*, lines 169–81: Gollancz, *Exeter Book*, I, pp. 210–11.

47 Heffernan, *The Phoenix at the Fountain*, pp. 65, 96. Heffernan does not translate the rest of this section.

48 Ibid., p. 13.

49 *The Phoenix*, lines 65–8, 106–7, 111–16: Gollancz, *Exeter Book*, I, pp. 204, 206, 207; first and third stanzas trans. Heffernan, pp. 52, 59, second stanza Gollancz, p. 207.

50 Heffernan, *The Phoenix at the Fountain*, pp. 61–2.

51 Riddle 30, *Exeter Book II*: Mackie, *Exeter Book*, II, p. 120; trans. Baum, *Anglo-Saxon Riddles*, Riddle 14, pp. 17–18.

52 King Alfred, *Boethius*, C.XXXIV.VIII: *King Alfred's Anglo-Saxon Version of Boethius de Consolatione Philosophiae*, trans. J. S. Cardale (London, 1829), pp. 226–7.

53 Ibid., C.XII: Cardale, *Boethius*, pp. 56–7.

54 J. Neville, *Representations of the Natural World in Old English Poetry* (Cambridge, 1999), pp. 148–9.

55 Ibid., p. 127, citing *Guthlac, Exeter Book*, lines 296–8, trans. n. 165.

56 *Durham*, lines 6–8: E. van K. Dobbie, ed., *The Anglo-Saxon Minor Poems*, Anglo-Saxon Poetic Records VI (New York, 1942), p. 27; trans. K. Crossley-Holland, *The Anglo-Saxon World: Writings* (Woodbridge, 1982), p. 185.

57 *Gnomic Verses*: Hamer, *A Choice of Anglo-Saxon Verse*, pp. 110–11.

58 *The Battle of Brunanburh*, lines 60–5: Dobbie, *The Anglo-Saxon Minor Poems*, pp. 19–20 (alo noting variant manuscript readings of *hasupādan* and so forth); trans. Gordon, *Anglo-Saxon Poetry*, p. 328.

59 Neville, *Representations of the Natural World*, p. 24, citing *Historia ecclesiastica* II.13: Miller, *The Old English Version of Bede's Ecclesiastical History of the English People*, pp. 134–7. An Old English version of Bede's *Historia ecclesiastica* is thought to have been in circulation by the early tenth century: L. Taylor, 'The Old English Bede texts: negotiating the interface', in *Proceedings of Borderline Interdisciplinary Postgraduate Conference 2003*, ed. J. Nyhan, C. Griffin and K. Rooney, www.epu.ucc.ie/borderlines/taylor. The original Latin reads (Colgrave and Mynors, pp. 182–5): quale cum te residente ad caenam cum ducibus ac ministris tuis tempore brumali, accenso quidem foco in medio et calido effecto cenaculo, furentibus autem foris per omnia turbinibus hiemalium pluuuiarum uel niuium, adueniens unus passerum domum citissime peruolauerit; qui cum per unum ostium ingrediens mox per aliud exierit, ipso quidem tempore quo intus est hiemus tempestate non tangitur, sed tamen paruissimo spatio serenitatis ad momentum excurso, mox de hieme in hiemem regrediens tuis oculis elabitur. Ita haec uita hominum ad modicum apparet; quid autem sequatur, quidue praecesserit, prorsus ingnoramus.

60 *The Wanderer*, *Exeter Book*, lines 101–6: Neville, *Representations of the Natural World*, pp. 48–99, trans. p. 49, n. 120.

61 *Beowulf*, lines 1357–64: M. Swanton, *Beowulf, Edited with an Introduction, Notes and a New Prose Translation* (Manchester, 1978), pp. 102–3.

62 *Beowulf*, lines 1414–16: Swanton, pp. 102–3.

63 *Judgement Day* II: Neville, *Representations of the Natural World*, p. 110, trans. n. 95.

64 Neville, *Representations of the Natural World*, ibid.

65 Bede, *De die indicii*: Neville, *Representations of the Natural World*, p. 111, trans. n. 97.

66 Morris, *The Blickling Homilies*, pp. vi–vii.

67 *Blickling Homilies* XVII, 'Dedication to St Michael's church': Morris, *The Blickling Homilies*, pp. 208–11.

68 Neville, *Represention of the Natural World*, p. 43.

69 *Twelfth-Century Homilies* XII, 'A Message from the Tomb': A. O. Belfour, ed., *Twelfth-Century Homilies in MS. Bodley 343*, EETS, OS 137 (London, 1909), pp. 130–1.

70 *Vercelli manuscript 10*, lines 156–9: P. E. Szarmach, ed., *Vercelli Homilies, IX–XXIII* (Toronto, 1981), pp. 14–15; trans. from L. E. Nicholson, ed., *The Vercelli Book Homilies: Translations from the Anglo-Saxon* (London, 1991), p. 78.

71 'The Fifth Sunday in Lent', *Blickling Homilies* V: Morris, pp. 56–9.

72 *The Wanderer*, 62b-3: Neville, *Representations of the Natural World*, pp. 49–50.

73 Neville, pp. 9–50.

74 *Vercelli homily* IX, lines 122–30: D. G. Scragg, ed., *The Vercelli Homilies and Related Texts*, EETS, OS 300 (Oxford, 1992), p. 170; Neville, *Representations of the Natural World*, p. 51, trans. n. 125.

75 *The Wife's Lament*, *Exeter Book*, lines 27–32a: Neville, *Representations of the Natural World*, p. 87, trans. n. 140.

76 *The Fates of Men*, *Exeter Book II*, lines 33–42: Mackie, *Exeter Book*, II, pp. 28–9.

77 *Gnomic Verses*, lines 25–39: Mackie, *Exeter Book*, II, pp. 32–5.

78 King Alfred, *Boethius*, C.XXXII, lines 314–318: Cardale, *Boethius*, pp. 180–1.

79 *Solomon and Saturn*, II.314: Dobbie, *The Anglo-Saxon Minor Poems*, p. 42; J. K. H. Jackson, *Studies in Early Celtic Nature Poetry* (Cambridge, 1935), p. 132.

80 D. W. Rollason, 'The cults of murdered royal saints in Anglo-Saxon England', in *Anglo-Saxon England*, ed. P. Clemoes, 11 (Cambridge, 1983), p. 8; Love, *Three Eleventh-Century Anglo-Latin Saints' Lives*, pp. xci, cxii–cxiii.

81 *Vita . . . Kenelmi*, 3: text and translation after Love, op. cit., pp. 56–7.

82 *Saint Kenelm*, lines 43–6: J. A. W. Bennett and G. V. Smithers, eds, *Early Middle English Verse and Prose* (Oxford, 1968), p. 99.

83 *Vita . . . Kenelmi*, 6: Love, pp. 58–9.

84 Ibid., 13: Love, pp. 68–9.

85 Blair, *The Church in Anglo-Saxon Society*, pp. 476–7.

86 Ibid., p. 477.

87 Ibid., pp. 91–3; Æthelwulf, *De Abbatibus*: A. Campbell, ed., *Æthelwulf, 'De Abbaticus'* (Oxford, 1967), pp. 1–13, 15.

88 *Gnomic Verses*, lines 159–160: Mackie, *Exeter Book*, II, pp. 42–3.

89 F. A. Payne, *King Alfred's Boethius* (Madison, Milwaukee and London, 1968), p. 23.

90 Alfred's version of Gegory's *Pastoral Care* (Cotton manuscripts) L, quoting John the Evangelist: H. Sweet, ed., *King Alfred's West-Saxon Version of Gregory's Pastoral Care*, I–II, EETS, OS 45 (London, 1871), p. 338, trans. pp. 338–9.

91 Ibid., XLV, p. 336, trans. pp. 336–7.

92 XXX. 'Passion of St. Eustace. Martyr', lines 190–2, *Ælfric's Lives of the Saints*, II: Skeat, pp. 202–3.

93 *Ælfric's Homilies*, XVI Dominica post Pasca ('First Sunday after Easter'), I, lines 120–1: P. Clemoes, ed., *Ælfric's Catholic Homilies. The First Series, Text*, EETS, SS 17 (Oxford, 1997), p. 311.

94 'S. Andreas', *Blickling Homilies*, II: Morris, pp. 244–5.

95 *Cambridge Psalter*: K. Wildhagen, *Der Cambridger Psalter* (Hamburg, 1910).

96 *St Augustine, Soliloquies*, I.10.2: W. Endter, *König Alfreds des Grossen Bearbeitung der Soliloquien des Augustinus*, Prosa 11 (Hamburg, 1922).

97 XII, 'Ash-Wednesday', lines 31–2, *Ælfric's Lives of the Saints*, I: Skeat, pp. 262–3.

98 *Homilies of Ælfric*, II: J. C. Pope, ed., *Homilies of Ælfric: A Supplementary Collection*, 2 vols, EETS, OS 260 (London, 1968), p. 623.

99 Alfred's version of Gregory's *Pastoral Care* (Cotton manuscripts), XL: Sweet, *Pastoral Care*, p. 292.

100 King Alfred, *Boethius*, C.IV: Cardale, *Boethius*, pp. 10–11.

101 First version ibid., C.XXV: Cardale, *Boethius*, pp. 138–9.

102 Version from *Meters of Boethius* 13, line 51: G. P. Krapp, ed., *The Paris Psalter and the Meters of Boethius*, Anglo-Saxon Poetic Records V (New York, 1932; London, 1933), p. 172.

103 King Alfred, *Boethius*, XXXIV: Cardale, *Boethius*, pp. 232–5.

104 C. A. M. Clarke, *Literary Landscapes and the Idea of England, 700–1400* (Cambridge, 2006), p. 27, referring to Evagrius, *Vita sancti Antonii, auctore sancto Athanasio interpret Evagrio*, PL 73, cols 125–70.

105 *Saint Guthlac, Exeter Book*, A II.148, V.429: Gollancz, *Exeter Book*, I, pp. 112–13, 130–1 (with differing trans. of *beorg*).

106 B. J. Muir, *The Exeter Anthology of Old English Poetry*, revised 2nd edn (Exeter, 2000), pp. 1–3.

107 Rees, *Celtic Saints*, pp. 28, 180; *Confession* 16, based on D. R. Howlett, *The Book of Letters of St Patrick the Bishop* (Dublin, 1994); J. Skinner, *The Confession of St Patrick and Letter to Coroticus* (New York, 1998); T. O'Loughlin, *St Patrick: The Man and His Works* (London, 1999).

108   *Saint Guthlac*, A.V.427–9: Gollancz, *Exeter Book*, I, pp. 130–1.

109   Ibid., A.VIII.760: Gollancz, *Exeter Book*, I, pp. 150–1.

110   Ibid., A.VIII.742–4: Gollancz, *Exeter Book*, I, pp. 148–9.

111   *Historia ecclesiastica* III.19; IV.13; V.2; IV.3: Sherley-Price, revised Latham, *A History of the English Church and People*, pp. 172, 228, 271, 208.

112   R. R. Darlington, ed., *The Vita Wulfstani of William of Malmesbury*, Royal Historical Society, Camden Society, 3rd series, 30 (London, 1928); *Victoria County History Worcestershire II*, 136; B. Smith, *A History of Malvern* (Leicester, 1964), pp. 41–2.

113   Geoffrey of Burton, *Life and Miracles of St Modwenna*, 35: Bartlett, pp. 145.143.

114   *Anglo-Saxon Chronicle* 894 for 893.

115   *Genesis B*, ls 840–1: Krapp, *Junius Manuscript*, Anglo-Saxon Poetic Records I, p. 28.

116   'Guaire and Marban': *A Marbáin, a díthrubaig*, manuscript Harl. 5280, fol. 42b: R. P. M. Lehmann, ed. and trans., *Early Irish Verse* (Austin, 1982), pp. 42–7.

117   Jackson, *Studies in Early Celtic Nature Poetry*, pp. 36, 96–100, 107.

118   Rees, *Celtic Saints*, p. 45.

119   Lehmann, *Early Irish Verse*, st. 8, 13–15, 19, pp. 43–5.

120   'Writing in the Wood': *Dom-farcai fidbaide fál*, Jackson, *Studies in Early Celtic Nature Poetry*, II, st. 1–2, p. 3. Rees, *Celtic Saints*, p. 41, notes how this poem was preserved on the margins of a ninth-century Latin grammar found in the monastery of St Gall in Switzerland.

121   *Vita Sancti Declani*, cited by Jackson, *Studies in Early Celtic Nature Poetry*, pp. 96–7.

122   '*Táinic sam slán sóer*, Summer Has Come (Four Songs)', tenth century: Jackson, *Studies in Early Celtic Nature Poetry*, XXVI, p. 25.

123   '*Fó sín samrad síthhaister*, Summer (The Four Seasons)', eleventh century: Jackson, *Studies in Early Celtic Nature Poetry*, p. 66.

124   Green, *Celtic Myths*, p. 39.

125   M. Dillon, *Early Irish Literature* (Chicago, 1948), p. 42.

126   Ibid., pp. 125–9.

127   Ibid., pp. 85–6.

128   Ibid., p. 53.

129   *Compert Conchoboir*, eighth century, version in Kinsella, *The Tain*, pp. 6, 255–6.

130   Dillon, *Early Irish Literature*, p. 110.

131   '*Tochmarc Emire*', tenth/eleventh century, version in Kinsella, *The Tain*, pp. 34, 259–60.

132   '*Serglige conCulainn inso sís /&/ Óenét Emire*': Dillon, *Early Irish Literature*, p. 121.

133   Dillon, *Early Irish Literature*, p. 6; translated by Kinsella as 'a spancel-hoop of challenge': Kinsella, *The Tain*, p. 68.

134   Dillon, *Early Irish Literature*, pp. 6–7; Kinsella, *The Tain*, pp. 72–6.

135   Kinsella, *The Tain*, p. 92.

136   Ó hÓgáin, *The Sacred Isle*, p. 90.

137   M. P. Brown, *Pagans and Priests* (Oxford, 2006), p. 19; D. McManus, *A Guide to Ogam* (Maynooth, 1991).

138   McManus, op. cit.

139   Book of Taliesin, Peniarth manuscript 98B, University of Wales, C16/167.

140   Graves, *The White Goddess*, see especially pp. 111, 160, 228–9, 251, 255.

141   Such as Marged Haycock and Mary Ann Constantine.

142   Graves, *The White Goddess*, pp. 41–3.

4

Trees, Mythology and National Consciousness: into the Future

TREES AND SYMBOLICAL PLACES OF ASSEMBLY

As shown in Chapters 1 and 2, trees had long been used, along with stones, mounds and other features (including giant posts) to mark places of assembly. In pre-Christian times diviners and enchanters met at large, significant trees which were held to be sacred to carry out their offices. As Flint expresses it, these were focal points of reverent expectation, places to which people came to stave off terrors, appease their anxieties, pour out their desires of their hearts, to seek comfort and help in sadness.[1] The giant oak at Geismar destroyed by Boniface, the Irminsul destroyed by Charlemagne, and the great sacred tree decorated with a golden image of a viper destroyed by St Barbatus of Benevento (d. 682), recorded in a ninth-century compilation, may have been examples of such trees, while in the Besle valley (Pays-de-la-Loire, France) St Valery found a great tree trunk 'carved with all kinds of images'.[2] After the acceptance of Christianity, however, the great mythological trees were to virtually disappear from the national consciousness of Western Europe, although the World Tree of Indo-European lore lingered on in Norse mythology as Yggdrasill until medieval times and remained central to many East European and other worldwide cultures. None survived in England with any degree of powerful symbolism. However, they lived on in Irish mythology.

Certain Celtic tribes in Gaul had been associated with particular species of tree. The Ebutones were the 'Yew Tribe', the Lemovices, 'the people of the elm',[3] and the five sacred trees of Ireland became legendary guardians of five Irish provinces. The five most sacred trees of mythology and legend: *Eó Mugna* (an oak which bore acorns, apples and nuts), *Eó Rossa*, 'the tree of Ross' (a yew), *Bile Tortan*, 'Tortu's tree' (an ash), *Craeb Daithi*, 'the branch of Dath-I' (also an ash), and *Bile* or *Craeb Uisnig* (another ash), had stood at the centre of five provinces. All were connected with legendary kings, only becoming manifest as these kings had been born, as in the stories of Conn Cétchathach, or had begun to establish their dynasties. It seems that a *bile* was regarded as an appropriate adjunct to a chiefly or kingly residence.[4] Thus, the sacred tree was intimately connected with the concept of kingship, wisdom and sovereignty and possibly marked the site of the king's inauguration. 'As the center of its territory, the tree is functioning as an *axis mundi*. . . . The tree was a symbol for this central axis, which passed from the underworld through a "hole" or "opening" into the sky'.[5] Ó hÓgain sees the *bile*, metaphorically seen as 'a champion or a protector', as a symbol of the reigning king 'who stood between heaven and earth and thus kept both in equilibrium for the welfare of his subjects. It is no coincidence that the inauguration of a local king often took place at a special tree in the territory of his sept'.[6] The tree thus gave protection to the whole tribe of each province, but more: 'As one of the most ancient living things, it rooted the tribe in history and served, in concrete form, as a way of making time and its passage comprehensible to men'.[7] Joyce notes how 'Trees of this kind were regarded with intense reverence and affection; one of the greatest triumphs that a tribe could achieve over their enemies, was to cut down their inauguration tree, and no outrage was more keenly resented, or when possible, visited with sharper retribution'.[8] The Irish Annals record, under 981, how the *bile* ('large tree') of *Magh-adhar* in Clare, the great tree under which the O'Briens were inaugurated, was rooted out of the earth and cut up by Malachy, king of Ireland. Under 1111, the Ulidiands led an army to Tullahogue, the inauguration place of the O'Neills, and cut down the old trees, for which Niall O'Loughlin afterwards exacted a retribution of 3,000 cows.[9] Trees at sites of tribal significance may have been replaced by Christian symbols after conversion and an early-tenth-century stone cross, the West Cross at Clonmacnois, Co. Offaly, shows two figures who may represent Abbot Colmán and King Flann mac Máel Sechnaill planting a staff in the ground, in keeping with the hagiographic tradition noted in previous chapters.[10]

Another, probably real, tree found its way into national historical record as the site of the Battle of Hastings where King Harold encountered his adversary William of Normandy. According to the *Anglo-Saxon Chronicle*, William landed at Pevensey in 1066 and hastily threw up fortifications at Hastings. Upon hearing of this, Harold was forced to rush southwards immediately after his victory over another claimant to the English throne, Harald Hardrada (incorrectly named in the Chronicle Harold *Hār fagera* 'Harald Fine-hair', who had died *c.*936): *Þis wearð þa Harolde cynge gecydd. ꝺ he gaderade þa mycelne here. ꝺ com him togenes æt þære haran apuldran*, 'Then this became known to King Harold and he gathered a great raiding-army, and he came against him at the grey apple-tree'.[11] Harold was attacked on 14 October before he was fully prepared and ultimately lost the battle, ever since known as the Battle of Hastings. The site was subsequently granted, in 1094, by William to the Church for the foundation of an abbey following the Benedictine rule, with the high altar located on the spot where Harold fell. It was first known as Holy Trinity but later as Battle Abbey.

HOLY TREES IN FOLKLORE AND LEGEND

While the symbolical 'Tree of Life' meant to the Christians the cross of the cruci-fixion, 'the new life-bearing tree' (Chapter 2), to others it remained the tree linking the cosmos. It has been shown that such beliefs were not easily eliminated. In Siberia, the tree, 'with its roots in the ground, its trunk on the earth and the branches in the sky, was a model of the cosmos' (see Chapter 1).[12] It was rightly the burial place for wizards, linking the earth with the upper world, the link between death and life. The tree plays a fundamental role in shamanistic practices: 'The shaman has been nurtured in this tree, and his drum, fashioned of its wood, bears him back to it in his trance of ecstasy . . . While in this trance he is flying as a bird to the upper world, or descending as a reindeer, bull, or bear to the world beneath'.[13] Trees were also associated with healing; Karamzin notes how, in early times, 'the Slavs in Russia offered prayers to trees, especially hollow ones, binding their branches with lengths or pieces of cloth'.[14] Oak groves were still regarded as sacred places among the Prussians as late as the sixteenth century, when the god of thunder was worshipped among oak-trees, with images kept in the trunk of a tree and a fire which was never allowed to go out burnt before that of the thunder god.[15] In Russia, too, trees continued to be venerated in medieval times. In 1534 the archbishop of Novgorod instructed the clergy in an extensive region to extirpate ancestor worship, including 'praying in their obscene shrines to trees and stones'.[16] People still frequented certain groves on the first Monday after St Peter's Day (29 June in the Orthodox calendar) in the mid-sixteenth century, where they engaged in 'devilish amusements'.[17] This is not, however, the latest survival, as will be seen.

The miracle of the flowering staff that was so popular in hagiographical literature (see Chapters 2 and 3) was a part of many legendary saints' *Lives* when the cult of saints was active in medieval times. The staff thrust into the ground might burst into life and become a mature tree; a dead tree might be brought back to life at a saint's command; a sterile tree might bear fruit or a tree in winter might bear unseasonal fruit – these are common motifs in medieval saints' *Lives*. On one occasion, a saint caused an entire forest to come into rapid existence.[18] One kind of tree might meta-morphose into another species – thus Samthanne changed a willow into a pine tree.[19] The legend of the Glastonbury thorn, noted in Chapter 2, may have arisen as late as the sixteenth century. Associations of holy wells with trees also remained common (see the *Life of St Kenelm*, Chapter 3). This cult remained very much alive in the folklore of Ireland. In Irish lore, a hazel tree, the source of sacred wisdom, grew over the source of the Shannon, which was said to rise in a subaqueous land, and nine hazels over a well in 'the Celtic Land of Promise'. In Co. Tipperary Connla's well was surrounded by another nine hazels which fed with their nuts the sacred salmon[20] (for hazel as the tree of knowledge, see further Chapter 11). Medieval liter-ature also frequently refers to the tree-well cult, usually in a Christianised form. In the Arthurian cycle, trees invariably grew over holy wells, and in the tenth-century Irish text, *Navigatio sancti Brendani*, 'voyagers came to an island and found a well overshadowed by a tree whose branches were covered with birds which sang the canonical hours on holy days'.[21] Trees or groves also formed trysting places in many medieval tales (perhaps a lingering link with their earlier association with fertility).

The Tree of Life has been noted in earlier chapters as an originally Near-Eastern motif, which easily lent itself to Christian interpretation, associated with the awakening to knowledge in the Garden of Eden and the symbol of the cross of Jesus, which made an afterlife possible through Christ's death and reincarnation. Typically, the tree is represented as a stem from which sprout 'spiralling, volute-like branches', often accompanied by a pair of animals or fabulous creatures or birds. The representation of animals and beasts, parts of whose bodies turn into foliage, is fairly common in Anglo-Saxon and Romanesque sculpture, found, for instance, on the capitals in the retrochoir of Romsey Abbey where the beasts have humanoid faces. Usually it is the tail or rear legs that become foliate, although on occasions the beasts are found disgorging vegetation through the mouth or face, like the later 'green man' heads.

Leaf masks from a nearby ruined second-century Roman temple were incorporated into the piers of Trier cathedral as early as the sixth century by Bishop Nicetus and, probably initially admired for their attractiveness, brightly painted (they had been a feature of Roman art since the first century AD). The use of the leaf-mask motif thus became sanctioned by the Church. It was under an eighth-century theologian, Rabanus Maurus, abbot of Fulda and archbishop of Mainz, that the evil aspect of the mask became accentuated, for, according to him, 'the leaves represented the sins of the flesh or lustful and wicked men doomed to eternal damnation'.[22] In England 'green men' do not appear before the late Norman period; Basford recognises this lascivious aspect in some of those introduced into English churches. The earliest English examples appear to be of a 'stiff-leaf' type: that on the doorframe at Kilpeck dates from *c*.1140 and another at Much Marcle, Herefordshire, has been dated to 1260; they increase in number in the later medieval period.[23] These masks are usually shown as disgorging interlaced or scrolling foliage. To the medieval mind, the mouth was the orifice that gave direct access to the soul but also allowed the escape of sin, thereby achieving salvation.

Foliate heads were becoming widespread in the thirteenth century, especially in France.[24] In England, by that date, church decorative motifs were becoming increasingly naturalistic, ornamented with wild plants such as the hawthorn, hop, buttercup, maple or oak, sometimes pouring out from the masks. The 'Green Man' was thus another cult associated with natural greenery. By the thirteenth to fifteenth centuries, throughout the churches and cathedrals of Britain and Western Europe the image of a (usually frowning) male face spewing out such greenery is tucked away for example on roof bosses, capitals, corbels, bench ends or misericords. Many have interpreted this as an ancient representation of fertility, the legendary 'Jack in the Green', hijacked by the Church from pagan myth, the foliate designs, associated with beasts and human heads, being an expression of tree symbolism often attributed to lingering superstition. Some even believe that the myth may have drawn upon the more sinister background of the Celtic head cult, hinted at in the medieval poem *Sir Gawain and the Green Knight*.[25] But the iconography was taken willingly into the Christian Church and was obviously to become part of medieval ecclesiastical iconography.

Basford rejects the Green Man as the popular May King of folklore, the symbol of the renewal of life in springtime. Rather, she argues that the Church saw him as 'the darkness of unredeemed nature as opposed to the shimmering light of Christian revelation' or, 'an image of death and ruin rather than life and resurrection'.[26] She continues:

> The use of the foliate head on Christian tombs and memorials (a use continued long after the motif had fallen out of favour as an ornament in church architecture) might suggest the idea of resurrection – a life out of death symbol, but could equally well suggest: 'For all flesh is as grass and all the glory of man as the flower of grass. The grass withereth and the flower thereof falleth away', Peter 1.24. The Christian soul, having renounced sinful nature – the World, the Flesh and the Devil – at baptism, hoped for salvation through grace after death. A foliate head carved on a font or a tomb could allude to man's fallen and concupiscent nature, or to his brief life on earth – a reminder that 'All greenness comes to withering'.[27]

Thus this may be another example of the Church's rejection of nature and the mythological symbolism of sacrifice and immortality. Woodcock, in a recent study of medieval ecclesiastical sculpture, also comments upon such symbolism and agrees that the regurgitation of foliage might be associated with the themes of renewal and resurrection, 'of dying in this world to be reborn in another', not shrinking from the imagery of physical suffering and decay. Death was a major theme of religious symbolism and the Green Man was therefore often used on high-status tombs in later medieval times, 'alchemically blending together otherworldly ecstasy with physical suffering'.[28] Others maintain a rather more benign view than that of Basford, interpreting the Green Man in Christian iconography as perhaps representing the belief that God is also the God of nature, 'forgotten at our peril'.[29]

The forest, too, continued to have a fearsome aspect in medieval Christian iconography. In a recent study of the fourteenth-century carved roof bosses of Norwich Cathedral, Sally Mittuch[30] shows how the bosses of the east walk of the cloister mark a progression within a forest towards the soul's judgement, for they are carved with spirals formed by the leaves of hawthorn, oak, maple and vine, in sequences symbolising either death or rebirth and salvation. The first progress leads towards a 'dark entry', symbolising the judgement of the soul, and is marked by a series of bosses depicting, in turn, an anticlockwise leaf spiral (the direction symbolising death), then motherwort and hawthorn, oak, hawthorn and maple, a hawthorn swirl, and a vine, leading towards the 'dark entry', the access to a dark chamber where corpses would have been laid out on biers awaiting burial. Mittuch sees this as related to Bede's eighth-century description of the near-death experience of the Irish saint, Fursey, who saw below him a dark, and thus perhaps forested, valley with the fires of damnation burning, but was judged by angelic spirits and returned to life, having been instructed on how to give salvation to the dying. This perilous battle between angels and demons at the time of death is the medieval concept that perhaps underlies the cloister walk of Norwich Cathedral, illustrating the soul travelling 'deep into a forest' until it heads for a glimmer of light, emerging at the dark entry beneath 'a glimmering green-man boss', which Mittuch sees as guiding the way. Here the battle for the soul erupts in fury with demons, including fighting wyverns, and angels at the point of judgement. The mouth of the green man gives access to the soul, and whatever he signifies, he is a Christian symbol and not a pagan effigy somehow sneaked into the Church, even if one borrowed from earlier beliefs. Another enigmatic woodwose, 'wild man' or satyr, is a hairy, but different, creature who appears in some East Anglian churches, apparently suggesting savagery, lust and uncontrolled passions.

TREES IN SEASONAL RITUAL

Tree symbolism continued to play a part in countryside ritual. One of Eliade's vegetation cult types was 'the tree as symbol of the resurrection of vegetation, of spring and of the "rebirth" of the year'. Some have argued that this concept may have underlain ceremonies in which trees have been ritually decorated.[31] These have often been centred upon the oak, as in some of the ceremonies carried out on Oak Apple Day, but the antiquity of such ceremonies can rarely be proven. It is a black poplar that is adorned on 29 May at Aston-on-Clun in Shropshire.[32] Dancing was often an integral part of such ceremonies. The Maypole dances, initially around a new tree brought in each year, undoubtedly reflect this tradition and were widespread throughout Europe; the new tree and the fresh foliage which was used to deck farms and buildings may have represented the newly awakened spirit of vegetation. The ceremonies were often blatantly orgiastic; the link with fertility also appears to be reflected in the many trysting trees. The milky liquid of the mistletoe and the shape of the cupped acorn had direct visual links with male sexual activity,[33] but in most cases the link was more subtle: certain oaks known as Marriage Oaks would be visited after a wedding, again to be danced around, but in a Christianising ceremony a cross would be cut into the bark.[34]

The bringing in of greenery played a significant part in such seasonal ritual, although this is rarely documented before medieval times. Evergreens were brought into homes and churches at Christmastime in the sixteenth century, particularly the holly and the ivy, the former sometimes into the interior, the latter into the porch.[35] The holly, with its sharp spines and red berries, may have symbolised the crown of thorns, and Christ's blood and was not, like the ivy, without echoes of earlier pagan symbolism.[36] Hutton notes that this is a custom 'of demonstrable pagan origin', and, as such, was to be largely discontinued under the wave of Protestantism and, more especially, Puritanism, that spread in the sixteenth and seventeenth centuries.[37] At Eastertide the palms used elsewhere were not available and in England fronds of willow or sallow in fresh leaf, or box, yew or other evergreens, might be substituted and consecrated. Palm Sunday itself might be known as 'Branch', 'Sallow', 'Willow' or 'Yew' Sunday. The earliest record of the hallowing of fronds was in the mid-eighth century, enjoined in a pontifical of Archbishop Egbert of York.[38] In May, the raising of a maypole was recorded by the early fifteenth century but the gathering of may garlands was undoubtedly a much older practice and again, at midsummer, garlands, including the green birch (and sometimes the broom), together with flowers, might be hung over doors.[39] After the Restoration such practices were revived and were particularly enjoyed in Victorian England, when the practice of decorating an evergreen Christmas tree became widely favoured. The bringing-in of the Yule log was also popular in nineteenth-century Britain, first recorded in the 1620s or 1630s but by then a well-established tradition, perhaps regarded as conferring some kind of magical protection upon the house. The tradition was first recorded in Germany in the twelfth century.[40] The tradition of bringing in greenery continues today; at Charlton-on-Otmoor, near Oxford, for instance, a large wooden cross known as 'The Garland', solidly covered in greenery, stands on the sixteenth-century roodscreen and is redecorated twice a year (including at the May Day celebrations) with a fresh garland of yew and box foliage.[41]

In southern England wassailing was carried out to bring health to crops and animals and may have descended directly from pagan practices (in the Western Isles and coastal Highlands a similar practice was known as saining). To secure good yields, fruit trees were 'wassailed' in parts of the south-west and south-east, and in western Worcestershire; from at least the seventeenth century, offerings of food to the trees were made, later explained as gifts 'for the robins'. The custom of wassailing orchards and fruit trees is documented by the sixteenth century (in 1581 in Fordwich, Kent) but might be older:

> Wassail the Trees, that they may bear
> You many a plum, and many a pear . . .[42]

The custom only declined in the middle of the nineteenth century, but revivals persist at Carhampton and Norton Fitzwarren in Somerset, carried out in January,[43] and the tradition has been restored at Leominster in Herefordshire on Twelfth Night. Bonfires were often lit and the ceremonies carried out on 17 January, the old Twelfth Eve.

'SACRED' OR 'FAIRY' TREES

The presence of yews within Christian graveyards, possibly reflecting the belief that they offered protection against supernatural forces, has already been discussed; comments upon the legendary role of individual tree species will appear in Chapters 8 to 12: only brief mention of primarily legendary associations will, therefore, be included here.

Some trees received protection because of their magical powers. Lucas notes how trees or woods 'which were treated with a certain reverence' might be 'protected . . . from wilful damage'.[44] Lucas notes a *bile* or 'sacred' ash tree growing in Borrisokane parish in Co. Tipperary in the nineteenth century. It had come to be known as the 'bellow-tree' or even the 'Big Bell Tree'. It was thought that if any part of it were to be burnt as fuel for the house the latter would itself be destroyed by fire; any water lodging in the hollow between its branches was regarded as holy.[45] Of the ash growing beside a well close to the tomb of St Bertram at Ilam in Staffordshire it was reputed: 'in olden times the ash was so venerated that the people deemed it extremely unlucky, if not positively dangerous, to break a bough of it'.[46] There are myriad tales in Ireland about fairy trees causing misfortune to those that damage or destroy them and in some places roads have even been re-routed to avoid such a tree. Vaughan Cornish has noted the 'Fairy Thorns' of Co. Armagh where, it was believed, to cut the thorn would bring injury or death.[47] Some trees exude red-coloured sap when cut, a feature that has been linked with the Earth Mother's menstruation or the life-blood of the tree itself, especially in the case of elders, which might be witches in disguise. Some trees were imbued with strong magical powers – it was believed that anyone in possession of even the smallest fragment of a famous ash tree which used to stand at Killura in Co. Cork could never die by drowning and in the nineteenth century large numbers of would-be emigrants would try to obtain chips or twigs from it.[48] The oak, too, retained much of its earlier awe: in addition to the Marriage Oaks, its link with the spirit world is manifest in the old folk rhyme 'Fairy folk/ Are in old oaks'[49] and its protective capacity is recognised in local rhymes in Wales, such as that applied to an old, dead oak stump now preserved within railings at Carmarthen:

> When Merlin's oak shall tumble down
> Then shall fall Carmarthen town[50]

Most commonly, it was a whitethorn growing alone in an open space to which damage was to be avoided, especially in Ireland, a superstition that continues unabated today. These were often thought to be under the protection of the fairies, who were the agents bringing retribution on persons who injured them, often causing death.[51] Thorns of any kind had suffered from their connection with the crucifixion and the crown of thorns – a Swiss tradition records how the palms spread on the road as Jesus entered Jerusalem grew spikes as they heard some calling for his crucifixion, thus giving rise to the holly.[52] This is a tree that enjoyed a special status in religious folklore in later times.

It is interesting to note that as the belief in the sanctity of trees waned over the ages, many became increasingly associated with famous historical figures. Many examples – far too many to be noted here – of the oak in particular, a tree that has over the ages inspired awe and symbolised steadfastness and courage, have been recorded over the centuries, acting as a site of of lovers' trysts, of execution, of preaching or associated with famous individuals in some way. The Abbot's Oak, Woburn, still alive, was what is known as a 'dool' or 'grief' tree: the abbot and prior of Woburn were hung from its branches by order of Henry VIII for denying the king's supremacy in objecting to Henry's marriage to Anne Boleyn.[53] Others stood at cross-roads or track-junctions, such as Wyndham's Oak in Silton, Dorset, where two of the followers of the duke of Monmouth were hanged in the seventeenth century after the Monmouth Rebellion. More of the duke's followers met their end on the Heddon Oak between Crowcombe and Stogumber in Somerset. Petty felons, thieves, highwaymen and murderers were hung at the Felon's Oak near Withycombe and Old Cleeve in Somerset. Many oaks marked preaching places: John Bunyan used to preach under an old oak at Samshill, Bedfordshire, only recently removed, holding his last service there before his arrest.[54] Other oaks used as preaching places included the Meavy Oak of Devon, still extant but heavily supported. Gospel oaks were widespread, usually on boundaries, where the Lord's Prayer would be read out during a perambulation of the parish boundaries in Rogation Week. Many oaks were associated with royalty. At Boscobel in Shropshire Charles II was said to have hidden in the leaves of a flourishing oak when being sought by Cromwell's troops; its descendant, grown from an acorn of the original tree, still stands. There are myriad other oaks associated with royal and important personages and the oak is regarded as the most English of trees, something of a national symbol. An interesting feature here, in the Western world, is the way that the tree's mythological associations, first established within pre-Christian belief, were maintained in Christian traditions but have subsequently given way to more secular associations, especially with well-known personages, as society has itself become more secularised. At the same time, the role of the oak as a rich wildlife habitat has given the tree a leading role in conservation circles.

THE TREE AND THE WELL

Folk customs associated with the tree and the well have also continued into recent times, the trees involved usually the ash, thorn, rowan, oak, holly or yew. Sometimes the tree and the well would be invoked to offer protection and the well or spring was frequently reputed to possess healing powers. Unfortunately, it is rarely possible to ascertain how old such customs might be. In Wales, near Narberth, the so-called Priest's Well was decorated with mountain ash and cowslips on May Day by the children in order to keep 'the witch' away from those families who drew water from it, a practice apparently connected with the English custom of well-dressing.[55] In Scotland, on an island in Loch Maree in Ross and Cromerty, people worshipped a sacred well and tree and on 25 August, the day dedicated to 'St Mourie' (perhaps a supposedly seventh-century saint, Maelrubha), sacrificed a bull. The well water was said to be a cure for lunacy and was visited by the afflicted as late as the mid-nineteenth century.[56] Over the centuries, trees and wells have remained active in folk custom as a source of healing power. Often a tree was a part of the ritual: at Easter Rarichie in Ross and Cromerty the spring known as the Well of the Yew was reputed to cure the 'white swelling' but only so long as the tree stood beside it. Some healing wells, especially in Ireland, consisted of water-filled stumps.[57] In the seventeenth century, St Fagan's Well in South Wales also lay beneath a sheltering yew and was frequented by many seeking a cure 'for the falling sickness [epilepsy] . . . Many come a yeare after they have drank of [it] and relate there [*sic*] health ever since'.[58] Frequently rags which had been used to bind a wound, or wool gathered from the hedges, were hung on the overhanging branches of such trees: the traveller John Aubrey reports crutches seen hanging on an old oak tree above the well of Ffynnon Llancarfon in Glamorgan in 1697.[59] Children were bathed in the holy well of Ffynnon Bedr near the church of Llanbedrycennin, Caernarfonshire, which was overshadowed by a yew, until the mid-nineteenth century.[60] Another well, Ffynnon Elias in Llansantffraid Deuddwr, Montgomeryshire, also overhung by a large yew, was visited by people with weak eyes; the waters of St Patrick's Well near Enfield in Co. West Meath, Ireland, emerging between the roots of an ancient tree, are also claimed to cure eye disease.[61] Spirits associated with the wells or trees are less in evidence in Wales, although a sprite called the Bwgan was said to live in the roots of a tree beside a well on the Lower Lliw in the district of Llanllugan-Adfa-Cefn Coch in Montgomeryshire.[62] Today a renewed interest in 'neo-paganism' is frequently expressed by the hanging of shreds of cloth on trees and bushes overhanging a 'holy' or 'healing' spring by those seeking the benefits of its waters.

CONCEPTS OF TREE SYMBOLISM

Tree rituals continued, therefore, to play a part in rural life. Attitudes to the origin of such rituals have changed over time. Frazer's *Golden Bough*, published in 1890, built upon the ideas of such scholars as Wilhelm Mannhardt in Germany and Sir Edward Tylor in Britain and convinced many that rituals were survivals of ancient religion. The centre-piece of Frazer's argument was the slaughter of *Rex Nemorensis*, the King of the Wood, which he argued took place in the sacred grove of Diana at Nemi in Italy where the priest-king protected the mistletoe – the golden bough – growing on a sacred oak:

> In the sacred grove there grew a certain tree round which at any time of the day, and probably far into the night, a grim figure might be seen to prowl. In his hand he carried a drawn sword, and he kept peering warily about him as if at every instant he expected to be set upon by an enemy. He was a priest and a murderer; and the man for whom he looked was sooner or later to murder him and hold the priesthood in his stead. Such was the rule of the sanctuary.[63]

But why had the king to die? To explain this, Frazer argued that the king was the personification of the oak-spirit, the symbol of fertility. He could only reign while his body was vigorous and youthful, although his spirit would pass to his successor. He could only be slain when the golden bough was broken, gold being the colour of the mistletoe branch once culled, and his body must then be burnt upon a great fire of oak-wood. Frazer collected myths from around the world to lend substance to his belief. He encountered the oak worship of the druids, the sacred groves of the Greeks and Romans, the sacred grove of Uppsala, the tree worship of the Slavs, and animistic beliefs of what he termed 'primitive' peoples. He found tribes who believed that the spirits of the dead took up their abode in trees; that the tree spirits gave rain and sunshine and made the crops grow. It was but a short step to associate the rural ceremonies he met in Britain with similar ceremonies found elsewhere in the world: most, he believed, were 'fossil' memories of pagan religion. He interpreted the effigy of a Green Man being cast into water as a mirror image of the sacrifice at Nemi, the May rituals which involved people dressed in green leaves, processing with may-boughs, as the bridegroom and bride who heralded the rebirth of vegetation in the spring. Many country rituals were fitted into this mould: Morris dancing, for instance, was thought to have descended from an ancient folk rite to induce fertility. The Yule log was added to his collection of 'putative pagan fire rituals from ancient Europe', again linked to 'agricultural fertility and the veneration of vegetation spirits' but the Yule log ritual could, as Hutton shows, have been introduced to Britain from Germany at the end of the Middle Ages. (In Devon the log was replaced by the ashen faggot, a bundle of ash stakes tied round with bands of bark – the latter of willow, ash or hazel).[64]

Frazer's *Golden Bough* influenced many twentieth-century writers such as Margaret Murray, Charlotte Burne and Nora Chadwick, and later archaeologists like Anne Ross. Only recently have the beliefs of early cultures been subject to more questioning scrutiny, such as Dáithí Ó hÓgáin's study of early Celtic belief in Ireland. One of the most original thinkers of the twentieth century was undoubtedly Robert Graves, although his works reveal a personal exploration of myth heavily coloured by both his own personal life and the knowledge and predilections of his age. In particular, his search for the White Goddess, first published as a book in 1948 but amended up until 1960, investigated an interpretation of Celtic lore which he believed encapsulated beliefs carried by migrating peoples from a Mediterranean homeland. Thus Math the son of Mathonwy, found in the Welsh stories, may have been a version of 'Amathus son of Amathaounta', the latter an Aegean Sea-goddess, carried by tribes emanating from Syria. The White Goddess was the early female 'earth-mother' who was to be supplanted and subordinated by the superior male gods of Ancient Greece and, ultimately, by Jehovah and the single Christian God. Many of the premises which underlay Graves's ideas of the transmission of legend and religion, such as the mass migration of peoples, are now questionable in the light of modern archaeology but his belief that older religions could find an outlet in legend remain. Such beliefs fell upon fertile ground in the atmosphere of the 1960s when many were ready to accept his ideas without question.

While it is now recognised that many rural customs may indeed be derived from very early beliefs, it can also be shown, as a result of today's more rigorous scholarship, that many were introduced in the Middle Ages. Morris dancing was a favourite court pastime in the reigns of Henry VII, Henry VIII and Elizabeth I.[65] Surges of more Puritanical belief drove many rituals from the Church, especially if they involved candles or bell-ringing, but many lived on within the homes and families of the rural countryside. Some were revived, or perhaps even introduced, in the later seventeenth and eighteenth centuries as part of the georgic movement, also represented in painting and literature, the rituals often encouraged upon the landed estates whose owners had the leisure and means to promulgate such attitudes and pastimes. With the continued Victorian empathy for the rural idyll, and romantic sympathy for the humble and obscure, rural ritual again underwent revival in the nineteenth century and was readily assimilated into the period's genuine concern with the education of the young, the working classes and the under-privileged. Neo-paganism during the twentieth century has attempted to revive much tradition perceived as ancient, much of it incorporating trees or springs. A present-day desire to enjoy the countryside, and all that represents it, has ensured the continuation of many folk customs, although relatively few incorporate the trees that are the subject of this book.

ENDNOTES

1   Flint, *The Rise of Magic*, p. 205.
2   Ibid., pp. 208–9, 266, citing *Vita Walarici Abbatis Leuconaensis* 22.
3   Green, *Celtic Myths*, p. 50.
4   Lucas, 'The sacred trees of Ireland', pp. 20.
5   Watson, 'The king', p. 170; M. Eliade, *Shamanism*, trans. W. R. Trask (London, 1964), p. 259.
6   Ó hÓgáin, *The Sacred Isle*, p. 168.
7   Watson, 'The king', p. 179.
8   P. W. Joyce, *The Origin and History of Irish Names of Places*, 4th edn (Dublin, 1875), p. 49.
9   Ibid.
10 N. Edwards, 1996. *The Archaeology of Early Medieval Ireland* (London, 1996), p. 84, fig. 36.
11 *The Anglo-Saxon Chronicle*, the Worcester Manuscript (D) 1066): C. Plummer, *Two of the Saxon Chronicles Parallel*, 2 vols (Oxford, 1892–9), p. 199; M. J. Swanton, trans., *The Anglo-Saxon Chronicle* (London, 1996), p. 199.
12 Smith, 'The Russian bear'; see, too, Tolley, *Shamanism in Norse Myth and Magic*, pp. 305, 366–8.
13 J. Campbell, *The Masks of God: Primitive Mythology* (London, 1973), p. 257.
14 N. M. Karamzin, *Istoriya gosudarstva rossiiskogo*, 12 vols, 5th edn (Moscow, 1989), I, pp. 55–6.
15 M. Todd, *The Barbarians, Goths, Franks and Vandals* (London and New York, 1972), p. 134.
16 *Dopolnenie k aktam istoricheskim*, I, no. 28 (St Petersburg, 1840), pp. 27–30, cited by Smith, 'The Russian bear'.
17 D. E. Kozhanchikova, ed., *Stoglav, Council of Moscow* (1863, repr. St Petersburg, 1911), p. 142.
18 This was St Coleta: *Acta Sanctortum quotquot orbe coluntir, vel . . .*, March I.547, ed J. Bollandus, cited by Loomis, *White Magic*, p. 94.
19 Loomis, *White Magic*, pp. 94–5. For Samthanne, see C. Plummer, *Vitae sanctorum Hiberniae*, vol. I (Oxford, 1910), p. 257.
20 Watson, 'The king', p. 166; F. Jones, *The Holy Wells of Wales*, 2nd edn (Cardiff, 1992), p. 18.
21 Jones, *The Holy Wells of Wales*, p. 51.
22 K. Basford, *The Green Man* (Ipswich, 1978), p. 12.
23 Ibid., p. 18; F. Doel, and G. Doel, *The Green Man in Britain* (Stroud, 2002).
24 S. Schama, *Landscape and Memory* (London, 1995), pp. 217–18.
25 Marshall, *Nature's Web*, p. 94.
26 Basford, *The Green Man*, pp. 20, 8.
27 Ibid., p. 21.
28 A. Woodcock, *Liminal Images. Aspects of Medieval Architectural Sculpture in the South of England from the Eleventh to the Sixteenth Centuries*, British Archaeological Reports, British Series 386 (Oxford, 2005), pp. 58–63.
29 The songs of Malcolm Guite, *ex inf.* Revd Nigel Cooper.
30 S. Mittuch, 'Medieval art of death and resurrection', *Current Archaeology* 209 (2007), pp. 34–40.
31 J. H. Wilks, *Trees of the British Isles in History and Legend* (London, 1972).
32 Bord and Bord, *Earth Rites*, p. 107.
33 Ibid., p. 112.
34 E. Radford and M. A. Radford, revised C. Hole, *Encyclopedia of Superstitions* (London, 1961), p. 253.

[35] R. Hutton, *The Stations of the Sun, A History of the Ritual Year in Britain* (Oxford, 1996), p. 35.

[36] R. Mabey, *Flora Britannica. The Concise Edition* (London, 1998), pp. 218, 225–8.

[37] Hutton, *The Stations of the Sun*, pp. 34–6.

[38] Ibid., p. 183, citing H. J. Feasey, *Ancient English Holy Week Ceremonial* (London, 1897), pp. 51–5.

[39] Ibid., pp. 227–8; R. Hutton, *The Rise and Fall of Merry England: The Ritual Year, 1400–1700* (Oxford, 1994), p. 39.

[40] Hutton, *Rise and Fall*, pp. 39–41, citing A. Tille, *Yule and Christmas, their Place in the Germanic Year* (London, 1889, 1899), pp. 92–3.

[41] *Ex inf.* Revd Nigel Cooper.

[42] Hutton, *Rise and Fall*, p. 14.

[43] Hutton, *The Stations of the Sun*, pp. 45–9.

[44] Lucas, 'The sacred trees of Ireland', p. 16.

[45] Ibid., p. 23.

[46] Bord and Bord, *Sacred Waters*, p. 99, citing the folklorist, F. W. Hackwood.

[47] V. Cornish, *Historic Thorn Trees in the British Isles* (London, 1941), pp. 50–7.

[48] J. Allegro, *Lost Gods* (London, 1977), pp. 12, 137–9.

[49] Wilks, *Trees of the British Isles*, p. 127.

[50] Ibid., p. 13.

[51] Hageneder, *The Heritage of Trees*, p. 161.

[52] Lucas, 'The sacred trees of Ireland', pp. 46–7.

[53] Wilks, *Trees of the British Isles*, pp. 77–8.

[54] Ibid., p. 13.

[55] Jones, *The Holy Wells of Wales*, p. 129.

[56] Bord and Bord, *Sacred Waters*, p. 34.

[57] Ibid., p. 59.

[58] *Diary of Richard Symonds*, 1645: C. E. Long, ed., *Diary of the Marches of the Royal Army During the Great Civil War Kept by Richard Symonds*, Camden Society 74 (London, 1859), cited in Jones, *The Holy Wells of Wales*, p. 66.

[59] Jones, *The Holy Wells of Wales*, pp. 186–7.

[60] Ibid., pp. 147, 153.

[61] Milner, *The Tree Book*, p. 139.

[62] Jones, *The Holy Wells of Wales*, pp. 131–2.

[63] Frazer, *The Illustrated Golden Bough*, p. 22.

[64] Hutton, *The Stations of the Sun*, pp. 39–40.

[65] Ibid., pp. 239–40, 62–5.

PART II

Trees and Woodland in the Anglo-Saxon Landscape

5

The Nature and Distribution of
Anglo-Saxon Woodland

ANCIENT WOODLAND

An unbroken cover of dense woodland waiting to be cleared and broken up by enterprising Anglo-Saxon colonists owes more to cinematic images of the American frontier than to reality; such a scenario is unlikely to have existed much longer than the early Holocene. Scholars like Vera and Rackham argue that the wildwood always consisted of an open woodland cover or even a park-like landscape, browsed heavily by herbivores. In temperate regions dense woodland will not form unless animals – both wild and domestic stock – are deliberately excluded.[1] Even before prehistoric farmers cut down trees to obtain land for agriculture, or allowed their animals to browse the woodland, mesolithic man was clearing and burning swathes of land to create open spaces which would attract the animals he wished to hunt. The open nature of the resulting woodland may explain why so much of it disappeared so quickly in the prehistoric period.

One outstanding problem concerns the date at which woodland cover was augmented. Most prehistorians argue that any English 'wildwood' had been removed by the late Bronze Age and that the amount of woodland then present was little greater than that found today. Although it was once claimed that woodland took over abandoned farmland once the Romans left, many environmentalists now believe that in most areas of at least southern and midland England there was relatively little regeneration of secondary woodland until very much later. A period of regeneration seems to have occurred in later Anglo-Saxon times when woodlands became an increasingly valued habitat for hunting. Woodland regeneration can be encouraged by a number of factors and is seldom straightforward: it can increase when farming becomes neglected in periods of natural stress or war; it can be deliberately fostered along tribal frontiers, either because these were felt to be areas insecure for farming or as a deliberate policy; it can express a recognition of the economic or cultural benefits of woodland for its own sake. Woodland has generally only been conserved when it has been considered of value, but the factors influencing this can be economic, cultural or a mixture of the two.

THE LOSS OF THE WILDWOOD

As soon as man began to settle the British Isles in considerable numbers at the beginning of the prehistoric period woodland began to recede. Although climatic change on a relatively small scale can affect the vegetation cover, and there seems to have been an increase in precipitation and a small drop in temperature about 4,000 years ago in the early to middle Bronze Age, it seems to have been man's influence that was the decisive factor. Woods were felled and cleared for agriculture, the leaves and branches of trees were gathered for fodder (often before the trees had set seed) and domestic stock was pastured within woodlands, inhibiting the regeneration of the trees. The more exposed marginal areas of western and northern Britain were irretrievably damaged at this time because tree clearance exposed thin soils that were prone to degradation: in some regions light soils were podsolised (exposed to the rain which leached down mineral layers until they formed a hard pan that tree roots could not easily penetrate) and in others peat formation created a landscape of barren moorland that was never to recover. Vegetational archaeology has now revealed the existence of the tree cover that met the earliest hunter-gatherers even, for instance, in the Outer Hebrides, Orkneys and Western Isles of Scotland. Here deforestation of the native hazel and birch woodland slowly took place in the face of peat formation and the deposition of blown sand to give way after 3550 BC to a more open 'machair' landscape, much used subsequently for agriculture.[2] The factors that led to woodland loss are incompletely understood, for the increasing influence of salt spray and storms must have contributed to the destruction of woodland by people, but the latter is likely to have played a major role. The deliberate burning of woodland and heath seems to have been an initial factor in the destruction of the hazel woodland of Fforest Fawr in south Wales, where raised bog began to form as early as c.8000 BC,[3] and on the granite boss of Dartmoor in southwest England, where oak, birch, alder or hazel woodland was cleared but failed to regenerate on the poor granite soils, heavily browsed by cattle and deer. In west Wales, too, loss of alder and oak woodland similarly coincided with clearance and increased pasturing of stock: increasing amounts of herbaceous and cereal pollen have been recorded from a number of sites in western Ardudwy (coastal west Wales) and indicate small-scale cultivation in the Iron Age and Roman periods, although pastoralism appears to have been the dominant activity and is likely to have been more effective in repressing tree regeneration.[4]

In general, therefore, woodland was in severe recession during the prehistoric period in Britain and, over the last few decades, air photography has revealed the extent to which large parts of England were virtually devoid of woodland by the end of the period. In particular, territorial boundaries consisting of linear banks often stretching over many kilometres, which could only have been constructed in an open landscape, have been identified in many regions, especially across eastern

England. Elsewhere soil profiles have regularly been those of open, farmed landscapes rather than ones rich in woodland humus. Even where woodland survived, its nature was to change, for the 'wildwood' was almost everywhere to give way to secondary woodland.

Loss of woodland continued in some areas during the Roman period, especially in regions where there were fresh demands upon it as a source of timber or fuel. In the areas around Hadrian's Wall and the Antonine Wall, two major linear fortifications in the far north of England and southern Scotland, massive amounts of timber and turf were used in wall construction. At Fozy Moss in Northumbria the land was almost totally deforested c.AD 125 and settlements associated with Hadrian's Wall perpetuated the need for agricultural land use until the fourth century AD.[5] Rackham (pers. comm.) has argued that woodcutting seldom led to any long-term deterioration in woodland – trees would regrow rapidly unless prevented by some other means, in this case probably the expansion of agriculture. Even when woodland was increasingly valued for the various other resources it offered, increasing population levels usually meant that it was constantly under threat of clearance unless it received specific protection. Agriculture was widespread in Roman times, when armies and towns had to be sustained and when a well-organised market was able to cope with the collection, distribution and marketing of produce, but woodland was also managed in this period to provide fuel for such industries as tile production and iron-working. The production of pottery and tiles in north-west Warwickshire, iron-smelting in areas such as south-eastern England and Northamptonshire, or the salt industry of Droitwich in the West Midlands, are all examples where evidence is as yet limited but where wood resources were undoubtedly valued. After the Roman withdrawal, areas of clay pits and iron-mining disturbance in places like the Weald or the Forest of Dean may also have rapidly become overgrown, increasing the woodland cover in these regions as industrial usage declined.

FACTORS LEADING TO WOODLAND REGENERATION

Whenever historical events led to a reduction in agriculture and farming, trees were waiting to regenerate unless irretrievable damage had adversely affected soil formation and structure. Periods of warfare and strife or the deliberate avoidance of frontier regions could all have led naturally to woodland regeneration entirely through neglect. There is, however, no clear evidence for this ever having taken place in Britain. One such period of political unrest followed the departure of the Roman legions in the fifth century AD. With the removal of the necessity to feed a standing army and the breakdown of Roman urban standards and large-scale marketing, the demand for agricultural produce was lessened, leading, for instance, to the abandonment of field systems over much of the higher downlands of southern England

and a return to more traditional methods of farming based more upon pastoralism. It is thought, however, that to a large extent open grassland replaced cropped fields and that in many regions woodland regeneration was minimal at this time. Had the countryside really been abandoned, secondary woodland would have covered most of the land area in less than thirty years.[6] British princes assumed political control over much of the area formerly controlled by Rome, although there were continuous onslaughts by the Picts, Scots and Irish and, with more long-lasting effect, by the Anglo-Saxons. The amount of political disruption varied regionally. There is evidence from northern England in particular that woodland regeneration did take place but often as part of a regular sequence of agricultural phases followed by localised woodland regeneration which was already established in Roman times, as evidenced at Tatton, Cheshire.[7] Similar oscillations in the balance between arable, pasture and woodland have been observed in parts of southern England but appear to be due to farming practices rather than political unrest. Many have argued, therefore, against wide-scale woodland regeneration in England after the collapse of Roman Britain, except perhaps in the north. On the Birmingham Plateau, an open wood-pasture habitat appears to have represented a return to traditional methods of farming in the vicinity of Metchley Roman fort after the gradual abandonment of the fort and its surrounding settlement. Scrub, mainly hawthorn and sloe, was encroaching upon open ground before the end of the Roman period but with increasing numbers of woodland species present (especially oak, hazel and alder), with a gradual transition to open woodland used mainly as wood-pasture.[8] In Anglo-Saxon times, there was more woodland in Britain than there is now, but even then, less than in most European countries today.

The presence of woodland along tribal boundaries is a frequently recognised phenomenon of early medieval England, likely to be rooted in a late prehistoric past. Woodland certainly seems to have marked some frontier regions both in this country and in Germany.[9] The presence of woodland usually reflects areas of more intractable soils, and the presence of 'more difficult' countryside may indeed have affected the lines followed by tribal boundaries, but such areas may themselves have been avoided by subsequent settlement because they represented unstable or vulnerable border zones. Woodland may even have been deliberately allowed to regenerate in such zones. The Wealden woodlands of south-eastern England appear to have separated a number of politically distinct regions which may have had their roots in Iron Age kingdoms and Roman *civitates*[10] and which were to underlie the early medieval tribal districts. The Weald is an area of difficult soils which forms the centre of an eroded anticline: Hastings Sands outcrop in the centre surrounded on the north, west and south by, in sequence, bands of heavy Wealden clays, greensand and chalk. The wooded core formed the boundary between the kingdom of Kent to the north and that of the South Saxons to the south, perhaps perpetuating a more ancient division. It has been argued that the woodlands of the Chilterns, a portion of

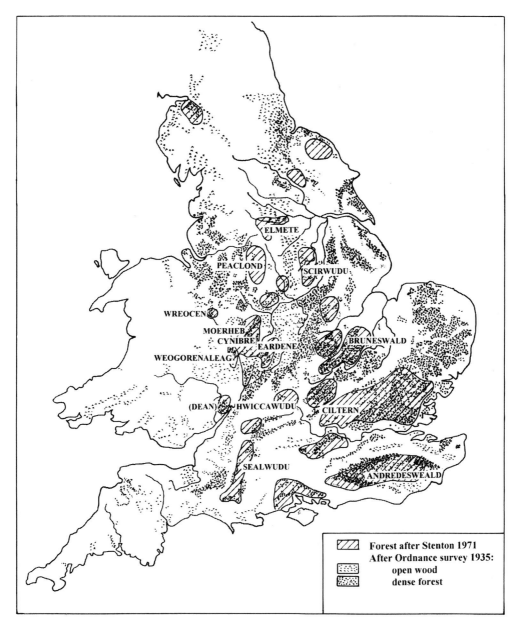

Figure 5. The distribution of Anglo-Saxon woodland (after Hill, *An Atlas of Anglo-Saxon England*, based upon the Ordnance Survey 1966 and Stenton, *Anglo-Saxon England*)

the great chalk escarpment of England, formed an effective barrier to Anglo-Saxon incursions[11] and Selwood, along the borders of what is now Wiltshire and Somerset (Fig. 5), marked the divide between the British and the Anglo-Saxons in the late sixth century – it was known to the British as *Coit Maur* 'the great wood'. It was such a marked divide that Aldhelm, bishop of Sherborne (the see of south-western England), was known as the bishop 'west of the wood' in 709.[12]

The kingdom of the Hwicce in the West Midlands was to be virtually encircled by wooded regions, among them Wychwood, 'the wood of the Hwicce', which lay to the south-east beyond its seventh-century boundary (Fig. 6). To the west, moving northwards, lay the woodlands which were to become the Forest of Dean, those of Corse and Malvern, *Weogorena leah* 'the *lēah* of the *Weogoran*', which merged northwards into Wyre, and, to the north, Kinver and Morfe (*Cynibre* and *Moerheb* on Fig. 5, as they appear in an eighth-century charter of Ismere).[13] Feckenham reached northwards towards the northern boundary and Arden limited the kingdom to the north-east – only the kingdom's south-eastern boundary across the Warwickshire Feldon passed through open country.[14] Similarly, the Magonsætan kingdom in Herefordshire and Shropshire was marked by thickly wooded countryside along its northern boundary with the Wreocensæte in Shropshire.[15] Regions of woodland and heath were usually lightly settled and are likely to have been areas of seasonal pasture rather than of permanent settlement. In general, therefore, political instability alone does not appear to have been an overriding factor in woodland regeneration, although this could result from cultural responses to such a situation. The picture will only become clearer as more environmental evidence accrues that will enable dates of regeneration to be more closely defined.

There is some evidence to suggest that woodland cover actually increased in some regions later in the Anglo-Saxon period, as in Oxfordshire at Sidlings Copse, later to form part of the royal Forest of Stowood.[16] Day attributes the regrowth of the woodland in Sidlings Copse to the place becoming unpopular for settlement due to the broken terrain left by the former (Roman) pottery industry.[17] In parts of the Wychwood area there is also evidence for an open landscape in Iron Age and Roman times and the site of a villa at Shakenoak did not revert to woodland for some three centuries after the Roman withdrawal.[18] However, extensive wooded areas were also being set aside for the increasingly popular pursuit of hunting in late Anglo-Saxon times; this rarely prevented them from being used for wood-pasture but probably deterred any deliberate clearance for farming and settlement.[19]

WOODLAND DISTRIBUTION: THE GENERAL PICTURE

Information about woodland distribution in early medieval England can be obtained from contemporary narrative sources: the Weald, for instance, is noted as a *mycclan*

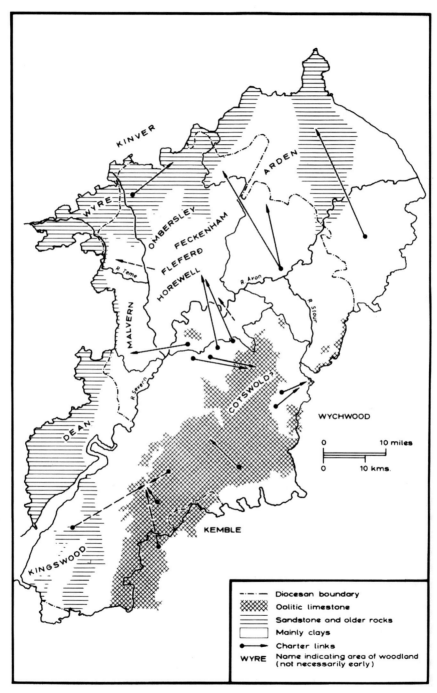

Figure 6. The kingdom of the Hwicce: frontier woodlands (from Hooke, *The Anglo-Saxon Landscape, The Kingdom of the Hwicce*)

wuda 'great wood' and was known as *Andredesweald* or *Andredesleah* (both containing 'wood' terms) and is noted as a wooded region of considerable extent in the *Anglo-Saxon Chronicle* (see Chapter 6).[20] Most of our present-day parish names and many of our minor place-names were coined in the Anglo-Saxon period and many contain woodland terms. More detailed local information can be derived from pre-Conquest charters, including references to trees and woodland in associated boundary clauses. In or shortly after 1086, a survey was made of estate ownership and manorial resources which was more comprehensive than anything that had previously been produced in Europe: Domesday Book, as it was called, covered all but the northern part of England and noted the quantities of woodland, ploughland, meadow, and so forth available on each manor or group of manors.

No authoritative map can yet be produced of the distribution of woodland in the early medieval period. Attempts by the Ordnance Survey in 1935 and 1966 and by Sir Frank Stenton in 1971 differ considerably, although there is little disagreement over the location of the best-known areas of woodland (Fig. 5);[21] Swanton also offers a map of 'areas of swamp and forest' to accompany his translation of the *Anglo-Saxon Chronicle*.[22] In his *Trees and Woodland in the British Landscape*, Oliver Rackham has mapped settlements whose names incorporate woodland terms to indicate a distribution which corresponds closely to the general picture suggested by the earlier sources, although by including the Old Norse term *þveit*, which may indicate a clearing produced by the felling of a wood but later appears to develop the meaning 'enclosed pasture' and 'meadow', he adds, questionably, a marked concentration in Cumbria not indicated earlier (but perhaps through lack of information).[23] The late Sir Clifford Darby mapped the woodland of 1086 from the Domesday Book statistics (not available for northern England),[24] although it is known that some woodland was omitted from the survey, usually because it had been taken into the king's forest but also for other unknown reasons (leading, for instance, to under-recording in north Hampshire and north-east Berkshire).[25] Most recently, Brian Roberts and Stuart Wrathmell have amalgamated the maps of Darby, Rackham and others to produce their own estimate of the woodland cover of England in this period, comparing this with common lands and woodlands recorded in the 1930s.[26] Further maps in the subsequent publication show the sources used for this map, including the distribution of woodland suggested by place-names and by woodland recorded in Domesday Book.[27] Together, these maps indicate well-wooded regions right across southern and south-eastern England, a second belt across the Midlands from Gloucestershire through Worcestershire and the Welsh Border region north-eastwards into Yorkshire east of the Pennines, and a scattering further to the north each side of the Pennines. The areas with least woodland included the intensively cultivated lowlands of the Midlands north-eastwards into Yorkshire and the uplands of northern England including the Pennine spine, the Lakeland hills and the border Cheviots.

This general picture can best be augmented by studies produced on a more local-ised, regional, basis in which the woodland terms can be investigated and in which place-name and charter recordings, where the latter are available, can be studied with greater accuracy. In time, environmental evidence from archaeological exca-vations will confirm or disprove an interpretation based solely upon documentary evidence but it will be a long time before such evidence accrues sufficiently to produce anything that is not localised and site-specific. Palaeobotany covers the inspection of pollen types to identify plant species present in a given sequence, although dating can be hazardous; identification of insect and mollusc remains can reveal much about the surrounding habitat and particularly whether the species present were those that preferred open or woodland condition; coprolites (faeces) can indicate plants that were eaten, and pollen grains on pottery show the plants collected or found close to sites of pottery manufacture. Soil horizons reveal much about the vegetation cover, which influenced soil composition and structure; alluvial deposits might indicate increased run-off with woodland clearance, for example. Such information is now collected systematically in any proper excavation but takes time and expense to quantify and analyse.

WOODLAND TERMS

The place-names of early medieval England are usually of Old English deriva-tion, although British names survived in some regions, especially for topographical features such as hills and rivers and also for some wooded areas, their numbers increasing westwards. The British (Primitive Welsh, Cornish, Cumbric) term for wood is *cęd*, *coid*, becoming *cos* in Cornish. It is preserved in a number of place-names. Lichfield, meaning 'the open land at or called *Lyccid*', for instance, is *Luit-coed* in an early Welsh poem, the latter the Primitive Welsh name for the former Roman town of Letocetum whose name meant 'the grey wood', possibly 'an area of woodland stretching from Wall to Lichfield'.[28] The *cęd* term is also in the wood names Chute and Melchet in southern England (both became the names of forests), and possibly in the name Dasset, *Dercetone* (PrW *derw* + *cęd*), in southern Warwick-shire where it may mean 'the oak-tree wood'.[29] Selwood continued to be referred to as *Coit Maur* 'the great wood' in Asser's *Life of King Alfred*.[30] Another *coit maur* and a *luhinn* (Welsh *llwyn*) *maur*, both 'great' woods or groves, are recorded in the Llandaff charters in the perambulations of Llandinabo in Herefordshire and Crick in Monmouthshire, both close to the Welsh border, where there seem to have been large stretches of woodland in the earlier part of the period.[31] Other woodland areas also retained British names, although these did not necessarily refer directly to woodland. Thus in the West Midlands Kinver is likely to be a British name, derived from *Cunobriga* and containing the Primitive Welsh *breʒ* 'hill' while Arden is British *ardu* 'high'.[32]

One British term that survived in place-names is *nemet*, discussed in Chapter 2. It is found most commonly in south-western England: a number of Nymet place-names are found in Devon, some taking their names from the Roman station of Nemeto Statio at North Tawton. The Latin term *nemus* is also occasionally used in the charters of southern England for a grove in which an estate possessed rights. Charters of Orchard in Dorset in 939 and Christian Malford in Wiltshire in 940 note rights in *silvis, silvorumque nemoribus* 'woods and groves of woods', and others of Ringwood in Hampshire and Burbage in Wiltshire, dated to 961, rights in *silvis silvarumque nemorum*.[33] As far as is known, there is no direct attestation of the use of the term *nemus* in the sense 'sacred grove', and it is highly unlikely that the Church would have used any term with such an implied meaning, but it is interesting that Christian Malford, *Cristemaleford*, is 'ford marked by a crucifix' (for whatever reason – see Chapter 2).

Many documents used Latin as their main language. The Latin terms used most frequently for woodland are *silva* and *saltus*, with *nemus* and *lucus* used for wood-land grove. In charters, Latin terms occur most often within the general body of charters as this was the language of all of these documents apart from their associated boundary clauses, which were usually in Old English; Latin is also the language of Domesday Book. Charter grants may specifically refer to rights in woodland and the term most commonly used is *silvae* 'woods', and occasionally *silviuncula* 'small woods'; *silvarum densitates*, 'thickets of woods', occurs in a number of Dorset, Wiltshire, Hampshire and Kentish charters.[34] A Warwickshire charter places two estates which were appendant to the main estate of Shottery in the central Avon valley in *ruris siluatici* 'wooded countryside', one lying in the Warwickshire Arden and the other in north Worcestershire.[35] Similarly, it is recorded in 930, of estates in the valley of the Isbourne in north Gloucestershire, *quinque nam locis habentur siluaticis ad fleferth*, 'they have five [*mansiunculae* (*mansæ*, 'hides')] in wooded places at Fleferth' in central Worcestershire.[36] A Worcestershire charter adds to an estate at Bentley, Holt, *siluam necessariam on Bradanlæge ad illam praeparationem salis* 'the woodland at Bradley necessary for the preparation of salt'.[37] *Silva* continues to be used in Domesday Book but often as *silva pastilis*, clearly indicating its use as wood-pasture: relatively open woodland in which stock could be pastured, including the taking of mast in oak- and beech-woods by herds of pigs; in some parts of the country Domesday Book measures the amount of woodland by the numbers of swine it can support. The woodland pastures, the *denbǣra*, of several Kent estates, were said to lie *in commune saltu* 'in the common wood',[38] *saltus* being another Latin term for wood, perhaps specifically 'upland wood or wood-pasture', as in the *saltu qui dicitur Andred*, another reference to the Kentish Weald.[39] The Old English *Orosius*, much of it a translation of a fifth-century Latin text, refers to *se weald*

Pireni as a translation of *Pyrenaei saltus* when referring to the Pyrenees.[40] Rights *in saltibus* at Wootton Wawen in the Warwickshire Arden appear to refer to wood-pastures on the rising land which gave its name to this region (Brit. **ardu* 'high land') and those *in saltuumque densitatibus* 'thickets of ?wood-pasture' belonging to an estate at Steeple Ashton, Wiltshire, may also have represented denser woodland, but in an uncertain location.[41]

The bulk of place-names known from this period, however, including those referring to woodland, contain Old English terms. One common Old English term for woodland was *wudu*, earlier *widu*, which could be used for large stretches of woodland but also for small woods and for 'woodland' in a general sense. The term is common in this sense in literary sources (Chapter 3). The Wealden woods are called *micla wudu* 'the great wood', called *Andred* in 892, and Selwood was *Sealwyda* in 878, *Sealwuda* in 894, 'sallow wood', both in the *Anglo-Saxon Chronicle*; Wychwood, in Oxfordshire, was recorded as *Huiccewudu* 'the wood of the Hwicce', in 840.[42] Rights in woodland are noted as *mid wuda* 'with woodland', rather than the more usual *siluis*, in a late writ concerning estates of Pershore and Deerhurst in the mid-eleventh century[43] and many charters refer to shares of *wudu landes ⁊ feld landes* 'woodland and open land',[44] or describe land *be wuda ⁊ be felde*, using the term to denote woodland in a general way. Patches of woodland may be added to an estate granted or leased by charter, and sometimes the wooded part of an estate may have its own boundary clause, such as Huddington in Worcestershire or Hawling in Gloucestershire.[45]

The term *wudu* occurs as a landmark feature in many boundary clauses but is more likely than other terms to be referred to without any distinguishing name. Of some 130 *wudu* features noted (this figure may include some repeated landmarks), only about 24 have descriptive names attached, while another 10 or so have *wudu* used as an adjective with another feature such as a ford, stream, marsh, bridge, gate or way. The descriptive names are usually those of people and places, revealing very little about the nature or use of the woodland. As individual woods, the *corna wudu* of Knighton, *ðæs bisceopes wuda* of Himbleton, *crohlea wuda* and *oddingalea wuda* of Crowle, and *ac wudu* of Salwarpe are examples which occur in Worcestershire boundary clauses, the latter another relatively rare example of *wudu* associated with a particular species of tree (here the oak; see also 'the sallow wood' above).[46] There are also additional references to 'wood' fords, 'wood' highways and so forth. In place-names the term is usually compounded with a habitative name such as *tūn*, perhaps indicating a settlement close to woodland which handled timber resources.[47]

Another term for areas of wooded countryside is *weald*, which again appears in literary sources with the meaning of 'woodland'. As a place-name it appears in *Andredesweald* (the south-eastern Weald) and, in charters, as *þeo weald æt Caldebek* 'the wood at Caldbeck', another wooded area in Cumberland which lay upon the boundary of Gospatric's land in the mid-eleventh century.[48] Bruneswald and its

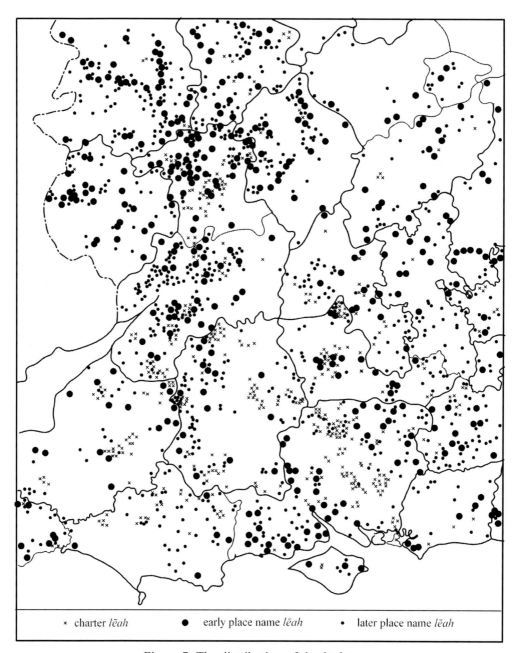

| × charter *lēah* | ● early place name *lēah* | • later place name *lēah* |

Figure 7. The distribution of the *lēah* term

outliers occupied the Bedfordshire and Cambridgeshire claylands (*Bruneswald* 1168: Leighton Bromswold, Huntingdonshire; *Bruneswold* C13: Witcham, Cambridgeshire; for what by then were separated areas of woodland). This term seems only rarely, if ever, to have been used for small individual woods and, as such, does not appear as an individual landmark in charters. There are indeed references to the Weald and the Caldbeck wood but in other cases the reference is to features associated with a wooded place: a ridge *wealdan hricg*, a coomb *wealdan cumbe*, and a spring *waldes wellan* (two other references to *oldan* may not be to this term).[49] This was a term that was to change its meaning to 'high open land', as represented by the later 'wold' names, but there is sufficient evidence to show that many such names were initially coined when the term was understood to refer to woodland and it does not appear in the later sense before the thirteenth century.[50] Cotswold was not recorded as a district name before the twelfth century when Giraldus Cambrensis referred to the *montana de Codueuualt* in referring, apparently, to the north Gloucestershire part of the oolitic limestone escarpment that runs through this county, but the name is likely to include a personal name from the early medieval period.[51] The scarp slope of the Cotswolds is still wooded today but the dip slope, like many other wold regions, was largely denuded of extensive woodland by the time of the Domesday survey. Fox has suggested that the correct way to interpret a *weald* is as 'a tract of countryside characterized by isolated stands of wood, perhaps amidst pasture and some cultivated land', that is 'loosely wooded countryside'.[52]

The commonest term for woodland is *lēah*. There have been many studies enquiring into the meaning of this term (the most comprehensive by the Swedish scholar Christer Johansson),[53] all agreeing that the term is indicative of wooded countryside. Strangely, the term does not seem to have been used for a wood or any other feature in literary sources, although it is one of the commonest place-name terms. Several *lēah* names are those of fairly extensive woodland regions, such as the Weald *Andredesleag/-leg*, *Ærmundeslea/Ermundeslea* in Hormer hundred, formerly north-east Berkshire but now part of Oxfordshire, and *Weogorena leah*, the woodland of the *Weogoran*, Worcestershire, i.e. the folk whose focus was Worcester (Fig. 7).[54] This name may survive as Wyre, now a wooded region of more limited extent to the north on the boundary of Worcestershire and Shropshire. These districts must have been ones of varied land use, also incorporating settlements and their fields with other scattered areas of rough pasture or heath, as the charters of *Weogorena leah* indeed show.[55] The term is the commonest of all wood terms in place-names and charter boundaries. Moreover, other terms compounded with *lēah* seem to indicate a variety of land use. It has been suggested that the word may derive from an Indo-European root *leuk-* 'light', as found in the Latin term for grove, *lucus*, but it is cognate with OSax, OHG *lōh*, 'copse, grove, undergrowth, scrub' and as it is frequently associated with other terms implying 'cutting off' and 'breaking',[56] intermittent clearing may be implied. The woodland cover might fluctuate according to the extent to which the wood was harvested or the intensity of grazing, which may help to explain some of the different names compounded with *lēah* and which could indicate that changes in the woodland cover were constantly taking place, with wood-pasture being the predominant usage.[57]

In charters the term occurs in compound names with tree species, where it probably means 'wood', and may suggest the use of the woods for building material and other uses: for wooden shingles (*spōn*) and rafters (*hrōst*) in Gloucestershire, rods (*gerd*) elsewhere. As noted in the previous paragraph, some names suggest woodland regeneration. In Worcestershire 'the thorny *lēah*' and *ympanleage* 'the *lēah* of the saplings' lay along the boundary between Martin Hussingtree and Smite in Hindlip, and their names seem to suggest the regeneration of cleared or over-grazed woodland areas.[58] Associations with gorse or broom, or even heath, *beonet* 'bent grass', *secg* 'sedge' or *þistel* 'thistle', may suggest that some areas remained relatively open. While domestic stock such as cattle, horses or even sheep were commonly pastured in woods, references to beans, barley, flax, wheat and so forth must surely refer to open spaces. However, of the 400 Gloucestershire names containing *lēah*, only 14 (4%) referred to crops, and Johansson noted the same percentage in the 700+ names that he examined.[59] Perhaps the implication is that the larger districts known as *lēah* were probably areas in which woodland was present but not necessarily ubiquitous, but where the *lēah* was a much smaller feature, as in many of the charter boundary locations, these may have been smaller pieces of land which were generally wooded but could be used for different purposes over time. This woodland could have been available for multiple uses (see Chapter 6) and may have been either periodically felled or thinned by its use as wood-pasture, but allowed subsequently to regrow – many of the charter *lēah* features are still woods today. Such a change could occur naturally on the margins of cultivation as agriculture advanced or retreated. Wager is probably correct to claim that *lēah* usually indicated secondary woodland.[60] To confuse matters further, by the date of the charters many such *lēah* names had, in effect, become minor place-names no longer necessarily illustrative of contemporary land use. Thus there were specific woods within the estate of Crowle named as *oddinga lea wuda* and *croh lea wuda*, suggesting an area of woodland divided between Oddingley and Crowle, Worcestershire, part of that which had already given rise to the place-names themselves – *Crohlea*, *lēah* perhaps compounded with **crōh* 'corner, bend', and Oddingley 'the *lēah* of the Oddingas, the people named after Odda'.[61] In another example, where a boundary runs *in hæðleage sceagan ðær he ðynnest is* 'to heath *lēah* shaw where it is thinnest' on the northern boundary of Alvechurch, Worcestershire, *hæðleage* may already have become the place-name Headley and it is the shaw, probably a small linear wood, that best describes the vegetation cover.[62] Subsequently, settlements that appear to have begun as medieval assarts also took the *lēah* name from their surroundings, although the woodland was cleared away, and many *lēah* names survive only as field-names in regions that are known to have been once well wooded.[63] A charter reference for an estate at Salwarpe in Worcestershire is, however, quite specific that both *ac wudu* and *pulle lea* ('pool *lēah*', to become a place-name Pulley) were woods.[64]

Other Old English terms found in place-names and charters include *bearu*, *grāf* and *holt*, all of which occur in literature, place-name and charters. The first of these, *bearu* 'small wood', perhaps the equivalent of the Latin *nemus*,[65] is not common in charters but occurs in place-names, especially in south-western England, although it is sometimes difficult to distinguish from *bǣr* 'swine-pasture' or *beorg* 'hill, tumulus'. Both *bearu* and *bǣr* may be compounded with *wudu*: a charter of Chilton, Berkshire, adds *ðæra wudebære landgemæru æt ðæclege* 'the boundaries of the ?woodgrove at *ðæclege*'.[66] Examples of names with *bearu* may include Beer in Devon and many of the 'Barrow' names, as in Barrow upon Trent, Derbyshire, Barrow upon Soar, Leicestershire, Barrow upon Humber, Lincolnshire, while Ogbear in Tavistock, Devon, is 'oak wood', although not recorded until 1238.

A much more common term is *grāf, grāfa, grāfe, grǣfa* 'grove', which seems to have been a wood of limited extent. The term is particularly common in place-names in midland England but occurs only occasionally in the south-west. Groves, like woods, could be added to estate grants and the grove belonging to an estate at *Gena-nofre*, Worcestershire, was large enough to have its own boundary clause, though only a few landmarks can be identified.[67] Another grove with its own boundary clause was that of Bredon's Norton in the same county, which lay within the parish of that name at the western end of Bredon Hill.[68] Most charter groves seem to have been specific small woods, and far more of these have their own distinguishing names. Of some 90 references to groves as boundary features only 23 are noted simply as 'the grove' (and some of these may be repetitions of groves named elsewhere). It is interesting to note that a grove could be 'common' or held by ceorls as if it was manorial woodland: a tenth-century lease of Thorne in Inkberrow, Worcestershire, refers to the *gemænan grafe to þordune* 'the common copse belonging to Thorne'[69] and only a few are associated with personal names. Some groves are descibed as 'black' or *hār* 'grey'; others are specifically stated to be of willows, hazels, sloes or elders, while one Warwickshire charter, anxious to identify a clearer boundary landmark, runs *on þa hehan æc on wulluht grafe middum* 'to the tall oak in the middle of *wulluht* grove'.[70] Groves seem to have been patches of woodland, managed to provide timber for an estate; some of them may have been managed by coppicing. The woods of the royal estate of Bromsgrove, 'Bremi's grove', in Worcestershire, supplied the salt industry of Droitwich, Domesday Book recording that the manor obtained 300 measures of salt for which, before the Conquest, it had supplied 300 cartloads of wood.[71] Some 500 years later, John Leland remarked that the wood used for salt production was 'yong pole wood for the moste parte, easy to be devidid in pecis [cloven]', i.e. coppiced.[72] Wager, in her study of medieval Warwickshire woodland, found that by medieval times many groves were in private, rather than common, ownership but that even in tenants' woods the lord retained rights to the timber and trees, leaving tenants only limited use of the underwood and pasture, and that such woods were usually enclosed for some years after cutting, forcing pasture to take second place.[73]

A further term, *holt*, may have been applied to a 'single-species wood' or, at least, a wood in which one species was dominant, when used in place-names and charters, for it appears more frequently than many of the other terms with individual tree species such as oak, ash, aspen, birch or beech.[74] In place-names it is most common in south-eastern and eastern England. This term is less common in charter boundary clauses, occurring only about 17 times, but most of these have specific names, one of them a *holt* called *Duddincbearu*, incorporating the *bearu* term as a place-name.[75] Few are associated with a personal name but holts with a specific species of tree named include an oak, hazel and beech holt (the latter as a named wood *Boc holt* in northern Kent). A tenth-century clause of *Teodeceslæge* in Ullenhall, Warwickshire, notes a *scyr holtes wæge* 'way of the *scīr holt*', in which the Old English term may have meant 'district, province, shire' rather than 'shining', for later field-names suggest a location close to the Hwiccan boundary in the northern part of Tanworth parish, while another wood called *Scyrhylte* lay in Leigh parish close to the western boundary of the Hwicce, noted in a boundary dispute of 825.[76] In both cases the woods were areas of wood-pasture and the adjective might even suggest intercommoning of community woodland in this period.

There are other Old English terms used in place-names and charters for particular kinds of woods. A *hangra* was what is still today known as a 'hanger', that is a wood on a slope. A *hyrst*, on the other hand, later 'hurst', was probably a wood upon rising ground, and many of the Kentish dens bore such a name. A *sceaga* was a small wood, or 'shaw'. In Kent this term was often applied to surviving linear woods left between cleared areas and in medieval Arden in Warwickshire the term was particularly common in the area in and around Tanworth where the land rose up to the drift-covered areas which probably supported a vegetation of mixed open pasture, woodland and heath. The term *fyrhð* is found largely in minor place-names and seems to indicate, according to Gelling and Cole, 'land overgrown with brushwood, scrubland on the edge of forest' while *þyfel* is 'a thicket'.[77] The term *fyrhð* survived in place-names over a considerable area of central Worcestershire, recorded in the parish names Grafton Flyford and Flyford Flavel and in two pre-Conquest estates, the first named as *Fleferð* but identified as Dormston, the second an area of five hides, identified as Kington, which was said to lie *in locis silvaticis* 'wooded places' on both sides of the River Piddle *æt Fleferht*, which was leased in the eleventh century with other estates located in the Vale of Evesham.[78]

Scandinavian terms for wood include *lundr*, *skógr* and *viðr*, found most commonly in place-names as charters are few in regions overtaken by the Danes and Norwegians. Gelling and Cole argue that *lundr* was a common name for woods of some economic significance, *skógr* used in much the same way as OE *sceaga* for a 'small wood' (common along the Pennine foothills), and *viðr*, a rare term in England, used as a cognate of *wudu*.[79]

Of all these terms, the term *lēah* is the most ubiquitous, occurring in place-names throughout the country. The evidence is augmented in those areas covered by charter boundary clauses. It is most common in place-names in a section through the centre of England extending northwards into Yorkshire, and is well represented to the west on the Cheshire plain and to the north-east in Durham east of the Pennines but less so over the higher parts of northern England such as the Pennines and the Lakeland hills (Fig. 7). It thins out dramatically eastwards in Lincolnshire and south-eastern England and is virtually absent from the south-west peninsula. However, charter evidence shows that the term did indeed extend further into Somerset, Dorset and Devon. Not surprisingly, it is found in the greatest concentrations where clays and similar soils supported abundant tree growth but were, perhaps, more difficult for agriculture, and there is a marked difference between such regions and those virtually cleared for intensive agriculture. In the West Midlands, Worcestershire, for instance, was a county estimated by Rackham to have been 40% wooded at the time of the Domesday survey,[80] with woodland absent only from the Vale of Evesham in the south-east, and this is exactly the area almost devoid of *lēah* names (with a few notable exceptions). In Warwickshire the term is largely absent, too, from the intensively cultivated south-eastern Feldon and it is less common over the more intensively cultivated dip slope of the Cotswolds in Gloucestershire; in Oxfordshire it is most frequent in the vicinity of Wychwood Forest (and in Hormer hundred, previously part of Berkshire). In south-central England, in Wiltshire, it occurs most frequently in the clay vale in the north-west of the county, over the clays of the Vale of Wardour in the south-west, and sporadically across the south of the county and in the eastern forest areas of Savernake, Chute, Clarendon and Melchet. It is fairly ubiquitous in Hampshire, occurring over the mixed sands and clays of the Hampshire basin in the south (including the area of the New Forest) and the London Basin in the north and also across the chalk downs, which in this region are often covered with clay-with-flints. In Dorset it is commonest over the clays of the Vale of Blackmoor. In Berkshire it is common except over the chalk downland. Yet there are some areas that are known to have been well wooded where the term only rarely occurs, if at all, such as the marshy Kennet-Lodden Vales of southern Berkshire. Only detailed regional studies can suggest why this should be so – in some cases the paucity of settlement may explain the absence of place-names of any kind, and late name recordings can often add evidence in areas where there was limited early settlement. There may have been a sort of hierarchy, too, in *lēah* names, ranging from those extensive areas such as *Ærmundeslea* and *Weogorena leah* noted above, and including the later recorded forest names of Groveley in Wiltshire and Dygherlye and Finkley in Hampshire, to the *lēah* areas that gave their name to estates or parishes, down to the remnant *lēah* features lying along the boundaries of such estates and the more limited areas of *lēah* noted in later place-names or even field-names. It remains one of the most useful place-name terms for the recognition of areas that were well wooded in the early medieval period.[81]

The scattered settlement pattern of these wooded regions, too, especially in those with an abundance of *lēah* place-names, probably reflected different cultural characteristics that only become clear through more detailed medieval documentation. The settlements themselves which were to acquire *lēah* names were usually dispersed in location and amorphous in shape, the term applied both to individual farms and straggling hamlets which took their names from the nature of the surrounding countryside (and, perhaps, their early role within it). Often the hamlets or groups of farms had no recognisable focus until later when some were to acquire a church. They tended to be poorer than the agricultural villages but the peasantry enjoyed a measure of independence and freedom not available to those closely tied into the obligations and seigneurial control of the closely knit agricultural village community.

THE NATURE OF ANGLO-SAXON WOODLAND

The picture of a primeval wildwood awaiting clearance and colonisation has now been firmly dispelled by modern archaeological and vegetational study. Certainly woodland was present and was probably increasing in amount in many regions in this period, while being whittled away in others: the ploughman is described as *har holtes feond* 'the hoar foe of the forest',[82] but over most of England the woodland was not impenetrable and rarely remote. Often the woods were pastured on a seasonal basis. In many areas domestic stock were driven away from the arable lands and hay meadows in late spring while in late summer and early autumn the acorns and beech-mast would be foraged by pigs, as shown by the Anglo-Saxon charter evidence (Chapter 6). In later times, in upland or moorland areas, stock were brought down from the open moorlands as winter approached and moved into the lowland woods for the winter season.[83] The presence of animals pasturing in the woods would create open woodland with glades. Indeed, the trees could only regenerate adequately if animals were deliberately excluded and this is unlikely to have been the case over large areas until the late Anglo-Saxon kings extended their hunting reserves. Even then, many had claims to pasture rights which could not be curtailed. Rackham discusses the apparent conflict between tree and animal and the balance that had to be achieved in the case of wood-pasture: 'The more trees there are, the less abundant and the worse will be the pasture; and the more animals there are, the less likely saplings or coppice shoots are to survive to produce a new generation of trees'.[84] Because of this, the woods used as wood-pasture had different kinds of trees and plants from those that were not pastured. However, Peterken notes that 'wood pasture could remain wooded for centuries without any natural regeneration taking place. Temporary reduction in grazing pressure, even at long intervals, would have been enough to initiate a new generation of trees'.[85] It will be argued in Chapter 6 that the wood-pastures, the *silva pastilis* of Domesday Book, probably constituted the greater part of Domesday woodland. Trees in wood-pasture will clearly show a distinct browse-line where animals eat the leaves that they can reach and the height of the line reflects the type of animal browsing. Whereas the roe-deer can only reach to about 4 feet (1.2 metres), the red deer can reach 5 feet (1.5 metres), but animals also have preferred tastes: deer enjoy ash, elm, hazel and hawthorn; the first three remain uncommon in wood-pasture but oak, beech, hornbeam and aspen are either left or rapidly recover while ash can also quickly recover if there is a lull in grazing.[86] Oaks, scattered as isolated trees, were to become one of the most characteristic features of medieval non-compartmental English parkland. In wood-pasture or parkland young oaklings tend to be avoided by stock because of their bitter tannin taste but, in any case, the long tap-root of a young tree can give resurgence to a bitten-off shoot.[87]

The dominant trees in the woods would vary from region to region, influenced by soil type, topography and local climatic conditions.[88] The most important distinction is between the mainly oakwood region of northern and western England and the more varied types of woodlands found in the Midlands, south and east. The English oak, *Quercus robur*, and sessile oak, *Quercus petraea*, are particularly common throughout England, the first in the English lowlands, the second dominant in the north and west. Most semi-natural woods are, however, mixed: oak is found commonly with birch on non-calcareous soils (as in Wales, the northern uplands and the south-west), with ash and beech (today) on calcareous (limy) ones and with alder and willow in damp situations. Birch woodland, often with rowan and hazel, is common on lighter soils. Oak is well represented in the west but scattered more thinly in woods and farmland over lowland Britain. Ash and wych-elm are often found together, and those growing on the calcareous limestones and chalk of southern England are amongst the richest woodlands found in Britain. Maple or hazel is also often a constituent of ashwoods or of mixed oak and ashwoods. Once very abundant, lime is now very rare in south-east England; the small-leaved lime can be found elsewhere in oakwoods and is often a relict of ancient woodland. Its rootstock can continue to produce new shooting trees for thousands of years (Chapter 8). Beech remains commonest in southern England, as it was in the Anglo-Saxon period, and hornbeam in the south-east. Until the outbreak of elm disease in recent decades, elm was ubiquitous throughout the country (but see Chapter 8) and could spread rapidly by suckering, driving out other species to dominate stands of

Plate III. A wood-pasture environment: a scene in the New Forest

woodland. Even after outbreaks of disease, the roots can survive to send out a new crop of suckers, although these may succumb in their turn.

TYPES OF PRESENT-DAY WOODLAND

Ancient primary woodland or 'wildwood' is that on a site that has never been ploughed or cultivated. Ancient semi-natural woodland is any woodland that has remained on an ancient site, preferably documented since at least the sixteenth century, with no obvious evidence of deliberate replanting. Secondary woodland is new woodland growing on formerly open ground, considered ancient secondary woodland if it had been rewooded before 1600 – this type of woodland has a less rich ground flora than does ancient primary woodland.[89] In practice, most ancient woods found today are a mixture of primary and secondary woodland and few, if any, could be termed natural, unaltered woodland, their very survival usually influenced by their usefulness to man. Many were regularly coppiced in the past. In the twentieth century a great deal of deciduous woodland was replaced by conifer plantations for more immediate economic return but the value of native deciduous woodland is now widely recognised (Chapter 6).

Patches of truly ancient woodland can be found throughout England but are usually of limited extent compared with plantations and replanted woodland. There are some larger patches of considerable interest: on the northern edge of Cannock Chase in Staffordshire, Brocton Coppice is over a kilometre across; in northern Somerset ancient woodland extends in a belt for some seven kilometres along the coastal fringe to the west of Porlock and in the valleys of Horner Water and its tributary Nutscale Water to the south; within the ancient forest of Sherwood in Nottinghamshire, to the north of Edwinstowe, are woods extending for nearly four kilometres from east to west, and there is also much ancient woodland remaining in the former forest areas of Grovely and Melchet in Wiltshire, Wychwood in Oxfordshire and Wyre on the Worcestershire/Shropshire border. Although ancient trees are not a prerequisite for such woods, ancient pollards are indeed found at Brocton and Edwinstowe. Ancient replanted woodland is more extensive, found, in midland and southern England, covering large areas in the old forest areas of northern Herefordshire, Savernake in Wiltshire and Dean in Gloucestershire (in the last area stretching for over 11km from north to south and over 6km from east to west).[90]

In my review of the landscape of Anglo-Saxon England I have suggested that an impression of what much of the early medieval wood-pasture regions may have looked like might be gained by visits to Epping Forest in Essex, Bradgate Park in Leicestershire or Sutton Park near Birmingham.[91] Here the countryside is largely open with clumps of trees and bushes scattered across open grassland. In Sutton Park there are areas with woods protected by woodbanks but the woods are now overrun by holly, a tree which survived much of the sixteenth-century clearance because of its value as forage for stock. Hatfield Forest in Essex also has good examples of compartmentation using woodbanks. Perhaps we should envisage rather more woodland than survives today in these locations – perhaps something closer to parts of the New Forest in Hampshire, where ancient areas of wood-pasture still survive (Plate III). This is the largest and least modified of the Norman forests in England, a landscape that has preserved much of its medieval forest heritage with an assemblage of ancient woods, heathland and valley bog. The woods are dominated by oak and beech with an understorey, again, of holly. Veteran trees are also a valued feature of such areas and the New Forest has the largest concentration of veteran trees found in England. The region includes some of England's (and, indeed, Europe's) best-preserved wood-pasture habitat to an unequalled degree – an ancient lowland landscape of heathland, bog, woodland and streams maintained through the grazing of thousands of New Forest ponies and cattle – that has resulted in one of the richest and most extensive wildlife habitats in Europe.

ENDNOTES

1   F. W. M. Vera, *Grazing Ecology and Forest History* (Wallingford and New York, 2000).
2   J. G. Evans, *Land and Archaeology: Histories of the Human Environment in the British Isles* (Stroud, 1999), pp. 49–53.
3   Ibid., pp. 24–6.
4   M. F. Walker and J. A. Taylor, 'Post-Neolithic vegetation changes in the western Rhinogau, Gwynedd, north-west Wales', *Transactions of the Institute of British Geographers*, n. s. 1 (1976), pp. 323–45.
5   Evans, *Land and Archaeology*, pp. 97–8.
6   O. Rackham, *Trees and Woodland in the British Landscape*, 2nd edn (London, 1996), p. 42.
7   F. Chambers, *A Reconstruction of the Postglacial Environmental History of Tatton Park, Cheshire, from Valley Mire Sediments*, University of Keele Department of Geography Occasional Paper 17 (Keele, 1991); N. Higham, *Rome, Britain and the Anglo-Saxons* (London, 1992), p. 78.
8   J. Greig, 'Pollen and waterlogged seeds', in A. Jones, 'Roman Birmingham 2 Excavations at Metchley Roman Forts 1998–2000 and 2002', *Transactions of the Birmingham and Warwickhire Archaeological Society* 108 (2005), pp. 75–80.
9   W. Metz, 'Das "gehagio regis" der Langobarden und die deutschen Hagenortsnamen', *Beiträge zur Namenforschung in Verbindung mit Ernst Dickenmann, herausgegeben von Hans Krahe*, Band 5 (Heidelburg, 1954), pp. 39–51.
10 M. Gardiner, 'The colonisation of the Weald of south-east England', *Medieval Settlement Group Annual Report* 12 (1997), pp. 6–8.
11 K. Rutherford-Davis, *Britons and Saxons. The Chiltern Region 400–700* (Chichester, 1982).
12 *Anglo-Saxon Chronicle* 709: Swanton, pp. 40–1.
13 S 89, B 154, *WoASCB*, pp. 61–3.
14 D. Hooke, *The Anglo-Saxon Landscape, the Kingdom of the Hwicce* (Manchester, 1985), p. 2; D. Hooke, *The Landscape of Anglo-Saxon England* (London and New York, 1998), pp. 139–42, fig. 47.
15 D. Hooke, 'Early units of government in Herefordshire and Shropshire', *Anglo-Saxon Studies in Archaeology and History* 5, ed. W. Filmer-Sankey (Oxford, 1992).
16 S. P. Day, 'Post-glacial vegetational history of the Oxford region', *New Phytologist* 119 (1991); S. P. Day, 'Woodland origin and "ancient woodland indicators": a case-study from Sidlings Copse, Oxfordshire, UK', *The Holocene* 3 (1993).
17 P. Dark, *The Environment of Britain in the First Millennium A.D.* (London, 2000), p. 121.
18 Rackham, *Trees and Woodland*, 2nd edn, p. 42; A. C. C. Brodribb, A. R. Hands and D. R. Walker, *Excavations at Shakenoak Farm, near Wilcote, Oxfordshire* (Oxford, 1968–73).
19 D. Hooke, 'Medieval forests and parks in southern and central England', in *European Woods and Forests, Studies in Cultural History*, ed. C. Watkins (New York, 1998), pp. 19–32.
20 *Anglo-Saxon Chronicle* 893 for 892: Swanton, pp. 84–5.
21 Ordnance Survey, *Map of Dark Age Britain* (London, 1966); F. M. Stenton, *Anglo-Saxon England*, 3rd edn (Oxford, 1971); see, also, D. Hill, *An Atlas of Anglo-Saxon England* (Oxford, 1981), p. 16.
22 Swanton, *Anglo-Saxon Chronicle*.
23 O. Rackham, 'Savanna in Europe', in *The Ecological History of European Forests*, ed. K. Kirby and C. Watkins (Wallingford, 1998), p. 47, fig. 11; Gelling and Cole, *The Landscape of Place-Names*, p. 249.
24 H. C. Darby, *Domesday England* (Cambridge, 1977), p. 193, fig. 64.

[25] D. Hooke, 'Regional variation in southern and central England in the Anglo-Saxon period and its relationship to land units and settlement', in *Anglo-Saxon Settlements*, ed. D. Hooke (Oxford, 1988), pp. 123–51.

[26] B. K. Roberts and S. Wrathmell, 'Peoples of wood and plain: an exploration of national and local regional contrasts', in *Landscape, the Richest Historical Record*, ed. D. Hooke, Society for Landscape Studies (Birmingham, 2000), p. 86, fig. 7.1; reproduced in B. K. Roberts and S. Wrathmell, *An Atlas of Rural Settlement in England* (London, 2000), p. 31, fig. 24, and B. K. Roberts and S. Wrathmell, *Region and Place. A Study of English Rural Settlement* (London, 2002), p. 28, fig. 1.13.

[27] Roberts and Wrathmell, *Region and Place*, pp. 19, 22, figs 1.9 and 1.10.

[28] *CDEPN*, p. 372; M. Gelling, *Signposts to the Past*, p. 57; Jackson, *Language and History*, pp. 332, 563.

[29] Domesday Book fol. 242c; *CDEPN*, p. 180, but the latter also offers an alternative suggestion.

[30] Asser, *De rebus gestis Ælfredi*: W. H. Stevenson, ed., *Asser's Life of King Alfred (De rebus gestis Aelfredi)* (Oxford, 1904), p. 45.

[31] W. Davies, *An Early Welsh Microcosm. Studies of the Llandaff Charters* (London, 1978), p. 29; Evans, *The Text of the Book of Llan Dâv*, pp. 73, 262. Other woods noted in this group of charters include *coit guent* Wentwood in Llanbedr (near Newport), possibly Mamilad Wood near the River Gamber (south-west Herefordshire), and a wood (*silue*) known as *Ynis Peithan* near Whitchurch (Herefordshire), the first and last of these to become part of the hunting forest for Chepstow Castle. But in general the woods named seem to have been relatively limited in extent and were often cut through by the boundaries: Davies, p. 30; e.g. Evans, pp. 173, 261. The dating of many of the Llandaff charters is still under discussion.

[32] *CDEPN*, pp. 349, 17.

[33] S 445, B 744, S. E. Kelly, ed., *The Charters of Shaftesbury Abbey*, Anglo-Saxon Charters V (Oxford, 1996), no. 10; S 466, B 752; S 690, B 1066, S. E. Kelly, ed., *Charters of Abingdon*, II, no. 87; S 688, B 1067, Kelly, op. cit., no. 88, the latter a forgery possibly based upon S 690: Electronic Sawyer.

[34] E.g. S 474, B 768; S 198, B 450; S 485, B 775, Kelly, *Charters of Shaftesbury*, no. 13; S 1013, J. M. Kemble, *Codex Diplomaticus Aevi Saxonici* (London, 1839–48), K 783 (hereafter given by K no.); S 671, B 1295, A. Campbell, ed., *Charters of Rochester*, Anglo-Saxon Charters I (London, 1973), no. 29 (the last possibly a tenth-century fabrication: Electronic Sawyer).

[35] S 64, B 123.

[36] S 404, B 667, B 668, Kelly, *Charters of Abingdon*, I, no. 22; *WoASCB*, pp. 158–62.

[37] S 1301, B 1087, *WoASCB*, p. 248.

[38] S 105, B 195, Campbell, *Charters of Rochester*, no. 6; S 33, B 194, Campbell, op. cit., no. 8; S 37, B 260, Campbell, op. cit., no. 15.

[39] S 168, B 335; S 123, B 247, S 25, B 191.

[40] *King Alfred's Orosius* 1.1: Sweet, *Pastoral Care*, pp. 24, 10.

[41] S 94, B 157, *WaASCB*, pp. 21–2; S 727, B 1127.

[42] *Anglo-Saxon Chronicle*, *Andred* 892, Selwood 878, 894; Wychwood: S 196, B 432 (for date see Electronic Sawyer).

[43] S 1146, K 829.

[44] S 1596, B 362, *WoASCB*, pp. 397–400 (sp, but based upon an authentic text); S 1372, K 682, *WoASCB*, pp. 299–301.

[45] S 1373, K 680, *WoASCB*, pp. 293–7; S 179, B 356, *WoASCB*, pp. 107–12 – that of Hawling is likely to be an eleventh-century fabrication: H. P. R. Finberg, *The Early Charters of the West Midlands*, 2nd edn (Leicester, 1972), no. 189, pp. 184–96.

46 S 1185, B 1007 (?untrustworthy), *WoASCB*, pp. 82–7; S 219, B 552, *WoASCB*, pp. 129–34; S 1591, K iii. 391, *WoASCB*, pp. 384–6; S 1596, B 362, *WoASCB*, pp. 397–400.

47 Gelling and Cole, *The Landscape of Place-Names*, p. 258.

48 *CDEPN*, p. 657; S 1243, F. E. Harmer, *Anglo-Saxon Writs* (Manchester, 1952), no. 121.

49 S 367, B 603; S 255, B 1331, B 1332, B 1333, *CBDC*, pp. 86–99; S 218, B 551 (?sp).

50 *CDEPN*, p. xlviii.

51 D. Hooke, 'Early Cotswold woodland', *Journal of Historical Geography* 4 (1978), pp. 333–41. Yeates, *Religion, Community and Territory*, pp. 86–8, has recently argued, upon slight evidence, for the region being named after an Iron Age goddess called *Cuda*.

52 H. S. A. Fox, 'The people of the wolds', in *The Rural Settlements of Medieval England*, ed. M. Aston, D. Austin and C. Dyer (Oxford, 1989), p. 84.

53 C. Johansson, *Old English Place-Names containing lēah* (Stockholm, 1975).

54 *Anglo-Saxon Chronicle* 477; M. Gelling, M., *The Place-Names of Berkshire*, parts I–III, English Place-Name Society 49–51 (Cambridge, 1974–82), III, p. 717; S 180, B 357, *WoASCB*, pp. 113–15; D. Hooke, 'Early medieval woodland and the place-name term *lēah*', in *A Commodity of Good Names. Essays in Honour of Margaret Gelling*, ed. O. J. Padel and D. N. Parsons (Donington, 2008), pp. 369–70.

55 *CDEPN*, p. xlvi.

56 Hooke, 'Early medieval woodland', pp. 367–8; *CDEPN*, p. xlvi.

57 D. Hooke, 'Anglo-Saxon landscapes of the West Midlands', *Journal of the English Place-Name Society* 11 (1978–9), pp. 3–23.

58 S 786, B 1282, *WoASCB*, pp. 196–8; S 1339, K 618, *WoASCB*, pp. 301–4.

59 Hooke, 'Early medieval woodland', pp. 375–6.

60 S. J. Wager, *Woods, Wolds and Groves. The Woodland of Medieval Warwickshire*, British Archaeological Reports, Br Ser 269 (Oxford, 1998), pp. 154–5.

61 *CDEPN*, pp. 172, 448.

62 S 1272, B 455 (1), *WoASCB*, pp. 135–42.

63 D. Hooke, 'Recent views on the Worcestershire landscape', *Transactions of the Worcestershire Archaeological Society*, 3rd ser. 21 (2008), pp. 92–3, fig. 2.

64 S 1596, B 362, *WoASCB*, pp. 397–9.

65 Gelling and Cole, *The Landscape of Place-Names*, p. 222.

66 S 1023, K 796, Kelly, *Charters of Abingdon*, II, no. 146 (sp).

67 S 1374, K 681, *WoASCB*, pp. 297–9.

68 S 1405, *WoASCB*, pp. 368–70.

69 S 1305, B 1110, *WoASCB*, pp. 261–4.

70 S 898, K 705, *WaASCB*, pp. 110–13.

71 Gelling and Cole, *The Landscape of Place-Names*, pp. 226–7; Domesday Book, fol. 172b: F. Thorn and C. Thorn, eds, *Domesday Book, 16, Worcestershire* (Chichester, 1982), 1.1a; D. Hooke, 'The Droitwich salt industry: an examination of the West Midland charter evidence', in *Anglo-Saxon Studies in Archaeology and History* 2, ed. J. Campbell, D. Brown and S. Hawkes, British Archaeological Reports, Br. Ser. 92 (Oxford, 1981), p. 141.

72 Leland, V, fol. 92: L. Toulmin Smith, ed., *The Itinerary of John Leland in or about the Years 1535–1543, Part V* (London, 1964), II.94.

73 Wager, *Woods, Wolds and Groves*, pp. 142–6.

74 Gelling and Cole, *The Landscape of Place-Names*, p. 233.

75 S 1819, Turner, 'Some Old English passages', p. 120.

76 S 1307, B 1111, *WaASCB*, pp. 78–81; S 1437, B 386, *WoASCB*, pp. 96–7.

77 Gelling and Cole, *The Landscape of Place-Names*, pp. 224–6.

[78] S 786, B 1282, *WoASCB*, pp. 194–6; S 901, K 1295, *WoASCB*, pp. 351–3.

[79] Gelling and Cole, *The Landscape of Place-Names*, pp. 242–3, 248–9, 252–3.

[80] Rackham, *Trees and Woodland*, p. 50.

[81] Hooke, 'Early medieval woodland'.

[82] Riddle 21, 13, *Exeter Book II*: Mackie, *Exeter Book*, II, p. 110; trans. Baum, *Anglo-Saxon Riddles*, p. 28.

[83] C. Watkins, *Woodland Management and Conservation (Britain's Ancient Woodland)*, Nature Conservancy Council (Newton Abbot and London, 1990), pp. 116–17.

[84] O. Rackham, *The History of the Countryside* (London, 1986), p. 120.

[85] G. F. Peterken, *Woodland Conservation and Management*, 2nd edn (London, 1993), p. 12.

[86] Watkins, *Woodland Management*, pp. 116–17, 122; Rackham, *The History of the Countryside*, p. 140; *Ancient Woodland*, revised edn, p. 513.

[87] Rackham, *Ancient Woodland*, revised edn, p. 293.

[88] More detailed information can be found in Peterken, *Woodland Conservation*, ch. 7.

[89] See maps prepared by the Nature Conservancy Council (now part of Natural England).

[90] D. Hooke, *England's Landscape. The West Midlands* (London, 2006), pp. 125–6, fig. 5.37.

[91] D. Hooke, *The Landscape of Anglo-Saxon England* (London and New York, 1998), pp. 162–4.

6

The Use of Anglo-Saxon Woodland:
Place-Name and Charter Evidence

WOODLAND AS A VALUED RESOURCE

As a wood-pasture and timber resource

After the Roman withdrawal, native farming turned more towards traditional methods of pastoralism and the use of resources gathered from the wild by hunting and fowling, and although the woods may have been less carefully managed they were valued, primarily as sources of timber and as areas of wood-pasture. In early medieval England, under the Anglo-Saxons, the use of wood-pasture was an important part of farming practice and herds of swine and cattle were taken to, or kept in, wooded regions across the country, the swine, in particular, feasting and fattening upon acorns and beech-mast in the late summer and autumn. Woods served as areas of wood-pasture for domestic stock to such an extent that their distribution influenced territorial divisions and communication networks.

By the time of the earliest reliable documentary evidence, in charters of the early eighth century, the Wealden woodland was partitioned between the folk groups of south-eastern England, used first as a community resource but later subdivided between individual manors, where each held wood-pasture units known as dens within their respective areas of woodland.[1] The wooded nature of the Weald is not in doubt: in the ninth century it is claimed in the *Anglo-Saxon Chronicle* (*s.a.* 893 for 892) of *þes mycclan wuda* 'the great wood' of the Weald: 'That wood is a hundred-and-twenty miles long or longer from east to west, and thirty miles broad'.[2] Links between royal vills and capital manors to such woodland dens persisted through the centuries, although the dens gave way to permanent settlement (Fig. 8).[3] Series of parallel trackways leading into the Weald represented the routes along which stock were driven to the seasonal pastures and can still be detected in the present-day road pattern. Similar estate links can be traced in other regions and are particularly clear in central England. Here, estates in the cleared Feldon region of Warwickshire held rights in the woodlands of Arden which gave rise to estate links clearly traceable into medieval times. A similar pattern of roughly parallel routes running from

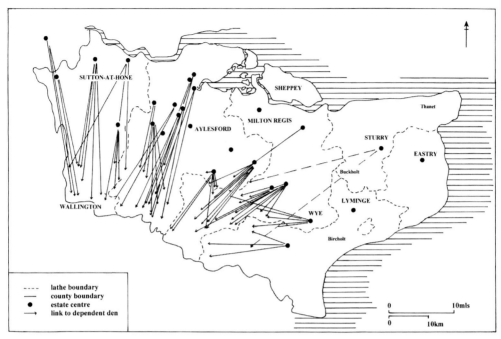

Figure 8. Estate links in the Kentish Weald

south-east to north-west linked the two regions and may again have originated in a system of droveways (see below).[4]

The Kentish charters offer ample evidence of the right to pasture stock in the wooded regions of south-eastern England, both on the North Downs and in the Weald (see below). Even the scattered trees of wood-pasture were of value: in Ine's laws, compiled in Wessex in the late seventh century, a tree that could shelter as many as thirty swine was regarded as twice as valuable as other trees.[5] Wood-pasture gave rise to a fairly open landscape of secondary woodland interspersed with open glades and scattered isolated trees rather than to extensive dense woodland, but might eventually give way under the pressure of grazing to open grassland or heathland common with scattered trees and scrubland (see Chapter 5).[6]

The sparse early medieval charter evidence for north Warwickshire clearly shows Arden to have been a region of scattered woods of limited extent rather than a region of unbroken woodland, and this seems to have been true for many other parts of the country traditionally regarded as 'woodland regions'. Groves of woodland would probably be temporarily protected from animals to allow the growth of underwood, a practice certainly followed in the medieval period. One way of producing timber from trees in areas open to grazing was to pollard them to provide timber above the reach of browsing animals (Fig. 9a) and there is evidence of this

Figure 9. Scenes from the Cotton Tiberius calendar (redrawn from the British Museum calendar manuscript BV, part 1): *a*. July – woodcutting; *b*. September – note the acorns being eaten by the pigs and the pollard tree on the right (although the figures have also been interpreted as huntsmen)

practice in early medieval England in references to *copped* trees in Anglo-Saxon boundary clauses (OE *copped* 'polled, lopped, pollard') (Plate IV). A late copy of an Old English boundary clause, of Chelworth in Crudwell, Wiltshire, notes *et ibi stat quidam truncus ex opposito in occidentali parte de la leye* 'and there stands a trunk across in the western part of the *lēah*', referring to a trunk of a tree that may again have been a pollard.[7] The leaves of such pollards could also be gathered for fodder – this was particularly valuable to help sustain stock over the long winters experienced in Scandinavia, and in this country the upper leaves of hollies might be gathered in winter for the same purpose. Generally, in this country, the medieval practice was to lop oak, ash and elm in summer as winter fodder or browse for cattle and deer, or in winter as iron rations. The pollards in the wood-pasture were

Plate IV. An ancient pollard in Whitcliff Park, Gloucestershire

a valuable source of pole wood. Wood for timber had been actively managed from prehistoric times with clear evidence of coppicing, and the evidence increases for the Roman period.[8] In the Anglo-Saxon period, timber and wood was widely used for all forms of construction and for most domestic and industrial utensils. Again, charters clearly indicate the value of woodland as a timber resource: eighth-century Kentish charters refer to rights to timber for building, as in a charter of Ickham and Palmstead, which included rights to wood for building and burning at Tenterden in the Weald and in other woodland at Hardres.[9] A ninth-century charter for a small estate at Seckley in Wolverley, Worcestershire, also granted 'five wainloads of good brushwood, one oak annually and other timber necessary for building' in addition to firewood.[10]

Woodland in its variety of forms was essential in the Anglo-Saxon economy. Almost all buildings were of timber, from palaces to hovels, as were ships; most common utensils and many ornamental features were carved from wood. Wood was the fuel for everything from cooking to industry. In the West Midlands, large quantities of wood continued to be needed throughout the early medieval period for the salt industry of Droitwich in order to evaporate the water from the brine which welled up naturally here. Another product from woodlands was honey from wild bees, an important source of this sweetener in early medieval England. 'Honey' brooks are noted in Worcestershire, where Beoley is 'bee wood' in a charter of 972 and a *hunig yrste* 'honey wooded hillock' appears as a landmark in a late boundary clause of Hardenhuish, Wiltshire.[11]

Woodlands for hunting

By the later part of the pre-Conquest period, woodland seems to have been regenerating in many regions of southern England. A likely reason for this is that it was being given added protection by Anglo-Saxon kings interested in conserving areas for hunting. In continental Europe, forests had been established in the Frankish kingdoms by the seventh century. England maintained close contact with these kingdoms and rapidly assimilated their cultural traditions. Some estates were singled out as of special importance for hunting, such as *illa uenatione uilla quae Saxonicae dicitur Bicanleag* 'that hunting vill which is called by the Saxons Bickleigh', recorded in 904.[12] This may have been Bickleigh in Devon, on the south-western fringe of Dartmoor, and the king probably had a lodge there. Hunting rights are included in other pre-Conquest charters and some areas of woodland appear to have been physically demarcated by wood-banks topped by hedges or fences – the OE *haga* (further discussed later in this chapter) – and these seem to have been closely related to the *haia* features of Domesday Book, noted as places in which deer might be captured. The *haga* features noted in woodland, therefore, appear to have been enclosures into which deer could be encouraged as a readily available source of venison and protected from marauding animals such as wolves (the later form *hayes* was used for 'a small hunting park, usually in a woodland area, enclosed for the retention of deer').[13] They seem to have been located, for the most part, in the more remote regions of woodland, often those which were later to fall within the Norman forests.[14] In Worcestershire, for instance, *haga* features occur most frequently in charter references in the area to the west of the River Severn, close to the west Hwiccan boundary; in Dorset they are concentrated within the north of the county in the area of the later forests of Gillingham and Blackmoor; they occur across Somerset and have been noted close to the forests of Mendip, Neroche and Selwood; they are widespread across Hampshire, a county with enormous areas of Norman forest; in Wiltshire they occur in the north-west of the county in the areas of the later forests of Kemble, Chippenham and Melksham and in the east in the area of the later forests of Savernake and Melchet. This association is less clear in the south-eastern counties, where both woodland and forest are incompletely recorded in Domesday Book: in Berkshire, Domesday woodland was plentiful across the south of the county but more woodland, oddly unrecorded, lay in Hormer hundred – all areas with *haga* features, with Domesday forests also in the southern part of the county, especially around Kintbury, Bucklebury and Windsor.[15] In Surrey, where forest was not adequately recorded and woodland only signified by swine renders, *haga* features are also noted in charters, especially upon the wooded estate of Chobham.[16]

Regions in which hunting was important can, therefore, be readily identified from the charter evidence, and by the time of Domesday Book the new Norman king was establishing forest law over many of these regions. In several, there is clear evidence of woodland regeneration post-dating the Roman and probably early Anglo-Saxon period. In Wychwood in Oxfordshire, for instance (Fig. 6), named by the Anglo-Saxons as 'the wood of the Hwicce', there were defended Iron Age enclosures and linear boundary defences associated with a probable late Iron Age *oppidum*, as well as Roman settlements, well within the later forest, but Anglo-Saxon settlement names around the forest core include many *lēah* and *feld* names, clearly indicating the presence of woodland by that date on the sands and clays that overlie the limestone rocks in the core area. Much of the woodland had been put 'within the king's enclosure', i.e. declared forest, by 1086.[17] Similarly, in northern Hampshire, evidence of Iron Age occupation and the lynchets of late Iron Age field systems were to give way to woodland by late Saxon times in the region to the north-east of Andover, an area where clay-with-flints covers much of the underlying chalk. On the estate of Faccombe Netherton, a late Saxon manor-house was to become the nucleus of a royal lodge within the Forest of Chute. At first, it was the bones of the red and roe deer that predominated, but from the mid-twelfth century the fallow deer, the species favoured by the Normans, increase in numbers.[18]

CHARTER EVIDENCE IN SOUTH-EASTERN ENGLAND

The charters of south-eastern England provide some of the most interesting references to the use of timber, and also indicate the role wood-pasture was to play in territorial organisation. Rights *in silvis* were fairly standard in the scribal formulae of pre-Conquest charters, alongside rights in fields and meadows, and sometimes marshes and rivers, but always based upon genuine resources available. In early medieval times the Wealden woodland was extensive (see above). Iron had been worked on its northern and southern fringes in prehistoric times but not in the High Weald itself. Many more bloomery sites worked in Roman times have, however, been identified: at least sixty when Cleere and Crossley published their study of the Wealden iron industry in 1985. However, the industry flourished only between the latter part of the first century and the middle of the third century. In spite of the need for charcoal to work the bloomeries, it is not thought by some present-day archaeologists that this led to widespread woodland devastation in the area, but examination of charcoal found at some of the sites provides ample evidence of the use of many species of trees for charcoal-burning, among them oak, ash, beech, hornbeam, birch, hazel, hawthorn and elder, with oak predominating.[19] In this period the pattern of roads was largely north–south with east–west linkages, but many of these, perhaps with the exception of some in the east, were established irrespective of the iron industry (if used by it), which was largely concentrated at the headwaters of the rivers Rother and Cuckmere. It has been suggested that the eastern group of iron-making sites may have operated under the direct control of the *Classis Britannica*, producing iron for the Roman fleet, and were abandoned in favour of more secure sites elsewhere (such as the Forest of Dean) in the second half of the third century.[20] The industry presumably continued on a local scale; a charter of 689 records the grant of *unum aratrum in quo mina ferri haberi cognoscitur* '1 *aratrum* [or *sulung*, the Kentish ploughland] in which it is known an iron mine is known to be held' by the estate of Lyminge,[21] as if iron extraction was continuing at that date. Few early medieval ironworking sites have been identified but a small-scale iron smelting site is known from Ashdown Forest.[22] Domesday Book mentions only one *feraria* 'ironworks' in Sussex but it is possible that small-scale ironworking was then so widespread as to be of little economic value in comparison with such regions as the Forest of Dean or the Forest of Rockingham.

But the main usage of the Weald in the Anglo-Saxon period was undoubtedly as wood-pasture (Fig. 9b). This is usually *pascua porcorum*, swine pasture, as the charters specify, although another term used for these is *denbera, -bǽra*, often shortened to *den*: a charter of Wassingwell, Kent, in 858 explicitly states *pascua porcorum quot nostra lingua denbera nominamus* 'swine pastures which in our language we call *denbera*'.[23] Occasionally the term used is *wealdbǽra*, as in a charter of 814 of Chart Sutton, Kent, or as specifically stated earlier, in 788 in a charter of Trottiscliffe, Kent, where the pasture was scattered in three different places, *in diuersis locis porcorum pastus id est uueald-baera'*.[24] Most of the Wealden dens were for swine pasture, the pigs particularly foraging on the oak- and beech-mast each autumn. One of the earliest Kentish charters granting swine pastures is that of 724 (an authentic charter) in which Æthelberht grants land by the River Limen to Mildred, the abbess of Minster-in-Thanet, together with *pasca porcorum* in the woods of *Blean* and *Bocholt* on the North Downs and in the *Weowerawealde* 'the wood of the men of Wye'.[25] From the middle of the eighth century such grants increase in number and many of the named dens can be identified (Fig. 8).[26] The rights to pasture pigs are normally recorded but other stock could also be pastured in the woods and woodland glades. In addition to 'boars and sows', other animals (horse and cattle or sheep) are noted in a supposedly eighth-century charter of Beauxfield in Shepherdswell: it is claimed that Offa gave grazing rights to the abbot of Saints Peter and Paul at Canterbury, which included the right *ad pascendum porcos et pecora et iumenta in silua regali* 'to pasture pigs and cattle and oxen in the king's wood'.[27] Swine pastures granted by King Cuthred to Archbishop Wulfred in the early ninth century appear to have lain in Petham within Buckholt but one wood in the 'west wood' was known as *Cinges culand* 'the king's cow land', set aside for *pasturam uaccarum regis* 'pasture of the king's cows' (possibly referring to a lost Kingland in Faversham hundred).[28] Another ninth-century charter grants land at a lost Milton in Otford, Kent, with *in ondrede pastum et pascua porcorum* 'pasture and grazings for pigs in Andred [the Weald]' but adds: *et armentum seu caprorum* 'and [for] plough-beasts or goats in these places: Ewehurst, *Sciofing den* and Snodhurst'.[29]

Linking the estates along the Kentish coast or in the inland Vale of Holmesdale to their woodland dens, a series of parallel roads developed, a feature mirrored also in Sussex and, indeed, all around the Weald.[30] Estate linkages also developed but initially the woodland seems to have been pastured in common by the men of the various folk regions. It is the charter evidence that appears to suggest that the wood-pastures were held in common by the folk of these districts – by whole communities. The church of St Andrew at Rochester was to obtain pasture rights for 12 herds of swine *in silba quae appellatus est Cæstruuarouualth*, the latter 'the wood of the men of the *ceaster* – Rochester' in 747; others *in commune saltu . . . on Cæstersætawalda* were granted by Cœnwulf to Swiðhun, *minsiter*, in 801 (who later made a bequest of the land to St Andrew's).[31] However, in time, the Weald was to be carved up into districts appendant to the large estate foci of the early medieval period. Only later were the dens to be appropriated by particular estates. Thus, in Kent, the district which included the ecclesiastical focus of Rochester also included the royal vill of Aylesford, a division later to be represented by the lathes of Aylesford, Sutton and Milton,[32] and the folk named as the *Weowara* were centred upon the royal vill of Wye in the Stour valley. Other groups included the *Limenwara* of the Lyminge region and the *Burhwara* around Canterbury in the northeast of the county, while the district around Eastry is referred to in charters as *in regione eastrgena/easterege*.[33] The lathe (OE *lǣð* 'an area over which authority is exercised') as an administrative district may, Joliffe believed, go back to the sixth century; Brooks has examined the evidence rather more critically but agrees that the four lathes of east Kent indeed existed from the early days of the kingdom, but not necessarily those of west Kent.[34] The date of the origin of the lathes is still, therefore, in dispute but the pattern of transhumance routes and the estate linkages revealed in the charters hints at the existence of some intercommoning in parts of the Weald before boundaries were more sharply defined. The pattern is mirrored in Sussex, and a charter of 953 also hints at common ownership when King Eadred grants 30 hides at Felpham, adding *pascua porcorum* (swine pastures) *at Hidhurst in silua* 'in the wood of Idehurst' (in Kirdford) *et in communa silua pascuale quod dicitur Palinga schittas* 'in the common woodland called *Palinga schittas*', perhaps 'the pig-sties of the *Palingas*'.[35] While most links between estate centres and their dens fall within prescribed boundaries, in some areas there is some intermingling of the dens, as in those belonging to the estates of the *Weowara* and the *Limenwara* in the Wealden region to the south of Chart Sutton.[36]

Wild animals, particularly deer, are likely to have frequented the woods, and hunting rights, *venationes*, are specified in a number of Kentish charters, appearing among the appurtenances of *Perhamstede* (?Palmstead) in *c.*767, alongside rights in fishing and fowling, or in charters of Westwood, Halling, Lyminge, Little Chart, *Ulaham*, *Eastre(a)stadelham* and Mersham.[37]

Timber extraction is also recorded in Kentish charters, some of it apparently destined for the production of salt. A genuine charter of Offa, dated 785, grants land at Ickham with woodland in Andred, Bocholt and Blean for swine pasture to Ealdbeorht, *minister*, and his sister Seleþryð specifying, in addition to pasture for one herd in one wood (possibly at Tenterden) and 50 pigs in another, also *ligna ad cedendum ad edificium seu ad conburendam sine contradictione similiterque siluam afundanter* [sic] *ad coquendum sal . . . et in haredum .C. plaustra onusti et duos carras ambulantes per totum annum* 'wood for felling for a building or for burning, without hindrance, and similarly wood is set aside for boiling salt . . . and at Hardres 100 loaded wagons and two carts all year round'.[38]

Salt was evaporated at several places around the coasts of southern and eastern England. The following year another less certainly authentic charter of Offa refers to the woodland rights of Hardres as *C. foðra uuido. ꝺ tuegro uuegna gang uuintres sumeres. ꝺ in boc holte timber geweorc. ꝺ uuidigunge* '100 "fothers" (cart-loads) of wood and [the right] to fetch wood twice [literally "passage for wagons"], in winter and summer, and in Buckholt ['beech wood'] timber work and the right to fetch wood'.[39] Another charter notes 50 cartloads of wood granted to Bishop Beornmod by King Ecgbert, supposedly in 838.[40] In an authentic charter of Æthelberht dated 863, Æthelred, *minister* and *princeps*, receives rights to estates at Mersham and Willesborough (including rights in woods, swine pastures and hunting) which include a *salis coquinariam hoc est .I. sealternsteall* 'place to boil salt, that is one salt place' with cottages belonging to it at *herewic*, and *IIII. carris transductionem in silba regis sex ebdomades a die pentecosten hubi alteri homines silbam cedunt hoc est in regis communione* 'passage for 4 carts in the king's wood for six weeks from the day of Pentecost where the other men are felling the wood, i.e. in the king's commonage' (*herewic* may be Harwick Street in Whitstable).[41] In 858 another charter of Æthelberht notes the wood belonging to the salterns at Faversham, probably in Blean Wood.[42] The abbot of Saints Peter and Paul at Canterbury also claimed rights in a spurious charter of 839 x 855 together with an estate at Lenham, Kent, which included *gressu trium carrorum in silua qui dicitur blean* 'ingress for three carts in the wood called Blean', to obtain wood for salt manufacture.[43] The owner of an estate at Oxney in Kent in the mid-tenth century had woodland 'outside the island' to which he had the right to every third tree.[44] Some estates had to pay renders from their land: an estate at Brabourne in Kent had to pay yearly to St Augustine's Abbey in 844 x 864 renders which included 40 'ambers' of malt, a full-grown bullock, 4 wethers, 240 loaves, a wey of lard and cheese 4 'fothers' of wood and 20 hens.[45] In 852, it is recorded in the *Anglo-Saxon Chronicle* that the abbot of Peterborough and the monks leased an estate to a certain Wulfred on the condition that he should return it later to the monastery with land at Sleaford, but also paid an annual render to the community:

> ˥ elce gere sextig foðra wuda to ðæm ham on Hornan ðæm wuda. ˥ tuelf foðer græfan. ˥ sex foður gerda.

> 'and he should give every year to the minster sixty wagon-loads of wood and twelve wagon-loads of brushwood and six wagon-loads of faggots.'

This was in addition to 'two casks of clear ale and two cattle for slaughter and six hundred loaves and ten *mittan* [measures] of Welsh ale; and to the lord of the church he shall render every year a horse and thirty shillings, and supply him with one day's food-rent [provisions] – fifteen *mittan* of clear ale and five *mittan* of Welsh ale and fifteen sesters of mild ale'.[46]

Timber for building is one of the requirements for the upkeep of Rochester bridge in the *Textus Roffensis* of *c*.975 when various estates were responsible for individual piers: for instance,

> ærest þære burge biscop fehð on þone earm to wercene þa land peran. ˥ þreo gyrda to þillianæ. ˥ .III. sylla to lyccanne. þ is of Borcstealle. ˥ of Cucclestane. ˥ of Frinondesbyrig. ˥ of Stoce.

> 'First, the bishop of the city undertakes to construct the land-piers at the [eastern] extremity, and to provide planks for 3 poles and put 3 beams in position; and this is due from Borstall, Cuxton, Frinsbury and Stoke.'

> Þanne seo oðer per gebyrað to Gyllingeham. ˥ to Cætham. ˥ an gyrd to þillanne. ˥ III sylla to leccanne.

> 'Then the second pier belongs to Gillingham and to Chatham, and to provide planks for 1 pole and put 3 beams in position.'

> Þonne seo þridde per gebyrað eft þam biscope. ˥ þridde healf gyrd to þillianne. ˥ III. sylla to leccenne. of Heallingan. ˥ of Trotescliue. ˥ of Meallingan. ˥ of Fliote. ˥ of Stane. ˥ of Pinindene. ˥ of Falchenham.

> 'Then the third pier again belongs to the bishop, and to provide planks for 2½ poles and put 3 beams in position. [This is due] from Halling and from Trottiscliffe and from Malling and from Fleet and from Stone and from Pinden and from Fawkham.'[47]

and so on to the ninth pier which is the last 'at the west end'. A little later, in 995, Æthelred II restored to the bishopric of Rochester rights in estates at Wouldham and Littlebrook, the latter including a mill place with a wood and *ælc geare fiftig foðra*.

⁊ *an hund of þæs cinges acholte* 'another 150 fothers (wagon-loads) each year from the king's oak wood'.[48]

WOODLAND USAGE ELSEWHERE

The main economic uses of woodland regions are well exemplified in the Kentish charters, but similar transhumance patterns to those found in south-eastern England can also be identified between the Warwickshire Arden and more heavily developed estates in the south-east of that county with a similar north-west to south-east pattern of droveways linking the two (Fig. 10) and an east–west pattern in the well-wooded region to the west of the River Severn in Worcestershire, leading from the Severn valley into a region known as *Weogorena leah*, 'the wood-pasture of the *Weogoran*' (the folk whose territory was centred upon Worcester).[49] Indeed, the linked estate pattern formed through the use of woodland resources by estates in more heavily cultivated regions was to influence territorial organisation across many parts of England, perpetuated in later manorial and ecclesiastical links. Much of this evidence has been discussed by the author elsewhere and will not be repeated here.[50] Many of the regions at the remoter ends of the links were well wooded in this period but others, like Dartmoor, consisted of moorland and hill pasture. The charter evidence is similar to that of Kent discussed above. A charter of Ombersley, Worcestershire, allegedly of 706 but a forged document, notes the grant of land here beside the River Severn to Bishop Ecgwine for his church at Evesham *Excepto eo ut si quando in insula eidem ruri pertinente prouentus copiosior glandis accideret, uni solummodo gregi porcorum fagine pastus regi concederetur* 'except that if at any time a more abundant crop of acorns should occur on the island belonging to the same estate, a provender-rent of mast sufficient for one herd of swine only shall be contributed to the king'.[51] Swine pastures were valuable and were the cause of dispute on other occasions. Thus, a dispute which arose between the king's swine-reeve and the bishop of Worcester over swine pastures at Sinton in Leigh, Worcestershire, involving *wudu leswe to suþtune ongægum west on scirhylte* 'wood-pasture pertaining to Sinton, towards the west in *Scyrhylte*' (on the plain below the Malverns in the south-west of the county), was resolved in 825: 'The reeves in charge of the swineherds wished to extend the pasture farther, and take in more of the wood (*ðone wudu*) than the ancient rights permitted. Then the bishop and the advisers of the community said that they would not admit liability for more than had been appointed in Æthelbald's day, namely mast for 300 swine, and the bishop and the community should have two-thirds of the wood and of the mast.'[52] Another Worcestershire charter granted freedom from *pascua porcorum re[g]is quod nominamus fearnleswe* 'the pasturing of the king's swine which we call "fern-pasture"' at Bentley in Holt in 855 to the community at Worcester.[53]

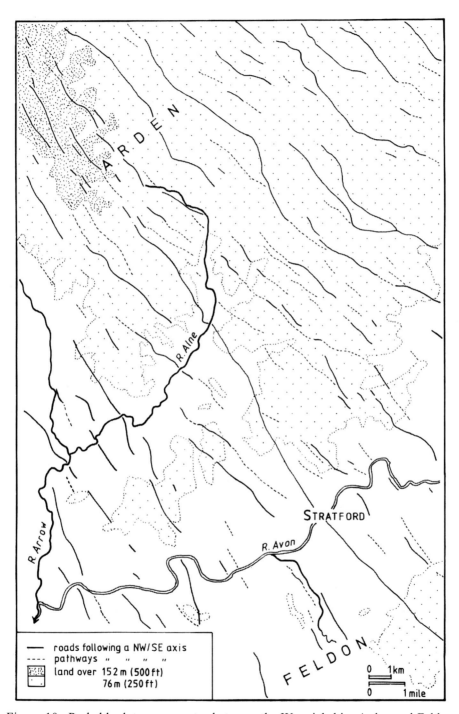

Figure 10. Probable droveway routes between the Warwickshire Arden and Feldon

The Worcestershire woods also supplied fuel to the salt ovens at Droitwich, where the salt would be evaporated over 'ovens' in leaden pans.[54] Considerable quantities of wood were required and were certainly carried by the cartload from woods at least five miles distant, as the charter of Bradley in 962 confirms.[55] It may not be coincidental that one of the chief recipients of salt was the royal manor of Bromsgrove, which had received 300 *mitts* of salt in exchange for 300 cartloads/mitts of wood according to Domesday Book[56] – here the *grāf* term probably indicated the type of managed woodland required to provide such a quantity of fuel. Long-distance routeways known as saltways radiated outwards from Droitwich, which was the main inland salt-producing area in the country before the Norman Conquest.[57] Some of the distant estates in Herefordshire may initially have sent wood to Droitwich, but by 1086 were selling the timber closer to home and sending payment instead. Most of the more distant places possessing salt rights, such as Princes Risborough in Buckinghamshire, lay in wooded regions but there may have been an additional factor underlying their connection with Droitwich. They all seem to have been royal estates in wooded regions and it seems that salt may have been an essential requirement to preserve deer taken by hunting, as was apparently essential in medieval times.[58]

Timber, especially oak, was the main constituent of buildings from palace ranges to churches: Bede notes how King Edwin was baptised at York on Easter day, 627, 'in the church of Saint Peter the Apostle, which the king had hastily built of timber'[59] and although important churches were often built of stone Bishop Aidan 'built a church on the isle of Lindisfarne suitable for the episcopal see, constructing it, however, not of stone, but of hewn oak thatched with reeds after the Scots manner'. The thatched roof and the walls were later to be covered with 'sheets of lead' by Bishop Eadbert.[60] Large timbered halls have now been identified in many locations and were either royal, episcopal, or even thegnly palaces. It is clear that most of the buildings in rural settlements were built of wood for when Penda attacked the royal city of Bamburgh in the mid-seventh century Bede notes: 'Pulling down all the neighbouring villages, he carried to Bamburgh a vast quantity of beams, rafters, wattled walls, and thatched roofs, piling it high around the city wall on the landward side. Directly the wind became favourable, he set fire to this mass, intending to destroy the city'.[61] Towns, too, were full of wooden buildings and fire was a constant threat. Bede notes how, in 619, the city of Canterbury was in danger of being destroyed by fire until the wind changed direction.[62] Although sunken-floored buildings represent a type of building found on many early Anglo-Saxon settlement sites, few excavated settlements of the fifth to the eighth centuries have been found without larger rectangular buildings constructed mostly of timber. Closely set postholes which would have carried substantial uprights mark the house/hall sites at West Stow.[63] Reconstructions of buildings at the high-ranking site of Cowdery's Down in Hampshire propose timber superstructures based on deeply founded but low timber walls with a possible framework of cruck blades;[64] other excavations elsewhere suggest stave building with vertical uprights set into the earth. Techniques became more varied in time with an increasing use of sill beams and a move towards the fully framed buildings of later periods. Sill-beam construction was standard in the eleventh-century *Byrhtferth's Manual*.[65] Post and wattle buildings were identified in the mid-tenth century at York and at the Guildhall site in London, and oak clapboarding was also being used in London from the 970s onwards. Excavations within *Lundenburh* at the Bull Wharf site at Queenhithe have revealed a more unusual type of building. Large oak arcade posts are thought to have supported a tiered tenth-century aisled building. More dramatically, the lower parts of the major branches were retained at the top of an arcade post with non-structural planking fastened to it as if to resemble a living tree; other similar reused arcade posts have also been identified at Vinter's Place, London. Those from Bull Wharf date from the mid-tenth century and are now shown in reconstructions at the Museum of London. These were to have their closest parallels in the stave 'mast' churches of Scandinavia, although many of the latter appear to be later in date.[66]

The West Midland charters also refer to the taking of timber for building. A grant of land at Seckley in Wolverley, northern Worcestershire, to one Wulferd by King Burgred of Mercia in 866 not only added *LXX. porcis saginam in commone illa saluatica taxatione hubi ruricoli. Wulfferdinleh. nominant* 'feeding for 70 pigs in that common woodland allotment, where the inhabitants call [it] Wolverley', but *V. plaustros plenas de uirgis bonis et hunicuique anno unum roborem ad aedificium ⁊ alias materias necessarias. ⁊ lignaria exabuntia ad ignem sicut illi necesse sit* '5 cartloads of good rods, and every year one oak tree for building and other necessary materials and wood in plenty for fire as may be necessary for it'.[67] Others refer to common woodland: an early-tenth-century lease of Elmstone Hardwick in Gloucestershire included *ða wudu rædenne in ðæm wuda ðe ða ceorlas brucaþ* 'the right of cutting timber in the wood which the peasants make use of', and another tenth-century lease of Thorne in Inkberrow, Worcestershire, stated that *seo wudung on gemænan grafe to þordune* 'the right of cutting wood in the common copse [shall belong] to Thorne'.[68] When Bishop Oswald leased land at Cotheridge in Worcestershire to his *minister*, Ælfric, in 963 he specified that that the lease should be on the condition that the lessee should plough two acres of the land and sow the grain for his church dues, afterwards reaping it and bringing it in, but the bishop would grant *ælce geare on minum wudu. XII. foþre wudas butan ceape* 'every year 12 fothers [wagon-loads] of wood in my wood without payment'.[69] In the tenth century King Edgar granted land at Sunbury, Middlesex, to which belonged *ælce geare into sunnanbyrig of burhwuda fiftig foðra wudes ⁊ fiftig swina mæsten* 'every year to Sunbury 50 fothers of wood from *burhwuda* and mast for 50 swine'.[70] Two late-tenth- to early-eleventh-century wills in which Siflæd bequeathed land at Marlingford, Norfolk, also refer to rights in woodland. One granted five acres and a homestead plus two acres of meadow and *to wayne gong to wude* 'two wagon-loads of wood' (i.e. the right to fetch wood, literally 'wagon passage') to the village church at Marlingford, while each of her brothers was to have *ane wayne gong* 'a wagon-load of wood' (literally, 'one wagon passage').[71] The other granted Marlingford to St Edmund's Abbey but exempted 20 acres of land and *tueye Waine gong wudes and þere Wude norþouer* 'two wagon-loads of wood [i.e. the right to fetch wood twice / wagon passage twice] and the woods over to the north'.[72] (Since the first was written as she 'went across the sea' and the second 'after her death', perhaps the one to the church preceded that to the abbey.) It has already been noted above that renders from an estate might include wood, and the church at Lambourne required dues which, apart from tithes of corn, lambs, piglets, cheese and so forth, and pasture for cattle, sheep, horses and pigs, included *ælce dæge on hors berinde . oðde twegen men. of þæes kynges wude to dæes preostes fyre* 'every day 1 horse or 2 men carrying wood from the king's wood for the priest's fire', but this document dates from after the Norman Conquest.[73]

Woods may also have been coppiced to provide wood for charcoal production. Two references in charter boundary clauses to *col* ('charcoal') fords across the River Salwarpe near Droitwich may suggest the carriage of charcoal to the salt ovens there[74] and other early *col* names such as Coldred ('charcoal clearing') in Kent or Coldridge ('charcoal ridge') in Devon probably refer to the same resource. There is ample archaeological evidence for charcoal-burning in prehistoric and Roman contexts, and Rackham has suggested that some of the 'burnt' woods referred to in place-names and charters may refer to this practice.[75]

The rights allotted by charter which covered estates in wooded regions sometimes specifically included hunting, and the importance of this in Anglo-Saxon England has often been underestimated. While all were theoretically free to hunt on their own land, there seem to have been deer enclosures more often at first on royal estates. In the time of King Cnut every man was entitled to hunt in the woods and fields on his own property but it was added *ꝺ forgá ælc man minne huntnoð lochwar ic hit gefriðod wille habban [on minon agenan], be fullan wite*, 'But everyone, under pain of incurring the full penalty, shall avoid hunting on my preserves, wherever they may be'.[76] Unfortunately there may have been additions made to these laws after the Norman Conquest, so this ordinance cannot be taken as proof of the existence of royal hunting reserves subject to special law at this date. Of the importance of hunting to the Anglo-Saxon kings there can, however, be little doubt. The king maintained huntsmen, falconers and dog-handlers, and three Mercian charters freed estates from the duty of providing hospitality for these huntsmen. The first is a grant of 844 in which King Berhtwulf frees an estate at Pangbourne, Berkshire, *a pastu principum ꝺ a difficultate illa quot nos Saxonice dicimus festigmen nec homines illuc mittant qui osceptros uel falcones portant aut canes aut cabellos ducunt* 'from the entertainment of ealdormen and from that burden which we call in Saxon *fæst-*

ingmen; neither are to be sent there men who bear hawks or falcons, or lead dogs or horses'.[77] Pangbourne lay at the south-western end of the wooded Chilterns. A more questionable charter of King Berhtwulf, allegedly of 845, grants similar privileges to the monastery of *Ufera Stretford*, at Stratford-upon-Avon in Warwickshire,[78] and a further authentic charter issued by Burgred, king of Mercia, in 855 exempted the minster at Blockley, Gloucestershire, in the north Cotswolds, from dues which included *pastu. et ab refectione omnium ancipitrum et falconum in terra Mercensium et omnium uenatorum regis uel principis nisi ipsorum tantum qui in prouincia Hwicciorum sunt* 'the feeding and maintenance of all the hawks and falcons in the land of the Mercians, and of all huntsmen of the king or ealdorman except only those who are in the province of the Hwicce'.[79] Also in the Hwiccan kingdom (part of Greater Mercia), rights *in siluis uenationibus*, 'woods for hunting', are leased with an estate at Grimley in Worcestershire in the tenth century by the bishop of Worcester.[80] The woods, which became known as Monk Wood, had a *haga* boundary along their western edge and were officially imparked in the fourteenth century.

The curtailing of general hunting rights by forest law, an innovation of the Norman kings, was extremely unpopular. For a while, William reinstated some of the earlier freedoms, as noted in the *Anglo-Saxon Chronicle* under 1087 (for 1088), but only temporarily: *geatte mannan heora wudas. and slǽtinge. ac hit ne stod nane hwile* 'granted men their woods and coursing [hunting or baiting with dogs] – but it did not last long'.[81]

There is, however, other evidence for the existence of hunting reserves in late Anglo-Saxon England, especially on royal estates. The maintenance of the (?)deer-fence, the *deorhege*, was a recognised part of a landholder's duties at the king's residence.[82] As noted previously, a feature referred to as a *haga* may indeed have been the term used for a game enclosure rather than, as some place-name specialists have argued, just another word for a hedge; the arguments have been presented elsewhere.[83] The term occurs in different types of countryside from other 'hedge' terms in the same county, or even in the same charter,[84] and seems to have been confined to the wilder, more remote regions, often areas with many *lēah* features. While some stretches of *haga* boundaries seem to have been quite short, others extended for miles, as in north Hampshire, and were found in areas where there was other evidence for hunting. While chalk underlies much of northern Hampshire, it is extensively covered with intractable clay-with-flint soils, and was an area that was marginal for farming. Although evidence of 'Celtic' fields used in late Iron Age and Roman times abounds, their lynchets were overgrown with woodland by medieval times, and a region around Hurstbourne Tarrant and the royal estate of Faccombe lay within the Norman forests of Dygherlye and Finkley (the latter part of Chute Forest) after the Conquest; Crux Easton parish, its southern boundary following a *haga* for several kilometres (Fig. 11), was held by a huntsman in 1086. Although *lēah* names are present and were in locations that were well wooded in medieval times, little

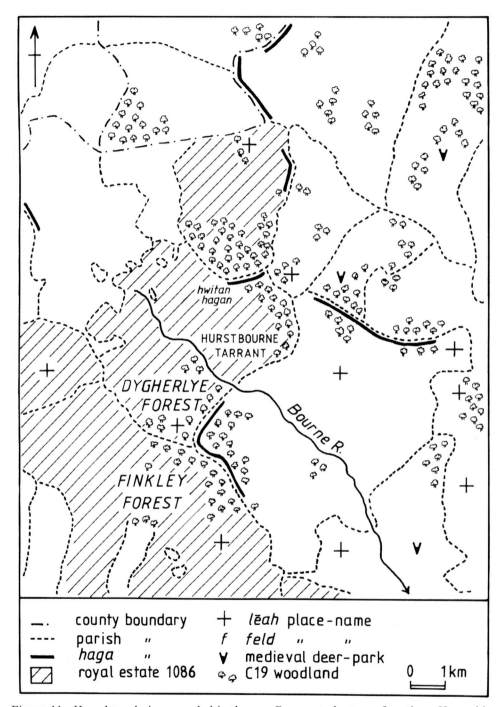

Figure 11. *Haga* boundaries recorded in the pre-Conquest charters of northern Hampshire

woodland is recorded here in Domesday Book. Paradoxically, this does not mean that woodland was not present – it had probably already been taken into the king's hands as forest and was not available for the peasants to use.[85]

A *haga* seems to have been an enclosure; indeed, the term was used in the newly defended burhs of the ninth century to describe property enclosures within them. Its boundary is likely to have been a substantial feature, for in Worcestershire there is reference to a 'swine' and a 'wolf' *haga*. While OE *dēor* could mean any animal, it may be suspected that deer were often involved. In the field, wood banks often lie along such a boundary today but if the Anglo-Saxon *haga* consisted of a bank and ditch this is likely to have been surmounted by a substantial timber pale or by a dead or living hedge (possibly of thorns as the hawthorn is the *hagaþorn*). One of the earliest animal-parks to be recorded was at Ongar in Essex, and an eleventh-century will of Thurstan states: *ic an mine cnihtes þat wude at Aungre butan þat derhage ⁊ þat stod þe ic þer habbe* 'I give to my page the wood at Ongar, except the (?)deer-park and the stud which I have there'.[86] The Worcestershire examples are largely concentrated in the wilder country to the west of the River Severn (see above) and many ran along estate boundaries on the Worcestershire plain at the foot of the Malvern Hills in an area that was to become the Forest of Malvern by 1086. The term *haga* does not occur in Domesday Book, and the closest Norman term available appears to have been *haia*: Domesday Book notes the presence of 'fixed' *haias* in such places as Herefordshire. Originally the enclosing fence or hedge may have been used in the capture of game for Ælfric records in his *Colloquy* how game, especially harts, might be driven with dogs towards a gap in a hedge where archers would be waiting or where nets had been spread:

> Ic brede me max ⁊ sette hig on stowe gehæppre, ⁊ getihte hundas mine þæt wildeor hig ehton, oþþæt þe hig becuman to þam nettan unforsceawodlice ⁊ þæt hig swa beon begrynode, ⁊ ic ofslea hig on þam maxum . . . Mid swiftum hundum ic betæce wildeor.

> 'I weave myself nets and set them in a suitable place, and urge on my dogs so that they chase the wild animals until they come into the nets unawares and are thus ensnared; and I kill them in the nets . . . I hunt for wild animals with fast dogs.'[87]

The term continues in use on occasions for a deer-park in medieval times. A deer-park in Wotton under Edge, Gloucestershire, was called the *bosc' de Haga* c.1130 (later Hawpark).[88] There was, however, another term for 'park' coming into use in Domesday Book – *parcus* (Old French *parc/park*). The park at the heart of the royal Forest of Feckenham in Worcestershire was decribed as a *parcus ferarum* 'park for wild animals' and lay in the parish of Hanbury and the manor of Holloway, but in 1306 it was referred to as 'the king's hay called *le Park*'.[89] This term *parcus* seems to be derived from the same root as another Old English place-name term *pearroc*, glossed with the Latin *clatri* 'bars (as of a cage)', while OE *fald* 'a fold for animals' includes a type described specifically as a *dēorfald* 'enclosure for wild beasts; ?deer-fold'. It is difficult to detect any specific difference in the use of these terms but the park is likely ultimately to have become a rather more officially organised affair, probably with a resident parker. It seems likely that deer were the game to be protected in the parks and enclosures, although the native red deer was to be replaced by the fallow deer after the Conquest, an animal which takes more kindly to living in a restricted space. The Domesday folios for the Welsh borderland occasionally also mention the capture of roe-deer in the hays.

WOODLAND MANAGEMENT

Attempts to give legal protection to trees are first encountered in the laws of Ine of Wessex compiled between 688 and 694.[90]

> 43. [Be wude bærnete.]
> Ðonne mon beam on wuda forbærne, ꝝ weorðe yppe on þone ðe hit dyde, gielde he fulwite: geselle LX scill., forþamþe fýr bið þeof.
> •1. Gif mon afelle on wuda wel monega treowa, ꝝ wyrð eft undierne, forgielde III treowu ælc mid XXX scill., ne ðearf he hiora má geldan, wære hiora swa fela swa hiora wære; forþon sio æsc bið melda, nalles ðeof.

> 44. [Be wudu andfenge.]
> Gif mon þonne aceorfe an treow, þæt mæge XXX swina undergestandan, ꝝ wyrð undierne, geselle LX scill.

> 43. 'If anyone destroys a tree in a wood by fire, and it becomes known who did it, he shall pay a full fine. He shall pay 60 shillings, because fire is a thief.
> •1. If anyone fells a large number of trees in a wood, and it afterwards becomes known, he shall pay 30 shillings for each of three trees. He need not pay for more, however many there may be, because the axe is an informer and not a thief.

> 44. If, however, anyone cuts down a tree that can shelter thirty swine, and it becomes known, he shall pay 60 shillings.'[91]

Illicit woodland clearance by burning or cutting down trees is obviously covered here but it is interesting to note the importance placed on large, and sometimes presumably old, trees that could provide shelter for a large number of swine. The latter had also to be supervised by a swineherd, for heavy fines were due if they intruded into another's *mæstenne*, mast pasture.[92] Protection of trees is a feature again of Alfred's laws in the later ninth century:

12. [Be wudebernete, Ᵹ gif man afylled bið on gemænum weorce.]
Gif mon oðres wudu bærneð oððe heaweð unaliefedne, forgielde ælc great
treow mid V scill., Ᵹ siððan æghwylc, sie swa fela swa hiora sie, mid V
pænigum; Ᵹ XXX scill. to wite.

'If one man burns or fells the trees of another, without permission [to do
so], he shall pay 5 shillings for each big tree, and 5 pence for each of the
rest, however many there may be; and [he shall pay] 30 shillings as a fine.'[93]

If anyone was killed unintentionally by someone felling a tree then the dead man's
kindred had the right to take the tree.

Timber and wood used in Neolithic trackways in the Somerset Levels provides
clear evidence of woodmanship. The Sweet Track, dating from around 4000 BC,
made use of small timber trees of oak, large underwood poles of ash, lime, elm, oak
and alder, and small poles of hazel and holly. Significantly, there is evidence of the
coppicing of ash, oak and hazel. Coppicing entails cutting trees back to the base
periodically to encourage the growth of new young shoots. Several other trackways
in this region, of Neolithic to Iron Age date, made use of hurdles formed of inter-
woven hazel rods produced by coppicing. The rods used in the hurdles at Walton
Heath were produced from coppiced, and occasionally pollarded, trees, mainly of
hazel but also consisting of ash and birch.[94] It is likely that this form of management
continued through ensuing centuries. Extensive remains of wattle-work hurdles,
walling and fencing were found at the late Iron Age 'lake villages' of Glastonbury
and Meare but do not always indicate coppicing.[95] However, ring counts on some
of the smaller wood from Roman sites at Castle Street, Carlisle, suggests that some
of the stems of alder and hazel used in wattle-work appear to have been cut from
coppiced wood after less than ten years of growth, and evidence of short-rotation
coppicing of hazel has also been found for the same period at York and London.[96]
Dark further suggests that in the Roman period certain species may have been deliberately grown for particular purposes, such as willows as a renewable source of fuel
for the Oxfordshire pottery industry, or oak for timber, while other species, such as
chestnut, may have been deliberately introduced to this country in that period – the
latter, like oak, was a large tree but could be coppiced. Construction in the post-
Roman period relied heavily upon the use of timber and wattle-work, as previously
noted, but Dark reviews evidence which seems to reflect the cessation of coppicing
at some sites with wattles of hazel and willow produced from roundwood of vari-
able size gathered from hedges and scrub and with trees being allowed to grow on
to flower and produce pollen, but argues that this does not mean that the woodland
was unmanaged.[97]

Some species of tree provided more valuable timber than others. The oak has
already been noted as the major source of timber for buildings, including churches,
and also provided timber for building ships, as referred to in the *Rune Poem* in

Chapter 3. It was an oak for building that was allowed each year to the grantee of the estate at Seckley in Wolverley, Worcestershire, in 866.[98] It was also worked into roof shingles at Winchester.[99] Oak remained the chief building material, especially for high-status buildings, throughout the early medieval period. Ash, on the other hand, can easily be bent into shape and was useful for wagon wheels throughout medieval times, elm for the shafts of carts and wagons, while the alder, naturally resistant to alternate wetting and drying, was useful for many items. The use of ash in relatively small quantities at the doors of buildings, as in the Middle Saxon halls at Brandon, Suffolk, and within *Lundenburh* (London), may have been a deliberate choice for some ritualistic reason.[100] The lime provided light wood suitable for making into shields. From some species, it was the bark that was particularly useful – thus oak and birch were used for tanning leather. Fine-grained or even textured woods were probably reserved for specialist items, such as the box or maple (the latter used for cups in the royal burial of Sutton Hoo).[101]

A recent reappraisal by Martin Comey[102] of the timber drinking vessels found with the seventh-century Sutton Hoo Mound 1 ship burial suggests that the choice of wood may have reflected the use of the vessels for specific drinks in an established etiquette involved in feasting and more particularly in the burial ritual. The objects found within the burial chamber include yew buckets, cups of horn and walnut burrwood, silver bowls, drinking horns and maple-wood flasks. Comey suggests that while the silver bowls may have held wine, the horns and maple flasks occupied a position in the central burial chamber and may have held mead and ale; the burr-wood cups, he suggests, held *bēor*, a drink made from fruits and honey.

Many different kinds of woodworking tools have now been found on excavated sites, clearly indicative of a sophisticated and specialised craft.[103] Wattles for building, hurdles and so forth were commonly made from hazel or willow but occasionally other woods such as poplar are found, and many different kinds of wood could be burnt for charcoal. The leaf fodder taken from species like the holly, ash or lime has been noted above, while fruit and nut trees, of course, provided food for people and animals.

There is little in the literature to reveal how woodland trees were managed in early medieval times but two estate memoranda, probably drawn up some time in the tenth or eleventh century, do discuss such management. It is noted in the *Recitudines* that *Wuduweade gebyreð ælc windfylled treow* 'the forester ought to have every tree brought down by the wind', while the *Gerefa*, which lists the duties of 'the discriminating reeve', states that wood was cut in May and June but winter was the time to *timber cleofan . . . wudu cleofan . . . deorhege heawan* to 'chop timber . . . chop wood . . . cut a deer-fence'.[104] Calendar pictures, too, illustrate the cutting of timber in July and show pollarded trees (Fig. 9a).[105] Both the *Recitudines* and the calendar pictures are based upon Classical exemplars, and may be seasonally unreliable, but the calendar pictures appear to have been adjusted to display English practices.[106] Pollarding, the removal of the crown of the tree, can prolong the life of a tree for many centuries. While charters clearly show the exploitation of woodland for all manner of uses, the boundary clauses, too, hint on occasions at methods of tree management. Some of the trees referred to as 'copped' may have been pollarded to produce new shoots beyond the reach of animals, clearly indicating the management of trees for timber and perhaps fodder. In Hampshire, a *coppedan ac* is noted on the boundary of Stoke by Hurstbourne, a *coppenthorn* on the boundary of South Damerham and another *coppedan þornæ* on the boundary of Worthy, with another *coppedan þorne* on the boundary of Altwalton in Huntingdonshire (all in tenth-century documents).[107] At Ecchinswell, Hampshire, where the bounds run *to ðon hnottan seale on searleage stent* 'to the pollard (literally 'close-cut') sallow standing at ?*sear* wood', the reference may also have been to a pollarded sallow (Chapter 9).[108] Some of those landmarks described as *stocc* or *stubb/stybb* features may also have been the trunks of pollarded trees, one suggestion made by Crick in her study of the charters of St Albans, but these terms are more likely to refer to stumps of trees, perhaps even ones left deliberately as a marker of some sort – a boundary clause of Kingsbury, Hertfordshire, refers to both *þæne æcenan stybb* and *þæne æcene stocc*.[109]

Evidence from excavations, especially from water-logged deposits such as those at Bull Wharf in London, can also help to suggest how timber trees may have been managed. There appears to have been ample timber available from large trees, often oaks, for the buildings of early medieval London, although lesser timbers, wattles and so forth made abundant use of other woods such as ash and beech (a cheaper alternative to oak), hazel, poplar and willow. It was only later that the timber from large trees became scarce. Much of the oak was apparently growing within wood-land, some of it quite dense, but at Hemington near Castle Donington in Leicester-shire the shape of much of the timber used in the bridges there suggests that it had come from trees growing singly within wood-pasture or hedgerows (these had been felled in 1100 but as trees well over a hundred years old).[110] Coppiced wood also seems to have been available but at Coppergate, York, the excavated timber seems to imply rather casual management with no organised system of regular coppicing for the production of the rods used. At Coppergate the chief structural wood used for all substantial timbers was, as elsewhere, oak but lesser structures made use of willow with lesser amounts of oak, alder, birch, poplar/aspen, ash and Pomoideae (which include apple, hawthorn and rowan, although none of these could be iden-tified specifically). Few buildings were intended to have a long lifespan and it is reckoned that many would have been structurally weak after 10–15 years.[111]

Woods managed for timber were probably also banked to exclude animals, although one type of boundary, the *haga* discussed above, was probably more intended to exclude wild animals that might take game or to fence in the deer themselves. For effective coppicing, managed groves would need to have been enclosed at different stages in the coppice cycle.

With the Church permeating every aspect of early medieval rural life, it is not perhaps surprising to find opinions expressed upon the best way to cut timber. The following is taken from *Byrhtferth's Manual*, a compilation of late-ninth/early-tenth-century writings gathered under the name of Byrhtferth, a monk of Ramsey: *Eac þa treowa þe beoð aheawen(e) on fullum monan beoð heardran wið wyrmætan ⁊ langferran þonne þaþe beoð on niwum monan aheawene*, 'Also the trees which are cut down at full moon are harder against worm-eating, and more durable than those which are cut down at a new moon'[112] Jolly quotes a fuller version of this homily, found amongst the homilies of Ælfric, abbot of Eynsham (*c.*955–*c.*1010), which adds the comment that this must not be deemed sorcery: *Swa eac treowe gif hi beoð on fullum monan geheawene hi beoð heardran and langfærran to getimbrunge and swiþost gif hi beoð unsæpige geworhte. Nis þis nan wiglung ac is gecyndelic þing þurh gesceapenysse*, 'As also trees, if they be hewed in a full moon, are harder and longer-lasting for building, and strongest if they are worked when sapless. This is no sorcery, but it is a natural thing through the created order.'[113] This is an expression of the Augustinian approach to nature – that God is ultimately responsible for all phenomena of nature that affected mankind.

ENDNOTES

1   D. Hooke, 'Pre-Conquest woodland: its distribution and usage', *Agricultural History Review* 37 (1989), pp. 113–29; D. Hooke, 'The woodland landscape of early medieval England', in *Anglo-Saxon Landscapes, II: Written Landscapes*, ed. N. Higham and M. Ryan (Woodbridge, forthcoming).

2   *Anglo-Saxon Chronicle* 892: Plummer, *Two of the Saxon Chronicles Parallel*, p. 85; Swanton, *Anglo-Saxon Chronicle*, p. 84.

3   A. Everitt, *Continuity and Colonization: The Evolution of Kentish Settlement* (Leicester, 1986). Critical analysis of the documents has now shown how the names of some dens might occasionally be transferred later to other estates. This does not affect most of the links shown here but Campbell notes how Islingham was to acquire the dens of Rochester, which were subsequently appended, among others, to a grant of Malling (see Campbell, *Charters of Rochester*, p. xviii). All were Church of Rochester estates in the lathe of Aylesford.

4   W. J. Ford, 'Settlement patterns in the central region of the Warwickshire Avon', in *Medieval Settlement, Continuity and Change*, ed. P. H. Sawyer (London, 1976), pp. 274–94; Hooke, *The Anglo-Saxon Landscape*.

5   Ine 43: F. L. Attenborough, *The Laws of the Earliest English Kings* (Cambridge, 1922), pp. 22, 50–1.

6   Rackham, *The History of the Countryside*, p. 121.

7   S 1582, Kelly, *Charters of Malmesbury*, no. 38.

8   Dark, *The Environment of Britain*, pp. 79, 122.

9   S 123, B 247.

[10] S 212, B 513.

[11] S 786, B 1282; S 308, B 409, Kelly, *Charters of Malmesbury*, no. 50.

[12] S 372, B 613.

[13] Hooke, 'Pre-Conquest woodland'; I. H. Adams, *Agrarian Landscape Terms: A Glossary for Historical Geography*, Institute of British Geographers Special Publication no. 9 (London, 1976), p. 108.

[14] Hooke, 'Medieval forests and parks'.

[15] Hooke, *The Landscape of Anglo-Saxon England*, pp. 150–4; Hooke, 'Regional variation'.

[16] S 1165, B 34.

[17] D. Hooke, 'Historical Landscapes Project: pilot study in methodologies: Oxfordshire' (unpublished report for English Heritage, 1993).

[18] J. R. Fairbrother, 'Faccombe Netherton', *Archaeology and Historical Research* 1, City of London Archaeological Society (London, 1984).

[19] H. Cleere and D. Crossley, *The Iron Industry of the Weald* (Leicester, 1985), p. 37.

[20] Ibid., pp. 57–60, 65, fig. 19.

[21] S 12, B 73, S. E. Kelly, ed., *Charters of St Augustine's Abbey*, no. 8; D. Hooke, 'The Early Charters of Kent' (unpubl. typescript, 1994); Hooke, 'The woodland landscape of early medieval England'.

[22] C. F. Tebbutt, 'A Middle Saxon iron-smelting site at Millbrook, Ashdown Forest, Sussex', *Sussex Archaeological Collections* 120 (1982), pp. 19–36.

[23] S 328, B 496.

[24] S 173, B 343; S 129, B 253, Campbell, *Rochester Charters*, no. 12, pp. 14–15.

[25] S 1180, B 141, Kelly, *Charters of St Augustine's*, no. 47 (the swine pastures were probably a later addition to the grant: Kelly, op. cit., pp. 163–5 and Electronic Sawyer).

[26] K. P. Witney, *The Jutish Forest: A Study of the Weald of Kent from 450 to 1380 AD* (London, 1976).

[27] S 140, B 207, Kelly, *Charters of St Augustine's*, no. 14 (likely to be later than claimed with alterations in the name of the beneficiary: Kelly, pp. ciii, 57–60).

[28] S 40, B 322; S 1615, B 323; J. K. Wallenberg, *Kentish Place-Names*, Uppsala Universitets Årsskrift (Uppsala, 1931), p. 106.

[29] S 186, B 370, B 371. The property is the lost Milton in Otford (Kent) with detached woodland in the Wildernesse district of Sevenoaks that lay to the west of Seal Chart (*ex inf.* N. Brooks).

[30] Everitt, *Continuity and Colonization*.

[31] S 30, B 175, *Charters of Rochester*, no. 4, p. 5; S 157, B 303, Campbell, no. 16, pp. 19–20.

[32] N. Brooks, 'The creation and early structure of the kingdom of Kent', in *The Origins of Anglo-Saxon Kingdoms*, ed. S. Bassett (Leicester, 1989), pp. 70–3.

[33] S 128, B 254; S 1264, B 332.

[34] J. E. A. Jolliffe, *Pre-feudal England: The Jutes* (London, 1933); Brooks, 'The creation and early structure', pp. 71–4.

[35] S 562, B 989, Kelly, *Charters of Shaftesbury*, no. 17, pp. 70, 72.

[36] As noted in n. 3 of this chapter, analysis of the documents is showing that in some charters the swine pastures were a later addition and on occasions were copied from earlier documents pertaining to different estates. Such linkages must, therefore, be treated with caution. See discussion in Campbell, *Charters of Rochester*, pp. xvii–xix.

[37] S 31, B 176, B 199; S 37, B 260; S 177, B 348; S 286, B 419, B 420; S 293, B 442; S 316, B 467; S 332, B 507.

[38] S 123, B 247.

[39] S 125, B 248 (sp).

[40] S 280, B 418, Campbell, *Charters of Rochester*, no. 19 (sp, likely to be a tenth-century altered copy: Electronic Sawyer).

[41] S 332, B 507.

[42] S 328, B 496 and endorsement.

[43] S 324, B 854, Kelly, *Charters of St Augustine's Abbey Canterbury, and Minster-in-Thanet*, Anglo-Saxon Charters IV (Oxford, 1995), no. 21 (but a spurious charter with the name of the beneficiary altered: Kelly, op. cit., pp. 84–7 and Electronic Sawyer).

[44] A. J. Robertson, *Anglo-Saxon Charters* (Cambridge, 1939), XL, p. 81.

[45] S 1198, B 501, F. E. Harmer, *Select English Historical Documents of the Ninth and Tenth Centuries* (Cambridge, 1914), pp. 9–10 (no. 6), 43–4. An 'amber' was the equivalent of four bushels of dry weight; a 'wey' was a measure for dry goods which varied with different commodities, and a 'fother' was a cartload – see Kelly, *Charters of St Augustine's*, no. 24, pp. 95–7.

[46] Robertson, *Anglo-Saxon Charters*, VII, pp. 12–13; a summary of this agreement is also inserted into the *Anglo-Saxon Chronicle*, Peterborough manuscript (E) 852: Swanton, *Anglo-Saxon Chronicle*, p. 65.

[47] *Textus Roffensis* (twelfth century), fols 164b, 166b: Robertson, *Anglo-Saxon Charters*, LII, pp. 106–9, 351–4.

[48] *Textus Roffensis*, fols 152–5; S 885, K 688, Campbell, *Charters of Rochester*, no. 31, p. 41.

[49] Hooke, 'Pre-Conquest woodland'; D. Hooke, 'Recent views on the Worcestershire landscape', pp. 91–106.

[50] See, for instance, Hooke, *The Anglo-Saxon Landscape*.

[51] S 54, B 116 (sp), *WoASCB*, p. 36.

[52] S 1437, B 386, *WoASCB*, pp. 96–7; Robertson, *Anglo-Saxon Charters* (1956), no. 5, pp. 8, 9.

[53] S 206, B 487.

[54] Hooke, 'The Droitwich salt industry'.

[55] S 1301, B 1087; Hooke, 'The Droitwich salt industry'; *WoASCB*, p. 248.

[56] Domesday Book, fol. 172b.

[57] D. Hooke, *The Landscape of Anglo-Saxon England*, p. 8, fig. 4.

[58] Ex inf. J. Birrell.

[59] *Historia ecclesiastica* II.14: Sherley-Price, p. 128.

[60] *Historia ecclesiastica* III.25: Sherley-Price, pp. 185–6.

[61] *Historia ecclesiastica* III.16: Sherley-Price, p. 167.

[62] *Historia ecclesiastica* II.7: Sherley-Price, pp. 111–12.

[63] S. West, *West Stow. The Anglo-Saxon Village*, 2 vols, East Anglian Archaeology 24 (Ipswich, 1985).

[64] M. Millett, 'Excavations at Cowdery's Down, Basingstoke, 1978–1981', *Archaeological Journal* 140 (1983), pp. 151–279.

[65] *Byrtferth's Manual*, I: S. J. Crawford, ed., *Byrhtferth's Manual*, EETS, OS 177 (London, 1929).

[66] D. M. Goodburn, 'London's early medieval timber buildings: little known traditions of construction', in *Urbanism in Medieval Europe: Papers of the 'Medieval Europe Brugge 1997' Conference*, ed. G. de Boe and F. Verhaeghe, Instituut voor het Archeologisch Patrimomium Rapporten 1 (Zellik, 1997), pp. 249–57; 'Fragments of a 10th-century timber arcade from Vinter's Place on the London waterfront', *Medieval Archaeology* 37 (1993), pp. 78–92.

[67] S 212, B 513, *WoASCB*, pp. 120–1.

[68] S 1283, B 560; S 1305, B 1110, *WoASCB*, pp. 261–4.

[69] S 1303, B 1106, *WoASCB*, pp. 256–7.

[70] S 702, B 1085; on the date see N. Brooks, *The Early History of the Church of Canterbury: Christ Church from 597 to 1066* (Leicester, 1984), p. 252.

[71] D. Whitelock, *Anglo-Saxon Wills* (Cambridge, 1930), no. 38, pp. 94–5; S 1525, B 1014, B 1015, B 1016.

[72] Ibid., no. 37, pp. 92–3.

[73] A. J. Robertson, *Anglo-Saxon Charters*, pp. 240–1, 490–3.

[74] S 1596, B 362, *WoASCB*, pp. 397–400.

[75] Rackham, *Ancient Woodland*, revised edn, p. 143.

[76] Cnut II.80.1, after 1027; Robertson, *The Laws of the Kings of England*, pp. 214–15.

[77] S 1271, B 443.

[78] S 198, B 450.

[79] S 207, B 489.

[80] S 1370, B 1139.

[81] *Anglo-Saxon Chronicle*, Peterborough manuscript (E), fol. 66b [1087]: Plummer, *Chronicles*, p. 223; Swanton, *Anglo-Saxon Chronicle*, p. 223.

[82] Liebermannn, *Die Gesetze*, I, pp. 444–55. OE *dēor* can refer to any animal but reference to deer seems most likely.

[83] Hooke, 'Pre-Conquest woodland'.

[84] See, for example, S 492, B 782: 'Frustfield' Whitparish, Wiltshire.

[85] R. Welldon-Finn, 'Hampshire', in *The Domesday Geography of South-East England*, ed. H. C. Darby and E. M. J. Campbell (Cambridge, 1971), pp. 320–1.

[86] B. Thorpe, *Diplomatarium Anglicum aevi Saxonici* (London, 1865), p. 574.

[87] G. N. Garmonsway, ed., *Ælfric's Colloquy*, revised edn (Exeter, 1991), pp. 23–4; trans. Swanton, *Anglo-Saxon Prose*, p. 109.

[88] A. H. Smith, *The Place-Names of Gloucestershire, Part I*, English Place-Name Society 38 (Cambridge, 1964), p. 257.

[89] A. Mawer and F. M. Stenton, with F. T. S. Houghton, *The Place-Names of Worcestershire*, English Place-Name Society 4 (Cambridge, 1927), p. 319.

[90] Attenborough, *The Laws of the Earliest English Kings*, p. 34.

[91] Ine, 43–4: Attenborough, *The Laws*, pp. 50–1.

[92] Ine 49: Attenborough, *The Laws*, pp. 52–3.

[93] Alfred 12: Attenborough, *The Laws*, pp. 70–1.

[94] Rackham, *Ancient Woodland*, revised edn, pp. 106–7.

[95] Dark, *The Environment of Britain*, pp. 78–9.

[96] Ibid., pp. 120–2.

[97] Ibid., pp. 154–5, 166.

[98] S 212, B 513, *WoASCB*, pp. 120–1.

[99] M. Biddle and R. N. Quirk, 'Excavations near Winchester Cathedral 1961', *Archaeological Journal* 119 (1962), pp. 192–3.

[100] Richard Darrah and Damian Goodburn pers. comm. See further, for instance, A. Tester, S. Anderson and R. A. Carr, 'A high status Middle Saxon settlement on the Fen Edge: excavations at Brandon 1979–88' (forthcoming).

[101] D. M. Wilson, 'Craft and industry', in *The Archaeology of Anglo-Saxon England*, ed. D. M. Wilson (Cambridge, 1976), pp. 253–4; P. Nelson, 'An ancient box-wood casket', *Archaeologia* 86 (1937), pp. 91–100; R. L. S. Bruce-Mitford, *The Sutton Hoo Ship Burial: A Handbook*, 2nd edn (London, 1972), fig. 11.

[102] M. Comey, 'The wooden drinking vessels in the Sutton Hoo ship burial: materials, morphology

and usage', University College of London conference, 'Woodlands, trees, and timber in the Anglo-Saxon world', 13–15 November, 2009.

[103] Wilson, 'Craft and industry', pp. 253–9; C. A. Morris, *The Archaeology of York. Vol. 17, The Small Finds. Wood and Woodworking in Anglo-Scandinavian and Medieval York.* Fascicule 13, Craft, Industry and Everyday Life. (York, 2000).

[104] *Rectitudines* 19, *Gerefe* 11: Liebermann, *Die Gesteze*, I, pp. 452, 454; Swanton, *Anglo-Saxon Prose*, p. 22.

[105] British Library, Cotton Tiberius B.V.

[106] P. McGurk, 'The labours of the months', in *An Eleventh-Century Anglo-Saxon Illustrated Miscellany: British Library Cotton Tiberius B. V, pt. 1*, ed. D. M. Dumville, M. R. Godden and A. Knock, Early English Manuscripts in Facsimile, ed. G. Harlow, no. 21 (Copenhagen, 1983), pp. 40–3.

[107] S 276, B 393 (sp but based upon a charter of the mid-820s); S 446, B 742; S 513, B 817; S 351, B 740 (sp); S 566, B 909.

[108] S 412, B 674.

[109] J. Crick, ed., *Charters of St Albans*. Anglo-Saxon Charters XII (Oxford, 2007), p. 197; S 912, Crick, op. cit., no. 11, pp. 180–1, 188. For a discussion of these terms see D. Hooke, 'Trees in Anglo-Saxon charters: some comments and some uncertainties', in *Old Names – New Growth. Proceedings of the 2nd ASPNS Conference, University of Graz, Austria, 6–10 June 2007, and Related Essays*, ed. P. Bierbaumer and H. W. Klug (Frankfurt am Main, 2009), pp. 90–3.

[110] S. Ripper and L. P. Cooper, *The Hemington Bridges: The Excavation of three medieval bridges at Hemington Quarry, near Castle Donington, Leicestershire*, Leicester Archaeology Monograph 16 (Leicester, 2009).

[111] H. K. Kenward and A. R. Hall, *The Archaeology of York, Volume 14: The Past Environment of York*, 14/7. Biological Evidence from Anglo-Scandinavian Deposits at 16–22 Coppergate (York 1995), p. 722.

[112] *Byrhtferth's Manual*, I, lines 33–6 [p. 161]: Crawford, pp.158–9.

[113] Jolly, *Popular Religion*, p. 88; *Homilies of Ælfric*, 1: B. Thorpe, ed., *The Sermones Catholici, or, Homilies of Ælfric: In the Original Anglo-Saxon, Vol. I*, 6 (London, 1844), pp. 100–2.

7

Trees in the Landscape

INDIVIDUAL OR GROUPS OF TREES

There must have been numerous clumps of trees and individual trees scattered across the early medieval landscape of England, both in farming regions and as prominent features in more heavily wooded areas. It is likely that the regional *pays* (landscape regions) of England were strongly recognisable in the Anglo-Saxon landscape, probably more so than in many later periods. Arable had retreated from the downlands of southern England, the Weald and elsewhere to be replaced by pasture and woodland. Many regions in which woodland had once again regenerated became typical of the kind of landscape associated with 'ancient countryside', a landscape of woodland intermixed with enclosed fields and scattered settlement.[1] In contrast, in other regions, open field agriculture seems to have led to the intensification of agriculture and, ultimately, to the creation of broad swathes of cultivated land with few boundary hedges and, probably, fewer scattered trees. Close examination of pre-Conquest charters and place-names helps to identify the nature of such regional *pays*.[2]

Place-names recorded before the end of the eleventh century are one source for the identification of tree species. They are ubiquitous across England, although only those recorded before 1100 will be included in this study as 'early' names; most here pre-date the Norman Conquest of 1066. Very few early place-names, however, are recorded in the far north of England beyond the reach of Domesday Book, and of these hardly any are tree names, although Helsington (*Helsingetune* 1086), in Westmorland, may be derived from *tūn* with *hæsling* 'hazel copse'.[3] Only a relatively small percentage of place-names take their names from trees, although it is noticeable how frequently these occur in Yorkshire, for instance, where the Domesday survey picks up many relatively minor names, or in the swine pastures of the Weald (Figs. 12a and 12b). The main sources of place-name recordings are the volumes of the English Place-Name Society but as coverage of the country has not been completed the lists offered here cannot be guaranteed to be comprehensive.

Charters associated with the transfer of rights over land and estates survive most frequently for southern and central England but are less common in the east and north of the country, being almost entirely absent from much of the area. Here,

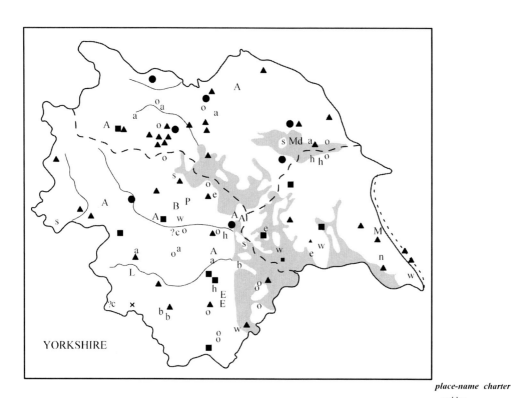

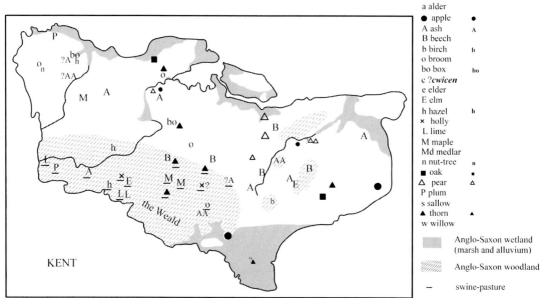

Figure 12. Trees recorded in the charters and early place-names of *a*. Yorkshire and *b*. Kent

ecclesiastical records were probably destroyed in the period of Danish raids when the Church, in any case, underwent considerable upheaval in these regions. There are only a limited number of boundary clauses available, also, for parts of south-eastern England (many charters here pre-dated the conception of detailed boundary clauses). In addition, some religious houses produced only a few boundary clauses – St Augustine's Abbey, Canterbury, had few in its cartulary and Minster-in-Thanet none.[4] Boundary clauses, too, tended to become more detailed over time, some of the earliest consisting of no more than four landmarks at cardinal points.[5] Trees become common features in the detailed clauses (Table 1) but the distributions of the individual 'tree' species become more meaningful when viewed on a county scale within a county that is well supplied with charters – such as Worcestershire (shown on Fig. 18), where they can be examined against geology, soils and other factors.

Historians have long been examining charters in order to ascertain authenticity and it can now be shown that a small percentage of these documents are not as reliable as claimed by their recipients. However, alterations usually affect matters such as date, or even entitlement to rights over a named estate, and the fact that they have been altered in some way rarely affects the language of the boundary clauses – which are normally of pre-Conquest origin – or the landmarks referred to in the present discussion. Only a very small number indeed can be shown to be post-Conquest fabrications (and this will be noted in the footnotes), although a few, such as the detached boundary clauses of Malmesbury Abbey, are later copies dependent on lost Old English bounds;[6] clauses in obvious Middle English spellings, undoubted additions, are not included here.

Of the 1602 texts listed by Sawyer (excluding lost and incomplete texts)[7] some 47% have added boundary clauses (sometimes several sets of bounds); a small number have since been added by the more detailed studies currently being carried out under a British Academy research programme on the cartularies of individual ecclesiastical houses.[8] All published sources available at the time of writing have been examined here for mention of trees by species. The distribution lists are clearly influenced by the survival of charters and reflect the fact that few charter-bounds survive for the East Midlands and eastern or northern England. Statistical analysis of tree names in either charters or place-names is not feasible, affected by both the varying and patchy nature of the evidence and by difficulties of linguistic interpretation, with the added difficulty of identifying repeated landmarks in charter bounds, but the lists in Table 1 do offer scope for discussion.

While place-names and charters frequently contain references to species of trees, unless this is associated with a further term describing woodland or a similar feature it is often quite impossible to know whether the name refers to one or any number of trees. It is also sometimes difficult to tell even from charter boundary clause references whether the trees associated with a particular topographical feature refer

Table 1. Early medieval tree list: the incidence of recorded tree species in charters and early place-names

	WMids	SW	SE	EMids	E	N	Llandaff	Total	Ch /PN
Ash	7/10	43/34	34/22	1/26	6/14	–/10	4/	95	117
Alder	12/5	21/9	7/4	–/1	–/1	–/10	–	40	30
Apple	5/2	36/?5	23/5	1/3	5/1	–/7	1/	71	?23
Ash–apple	1/–	–/–	–	–	–	–	–	1	–
Aspen	2/2	–/2	2/2	–/–	–/4	–	–	4	10
Birch	4/1	6/1	6/2	–/3	1/7	–/3		17	17
Beech	–/1	?3/2	?14/12	–/–	2/1	–/2		?19	18
Box	–/–	–/1	2/8	–/–	–/1	–	–	2	10
Broom	3/14	5/4	12/13	–/3	–/9	–/18	1/	21	57
Cherry	– –	–	?1/–	–	–	–/		?1	
Ceacga		2/1	2/1					4	2
?Cwic						–/?2		–	?2
Elebeam	–	1/–	?9/–	–	–	–		?10	–
Elder	2/–	30/2	14/1	–/–	2/–	–/1		48	4
Elm	–/5	4/2	–/2	–/1	–/3	–/2		4	15
Furze/gorse	–/–	6/4	1/–	–	–/1	1/		8	5
Hazel	1/3	9/3	20/11	–/3	1/–	–/8	1/	32	28
Holly	3/1	5/5	1/2	–/1	–/–	–/2		9	11
Lime	8/2	15/5	?4/8	–/3	–/?3	–/1		?27	?21
Maple	2/1	17/5	8/8	–/3	3/2	–/1		30	20
Medlar							–/?1	–	?1
Nut–tree	1/1	2/1	4/3	–/1	–/1	–/1		7	8
Oak	38/16	33/13	36/13	1/8	7/7	1/14		116	69
Pear	8/5	11/4	?8/12	–/2	–/5	–/–	27	27	29
Plum	1/1	–/3	1/3	–/2	1/4	–/1		3	14
Privet	–	–	1/1					1	1
Sallow	1/2	6/2	5/2	–/2	1/3	–/6		13	17
Service tree	1/–	–	2/–	–	–/1	–		4	–
Sloe	1/–	3/–	1/3	–/–	1/1	–/–		6	4
Thorn	41/10	125/36	113/20	6/14	9/16	1/42	1/	296	138
Willow	8/11	47/6	26/3	3/7	7/6	–/5	4/	95	38
Wych–elm	–/1	?4/–	1/–	–/–	2/2			?7	3
Yew	1/1	4/5	3/7	–	1/–	–/–	1/–	10	13

Total charter recordings: 1028

Total early place–name recordings: 725

Counties covered in this analysis:
WMids: Worcestershire, Warwickshire, Herefordshire, Shropshire, Staffordshire.
SW: Dorset, Somerset, Devon, Cornwall, Wiltshire, Gloucestershire.
SE: Sussex, Surrey, Kent, Hants, Berks, Bucks, Oxfordshire, Middlesex.
E Mids: Derbyshire, Nottinghamshire, Leicestershire & Rutland, Northamptonshire, Lincolnshire.
E: Huntingdonshire, Cambridgeshire, Norfolk, Suffolk, Essex, Hertfordshire.
N: Cheshire, Lancashire, Yorkshire North Riding, West Riding & East Riding, Westmorland.
S Wales (Llandaff charters; no place–names noted; the date of these charters is still disputed).
'Early' place–names are taken here as C11 or earlier (N counties without early names omitted).
Names of Wealden swine–pastures are read as place–names.

to single trees or groups. A coomb or valley associated with a particular species of tree, for instance, is likely to have been a place where that tree was found in abundance but it is not impossible that one outstanding specimen or a tree sited in a prominent spot might have given its name to the feature, especially a tree upon a hill-top. In the charters of southern England, *dūn* is associated with thorn, *hyll* with the maple, oak and hazel, *ōra* with hazel and lime, and *cnæpp* with the maple; in the West Midlands *dūn* is associated with thorn on two separate occasions, and with broom and sallow, *hyll* with oak and sloe, *ofer* with lime, and *hrycg* with lime, yew and plum. In valley locations, coombs in southern England are associated with maples, alders, broom, furze/gorse, yews, nut trees, willows, sloes, limes and thorns; *denu*-type valleys with oak and broom; and *slæd* with willow. In the West Midlands, coombs are associated with yew and alder, and *denu*-type valleys with yew. Often trees were associated with watery locations: meres or lakes, streams and other watercourses, the commonest trees in this category willow (with *broc, mere, wylle*), alder (with *broc, burna*), but also broom (with *burna*), hazel (with *broc*), ash (with *lacu, burna, wylla/wella*) and thorn (with *lacu, wylle/wella*). Trees might also overhang springs: in southern England such trees include thorn, hazel, ash, elder and oak; marshland here was associated with willows. In the West Midlands, willow and alder are again common with *broc* and *mere*; thorn and ash are found in marshy situations and there is also a reference to a *hnutfen*, probably a boggy environment where hazels were found; springs were associated with hazel, ash and alder. The occurrence of individual trees in charter boundary clauses can cast light upon the distribution of particular species but this is best explored in later chapters.

TREES AS MARKERS: CENTRES OF ASSEMBLY

In Anglo-Saxon England, the choice of a site marked by a tree for an important meeting (see Chapter 4) is illustrated in England by the meeting of St Augustine in 603 with the British bishops at a place on the boundary between the Hwiccan and West Saxon kingdoms known to the English as *Augustinæs Āc*, 'Augustine's oak-tree'.[9] Several Gloucestershire sites for the oak have been suggested, among them The Oak in Down Ampney on the Wiltshire border and Aust on the River Severn; the first seems a more likely candidate but it has not been possible to identify the site with any certainty.[10] Other sites associated with the preachings of St Augustine lie close to the western boundary of the Hwicce but are of more dubious foundation: they include the Lady Oak at Cressage: *Cristesache* 1086 'Christ's oak-tree', near the Wrekin in Shropshire, which finally died in the winter of 1982 but whose stunted remains still stand beside a younger sapling in an open field beside the older route of the A458, close to the site of a now demolished Saxon church. This may indeed have been used as a preaching site by Christian missionaries and Morton notes the

Table 2. The incidence of recorded tree species in early hundred and wapentake names (to 1086) (after Anderson, *The English Hundred-Names*)

Pre-Conquest recording			Post-1086	
Oak	Acklam	Sx		
	Skyrack	Y	Tipnoak	Sx
Apple	Appletree	Db		
Ash (ashen)	*Asceleie*		So	
	Ashendon	Bucks	Broxash	He
	Barkston Ash	Y	Catsash	So
	Bromsash	He	*Chikenesse*	Wa
	Esch	Wo	?*Fnog(g)esesse*	He
	Esselei	Ha		
	Grumbalds's Ash	Gl		
	Ludes/Louthesk	Li		
Birch	Bircholt	K	Berkeley	Gl
Box(tree)	Bexhill	Sx		
	Box, Boxgrove	Sx		
Broom	Braunton	Dv		
	Bromley	K		
Elder	Elstub	W		
Gorse			*Gosefeld*	Bk
Hawthorn (haw)	Eyhorne	Dv	Haytor	Dv
			Hagmead	Gl
Hazel	Hasilor	Do		
	Hase/Hessle (N *hesli*)	YER		
	Hessle (N *hesli*)	YER		
	Hezetre	He		
Pear(tree)	Parham	Sf		
	Pyrton	O		
Plum	Plomesgate	Sf		
	Plympton	Dv		
Spracen			?*Sparkenhoe*	Le
Thorn (bush)	Aswardhurn (N)	Li	Crowthorne	Gl
	Blacheterne	So	Thornbury	Gl
	Celfledetorn	Gl	Thorngate	Ha
	Chechemetorn	W	*Ulethorn*	Ha
	Copthorne	Sr		
	Cvtethorn	He		
	Elthorne	Mx		
	Godderthorn	Do		
	Horethorne	So		
	Nachededorn	Bk		

	Spelthorne	Mx		
	Thorngrove	W		
	Thornhill	W		
	Thornlau	He		
	?*Witbrictesherna*	Ess		
willow (withy)	Wilford	Sf		
	Willey	Bd		
	Willybrook	Np		
	Witheridge	Dv		
wych-elm	Witchford	IoW	Witchford	Cam
bēam	1			
trēow	23 + ?1		7	

activities of the Welsh St Samson who travelled widely in this region in the sixth century. It seems difficult to believe that an oak could have lived that long and the tree may be a survivor from the edge of the Long Forest.[11] The Rock Oak at Rock in Worcestershire and a yew at Stanford Bishop in Herefordshire are other trees that have been connected with the preachings of St Augustine, and what was traditionally Augustine's oak chair was discovered at Stanford Bishop in the Victorian church tower (now in Canterbury Museum).[12]

Throughout the early medieval period and after the Norman Conquest, trees continued to mark places of assembly and, especially, hundred meeting places (Table 2). The hundred represented the basic unit of local governance, and although it is not named as such until the reign of King Edgar (ruled 957–75) – Edgar's Ordinance required the men of each hundred to attend a hundred court on a regular basis, ideally every four weeks, for the maintenance of law and order[13] – it appears to have been based on earlier kinds of administrative units. At the beginning of the period, folk regions can sometimes be identified but these were gradually being broken down into multi-hide units based upon recognisable central places,[14] some being quasi-hundreds. In Danish areas the hundred was to be replaced by the wapentake. Assemblies with administrative responsibility are noted in the later-seventh-century laws of Kings Hlothere and Eadric in Kent, and in 801 an estate in Middlesex, first granted in 767, was freed from the burden of *popularia concilia*, 'public assembly'.[15] Other assembly places are noted in pre-Conquest charter bounds but are not always associated with charters known to be completely authentic: on the boundary of Calborne on the Isle of Wight was a *gemot beorh* 'meeting barrow or mound', allegedly recorded in 826 but found as a boundary clause attached to a charter of dubious authenticity,[16] while a *spelstowe*, 'assembly place', is recorded upon the boundaries of Bourton-on-the-Water and Aston Blank in Gloucestershire in other rather doubtful charters.[17] In 963 three Worcestershire hundreds, *Cuðbergelawe*, *Wulfereslaw* and *Winburgetrowe*, were united under a combined hundred Oswaldslow, representing the holdings of the Church of Worcester.[18]

The early hundreds and wapentakes often took their name from the landmark at their meeting place. The actual location of a hundred meeting place was usually one in the open air close to the centre of the hundred at a spot made accessible by the road network; often this lay close to an estate boundary. The hundred meeting place of Longtree Hundred in Gloucestershire was at a 'tall tree' which stood 'at the highest point on the road from Tetbury to Avening near the spot where it is crossed by the ancient Roman road from Cirencester to Aust'.[19] There is an extensive view in every direction from the meeting-place. The site is not central to the Domesday hundred but reorganisation had widely affected midland territorial units. Indeed, the place of assembly might be moved to a central vill, especially as new hundred subdivisions, often based upon royal manors, became recognised. The choice of landmark marking such assembly points is often one of an archaic nature, some apparently referring to the head of an animal placed upon a post (such as Swineshead hundred in Gloucestershire). Very often, it was a tree that marked these assembly places. The name of *Ghidenetroi* hundred in Sussex (1086) seems to have incorporated OE *gyden*, 'goddess', implying an ancient place of worship, with 'tree', a possible heathen survival.[20] Ten Domesday or pre-Domesday hundreds in the West Midland Hwiccan kingdom contained the term *hlāw*, *hlēw* 'mound, tumulus', and a further three the term *beorg*, 'barrow, hill', but four incorporated the *trēow* term: Doddingtree and *Winburgetrowe* in Worcestershire (both associated with personal names) and Brentry and Longtree in Gloucestershire (the first either 'Beorna's tree' or 'the tree of the warriors' and the latter 'the tall tree', as noted above), while Chelthorn, *Celfledetorn*, 'Cēolflǣds's thorn-tree', in the Winchcombshire part of Gloucestershire, was a more direct reference to the thorn-tree.[21] The early place-name Matlock in Derbyshire appears to be 'speech oak', i.e. 'oak where the moot was held' (OE *mæþel* with *āc*), in Wirksworth Hundred by the time of Domesday Book.[22] Over the country as a whole some twenty-three hundreds or wapentakes recorded by 1086 had names incorporating the term *trēow* and seventeen of these may incorporate a personal name.[23]

While many early hundred or wapentake names, therefore, incorporate the term *trēow*, 'tree', some are more specific about the species of tree. The commonest species to be named in hundred names recorded before 1086 was undoubtedly the thorn, noted on fifteen occasions, with another referring specifically to the *hægþorn*, the hawthorn. The ash occurs in eight early hundred or wapentake names, the willow in four, the oak in two.[24] Amongst other early hundred or wapentake names the hazel occurs three times, the box twice (both in Sussex), plum and pear each twice, and the apple, birch and wych-elm each once, plus one elder stump. It is unlikely that any of these trees could have survived to the present day, although Anderson notes that 'a great thorn-tree, growing from an enormous old stump, still stands in a hedge-row near Down House on the brow of Horethorne Down' in Horethorne Hundred, Somerset, a location with extensive views eastwards across the hundred.[25] It was also often common practice to plant a young tree on the site of an old in an important location.

There were other meeting places on the boundaries of hundreds or even shires, perhaps representing a site chosen for more important lawsuits concerning the folk of a greater region than the hundred. One such duty which could be carried out at places of public assembly, but not usually at the hundred meeting place, involved the carrying out of judicial execution, and several execution sites have been identified in recent years, usually upon hundred boundaries. Sometimes these are described in charters as a *cwealmstōw*, 'killing place'; in others, a gallows is named as a *weargrōd*, 'felons' cross' (OE *wearg* 'a felon, a criminal, an outlaw' with *rōd* 'gallows, a scaffold'). One such landmark, *þa wearh roda on wodnes dic*, is noted on the great linear earthwork of Wansdyke on the boundary of Stanton St Bernard, Wiltshire, in 957 and another, *þare ealden werhrode* 'the old gallows', occurs on the boundary of *Berewican*, perhaps near Tyburn, Middlesex, in 1002.[26] A *weargtrēow* 'gallows tree' may have given its name to Warter Hundred in Yorkshire East Riding, named after the Domesday vill of that name, although alternatively this may have been from OE *w(e)arr* 'a knot', hence 'the gnarled tree'.[27] Another *waritroe* stood at the end of a long spur of high land on the eastern boundary of Childswickham on the Worcestershire/Gloucestershire boundary, a location still known a Gibb's Hill in the nineteenth century.[28] In Northamptonshire, the boundary of Kettering ran *to þam galhtreowe* 'to the gallows tree'.[29] Kelly suggests that *frigedæges treow* 'Friday's tree' on the boundary of Ginge in Berkshire, standing beside a highway, may also have been 'a lonely tree that was deemed unlucky or unproductive or used as a gallows'.[30] Reynolds[31] has suggested that the term *hæðenan byrgels* 'heathen burials' might indicate the same kind of site, although this could conceivably have described a collection of earlier barrows (which may, however, have attracted later non-Christian burial). It is possible that the *syl beame* 'pillar tree', noted in a tenth-century clause of Leigh, Worcestershire, was also a gallows standing high on Crumpton Hill at the northern end of the Malvern Hills. Another reference, to *þone hlædredan beam*, '?laddered tree', in a charter of Bedwyn, Wiltshire, raises the same possibility.[32] In two cases, it was again a thorn-tree that marked the execution place: the *weawan þorn* of Meon and Privett in Hampshire may have been a felons' thorn and certainly *ðan þorne þer ða þeofes licgan*, 'the thorn where the thieves lie', which stood beside a major crossing place of the River Trent at Burton, noted in the boundary clause of Rolleston in 1008, is likely to have been the burial ground for a nearby execution site.[33] Other place-names also contain these terms, and include Worgret in Dorset (*Vergroh* 1086, from *weargrōd*).[34] Place-names referring to thieves and felons are much more numerous, although most are recorded in medieval records. OE *þēof* is found in charter-bounds: *þeofa cumb* in Meon, Hampshire, and *þeofa dene* in Hallow, Gloucestershire, are pre-Conquest boundary landmarks, both referring to valleys associated with thieves.[35] Reference to felons (OE *wearg*) may also occur in the name Warnborough, Hampshire (*Weargeburnan* 973–4), and is interpreted by Mills as 'stream where criminals were drowned', like the later recorded Wreigh Burn in Northumberland. Watts notes that this may refer to the ancient custom of executing felons by drowning, the hands tied beneath their knees, in a stream (see Chapter 2).[36]

The place-name element *bēam*, which could refer to a tree, is much less common than *trēow*; neither is it always clear whether it referred to a particular tree or a beam of wood. Thus Bampford in Derbyshire and Birtle cum Bamford in Lancashire could refer to fords marked by a prominent tree or to a ford that could be crossed by a beam; the various Bamptons (found in Oxfordshire and Cumbria) and Kirkbampton, also in Cumbria, might have been places where beams, as constructional timber, could have been made or obtained, although the suggestion made in Chapter 2, as a site marked by some kind of pillar, raises an interesting possibility. The other two occasions when *bēam* became incorporated into a parish name are North and South Benfleet in Essex, which may have been 'a tree-marked fleet'.[37]

Trees as boundary markers

Most references to trees in charter boundary clauses are purely pragmatic, merely referring to trees as convenient landmarks by which a boundary could be recognised on subsequent occasions.[38] The use of trees as boundary markers, along with other features, clearly follows Roman tradition: *Finitur secundum antiquam obseruationem fluminibus, fossis, montibus, uiis, arboribus ante missis, aquarum diuergiis et si qua loca ante a possessore potuerunt optineri*,[39] 'It is bounded according to ancient observance by watercourses, dykes, mountains/heights, ways, trees previously recorded, forkings of waters, and any places which it has previously been possible for the owner to hold'; *Eadem quasi magistra sit eorum quae [est] in quaestione[m] sunt: considerent, si cauis, si superciliis, cliuis, marginibus, ante missis arboribus, ita ut ipsa uicinitas terminatur, ut et his quae in quaestionem ueniunt praestet exemplum. Sed si caua defecerit aut <supercilium, cliuus, m>argo, arbores ante missae, solent termini occurrere*,[40] 'Let the same be like a mistress over those matters which are in question: they should consider whether there are hollows, banks, slopes, borders, trees previously planted, which limit neighbouring properties, so that, just like with those in question, it may serve as an example. But in the absence of hollows, banks, slopes, borders or trees previously planted, boundary markers are usually present'. These date from the first century AD, but such a tradition is very ancient; boundary stones bearing lists of features were also set up in northern Greece during the period of the Macedonian Empire (a boundary stone in the new Macedonian archaeological museum at Thessaloniki shows a list of land-marks delineating the boundary between 'certain cities' to the north of Chalkidiki, which dates from 350–300 BC).

Although woodland, as opposed to individual trees, does appear in many cases as a boundary landmark in the pre-Conquest charters of England (and, in the Llandaff charters, in Wales) the wood would need to have been either of limited extent or to have been named merely in passing, as it were. In fact, many references do just this, running along the 'eaves' of a wood (*efese*) or the plant/tree-roots (*wyrtruma*, *wyrtwala*). *Wyrtruma* or *-wala*, literally 'plant roots', might imply the lower side of a wood but there is little in the documents or literature to offer a decisive meaning and one interpretation of these terms is as 'wood-bank, bank defining the perimeter of a wood'.[41] Of the wood terms used, the general term *wudu* is surprisingly frequent, noted on some 130 occasions, but *lēah* is the most frequent of all; *grāf* (with variants such as *grǣfa*) occurs some ninety times, *holt* only about seventeen times; *weald*, *sceaga* and so forth are less frequent. Sometimes a boundary passed 'through' a wood, as in several Llandaff charters noted previously; and the boundary of Watchingwell on the Isle of Wight also ran to or through the middle of *Hrece leage*.[42] In one case, where a precise boundary mark was required, a Warwickshire clause of Long Itchington chose to note *þa hehan ǣc on wulluht grafe middum* 'the tall oak-tree in the middle of *wulluht* grove'.[43] Single trees which could be precisely located were the most useful boundary landmarks and these form the bulk of the tree references in charter boundary clauses. Despite suggestions that some trees may have been deliberately planted as boundary markers[44] it seems more likely that they were simply fortuitously growing on the boundary in an appropriate location and proved a suitable landmark; some were indeed described as 'solitary' (see below). The actual species of tree is not always given, for many references are simply to 'someone's' tree: *trēow* with a personal name. Where individual trees occur in association with a personal name this almost always denotes the ownership of nearby land or an association with a well-known local person. Like boundary stones, many such trees stood beside roads (see examples below).

Bēam occurs less frequently than *trēow* in charter boundary clauses but is not uncommon in Hampshire, where there are no fewer than nine references to *bēam*, including a *greatan beam* 'great tree' in Droxford and a *greatan mearc beam* 'great mark tree' in Meon (but nineteen references to *trēow*).[45] In Bucklebury, Berkshire, the *cristen mǣlbeam* is a tree bearing a crucifix[46] while the *syl beam* of Leigh in Worcestershire has already been noted above as a possible gallows site. In Creech, Somerset, *bēam* is again found associated with a ford, and in Purbeck and Corfe in Dorset *beam broc* is the name of the brook itself, as might be *Bromesbeam* in High Halden, Kent. Two other trees are noted as *bēam* features in Kent and Surrey and two more in Hertfordshire, while in Gloucestershire one finds a *bēamweg* in Withington, but *trēow* is always more common. Two tree names themselves incorporate the term – the *elebēam* and the *hnutbēam*, the first unidentified (see Chapter 12), the second the 'nut-tree'.

A discussion of the distribution of particular species of trees will form the content of the next few chapters. Particular tree species can be named in association with woodland as, for instance, in the *ac wudu* 'oak wood' of Salwarpe, Worcestershire, the *ellen grafan* 'elder grove' of Pewsey, Wiltshire, the *perhangran* 'pear hanger' of Abingdon, Oxfordshire (formerly Berkshire), the *aclieh* 'oak wood' of Nursling, Hampshire, or the *hæsel holt* 'hazel copse' of Droxford, Hampshire; many other similar incidences occur of a specific species being compounded with a wood term.[47] On other occasions, the occurrence of a particular tree type in a locality is probably suggested by its presence in valleys, marshes and so forth, as noted in the Crediton boundary clause. Other examples include the *thorncombe* 'thorn coomb' of Plush in Buckland Newton, Dorset, the *æsc dene* 'ash valley' of Hawkesbury in Gloucestershire or the *æscmor* 'ash marsh' of the Deerhurst estates in the same county.[48] Sometimes a single particular tree may have attracted attention, especially on a hill-top or ridge. Clumps of trees might be indicated as in the *wythybed* 'withy bed' of Dauntsey, Wiltshire, or the *þorn þiuel* (*þȳfel*) 'thorn thicket' of Mapperton in Almer, Dorset.[49]

It seems that some surveyors tended to refer to trees more than others, especially as boundary clauses became more detailed as the period progressed. The range of trees recorded along the boundaries of the Meon land units in central Hampshire is outstanding – in one boundary clause of a large 65-hide estate (probably East Meon, Froxfield, Steep, Langrish and part of Privett)[50] these include the oak, ash, alder, apple, *elebēam*, lime (?), thorn, and willows associated with a ford and a mere, plus an additional reference to *þone greatan mearc beam* 'the great mark/boundary tree' and to *beorhtulfes treowe*, a possible grove, a wood stream-name and three other references to woods, tree roots, an edge of a wood and three *lēah* features. A forked oak, 'a red-leaved beech', a lime (?) and two thorns occur in another clause of an eight-hide estate (probably parts of East Meon, West Meon and most of Privet including Farnfield)[51] plus two other undifferentiated trees, one of them *þam twisledan beame* (another 'forked tree'), the other *coggan beame*, 'Cogga's tree', plus two *lēah* features, a hanging wood and another 'thorny farmstead'. Oak and thorn plus two *lēah* features, tree roots, a wood stream-name and another wood are noted in a third clause (50 hides in Steep and Langrish and perhaps a small part of East Meon).[52] Box, *elebēam*, beech – two of the latter associated with *haga* boundaries – plus a 'green tree', a *ceorles beame*, two *lēah* features, a 'timber' ridge, another wood, a broomy valley and a willow mere appear in a fourth clause of a 22-hide estate (parts of Privett, Froxfield and East Meon).[53] A fifth clause of a 12-hide estate (most of West Meon)[54] has perhaps eight *lēah* features including a nut *lēah* and perhaps a lime *lēah*, another unspecified tree, an oak, a broomy valley and a 'little wood' or *sceaga*. A late clause of a single-hide estate that was probably Coomb in East Meon, granted by the king to the bishop of Winchester, refers to only one 'broad *lēah*'.[55] The late Professor Grundy attempted to resolve which estates were covered in these charters but with limited success: the parishes here were subdivided into tithings and his published work is not accompanied by maps; unfortunately few of these landmarks have been satisfactorily located despite the fact that several of the landmarks appear in different clauses.[56] Meon and its associated estates lie on the Hampshire downland in the east of the present county, extending eastwards onto the greensand and Gault clays. The chalk is also heavily overlain by clay-with-flints in the northern part of the estate. Patches of woodland were obviously numerous in the early medieval period and many of the boundaries in the north followed *haga* boundaries, suggesting land set aside as game reserves, often first documented on royal estates.[57] By 1086 most of the area belonged to the abbey of Westminster and, perhaps surprisingly, this area does not appear to have been put under forest law by the Norman kings (unlike many other regions with *haga* enclosures), although a medieval deer-park was officially enclosed at East Meon by the bishop of Winchester by 1279.[58] The trees mentioned in the boundary clauses appear to have been scattered around the boundaries of these estates and 'the great mark or boundary tree' to have stood beside the Winchester–Petersfield road on the southern boundary of Steep parish and on the boundary between East Meon and Chalton hundreds; *hyreðes treow* or *hyrdes treow* stood beside the same road on the west side of the large Meon estate where the boundary met that of Hinton Ampner. The boundary clause of Hinton Ampner with which West Meon was thus contiguous has trees or tree species mentioned in seven, possibly eight, of its twenty-three landmarks, while a further five landmarks are associated with woods (Fig. 13a).[59] It reads:

> Ðis synd ða landgemæro to Heantune. Ærest on ðone suðan hlinc. Of ðam hlince on elleford upp on ðone hricg. Andlang hricges on wines heafdes þorn. Of ðam þorne on colan treow. Of colan treowe on crawan þorne. Of crawan þorne innan ða bæc. Of ðam bæce on ðone middemestan beorh on bromdæne. Andlang bromdæne innam smalan dæne. Of smalan dæne on clinca leage. Of clinca leage on ða greatan bæce innon næddærheall. Of nedderheale on linleage. Of linleage on hyrdes treow. Of hurdes treowe on ðone grætan hlincg. Of ðam greatan hlince on acvstede leage. Of acstede leage on ðone rugan beorh. Of ðam beorga on weoleage. Of weoleage on Wulfredes wyrð. Of Wulfredes wyrðe on cadan hanger. Of cadan hangran on ræling beorgas. Of reling beorgan on ðone greatan hlincg.

This clause is probably authentic, dating from the mid-eleventh century, when clauses were often exceedingly detailed. Tree species named include elder (with a ford), oak, two thorns (the *wines heafdes þorn* 'thorn on Wyn's headland' of this charter replaces *ðære ænlypigan þorn* 'the solitary thorn' in the earlier, shorter boundary clause of the same estate), a broom valley, four *lēah* features (one of which may have been associated with the lime) and a hanger. The *lēah* features are all on the eastern boundary and the boundary of the adjacent estate of West Meon (above) also adds *hnut leage bære* 'nut wood pasture' in the same area; the hanger is a surviving wood on the south-western boundary; *colan treow* 'Cola's tree' may also have been another tree on the Winchester–Petersfield road but as often it is impossible to precisely locate such a landmark. There are still many patches of ancient woodland left in the region, especially in Froxfield and Steep, although a considerable number of the smaller woods in the west have been lost in recent decades.

The boundary clause of Stoke Prior in Worcestershire also refers to several trees:

> Ærest fram myðan in cyrstel mæl ac. Of cyrstel mæl ac in east ende teoue lege. Of teofe leage in þæt syrf treow. Of þam syrf treowe in þ rug maple treow in forweard werdune. Of foreweard wer dune oð midde wearde wer. Of midde wer dune in werdun broc. Of midde 'wer' dune broce in middan wearde langan dune. Of middan wearde langan dune in sceap weg. Of scearp weg in hwæta leage. Of hwæta lege in hens broc. Of hens broce in salwarpan. Of seal warpan in holan weg. Of þam weg in ða hwitan biricean. Of þære birican in alcherdes ford. Eft of salarpan in þa ifihtan ac. Of þære ac in þa mær ac. Of þære ac in bennic æcer. Of þam æcere in cærsa bæt. Of þam bæte in pipan. Of pipan in wiðui broc. Of þam broce in þæt þruh. Of þam þrug in holan weg. Of þam wege in bridenan brygge. Of þære brigge in cumb. Of þam cumbe in ale beardes ac. Of þære ac in þa heort sole. Of þære sole. In þa þistle. Of þære þistle eft in ða myþan.[60]

This is a spurious charter which was probably fabricated in the early medieval period to strengthen the claims of the Church of Worcester to the whole 10-hide parish-estate of Stoke Prior, as they were only able to prove by written charter their claim to the five *tributarii* in the north of the parish which lay at Aston, granted in an authentic charter of 770 by Uhtred, *regulus* of the Hwicce to Æthelmund, his faithful *minister*.[61] Of thirty landmarks, ten are to trees or *lēah* features: these include a crucifix oak (see above, Chapter 2, in relation to Tardebigge), the service-tree, the rough maple-tree, the white birch-tree, an ivy-grown oak and a boundary oak, a withy brook and 'Alebard's oak tree'. This document is a late forgery made by the Church but one has to commend the surveyor's eye for nature: he follows the lie of the land exactly as he moves 'from the front of a watch hill to the middle part of a watch hill (following a hill which sweeps around); from the middle of the watch hill to watch hill brook', and his other landmarks include a deeply incised valley aptly referred to as a 'trough' and 'the hart's wallowing place', another small valley on the eastern boundary. Close observance of nature is also portrayed by the Gloucestershire reference on the boundary of Bishops Cleeve to *wata cumb. þer stondað apeltreo ꝺ mapeltreo togædere gewæxen*, 'Wat's coomb where stands the apple-tree and maple-tree grown together'.[62]

The eleventh-century boundary clause of the Crediton estate also refers to several landmark trees.[63] As the southern boundary of the main part of this territory makes its way across the broken topography of central Devon, where tributary streams cut through hilly country to drain northwards into the River Yeo, landmarks include a crab-apple-tree, an alder and a birch coomb. Beyond, the broad ash-tree may have stood at a crossroads on the higher land at Easton Cross while an alder shaw lay in the valley of the Yeo itself; another 'willow slade' and an 'ash coomb' lay further along the boundary. Beorwynn's tree and Egsa's tree probably stood beside roads, a likely situation too for the eight oaks on the north-eastern boundary of Morchard Bishop. A further 'woody' landmark is 'Cæfca's grove' on the western boundary. It is almost impossible to give precise locations for the individual trees. Such a landscape is in marked contrast to the barren moorlands of much of Dartmoor to the south where trees are rarely mentioned. It seems easier to locate the trees that are noted along the boundary of the Berkshire Blewbury estate, which included the parishes of Blewbury, Aston Upthorpe, Tirrold and North and South Moreton. One landmark, *þam langan cyrstel mæle æt hafurc þorne*, 'the tall crucifix at hawk thorn', stood on the eastern boundary of Aston Tirrold, probably on a 'stone way' that led up Lollington Hill, while we are told that the next landmark, *þan langan þorne*, 'the tall thorn-tree', stood beside the Icknield Way, which crossed the boundary a little further to the south (Fig. 13b). These landmarks are rapidly followed by *þan þriddan þorne æt wirhangran*, 'the third thorn-tree at ?bog-myrtle hanger', *þam feorþan þorne on wrangan hylle* 'the fourth thorn-tree which stands on the front part of the crooked hill', *þam fiftan þorne* 'the fifth thorn-tree' to *þam elebeame* (upon the identification of this species see Chapter 12); after a 'little way' the boundary then reached yet another thorn-tree, and further landmarks in this boundary clause were a *wrocena stybba* 'wrocena tree-stump' (perhaps a corruption for 'stump of the fugitives'), and *þæt treow steall*, perhaps 'the tree place' (dictionaries translate this as 'plantation' but this is questionable, since the term *steall* is also compounded with words for barrow and mill and so forth). Both the last two landmarks lay on the top of the downs.[64] Most of the first group of thorn-trees may have lain at the edge of cultivated land as the boundary climbed the slope of the downs – a common location for this species, ever ready to colonise any available piece of undisturbed ground.

Of all the trees named in charters and early place-names, the thorn is the most common – over 290 are referred to in the boundary clauses making this almost three times as common as the next most frequent tree, the oak (the thorn comprising nearly 29% of trees mentioned in charters, the oak 11%: Table 1). The thorn is one of the first species to colonise abandoned arable, a factor that perhaps explains its frequency in agricultural regions; its ability to thrive on the edges of woods also makes it a forerunner in the regeneration of cleared land in woodland regions. The

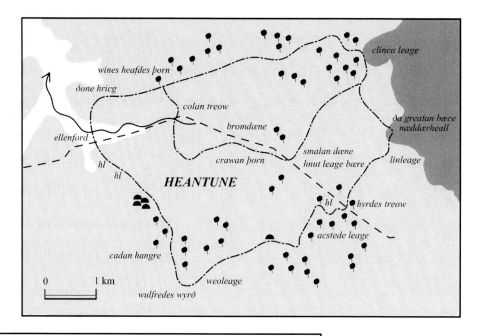

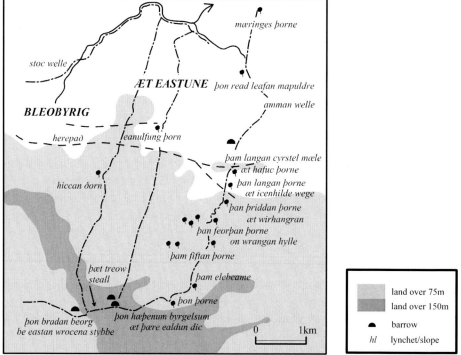

Figure 13. Boundary clauses of *a.* Hinton Ampner, Hampshire; and
b. Aston Tirrold and Aston Upthorpe, Berkshire

distribution of thorn references will be examined further in Chapter 10 but it is most frequently referred to in quite different regions from the two other common species – the oak and the ash. Willows are also frequently referred to. Some tree species only rarely appear and some are not obviously mentioned at all, the latter including the chestnut, hornbeam and rowan (see Chapter 11). The wild service-tree seldom appears but is little more than a shrub, and the sloe, too, falls into this category, although specimens may be included among the wider coverage of 'thorn'. Perhaps surprisingly, the apple is also a frequent landmark but its fruit, whether from the wild crab-apple or a cultivated variety, would have been of value. Trees are again found as boundary markers in the Llandaff charters that refer to south Wales and neighbouring parts of Herefordshire. Amongst those mentioned, the ash and the willow are the most common (but each only four times), generally referred to by their Welsh names *onnen* and *helygen*; other trees noted include a yew, a thorn, an apple and a hazel, plus a 'broom-bed, and a 'gorse moor'.[65]

Mǣre or *mearc* (often *(ge)mearcodan* or *mearcedon*) 'boundary' trees, are not uncommon in boundary clauses, referring mostly to oaks, beeches, limes or thorns. Others are referred to as a *landscearu* 'boundary' feature, like the *landchereþorn* of Ditcheat and Lottisham, Somerset, or the *land scor aac* of Fovant, Wiltshire.[66] Some stood at road junctions that were marked by a post, such as the *stapol þorn*, *stapola ðorne* and *stapol þornæ* of Easton near Winchester, Micheldever and Abbots Worthy, all in Hampshire, as was the *þam þorne þær se stapul stent* 'the thorn-tree where the ?signpost stands'.[67]

Adjectives used to describe individual trees in charter boundary clauses may have helped to identify them as boundary markers: 'the ivy-covered oak', for instance, noted above on the boundary of Stoke Prior in Worcestershire, or the *ifihtan stoc* 'ivy-covered stump' at Havant, Hampshire. At Crawley in Hampshire *sænget þorn* appears to have been 'burnt thorn' (many of these will be discussed further in later chapters under individual species). Some adjectives might describe form and shape such as the *niþer bogenan ac* 'bent-down oak' of Bentley in Worcestershire or trees described as *micel, grēat* 'great' (apple, alder, maple, many thorns, willow, lime, ash, beech, *elebēam*), *brād* 'broad, wide' (willow, oak, thorn, apple) or *gēap* 'spreading' (lime), *lang* 'tall' (thorn, beech) or *hēah* 'lofty' (oak, ash); or, alternatively, *smæl* 'small, narrow, thin' (thorn), *lȳtel* (maple), *scort* 'short (thorn, oak); others were described as *twisliht* 'forked' (oak, birch), *wōh* 'crooked' (an apple, oaks, an alder, a sallow), *holh* 'hollow' (ash); some as *eald* 'old, ancient' (maple, *elebēam*, thorn, willow, sallow, beech, ash, yew, and so forth), *radelod* '?having straight branches' (an oak), and *lopped* '?lopped' (a thorn) or *copped* 'polled, lopped or pollarded' (oak, thorn); some were *sīere* 'withered', *fūl* 'diseased' or *sēoc* 'sick' (a beech-tree, a thorn and an oak respectively). Some adjectives refer to colour, as in trees described as 'black', usually the blackthorn. There is also a reference to a *blake wiðig*, but this is perhaps a 'pale willow' (OE *blæc* 'dark, black' can be difficult to distinguish from *blāc* 'pale'). Other colours include 'grey' (especially the apple – see Chapter 11), 'red' or 'red-leaved' (a maple, a beech and a box), 'white' (the birch), or even 'green' (oaks). The nature of their bark may be expressed as 'rough' (oak and thorn) or 'smooth' (oak). Some trees were growing in particular locations or associated with particular kinds of birds (hawks, swallows, 'hens', crows, pigeons).

Some trees were solitary – often described as *anlīepig* 'single, solitary' like *ðære ænlypigan þorn* of another Hinton Ampner charter or *þa ænlypan ac* of Cern, Berkshire –, others in groups, as at the *æscbedd* 'ash-bed' in Himbleton, Worcestershire.[68] It seems to be oak-trees that were most often specified by number, perhaps because of their value: five oaks at Upper Arley, Staffordshire, and at Little Witley, Worcestershire; eight at Crediton, Devon; and three at both Cuddesdon and Eynsham, Oxfordshire.[69] Some trees were noted for their practical use: the *mest ac* of Hatherton in Staffordshire providing mast or forage for pigs from its acorns; the *spedige* thorn of Meon, Hampshire, may have been 'bounteous' in its fruits, as was the *feden þorn* of Liddington, Wiltshire, 'the nourishing thorn', while a thorn on the boundary of Overton and Conderton in Worcestershire was associated with 'earth/pig-nuts' (probably the edible tuber *Conopodium majus*).[70] Only rarely was a tree described as a thing of beauty – usefulness probably far outweighing such an impression, but two oaks and a thorn were described as 'fair' or 'beauteous'.

Many trees were associated with named individuals, as noted above. These probably referred to ownership or another well-known local person and often again stood beside roads. In Berkshire, for instance, some 23% of all trees noted as boundary markers fall into this category and in Wiltshire and Hampshire 15% and 13% respectively. Within this entire group, most – some 68% – of the references are to a tree of an unspecified species (usually referred to as a *trēow* but very occasionally as a *bēam*), although of the named species the commonest is again the thorn, followed by the oak and ash with single references only to a holly, pear and elder. In Wiltshire there are at least eighteen incidences of trees with a personal name, and sometimes the tree species is given. Of the Wiltshire examples, eight of them are thorn-trees, and, indeed, it is the thorn which is most frequently mentioned in such a context, although the oak, ash and pear have also been noted.

As boundary markers, trees may seem to be rather ephemeral features, especially with short-lived trees like the aspen. A reference to *þene licgendan stoc*, 'the lying tree-stump', on the boundary of *Weonfeld*, Wokefield and Sulhamstead Bannister, Berkshire,[71] seems to be even more dubious. Even worse, the 'old tree place' seems even more ephemeral if it indeed refers to a remembered tree – this occurs on the Wiltshire boundaries of Wanborough and of Beeching Stoke as *þone ealdan treow stede/ þone ealde treo stede*, and another *trēow steall*, 'tree place', occurs on the boundary of the Berkshire Blewbury estate, as noted above, but Biggam notes how a dead tree can remain as a recognisable grey-coloured trunk for at least 200 years.[72] It does not seem to have worried the Anglo-Saxons that some landmarks were relatively short-lived features (including a manure heap in Worcestershire) and it is doubtful whether they considered how long a particular tree might live. They knew the boundary line well and were content to name landmarks obvious to them as they walked or rode around the boundary.

Few trees can live a thousand years and perhaps the only likely candidates are the very few yews noted on boundaries. Even so, individual yew-trees known to be over 1,000 years old are rarely found in such a location, often standing within churchyards well within estate boundaries. A solitary yew appears on the boundary of an estate in Hampshire – the *ealde iw* that apparently stood in a small valley on the boundary of Mickelmersh, possibly to the south of the present Stubb's Copse,[73] and another is recorded as standing on a mound or barrow near Chepstow in the Llandaff charters, although yews are also noted in other locations (see Chapter 8). It is surprising, however, even with other shorter-lived species, how often the same species of tree can still be found close to one mentioned in a charter boundary clause. A young tree can replace an aged one naturally, although in the case of some historic trees it was traditional to plant a young one when the old one started to die. In Shropshire, a young sapling oak supports the old relic 'Lady Oak' at Cressage, possibly another survivor from the edge of the Long Forest (see above).[74] It is doubtful whether deliberate replanting was carried out in the case of boundary trees. However, tree species have been found to continue in a specific spot on many occasions: thorns still grow near the *hlangen* thorn of Ladbroke and Radbourne and the thorn bed of Long Itchington in Warwickshire and ashes at the ash bed of Himbleton, Worcestershire.[75] Field maples and oaks still stand close to the spots where they were recorded along the eastern boundary of Stoke Prior in Worcestershire. Since the trees noted were usually those common in the locality this is perhaps not surprising. In the following chapters reference is made to a number of so-called 'champion' trees – the largest now alive. While size cannot be a reliable indicator of the exact age of any species of tree, being dependent upon the soils and microclimate of a location, it can obviously often be a measure of antiquity. Size is normally recorded by girth (in centimetres in the Tree Register) and height (in metres).[76]

One wonders about the many stubs or stumps of trees recorded along charter boundaries. The elder is the tree mentioned most frequently in references to stubs, followed by the thorn: there are no fewer than sixteen elder stub references and three thorn stub references in Wiltshire (although some of these may possibly refer to the same feature). These may have been a type of pollard – the production of a stub by removing tree branches was a recognised form of management of the elder in later times, perhaps to more easily reach the flowers or fruit,[77] or the tree may have been deliberately cut down (see Chapter 2). The elder, the tree upon which Judas is said to have hung himself and upon which Christ was supposed to have been nailed, remained involved with magic, medicine and witchcraft in later centuries (it was thought that witches could transform themselves into elder trees).[78] It is certainly noted in the Old English *Penitentials* as a possible feature of heathen worship and may not have been generally liked; but this may be entirely fanciful and its flowers and fruits can of course be used (as a fruit drink or as a base for wine) and its leaves are eaten by sheep and cattle; it also grows readily in most situations and may have needed control. However, given the elder's unsavoury associations, it may be significant that one had been deliberately reduced to a stump in a medieval London churchyard.[79] A Berkshire clause, that of Chilton, with added woodland at West Ilsley, runs *innon rod stybban*, 'to the clearing stumps' (*rōd*[1]) as if these were trees that were being cut down, but the species is not named.[80] Oak, ash, alder, sallow, willow, elder and thorn stubs might result from pollarding, but what of the pear stub of *Winterburnan* or the apple stub of Dauntsey, both in Wiltshire?

Trees are, therefore, particularly prominent in those Old English documents that describe the landscape of the day – probably more so than any other natural feature apart from those of the local topography. These present us with information about the early medieval landscape that cannot be obtained from any other source and present us with images that are immediately recognisable to us today.

ENDNOTES

[1] Rackham, *The History of the Countryside*, pp. 4–5.
[2] Hooke, 'Anglo-Saxon landscapes of the West Midlands'; *The Anglo-Saxon Landscape*; 'Regional variation'; *The Landscape of Anglo-Saxon England*.
[3] A. H. Smith, *The Place-Names of Westmorland, Part I*, English Place-Name Society 42 (Cambridge, 1967), p. 108.
[4] Kelly, *Charters of St Augustine's*.
[5] F. M. Stenton, *The Latin Charters of the Anglo-Saxon Period* (Oxford, 1955).
[6] S. E. Kelly, *Charters of Malmesbury Abbey*, Anglo-Saxon Charters XI (Oxford, 2005).
[7] Sawyer, *Anglo-Saxon Charters*.
[8] In particular, Julia Crick's study of the St Albans manuscripts contains a number of Hertfordshire boundaries not hitherto in print: Crick, *Charters of St Albans*.
[9] *Historia ecclesiastica* II.2: Sherley-Price, pp. 100–1.
[10] Smith, *The Place-Names of Gloucestershire*, IV, p. 33, n.1.
[11] Morton, *The Trees of Shropshire*, pp. 50–4.
[12] Wilks, *Trees of the British Isles*, pp. 111–14.
[13] A. Reynolds, *Later Anglo-Saxon England, Life and Landscape* (Stroud, 1999), pp. 75–84.
[14] Hooke, *The Landscape of Anglo-Saxon England*.
[15] S 106, B 201.
[16] S 274, B 392 (possibly a tenth-century fabrication, see Electronic Sawyer).
[17] S 550, B 882; S 99, B 165.
[18] S 731, B 1135; *WoASCB*, pp. 145–7 (sp).
[19] Hooke, *The Anglo-Saxon Landscape*, pp. 102–3, fig. 26; Hooke, *The Landscape of Anglo-Saxon England*, p. 23.

[20] O. S. Anderson, *The English Hundred-Names, The South-Eastern Counties*, Lunds Universitets Årsskift, Bd 37 (Lund and Leipzig, 1939), pp. 69–70.

[21] Hooke, *The Anglo-Saxon Landscape*, pp. 99–102, table 2.

[22] *CDEPN*, p. 403.

[23] O. S. Anderson, *The English Hundred-Names*, Lunds Universitets Årsskift, Bd 30 (Lund, 1934).

[24] Ibid.

[25] O. S. Anderson, *The English Hundred-Names. The South-Western Counties*, Lunds Universitets Årsskrift. Bd 35 ((Lund and Leipzig, 1939), pp. 56–8.

[26] S 647, B 998; S 903, J. Armitage Robinson, *Gilbert Crispin, Abbot of Westminster* (Cambridge, 1911), p. 168.

[27] Anderson, *The English Hundred-Names*, p. 15; *CDEPN*, p. 653.

[28] S 1174, B 117(sp), *WoASCB*, pp. 40–3.

[29] S 592, B 943.

[30] S 583, B 981 and S 673, Kelly, *Charters of Abingdon*, II, nos 58 and 84, pp. 247, 250, 343.

[31] Reynolds, *Later Anglo-Saxon England*, p. 109.

[32] S 786, B 1282, *WoASCB*, pp. 26–7; S 756, B 1213, *Charters of Abingdon*, II, no. 108.

[33] S 754, B 1200; S 920, P. H. Sawyer, ed., *Charters of Burton Abbey*, Anglo-Saxon Charters II (Oxford, 1979), no. 31; Hooke, *The Landscape of Anglo-Saxon Staffordshire: The Charter Evidence* (Keele, 1983), pp. 93–7.

[34] A. D. Mills, *The Place-Names of Dorset, Part I*, English Place-Name Society 52 (Cambridge, 1977), p. 74.

[35] S 811, B 1319; S 179, B 356 (the first suspicious, the second a forgery of eleventh-century date: H. P. R. Finberg, *The Early Charters of the West Midlands*, no. 189, pp. 184–96).

[36] A. D. Mills, *A Dictionary of English Place-Names* (Oxford, 1991), pp. 346–7; *CDEPN*, p. 652.

[37] See *CDEPN* for the meanings of most place-names.

[38] Hooke, *The Landscape of Anglo-Saxon England*, pp. 84–92; C. P. Biggam, *Grey in Old English* (London, 1998), pp. 228–30.

[39] Frontin, *L'œuvre gromatique*, 11, AD 72–100: *L'œuvre gromatique, Corpus agrimensorum Romanorum IV Iulius Frontinus*, [Th. 2] 11, COST Action G2 (Luxembourg, 2000), pp. 6–7.

[40] Hygin, *L'œuvre gromatique, Corpus agrimensorum Romanorum V Hyginus*, [Th. 75] 30–1, COST Action G2 (Luxembourg, 2000), pp. 18–19 (dating from AD 97), with minor amendments to the translation given in this source (in French). The Latin text is somewhat obscure and possibly corrupt in places.

[41] See A. H. Baines, J., 'Wyrtruma and wyrtwala', *South Midlands Archaeology* 12 (1987), pp. 102–10 and P. E. Kitson, 'The root of the matter: OE *wyrt, wyrtwale, -a, wyrt(t)rum(a)* and cognates', in *Language, History and Linguistic Modelling: A Festschrift for Jacek Fisiak on his 60th birthday*, ed. R. Hickey and S. Puppel, 2 vols (Berlin, 1997), i.127–41.

[42] S 766, Dugdale, *Monasticon Anglicanum*, ii.323–4.

[43] S 898, K 705, *WaASCB*, pp. 110–13.

[44] G. B. Grundy, 'Saxon charters of Worcestershire', *Birmingham Archaeological Society Transactions and Proceedings* 52 (1927), p. 105; Muir, *Ancient Trees*, p. 50.

[45] S 276, B 393 (a forgery based on other charters: Electronic Sawyer); S 446, B 742; S 811, B 1319 (suspicious).

[46] S 607, Gelling, *Place-Names of Berkshire, Part III*, p. 645; S 786, S 1282.

[47] S 1596, B 362, *WoASCB*, pp. 397–400; S 1597, B 361, *WoASCB*, pp. 401–2; S 470, B 748; S 605, B 924, Kelly, *Charters of Abingdon*, II, no. 52; S 276, B 393 (sp); S 1277, B 544; S 446, B 742. Charter statistics for Berkshire are based upon the former county area.

48 S 347, B 564; S 786, B 1282 (sp); S 1551, Finberg, *Early Charters of the West Midlands*, pp. 79–84, no. 187.

49 S 1580, K iii. 392–3; S 490, B 781, Kelly, *Charters of Shaftesbury*, no. 14.

50 S 811, B 1319 (suspicious).

51 S 754, B 1200.

52 S 619, B 982.

53 S 283, B 377 (sp).

54 S 417, B 689.

55 S 994, K 763.

56 G. B. Grundy, 'The Saxon land charters of Hampshire with notes on place and field names', *Archaeological Journal*, 2nd ser. 33 (1926), pp. 192–230.

57 Hooke, 'Medieval forests and parks'.

58 Hooke, 'Medieval forests and parks'; *Victoria County History Hampshire III*, p. 67, n. 85; Hampshire County Council, *Hampshire's Countryside Heritage 2: Ancient Woodland* (Winchester, 1983), p. 34.

59 S 1007, K 780; some of the landmarks are also recorded in an earlier charter S 942, K 712 (990), which also records a *haga* boundary to the north of *huredes/hureðes/hurdes* tree around the north-eastern angle of Hinton Ampner parish; G. B. Grundy, 'The Saxon land charters of Hampshire', pp. 139–42.

60 S 60, B 204 (sp), *WoASCB*, pp. 65–6.

61 Ibid., S 59, B 203 (?sp), *WoASCB*, pp. 63–9.

62 S 1549, *Heming*: T. Hearne, ed., *Heming. Hemingi chartularium ecclesiae Wigorniensis* (Oxford, 1723), pp. 245–6.

63 S 255, B 1331, B 1332, B 1333, *CBDC*, pp. 86–99, no. 1.

64 S 496, B 801, Kelly, *Charters of Abingdon*, I, no. 36; Gelling, *Place-Names of Berkshire*, part III, pp. 758–61.

65 Davies, *An Early Welsh Microcosm*, p. 30; Evans, *The Text of the Book of Llan Dâv*. The date of the charters is still under discussion.

66 S 292, B 438; S 364, B 588.

67 S 695, B 1076; S 360, B 596, S. Miller, ed., *Charters of the New Minster, Winchester*. Anglo-Saxon Charters IX (Oxford, 2001), no. 3 (forgery of early C11); S 962, K 743; S 381, B 629 (sp).

68 S 942, K 712; S 651, B 1035, Kelly, *Charters of Abingdon*, II, no. 79; S 219, B 552 (?suspicious).

69 S 1380, Dugdale, *Monasticon Anglicanum*, vi.1443–6 (no. 1), D. Hooke, *The Landscape of Anglo-Saxon Staffordshire: The Charter Evidence* (Keele, 1983), pp. 68–70; S 1323, B 1242, *WoASCB*, pp. 278–81; S 255, B 1331, B 1332, B 1333, *CBDC*, pp. 86–99; S 587, B 945, Kelly, *Charters of Abingdon*, II, no. 70; S 911, K 714.

70 S 1380, Dugdale, *Monasticum Anglicanum*, vi.1443–6 (no. 1) (sp), Hooke, *The Landscape of Anglo-Saxon Staffordshire*, pp. 78–81; S 619, B 982; S 459, B 754, Kelly, *Charters of Shaftesbury*, no. 11; S 216, B 541, *WoASCB*, pp. 125–9.

71 S 578, B 888, Kelly, *Charters of Abingdon*, I, no. 46; Gelling, *Place-Names of Berkshire*,part III, pp. 641–2.

72 S 312, B 477 (sp); S 478, B 769, Kelly, *Charters of Shaftesbury*, no. 12; S 496, B 801, Kelly, *Charters of Abingdon*, I, no. 36; Biggam, *Grey in Old English*, pp. 228–9, citing Rackham, *The History of the Countryside*, p. 151.

73 S 857, K 652; Grundy, 'The Saxon land charters of Hampshire', p. 238; Evans, *The Text of the Book of Llan Dâv*, p. 166.

[74] Morton, *The Trees of Shropshire*, pp. 50–1.

[75] S 892, A. S. Napier and W. H. Stevenson, eds, *The Crawford Collection of Early Charters and Documents* (Oxford, 1895), pp. 19–22, no. 8; *WaASCB*, pp. 74–7; S 898, K 705, *WaASCB*, pp. 110–13; S 219, B 552, *WoASCB*, pp. 129–34 (suspicious).

[76] Tree Register at www.treeregister.org/pdf/Champion%20Trees

[77] Rackham, *Trees and Woodland*, 2nd edn, p. 9, fig. 2.

[78] Paterson, *Tree Wisdom*, pp. 276–94.

[79] Damian Goodburn, pers. comm. I. Howell, D. Bowsher, T. Dyson and N. Holder, *The London Guildhall: An Archaeological History of a Neighbourhood from Early Medieval to Modern Times* (London, 2007).

[80] S 934, B 1170, Kelly, *Charters of Abingdon*, II, no. 137; Gelling, *Place-Names of Berkshire*, part III, p. 767.

PART III

Individual Tree Species
in Anglo-Saxon England

8

Trees of Wood-Pasture and 'Ancient Countryside'

Most common species of trees are encountered in pre-Conquest charters and place-names but some were more common than others. The most frequently mentioned trees in boundary clauses are the oak, the ash and the thorn (see Chapter 7). This is mirrored in their incidence in place-names and as hundred names (trees often served to mark the meeting-places of these early territorial divisions, as noted in the previous chapter). Species distributions change dramatically, however, across England and one needs to ask whether any significance can be attached to this. Why, for instance do the oak and the ash occur so frequently in Worcestershire but much less often in Wiltshire and Berkshire? What trees take their place? What is the commonest, what is the rarest tree in pre-Conquest charters? These are questions already broached and partially answered but explored in more detail over the remaining chapters.

REGIONAL DISTRIBUTIONS AND LANDSCAPE CHARACTER

References to trees in charter boundaries may disclose much about landscape character. It can hardly be a coincidence that so few trees are mentioned as boundary landmarks in Cornwall. On this windswept peninsula landmarks are more likely to be remnant archaeological features such as stones, barrows and ancient settlement sites.[1] But move eastwards into Devon with its richer red sandstone soils and one boundary clause alone, that of Crediton, mentions an ivy grove, a crab-apple tree, an alder, a birch coomb, a broad ash-tree, an alder shaw, an ash coomb, a willow slade, eight oaks, and various trees associated with individuals (see Chapter 7).[2] Other Devon charters add broom, thorn, elder, oak, furze, hazel, lime and maple. Obviously, much of this must be pure chance but there is undoubtedly a clear indication of the landscape regions of early medieval England in pre-Conquest charters, and trees play not a small role in helping to identify these. It is only, however, when boundary clauses are plentiful that species distributions become meaningful, but place-names can help to extend this coverage.

Species distribution can be investigated on a broad scale. Rackham relates the incidence of species to 'ancient' and 'planned' countryside, noting how certain trees

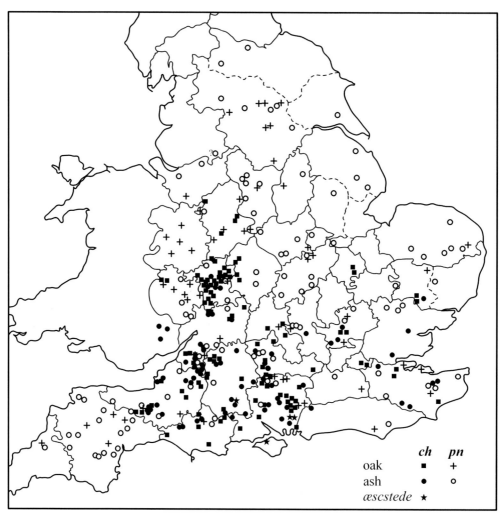

Figure 14. Trees of wood-pasture and 'Ancient Countryside': the distribution of oak and
ash in early medieval charters and place-names. The boundaries are those
of the 'traditional' i.e. pre-1974, counties

such as the oak, ash, alder, lime, birch, elm, yew and holly seem to have occurred
most often in the former type while the thorn, the sloe and the elder were much
commoner in the latter.[3] This is corroborated by the present study. The distribution
of species also clearly reflects local conditions of geology and topography as well
as land use. Obviously one has to locate individual charter boundary landmarks as
accurately as possible within a landscape that can vary topographically and geologi-
cally within a very short distance if any accurate assessment is to be made of regional

distributions, and this is a very time-consuming exercise. Only a detailed examination of the individual boundary clauses can identify all occurrences of a particular tree type and also trace whether individual landmarks are repeated on several occasions. For the present study all charter references have been collected and checked against the Old English Microfiche Concordance compiled by the University of Toronto, the whole corpus of early medieval charters thus being covered.

THE OAK AND THE ASH:
TREES OF WOOD-PASTURE REGIONS (Fig. 14)

The oak

The oak (OE *āc*, ON *eik*) is often met as a boundary landmark. It tends to have a majestic form, especially *Quercus robur*, and also had a mythological significance. In many cultures, it was seen as the tree of longevity and might, therefore, be linked to ancestral symbolism and perceptions of permanence.[4] It appears to have played a major role in early forms of tree worship and in pre-Christian religion (see Chapter 1): thus in Greek mythology oak-tree spirits were known as dryads. The tree itself was the tree of Zeus, Jupiter, Hercules, the chief of the elder Irish gods known as the Dagda, Þórr, Allah and, in part, of Jehovah.[5] In ancient Greece, many sacred groves were of oak, including the most hallowed sanctuary of Dodona. Here was a far-spreading (?)oak tree with evergreen leaves and sweet edible acorns, which stood within the grove, with a spring of cold crystal water gushing from the foot of the tree.[6] There are obvious similarities here with the Norse Yggdrasill, but that was reputed to be an ash; both trees were obviously closely linked in tree symbolism but far-removed from the real tree. The oak was also sacred to the ancient Hebrews. Paterson[7] notes how Abraham supposedly received his heavenly visitors under an oak, how Jacob buried all the idols of Shechem under an oak, and how it was under an oak that Gideon saw the angel who advised him to flee from Israel. Augustine's meeting with the British bishops in 603 below an oak may have deliberately continued this biblical symbolism (see Chapter 7), a tradition perpetuated in the numerous 'preaching' oaks of later years. The oak was closely associated with Norse and Germanic gods: with Þórr in north-western Europe, and with Donar in the form of the oak at Geismar, felled by Boniface.[8] Lightning striking an oak was believed to have been fire from heaven. The oak was supreme in the sacred groves of the Germanic races and of the Celts, thought by the druid priests to contain the energy, power and strength of their gods, likened to the male procreative force of the universe (the berries of the mistletoe growing upon an oak representing the sperm of the god). When the goddess Brigit became transmuted as St Brighid it is said that acorns were burnt on perpetual fires at a retreat known as the Cell of Oak at Kildare. In legend, Merlin continued to work his enchantments in a grove of oaks, using the topmost branch as his wand, but is said to have prophesied that the oak-cult would be swept away by Christianity.[9]

There is limited indication of any supernatural symbolism in Anglo-Saxon literature and thought (but for reasons for this, see Chapter 2). In a Leicestershire place-name, as previously noted, a holy oak appears to have been associated with the Saxon god Þunor. On the other hand, it was the only tree to be associated with a crucifix as a boundary marker, two recorded on the boundaries of Stoke Prior and Tardebigge in north Worcestershire (see also Chapter 2), although the reason for this remains unclear. Nevertheless the oak was a tree that was bound to draw attention because of its size and beauty and for the quality of its timber: the frequency with which it appears in charter boundary clauses and place-names is discussed below. The role of the oak in English lore has already been discussed in Chapter 4. Inevitably, its mythical associations appear to have lingered on or been revived in later periods. Interpretations of folklore presented at the turn of the nineteenth century tended, by today's more rigorous standards, to be over-imaginative, and Sir James Frazer, in his *Golden Bough*, made much of the sacrifice of the oak-king of Nemi on Misdummer Day. Midsummer bonfires remained a part of medieval ritual, sometimes fuelled by oak, and the month associated with the oak by Graves is *Duir*, 10 June to 7 July, with midway St John's Day, 24 June, the day on which he believed 'the oak-king was sacrificially burned alive'.[10] The role of the oak in Celtic druid tradition has been discussed earlier.

Parts of this tree were also ingredients in ancient herbal cures: its bark used in a green salve or ointment in the *Lacnunga*[11] and in other salves noted in Cockayne's *Leechdoms* (vol. II) for, amongst other things, 'secretion of the joints' or *bite* 'cancer'; its twigs were boiled in water to bathe a body suffering from leprosy or the powdered rind was mixed within a draught of liquid as a cure for shingles or lung disease. Oak bark is rich in tannins which protect the lining of the digestive tract from irritation and inflammation and was historically a remedy for gastric upsets.[12]

The importance of the oak in Anglo-Saxon thought is portrayed in the Old English *Rune Poem*:

> (ac) byþ on eorþan   elda bearnum
> flæsces fodor;   fereþ gelome
> ofer ganotes bæþ;   – garsecg fandaþ
> hwæþer ac hæbbe   æþele treowe.

> 'The oak nourishes meat on the land
> for the children of men; often it travels
> over the gannet's bath – the stormy sea tests
> whether the oak keeps faith nobly.'[13]

The oak was the most important timber tree for building (see Chapter 6). Its acorns were a major source of sustenance to the Anglo-Saxon herds of swine (nourishing 'meat on the land' in the *Rune Poem*) and rights to mast are often noted in pre-Conquest charters (see Chapter 6). Oak timber was valued above that of most other native trees, much used for the building of dwellings and ships (as indicated in the *Rune Poem* above, where *āc* refers to an oaken ship). In the Welsh laws attributed to Hywel Dda, an oak or a beech was valued more highly than any other tree apart from a 'holy yew' – at six-score pence.[14] The *coppeden ac* recorded upon the boundary of Stoke by Hurstbourne, Hampshire (see above), may be an early reference to the pollarding of this tree. Oak stumps (OE *stocc*) in Norton and Kingsbury, Oxfordshire, may also have been pollards (see discussion, Chapter 6).[15] Some of the oaks referred to in place-names and charters were found in woods in which they presumably formed the dominant tree: *āc* occurs frequently with *lēah* and occasionally with *hangra* and *holt*.

The noble appearance of this tree may have attracted interest, and it is, indeed, two oaks that were described as 'fair' or 'fine, elegant': the *feȝer ok* of Mells, Somerset (OE *fæger* 'fair, lovely, beautiful'), and the *smiceran æc* of Abbotts Wootton, Dorset (OE *smicer* 'beauteous, fair, elegant').[16] But it was also one of the most valuable of trees in its production of acorns, a valuable fodder crop, and for its timber.

In the charters, some oaks were associated with birds and animals. These include the *crawan ac* 'the crow's oak' of Westwood, Wiltshire, and perhaps *þa scip ac* of *Wican*, Worcestershire ('sheep oak'),[17] the latter a reminder that in Ine's laws a tree that could provide shelter for animals (in this case swine) was worth far more than ordinary trees;[18] a *mest ac* 'mast oak' is recorded on the boundary of Hatherton, Staffordshire, near the later Cannock Chase.[19] Others were described as tall, slender, broad, great, forked, *radeludan* (?*radelod* 'having straight branches'), or *rugan* (*rūh*) or *wærriht* (?*w(e)arr* 'a knot', *i.e.* 'rough-barked') and yet another as *smēþe* 'smooth'. However, others were described as *wōh* 'crooked, twisted' or, in the case of the *niþer bogenan ac* of Bentley, Holt, in Worcestershire, 'bent-down'.[20] Another at Stoke Prior, Worcestershire, was *īfihtan* 'ivy-covered' and another in Pennard Minster, Somerset, was decried as *þa seocan aac*, 'sick oak', one in North Stoneham, Hampshire, as *fortyhtan* 'large-rooted' and one in Abingdon, Oxfordshire (earlier Berkshire), as *fulan* (*fūl*) 'diseased'.[21] *Đare grene æc* of Balsdon, Suffolk, and *þan gren aken* of Langley, Wiltshire, both 'green' oaks,[22] remind one, perhaps, of the fresh colour of the male flowers seen in spring, unless this was related to green lichen on the trunk – an examination of the locations could be useful. An oak on the boundary of Overton, Hampshire, was called *þa hreadleafan æc* 'the red-leaved oak' and another in Abbots Bromley, Staffordshire, the *readan acon* 'red oak'.[23] Rackham notes the 'Red lyved ooke' of a Somerset perambulation of 1567, and suggests that these may be references to 'that rare and striking form of *Quercus robur* that produces bright scarlet lammas shoots every August'.[24] Only one oak stump is noted – at Fen Stanton in Huntingdonshire.

Some oaks stood in woods, like the Long Itchington oak mentioned earlier, while others were *anlipigan* 'solitary'; only two were associated with springs. The function of the trees as boundary landmarks is frequently indicated by reference to *mǣre* or *mærc* (also *gemearcodan*, *merkeden*) oaks and the *land scor aac*, of Fovant, Wiltshire,[25] and association with landownership by the many oaks associated with personal names. The oak, especially the English oak, *Quercus robur*, was obviously sufficiently distinctive to be picked out as a boundary landmark on many occasions: it occurs on twenty-eight separate occasions in Worcestershire charters alone and over hundred times in all recorded charter bounds, making this tree, after the thorn, the most oft-quoted of all the named species in this source, and is third commonest in the list of early place-names (some 9% of early tree place-names) – in total, over 10% of the tree species recorded along boundaries and in early place-names (Tables 1 and 3).

In spite of the high incidence of references to the oak in charter boundary clauses it occurs in only three hundred names (Table 2) – only two in a pre-Conquest source, both in Yorkshire: Acklam, the 'oak *lēah* or wood', and Skyrack to the north-west of Leeds, 'the bright oak' later interpreted as 'the oak where the shire meets';[26] a third reference, Tipnoak in Sussex, 'Tippa's oak-tree', is not recorded before 1262.[27] Other hundreds met at oak-trees but the hundred itself bore a different name, such as Holdshott Hundred, Hampshire, which later met at the 'Hundred Oak'. Matlock, Derbyshire, *Meslach* in 1086, in Wirksworth Hundred, is also 'oak-tree where meetings are held'.

OE *āc* in place-names recorded in or before 1086 is common throughout the country, most names being recorded in charters or in Domesday Book. They range from simplex forms such as Oak in Inwardleigh, Devon: *Acha* 1086; Oake, Somerset: *Acon* C11; Noke, Oxfordshire: *Acam* 1086; or Aike in Lockington, Yorkshire East Riding: *Ach* 1086, to forms in which *āc* is compounded with a descriptive term or one denoting location. Whitnage, Devon, *Witenes* in 1086 but *Witenech* c.1200, is 'white oak'; Shurnock, Worcestershire, *sciran/sciren ac* c.960, is 'at the bright oak', while other oaks at Oakford, Devon, or Okeford, Dorset, marked fords. *Āc* with the habitative term *tūn* is found in the many *Actun* names such as Aughton, Yorkshire West Riding: *Actone* 1086; Aughton, Yorkshire East Riding: *Actun* 1086; Acton Beauchamp, Hereford: *Aactune* 727; Iron Acton, Gloucestershire: *Actune* 1086; Acton Burnell and Pigott, *Actune* 1086, Acton Round: *Achetune* 1086, and Acton Scott: *Actune* 1086, all in Shropshire; and Acton Trussell, Staffordshire: *Actone* 1086; while Oakworth, Yorkshire West Riding: *Acurde* 1086, combines *āc* with *worð* 'farm, enclosure'. A more unusual association is found in Barnack, Cambridgeshire: *Beornican* c.980, *Bernac* 1086, which is probably '(place at) the oak-tree(s) of the warriors' (OE *beorn* with *āc*).[28] OE *āc* with *lēah* is also frequent, as in Oakleigh, Kent: *Acleah* 774; two lost Domesday manors, *Achelie* in the New Forest, and another, North Oakley in Kingsclere: *acleah* 824, both in Hampshire; Oakley, Somerset: *Achelai* 1086; Oakley, Buckinghamshire: *Achelei* 1086; Oakley,

Bedfordshire: *Accleya* 1060; Great and Little Oakley, Northamptonshire: *Aclea* C11; Great Oakley, Essex: *Accleia* 1086; Acklam, Yorkshire East Riding: *Aclun* 1086; West Acklam, Yorkshire North Riding: *Aclum* 1086; or Acle, Norfolk: *Acle* 1086. The Scandinavian term for oak, *eik, eiki,* is found in Aysgarth, Yorkshire North Riding: *Echescard* 1086, Ackton, Featherstone, Yorkshire West Riding: *Aitone* 1086, and in Aiskew, Bedale, Yorkshire North Riding: *Echescol* 1086 (with ON *skógr* 'wood'), while the Old Danish form *ek* is found in a lost Eckton in Otley, Yorkshire West Riding: *on Ectune c.*1030. Other terms for the oak are found in West Firle and Frog Firle in Sussex: *Ferle* and *Ferles* in 1086, which may be an Old English dialect term **fierel/fierol* 'place where oak-trees grow' or 'place covered with oaks' (cognate with OHG *fereh-eih* and Langobardic *fereha* 'oak', although a meaning of 'beech' has also been discussed); an alternative, but perhaps less likely, interpretation is 'the land of the Firolas or "the oak people"'.[29] The Cornish *glastan* found in the place-name Treglasta in Davidstow refers to 'fruiting oaks'.

The oak, one form, *Quercus robur,* sometimes referred to as the English or pedunculate oak, is a common woodland tree on the clay soils of the English lowlands but – usually as *Q. petraea,* the sessile oak – is also found on dry shallow soils and across highland Britain, common in both ancient and secondary woodland. It is a particularly robust tree, tolerating drought and other adverse conditions. By withdrawing nourishment from its uppermost branches it can survive conditions that would kill many other trees, leaving a specimen 'stag-headed' but otherwise unaffected. Sometimes the oak forms the dominant species in a wood; more often, especially in the case of *Q. robur,* it occurs in close association with lime, beech, ash, hazel or wych-elm; falling branches leave areas open for the growth of other species and for a shrub and herb layer. It grows readily across much of England and it is not therefore surprising that in some counties the oak appears so frequently as a boundary landmark, especially as it is often forms an imposing tree. It is particularly frequent not only in Worcestershire (and, according to early recorded place-names, in Herefordshire) but also in Hampshire. Both regions have extensive clay soils, although in Hampshire it is a layer of clay-with-flints which overlies the chalk. Interestingly, both were to become counties which were almost entirely to be designated royal forest after the Conquest and were almost certainly areas of hunting in pre-Conquest times[30] (Domesday Book coverage of forest is not comprehensive.) Large parts of the early medieval landscape of these counties are likely to have been wood-pasture regions in the early medieval period, open grassland liberally scattered with woodland trees interspersed with patches of ancient woodland. Throughout history, the oak has been a tree of wood-pasture able to withstand the pressures of grazing and able to colonise grassland,[31] and was often pollarded in medieval deer parks. It is, indeed, in Stoke by Hurstbourne in Hampshire that ones hears of *þa coppedan ac* in 900[32] (and, in the same county, of pollarded thorns).

The oak can be a long-lived tree, especially if kept pollarded; oaks over 500

Plate V. An old Windsor pollard oak

years old are known, especially in former areas of wood-pasture and parkland, as in the New Forest in Hampshire, Whitcliff Park in Gloucestershire, Moccas Park in Herefordshire, and Windsor Park (Plate V). An oak-tree grows rapidly for the first 80–150 years before slowing down; after about 250–350 years, decline sets in, and trees surviving beyond 400 years are often hollow.[33] As Dryden notes,[34]

> The monarch oak, the patriarch of trees,
> Shoots rising up, and spreads by slow degrees;
> Three centuries he grows, and three he stays,
> Supreme in state, and in three more decays.

If coppiced or pollarded, however, the oak can live for 900 years or more: the biggest and oldest oaks surviving today are all pollards. The Tree Register notes among its 'champion trees' an English oak with a girth of 1253 centimetres at Lydham Manor in Bishop's Castle, Shropshire, and another hollow oak with a girth of 1230 centimetres, at Bowthorpe, near Bourne in Lincolnshire: it is now only 12 metres tall but is hollow and the cavity has been used in the past as a pigeon house. Such trees may be at least 800 years old, possibly 1,000. Another large veteran which has been described as 'the finest oak in the British Isles' is to be found at Fredville Park in Kent (diameter 1216cm, height 20m), a pollard in which the central stem appears to have become dominant but is unlikely to be older than 450 years.[35] The girth of an oak is not a certain indication of a specific age, for growth can be exceedingly slow after pollarding. Rackham estimates that the Doodle Oak in Hatfield Forest, Essex, which died in 1858, may have dated from c.950, and the Queen's Oak at Huntingfield, Suffolk, together with some of the pollards in Windsor Great Park, may be about 1,000 years old.[36] The so-called Domesday Oak of Oldberrow, Warwickshire, in the Arden, is also of considerable age and lies within an early medieval estate which had 'the boundary oak' and 'five oaks' on its boundary in the ninth century.[37] Some of the largest oaks recorded are found in Sherwood Forest, Nottingham. These may be ancient but are now quite dead, although the younger Major Oak at Edwinstowe, its circumference over 1000cm, is still alive if only as a hollow pollarded dwarf supported by iron stays; a painting by J. Rodgers shows it as it once looked.[38]

Many of our most ancient oaks survive in areas that were formerly forest or wood-pasture: Savernake Forest in Wiltshire is considered to be one of the top five European forests for veteran trees, recorded as 'the woodland which is called *Safernoc*' in 934[39] and later a Norman forest. Within what remains of the forest, relict wood-pasture regions still remain and are represented by scattered sessile and pedunculate oaks, set amidst other areas of eighteenth- or nineteenth-century plantations of oak and beech or areas of secondary woodland in which the birch, ash, rowan and willow are common species. Some of the most ancient oaks show a basal stool and appear to have been coppiced in the distant past: a few have a basal circumference of over 8 metres. More have been pollarded, a practice systematically carried out from the fifteenth century or earlier. Today these ancient specimens are 'gnarled and nodular hulks, hollowed, mis-shapen and stag-horned, and show evidence of phases of management followed by long periods of neglect'.[40] One of the largest, the Big Belly Oak, appears to have been both coppiced and pollarded and has a girth of 1080 cm. (It also possesses its own folklore: anyone dancing naked around it twelve times anticlockwise at midnight will meet the devil!) This is but one of many equally impressive oaks to be found in Savernake but none here are likely to be as old as the early medieval period. However, throughout the country, many oaks are such impressive specimens that they attract admiration and awe, and the oak has come to be regarded as the 'national' tree (see Chapter 4). They are also the most valuable tree for the maintenance of biodiversity, providing a habitat for innumerable other species of wildlife.

The ash

Another tree which occurs frequently in the boundary clauses is the ash, *Fraxinus excelsior*, OE *æsc*, ON *askr*. This tree is described in the *Old English Rune Poem*:

> (æsc) biþ oferheah,   eldum dyre,
> stiþ on staþule;   stede rihte hylt,
> ðeah him feohtan on   firas monige.

> 'The ash is extremely tall, precious to mankind,
> strong on its base; it holds its ground as it should,
> although many men attack it.'[41]

The ash is also an excellent timber tree (the use of ash-wood for weapons, especially spears, may explain the reference in the *Rune Poem*)[42] and an *æscstede* may sometimes refer to 'a place of battle', several of which sites are referred to in charter boundary clauses (e.g. Meon, Hampshire, and Calbourne, Isle of Wight). In literary sources, *æsc* is occasionally used for 'spear', as in *The Battle of Maldon*. In this poem valiant Anglo-Saxon leaders fought a losing battle against the Danes in 991 near Maldon in Essex: ealdorman Byrhtnoth, fighting the Danes, before the battle *wand wacne æsc* 'brandished his slender spear', while one Offa, during the battle, *æscholt asceoc* 'shook his ash-wood spear', and an old warrior, Byrhtwold, later also *æsc ācwehte* 'shook his spear'.[43] The poem *Beowulf* also refers to *æscum* as 'with spears', as does the Old English *Genesis*, *Đe ðe æsca tir æt guðe forgeaf* 'who to thee gave glory of spears in battle'.[44] Related words include *æscplega* 'play of spears, battle', *æscðracu* 'battle', *æscwīga* '(spear-)warrior, *æscrōf* 'brave in battle', *æsctīr* 'glory in war', and *æscstede* 'place of battle'. Most of these are found in literary sources but the last also occurs in the charters of Wiltshire, Hampshire and the Isle of Wight.[45]

The ash is almost as powerful as the oak in mythology. Archaeologically, the presence of ash twigs has been found in prehistoric ritual shafts and its significance appears to have been recognised across Europe.[46] Aldhouse-Green[47] notes its association with healing. The role of the ash in mythology and tree worship has been touched upon in Chapter 1 and this tree played a role in many ancient religions. In

Greek mythology the tree was sacred to Poseidon, the second god of the Achaean trinity.[48] The Greek goddess Nemesis carried an ash branch 'as a symbol of the divine instrument of the justice of the gods', epitomising the female fates dispensing justice and measuring out mortal happiness or misery.[49] The tree was also regarded as one of the seasonal guises of Nemesis and associated with the watering of the earth. The Norse Tree of Life, Yggdrasill, sacred to Óðinn, was also seen to be an ash tree and Óðinn's hanging in the tree to receive wisdom and knowledge has strong shamanistic links; Paterson[50] claims that it was the Vikings' great reliance on the magic of the ash tree that led to them gaining their title of *Æscling* ('Men of Ash'). In Norse mythology, the first humans were brought to life by Óðinn and his brother from logs found on the sea-shore: the male became *Askr* 'ash', and the female *Embla* possibly 'elm' (or 'creeper'). Graves notes that the ash was also 'the tree of sea-power, or the power resident in water', and associates Óðinn's alias *Yggr*, from which Yggdrasill is derived, with *Hygra*, Greek for 'sea'.[51] Ash, *askr*, was also the Norse term often used to refer to a Viking ship, which may be another more pragmatic reason to refer to the Norse as 'ashmen'. In Celtic lore, three of the sacred trees guarding the provinces of Ireland were ashes: *Bile Tortan, Craeb Daithi* and *Bile* or *Craeb Uisnig*,[52] their fall symbolising the triumph of Christianity over paganism. The survival of tree reverence in association with this tree is, however, portrayed in south-western England in the boundary clause of the Taunton charter while, in the same county on the boundary of Manworthy in Milverton, there is also a charter reference to a 'pierced' ash which may indicate lingering superstition (below and Chapter 2). In Britain the ash remained associated in folklore with rebirth and new life. A 'Trysting Tree' stands close to the site of an Iron Age hillfort on Torberry Hill near West Harting in Hampshire, an old tree with a girth of 700cm but with a hollow centre. In past times – even as late as the nineteenth century – children could be passed through a deliberate split made in the trunk of a young ash to gain healing from the goddess of the tree.[53] The successful closure of the breach in the tree would indicate the effectiveness of the cure but this would only continue while the tree stayed alive and unharmed. The sap from a burnt ash stick was given to babies as their first spoonful of food in parts of Scotland.[54]

The 'holy ash' on the boundary of Taunton estates in Somerset and the 'pierced ash' in the same county have been discussed in Chapter 2, the first of these representing one of the rare examples of tree veneration to have crept into Old English documentary or literary sources. Moreover, the ash is also prominent in the folk legend that finds expression in saints' *Lives* and 'holy' wells. In the *Life of St Kenelm* (Cynehelm) it was an ash that grew when the boy-king planted his staff in the ground before his murder in the woods of Clent in north Worcestershire, and others are reputed to have grown from the staffs of other saints, among them those of Aldhelm, Eadwold at Cerne, Dorset, and St Oswald at Oswestry, Shropshire. At Ilam a bizarre narrative, depicted on the church font of *c.*1100, tells how Beorhthelm

Table 3. The frequency of individual tree species in charters
and early place-names

	Charters			Place-names			All names pre-1100	
	Total	%		Total	%		Total	%
Thorn	296	28.8	Thorn	138	19	Thorn	434	25
Oak	116	11.3	Ash	117	16	Ash	211	12
Willow	95	9	Oak	69	9.4	Oak	185	10.5
Ash	95	9	Broom	57	7.9	Willow	133	7.6
Apple	71	6.9	Willow	38	5.25	Apple	?94	5.4
Elder	48	4.7	Alder	30	4.1	Broom	78	4.5
Alder	40	3.9	Pear	29	4	Alder	70	4
Hazel	32	3.1	Hazel	28	3.9	Hazel	60	3.4
Maple	30	2.9	Apple	?23	3.2	Pear	56	3.2
Pear	27	2.9	Lime	?21	2.9	Elder	53	3
Lime	?27	2.6	Maple	20	2.8	Maple	50	2.8
Broom	21	2	Beech	18	2.5	Lime	48	2.7
Beech	19	1.8	Birch	17	2.4	Beech	37	2.1
Birch	17	1.7	Sallow	17	2.4	Birch	34	1.9
Sallow	13	1.7	Elm	15	2.3	Sallow	30	1.7
Elebēam	10	1.3	Plum	14	1.9	Holly	20	1.1
Yew	10	1	Yew	13	1.8	Elm	19	1
Holly	9	1	Holly	11	1.5	Plum	17	1
Gorse/Furze	?8		Box	10	1.4	Nut-tree	15	
Nut-tree	7		Aspen	10	1.4	Aspen	14	
Wych-elm	?7		Nut-tree	8	1.1	Yew	13	
Sloe	6		Furze/gorse	5		Furze/gorse	13	
Aspen	4		Elder	4		Box	12	
Service-tree	4		Sloe	4		*Elebēam*	10	
Ceacga	4		Wych-elm	3		Sloe	10	
Elm	4		*Ceacga*	2		Wych-elm	10	
Plum	3		*Cwicbēam*	?2		*Ceacga*	6	
Box	2		Privet	1		Service-tree	4	
Privet	1		Medlar	?1		Privet	2	
Cherry	?1		Ash-apple	–		*Cwicbēam*	?2	
Ash-apple	1		Cherry	–		Ash-apple	1	
Medlar	–		*Elebēam*	–		Cherry	?1	
Cwicbēam	–		Service-tree	–		Medlar	1	

Total charter recordings: 1028
Total early place-name recordings: 725
(% below 1 not given)

abducted an Irish princess but became a hermit after she had been eaten by wolves; the sacred tree of the saint was an ash that was still growing close to his well in the 1680s.[55] In herbals it is again the bark of the tree which seems most often to have been used, in the *Lacnunga* usually with the bark of other trees such as the 'quickbeam', willow, oak and so forth, either used as a salve (as for a sore or a headache) or drunk in ale and water.[56] In the *Leechdoms* the bark is used with that of other plants to produce a salve 'against blotch', leprosy, 'a penetrating worm', palsy and all wounds.[57]

The ash is a tree of considerable beauty with its delicate leaf pattern and fragile nature but is generous with its seeds, growing readily wherever it can remain undisturbed. It grows at its best only in suitable soils that are fertile, base rich and well drained but grows readily elsewhere as a poorer quality tree. Few ash-trees live longer than two hundred years but can readily be pollarded. A very large ash at Talley Abbey in Carmarthenshire, recently recorded and possibly the oldest ash-tree in Britain, has a girth of 1100cm, surpassing that found at Adfort House, Co. Tipperary in Ireland (girth 1056cm at 1.4m).[58] This tree is again common in charters and place-names. It is the fourth-commonest tree found as a charter boundary landmark, recorded at least 95 times (9% of tree names in this source) with four of these references occurring in the Welsh Llandaff charters under the tree's Latin name *fraxinus* or its Welsh name *onnen*, once as *rit yr onnenn* 'ash ford' (Table 3).[59] In several Latin bounds it appears under its Latin name *fraxinus*, as in two boundary clauses attached to a document 'adapted' in the tenth century, granting estates in West Sussex to Bishop Wilfrid: those of Tangmer and Pagham, or in the late bounds of Taunton.[60] In another late boundary clause, that of Purton, Wiltshire, it appears in a landmark *usque ad la freynne* 'to the ash-tree' (French *frêne*).[61] The ash is, however, the second-commonest tree recorded in early place-names, more common than oak, with over a hundred incidences, 16% of all early tree place-names and 12% of trees named in both charters and place-names. It is also more common than oak as the marker of hundred meeting-places, occurring in a pre-Conquest context in Herefordshire, Worcestershire, Somerset, Hampshire and Buckinghamshire (Tables 2 and 3).

In the charter boundary clauses, ashes are often referred to without any qualifying adjective, but they have been described as 'great' (Ham and Christian Malford, Wiltshire), 'tall' (Godmersham, Kent; Weston near Bath, Somerset), 'slender' (Pyrton, Oxfordshire), 'broad' (Crediton, Devon), 'old' (Havant, Hampshire), 'ivy-covered' (Winchester, Hampshire) or 'hollow' (Slackstead, Hampshire). They are found either singly, in groups, as in *þ æscbed* 'the ash-bed' of Himbleton, Worcestershire, and the ash 'hurst' of Hardenhuish, Wiltshire, and more rarely in woods – *æsclege* occurs on the boundaries of Halstock and Stalbridge Weston in Dorset.[62] In the boundary clauses, the tree is found associated with both hill and valley locations, probably where it was abundant, and with *beorg* 'hill or barrow' in Pucklechurch,

Gloucestershire, and Radstock, Somerset.[63] It is also found in watery locations such as alongside streams, meres and marshes. Various 'ashbourne' rivers are so-named, such as the earlier name for the River Yeo in Devon, which gave its name to Ashburton, or Ashbourne in Derbyshire (*Esseburne* in 1086), later to be known as the Henmore Brook, and Ashburnham in East Sussex (with *hamm*); it also occurs with the term *lacu* in Lyng, Somerset, and Rodbourne Cheney, Wiltshire.[64] The ash also occurs beside fords and springs – the latter on six separate occasions: in Baverstock, Wiltshire; Corston, Bleadon, Isle Abbots and Berrow in Somerset; Stoke Bishop, Gloucestershire, and with the streams issuing from ash springs in Topsham, Devon.[65] Only two ash-trees appear as stumps (both in Hampshire).[66] Landownership may be indicated by an association with personal names.

The ash is also found in some early hundred names, among them *Esch* in Worcestershire, Bromsash, 'Brōme's ash' in Herefordshire: *Bromesais* 1086, with *lēah* in *Ascleie* Somerset 1084 and *Esselei* Hampshire 1086, and with *dūn* in Ashendon in Buckinghamshire: *Essedene* 1086.[67] In early place-names it is also widespread, occurring far too frequently to discuss here in detail. It is probably the commonest tree to have given rise to a place-name and is especially frequent in more marginal areas, and common in Devon and Yorkshire. In a simplex form it is found, among many other such names, in Ash, Kent: *Ece* 1086; Ash in Stourpaine, Dorset: *Aisse* 1086; and Ash Priors, *Æsce* 1065, and Ashbrittle, *Aisse* 1086, in Somerset; in a dative plural form in Ashen, Essex: *Asce* 1086. Esher, Surrey, is 'district where ash-trees grow' (*Æscæron* 1005) incorporating *æsc* with OE *scearu* 'share, province' (as in OE *landscearu*). In place-names ash appears more frequently than oak in association with 'wood' terms, including names with *lēah* and *holt* (Aisholt, Somerset, *æscholt* 854), and, later, with 'grove'. *Æsc* with *lēah* is particularly common, as in East Ashley, Hampshire: *Esselie* 1086; Ashill, Norfolk: *Asscelea* 1086, and in many other early 'Ashley' names, found in Cambridgeshire, Gloucestershire, Cheshire, Northamptonshire and Staffordshire. The Old Norse term *viðr* 'wood' is found in the place-name Askwith in Weston, Yorkshire West Riding: *Ascvid* 1086 (with the ON form *askr*). With *feld*, open land close to a wooded region, it occurs in the names Ashfield and Great Ashfield, Suffolk: *Assefelda* and *Eascefelda* 1086. The ash-tree is often found associated with topographical terms for hills, probably where it occurred in some numbers: with *dūn* in Ashdon, Essex: *Ascenduna* 1086; and Ashendon, Buckinghamshire: *Assedune* 1086; with *hyll* in Ashill, Somerset: *Aisselle* 1086; with *hōh* 'hill spur' in Ashow, Warwickshire: *Asceshot* 1086; with *ofer* in Ashover, Derbyshire: *Essovre* 1086. It is also found with valley terms: with *denu* in a lost Ashden, Compton, Berkshire: *Assedone* 1086; with *cumb* in Ashcombe, Devon: *Aissecome* 1086; and in more watery locations with *mere* 'pool' in Ashmansworth, Hampshire: *Æscmaereswierthe* 909, and Ashmore, Dorset: *Aisemare* 1086; with *wella* 'spring or stream' in Ashwell, Hertfordshire: *Asceuuelle* 1086; Ashwellthorpe, Norfolk: *Æscewelle* c.1066, and Ashwell, Leicestershire, *Exewelle* 1086.

Compounded with the archaeological term *burh/burg* 'stronghold' it is found in Ashbury, Oxfordshire: *Eissesberie* 1086; a lost Asbury in Westerleigh, Gloucestershire: *on Æscburhg* 950, and Ashbury, Devon: *Esseberie* 1086; and with ford (the various Ashfords) in Derbyshire, Devon and Shropshire. It is extremely common with habitative terms, often occurring several times in one county so that additions were later made to the name to distinguish individual settlements. With the habitative term *tūn* it is found in Wiltshire in the names Ashton Keynes: *Æsctun* 880–5, and Steeple and West Ashton: *Æystone* 964, *Aistone* 1086; but other early Ashton names are found in Cheshire, Herefordshire, Northamptonshire (three examples), Gloucestershire, and Worcestershire. The OE *æsc* or ON *askr* with ON/ODan *býr/bȳ* is common in the east of the country with these terms found in Ashby St Mary, Norfolk: *Ascebei* 1086, for example. Such names are particularly common in the East Midlands. In Leicestershire are found Ashby de la Zouch: *Ascebi* 1086; Asby Folville: *Ascbi* 1086; and Ashby Magna and Parva: *Essebi* 1086. In Lincolnshire are found Ashby by Partney, Ashby de la Launde, Ashby cum Fenby, West Ashby and Ashby Puerorum, all *Aschebi* 1086. In Northamptonshire, the terms are met in Canons Ashby: *Ascebi* 1086; Castle Ashby: *Asebi* 1086; Cold Ashby: *Essebi* 1086; Mears Ashby: *Asbi* 1086; and Ashby St Ledgers: *Ascebi* 1086. Ash is found with *wīc* in Ashwick, Somerset: *Escewiche* 1086; and with *cot* in Ashcott, Somerset: *Aissecote* 1086. Askham names, *æsc* replaced by ON *askr* with *hām*, are found in Nottinghamshire and N Yorkshire. Only occasionally are personal names, presumably indicative of landownership, associated with the ash: Franche in Kidderminster, Worcestershire, may be 'Frea's ash-tree': *Frenesse* 1086, and Kippax, Yorkshire West Riding, is 'Cippa's or Cyppa's ash-tree': *Chipesch* 1086. Descriptive adjectives are also rare but Whitnash, Warwickshire, may be '(place at) the white ash-tree': *Witenas* 1086. The Cornish term for ash, *onnen*, has given rise to the river-name Inny (*Æni* 1044) 'ash-river'.

In charters and early place-names, the ash occurs in similar regions to the oak but is more frequent in a band across Somerset, west Berkshire and south Gloucestershire, regions where woodland was being actively assarted in the early medieval period.[68] It is particularly abundant in south Gloucestershire on the claylands around the area of the later forest of Kingswood, part of the band described above (Fig. 14). The ash is a tree that has increased over the centuries, often as secondary woodland on former farmland but also within areas of ancient woodland where it has replaced other species.[69] Ash today is still usually found in woodlands mixed with other trees. Ash-hazel woods are a feature of the both the damper areas of the East Midlands and East Anglia, of lower slopes from Cornwall to northern Scotland, and of drier limestone areas; dry ash-maple woods are found on the Mendips and elsewhere; ash with wych-elm is found in scattered locations from Devon and Somerset through Yorkshire into Scotland, including areas of heavy soils in Shropshire and Herefordshire; ash with lime to the north of the Thames and in the Mendips, with oak and

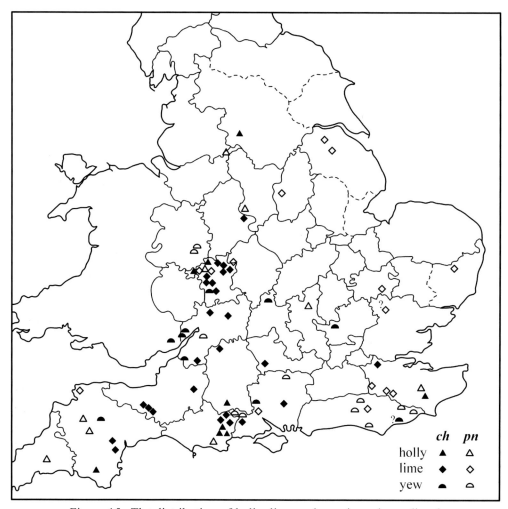

Figure 15. The distribution of holly, lime and yew in early medieval
charters and place-names

wych-elm in mid-south England, with oak and beech on the Cotswolds, Chilterns
and in mid-south England with outliers in south-east England, with beech in the
Wye Gorge, and with hornbeam in north-east and south-east Norfolk.[70] Given such
a widespread distribution, it is not perhaps surprising that this tree enjoys such a
wide coverage in charters and place-names.

The West Midlands is very much oak and ash countryside. Worcestershire was
one of the most heavily wooded counties at the time of the Domesday survey and
in the medieval period; Rackham estimates that woodland covered 40% of the land

area of the county in 1086 (as noted in Chapter 5).[71] All but the south-eastern part, the Vale of Evesham, was to become royal forest after the Conquest. It is the occurrence of the *lēah* term (Fig. 7) that provides the surest indication of the presence of woodland in the pre-Conquest period and the distribution of oak and ash in West Midland charters tends to mirror the distribution of this term, making allowance for gaps caused by the absence of charters (there are few charters for northern Warwickshire and a gap in central Gloucestershire). The oak and ash are two of the trees most commonly mentioned in charters. Rackham notes their presence in both 'ancient' and 'planned' landscapes, although they appear most often in the former, with 75% of the oaks, and 50% of the ashes, that he noted standing in 'ancient' countryside.[72] The distribution of these species may, therefore, be an important indication of landscape character and land use worthy of closer investigation.

OTHER TREES FREQUENT IN ANCIENT COUNTRYSIDE

The yew

Whereas the oak and ash are common in charters and place-names and are found scattered throughout the country, there are other species of ancient countryside which appear in more restricted areas. These include species which tend to be less tolerant of soil type or more sensitive to climatic exposure. The yew, *Taxus baccata* (OE *īw*, *ēow*, **īg*), has been noted most frequently in the charters and early place-names of southern England (although this is a distribution which may be affected by the availability of the charter evidence) (Table 3, Fig. 15). In the total number of tree names recorded here it occurs only ten times as a charter landmark with thirteen other early place-name recordings: only 1% of the trees noted as boundary landmarks and only 1.8% of those noted in early place-names.

The yew is one of the longest-lived trees and, apart from the possible exception of a very small number of oak trees, the only one likely, on occasions, to have survived as a living tree from Anglo-Saxon times, although yews are notoriously difficult to date. 'It shares with the oak the reputation of taking longer than any other tree to come to maturity, but is longer lived even than the oak'.[73] The symbolism of the yew as a tree associated with death and regeneration has already been mentioned in Chapter 2. This tree was held in veneration in many Indo-European cultures and was associated with death and the underworld in Roman literary tradition, an association found, too, in Germanic and Celtic tradition but with immortality and protection against evil enhancing its sacred role. It was, apparently, in Britain that the yew cult flourished and yew wands were said to have been used for divination in combination with ogham characters (see Chapter 3).[74] A yew was one of the sacred trees of Ireland. The Church accepted the yew as a symbol of the resurrection and used yew in its Easter and Palm Sunday rituals.

It was perhaps the association with resurrection, together perhaps with a belief in its protective power against evil influences, which accounts for the presence of the yew in many Christian graveyards, although the church may also have been sited on occasions close to an existing revered tree, perhaps a traditional meeting place or site of ritual. It has been claimed by some that a substantial number of yews appear to pre-date the nearby churches (see Chapter 2), but the suggested age of these trees has never been substantiated. Even if dating by dendrochronology were permitted, the majority of them today are hollow. In Much Marcle, in Hereford-shire, a giant hollow yew close to the church door may be over 1,000 years old. At Claverley, Shropshire, a yew with a girth of over 800cm may have been asso-ciated with a probable Romano-British burial site before the construction of the Norman church, and Alan Meredith has claimed a date for a yew of such girth in the region of 1,500 years.[75] At Loughton, Shropshire, below Clee Hill, a massive, contorted yew has produced a radiocarbon age of 550 +/-50 years from inside its hollow bole (girth over 1000cm, but from a spot which may have taken over 400 years to grow to this point, indicating again an age of over 1,000 years).[76] Other ancient yews stand in the Shropshire churchyards of Ashford Carbonel, Church Preen, Acton Scott and Uppington, and among the oldest are others at Clun (girth over 1000cm but very decayed) and Norbury (girth 1070cm at base). At Tandridge church in Surrey, the foundations of the possible Saxon building arch over the root of a yew which must have been large when the church was built (the present girth at 1.3m is 1100cm).[77] Another large churchyard yew can be found near Ashbrittle parish church in Somerset; this tree has girth at ground level of 1219cm (1158cm at 0.1m). It is surpassed in size, however, by the yew-tree at Brabourne parish church in Kent, which has a girth of 1797cm and one at Hampstead Marshall, Berkshire, with a girth of 1433cm. Other large churchyard yews include one at Kenn in Devon and, in Wales, at Discoed and Defynnoc in Powys and at Llangernyw in Conwy. The Ashbrittle yew grows on a mound said to be a tumulus and today consists of a central stem with six others, probably parts of a long decayed central trunk, but the central stem may have grown separately and represent a second tree (Tim Hills: TR). Another churchyard yew (or, more likely, yews) of considerable age is found at Llanerfyl, Powys, its trunk split into four huge twisted parts, and it has been found to overshadow a Christian grave from the fifth or sixth century, dedicated to 'Rustece, daughter of Paterninus'. The four trunks are, however, divided into three female and one male and may have again been derived from more than one original tree, the multiple boles fusing together; it shares the popular tradition of having grown from a saint's staff – here that of St Erfyl – planted in the ground. It became common for yews to be newly planted beside later churches, a practice recently being encouraged afresh. An even older date has been claimed for the Fortingall Yew found in a Perthshire churchyard; it is now in two distinct pieces with the old shell sending up new growth, and has been described as 'reputedly the oldest living thing in Europe' (girth said to be 1700cm in 1796).[78]

As the tree of resurrection, Graves notes how, in the Irish romance of *Naoise and Deidre*, yew stakes were driven through the corpses of the lovers to keep them apart, but the stakes sprouted and became trees whose tops eventually embraced over the cathedral of Armagh.[79] In a darker aspect, this tree was the death-tree of European countries, sacred to Hecate in Greece and Italy: black bulls wreathed with yew were sacrificed to this goddess. The Roman association of the yew with the goddess Hecate linked the yew with witches (as in Shakespeare's *Macbeth*), an association perhaps enhanced by its poisonous nature. A compound of the yew-berry, hellebore and devil's bit is said to have been used for poisoning weapons in early Ireland.[80] The sticky juice from beneath the bark was also a formidable arrow poison but as it took several hours to take effect its use in hunting animals was limited.[81] Unsurprisingly, the yew seldom appears in herbal cures, and the *eowberge* 'yew berry' appears only once, with other ingredients, in a cure for 'water elf disease', one of the 'cures' probably adopted from a pre-Christian past, for to effect the cure ale had to be poured over and a charm sung over the confection, but holy water had to be added.[82]

Reference to yew occurs in several versions of the *Rune Poem*, referring to its supposed properties or uses:

> (eoh) byputan   unsmeþe treow,
> heard hrusan fæst,   hyrde fyres,
> wyrtruman underwreþyd,   wynn on eþle.

> 'The yew is a tree with rough bark,
> hard and firm in the earth, a keeper of flame,
> well-supported by its roots, a pleasure to have on one's land'
> (The Old English *Rune Poem* XIII)[83]

> (ýr) er vetrgrønstre víða;
> vant er, er brennr, at svíða.

> '(yew) is the greenest of trees in winter;
> when it burns, it sputters.'   (The Norwegian *Rune Poem* XVI)[84]

> (ýr) er bendr bogi
> ok brotgjarnt járn
> ok fífu fárbauti

> '(yew) is bent bow
> and brittle iron
> and Farbauti (giant) of the arrow.'   (The Icelandic *Rune Poem* XVI)[85]

Today, however, it is known that the yew contains a substance (taxol) that can help to alleviate cancer. The association of the yew with bow wood is already established in Roman literature (e.g. Virgil's *Georgics* II).[86] The British yew was, however, later considered inferior to Spanish or Portuguese yew for this purpose, becoming brittle with age and with less pull. It has been claimed that in the reign of Richard III in 1483 it was ordered that yew should be planted in England for the use of archers but these references have never been substantiated by modern researchers.[87] The *Rune Poem* appears to suggest that the yew was a guardian of fire, i.e. a yew log on the hearth – which, incidentally, throws out great heat – but in folklore branches of yew were often kept as a protection against fire. In the main Sutton Hoo ship-burial (Mound 1), yew had been used for a number of buckets; these were bound with iron hoops and may have been used for the fermentation of an alcoholic drink associated with the burial ritual (Martin Comey, pers. comm.).

Although many probable ancient yews are known today, some supposedly 1,100 or more years old,[88] none of these seems to correspond with charter references; most probably stood well within estate boundaries, often close to a central church site. One 'old yew' *ðone ealde iw*, in Mickelmersh, Hampshire,[89] may recognise the longevity of this species, and on the boundary of this estate there was also a *iww cumb* but there are only a relatively small number of certain references to this tree in the boundary clauses – four of them on the margins of the Severn Basin. One yew is recorded in the Llandaff charters (Welsh *yw*, *ywen*) standing on a mound or a barrow on a Chepstow estate (see Chapter 2): the bounds run *ad cumulum iriuenn* 'to the mound of the yew-tree'.[90] In addition, a few references in Old English charters are to valleys with yews: *eow cumb* in Stoke Bishop, Gloucestershire; *iwdene* (and also, perhaps, *iwes heafdan*) in Tidenham, Gloucestershire, and *idene* in Flamstead, Hertfordshire, while yew or yews located upon high ground are noted in the *eowrhyc* 'yew ridge' on the boundary of Upton-on-Severn, Worcestershire.[91] The yew prefers (but is not restricted to) neutral or alkaline soils and its two locations in Gloucestershire, in Tidenham and Stoke Bishop, are located upon restricted outcrops of carboniferous limestone. The River Yeo in Crediton is referred to in the landmark *(on) eowan*, a name derived from the OE *īow* or a British equivalent, as is the River Iwerne in Dorset, *Iwern broc* 958, probably derived from Brit. *īwo-* 'yew', which gave its name to the estates of Iwerne Minster and Iwerne Courtney,[92] and *eow anwelles stream* may be a yew stream in Tadmarton, Oxfordshire (but a variant is *on eoppan welles stream*, now regarded as containing a personal name Eoppa).[93] There are other early 'yew' place-names. In Hampshire, Ewhurst: *(on) ywyrstae (stigele)* 1023, *Werste* in 1086, took its name from a wood and one still bears this name today, while Eyeworth: *Iuare* 1086, probably *Īwwaru*, is yew *īw* with *waru*, *wer*, which becomes modern 'weir' or fishpond. The trees referred to in these names were obviously often not single individuals, and yew woods are noted on several occasions – *īw* with *lēah* in the name of Uley, Gloucestershire: *Euuelege*

1086, and *īw* with *hyrst* in Ewhurst Manor, Shermanbury, West Sussex: *Luvehest* 1073; Ewhurst, Hampshire (above) and Ewhurst, East Sussex: both *Werste* 1086. Other early Sussex yew names are Ifield, West Sussex: *Ifelt* 1086 (with *feld*), Iford: *Niworde* 1086, and Iden (both East Sussex): *Idene* 1086 where *īw* is compounded with *denn*. In Shropshire *īw*, *ēow*, is compounded with *dūn* 'hill' in the names Eudon Burnell and Eudon George. Although the yew has sometimes been interpreted as a species of tree likely to mark a meeting-place, there are no early hundred names referring to this species.

Today, the yew is found on limestone soils within sessile-oak–ash–lime woods (stand type 4C), mostly in the Severn Basin, which is where it occurs in pre-Conquest charters, and in the beechwoods of southern England and the lower Severn estuary (stand types 8C, 8Eb). On light acid but freely drained soils it is found in sessile-oak–lime woods (stand type 5B), mostly in south-east Wales and parts of Lancashire and Cumbria, and in sessile-oak–hornbeam woods (stand subtype 9Ba) in south-eastern England.[94] Throughout history, individual specimens have been regarded with considerable interest, partly because with age and suitable conditions the tree can become particularly distinctive in form and partly because of its traditional symbolism, which has already been noted in Chapter 2. In West Sussex, near Chichester, in a chalk coomb known as Kingley Vale, now a nature reserve, yews grow so thickly that little light pierces the canopy. A dubious tradition claims that the trees were planted early in the ninth century to commemorate a defeat of the Vikings by the men of Chichester, but the trees may well be older (some twenty or so large old trees exist).[95] Here, several enormous old trees have branches that bend down to touch the ground, rooting to give rise to new young trees encircling the parent tree.

The holly

The holly, *Ilex aquifolium*, is not a tree commonly found in either early place-names or charters, but the references that do occur are mostly related to ancient countryside (in Rackham's lists, 11% of all trees in ancient countryside against 0.05% in planned countryside),[96] although *holen*, *holegn* 'holly' is often difficult to differentiate from *holh*, *holinga*, *holnes*, other words for 'hole, hollow, hollow place', as in the place-name Hollingden in Soulbury, Buckinghamshire, *Holendone* 1086, which could be either 'holly' or 'hollow' with *denu* 'valley'. Its frequency in charters and early place-names is similar to that of the yew (only 1% of the charter recordings referring to tree species and 1.5% of the early place-names: Table 3). In later names it may appear as *holm* or *hulver*. The *holenbedde*, *holne stoke*, *holen wicken* of Corfe, Dorset,[97] may all be references to the presence of hollies, also met in this county in the name of East and West Holme: *Holne* 1086. References to *þam gemæra æt þam holignan* 'the boundary at the hollies' (a place-name *Hollim* in the adjacent parish of Rock recorded by 1086), at Knighton-on-Teme and *ymman holig/holigne*,

Plate VI. Aged hollies on Lord's Hill, Shropshire

'Ymma's holly' at Old Swinford, both in Worcestershire, are undoubtedly to this tree, as is *ðæm beorge ðe mon hateð æt ðæm holne* 'the barrow which is called "at the holly"' in South Hams, Devon,[98] where early holly place-names are Hollam in Little Torrington: *Holnham* 1086, and Holne: *Holle* 1086. Hollington in Derbyshire and Hollington in East Sussex (both recorded as *Holintune* in 1086) are both 'farmstead where holly grows', Hollingworth, now Greater Manchester: *Holisurde* 1086, is 'holly enclosure'. The Cornish term for holly is *kelin*, found in the early recorded place-names of Kelynack in St Just in Penwith: *Chelenoch* 'holly-grove' 1086, and perhaps Clinnick in Braddock: *Clvnewic* 1086. A holly wood appears to be referred to in *holen hyrst*, a Wealden den, probably in the parish of Smarden, Kent, and another den is *Holanspic*, possibly in Brenchley, also in Kent.

Holly is a tree of woodland, wood-pasture and ancient hedgerows. It was once widely coppiced and pollarded to provide fodder for sheep and deer and might be protected for this reason in some royal forests. Above the reach of browsing animals, the holly's thorns are much less sharp and provided a valuable crop of leaf fodder that could be stored for the winter season. The frequency with which holly occurs in the medieval place-names of the West Riding of Yorkshire may reflect this value attached to it as a fodder tree in hilly districts: the leaves were often mashed to make them more edible, although the upper leaves are often without prickles. Holly woods are almost unique to the British Isles. Disliking hard winters, the holly is mainly a tree of western Britain but occurs commonly in eastern England as a woodland tree; it can be long-lived. It is found in many kinds of woodland, especially oakwoods, and is usually a tree of the understorey, common in the New Forest and Epping Forest and in other areas of wood-pasture, encountered, indeed, by Rackham in 'every forest and wooded common'.[99] There are still scatters of ancient hollies in what used to be the Stiperstones Forest of Shropshire, especially at Lords Hill on the north side of the Stiperstones above Snailbeach (Plate VI), although many are now in an advanced state of decay, contorted with age, perhaps the survivors of a once extensive oakwood.[100] Peterken has noted the remarkable size of hollies in Staverton Park, Suffolk, which have grown up since grazing diminished when sheep were excluded *c.*1820 (the Tree Register notes one 22.5m high with a girth of 236cm).[101] Of surviving trees, that with the widest girth recorded in the Tree Register is a specimen at Knightshayes, Tiverton in Devon (girth 713cm at 0.4m, height 12.0m), followed by another at Dundonnell House, Highland Region (girth 393cm at 1.3m, height 14m).

The evergreen leaves of the holly have represented immortality in some cultures and in England it was often considered unlucky to cut down a holly. The tree was sacred to the druids and the Romans (gifts of holly were given at the festival of Saturnalia which celebrated the birth of the sun-god at the time of the winter Solstice). It was thought to offer protection against elves and fairies if brought into the home over the midwinter festive season but had to be removed by Imbolc Eve (31 January), a custom transferred into the Christian beliefs associated with Twelfth Night, and the berries became associated with Christ's passion. The holly king appears in pagan belief as a manifestation of the tenacity of life, sometimes twinned with the oak king where the former reigned over the waxing tide from midwinter to midsummer while the holly king reigned over the waning tide from midsummer to midwinter.[102] Much of this was suppressed by the Church, which recognised these as blatantly erotic images. Graves notes the age-old mythological battle between the oak knight and the holly knight, the latter, as midwinter, sparing the former, midsummer, and argues that while the oak was taken over by John the Baptist so the latter was taken over by Jesus as 'John's merciful successor' and hence glorified beyond the oak:[103]

> Of all the trees that are in the wood
> The holly bears the crown.

He adds, however, that the holly may have replaced the scarlet-oak or holly oak, a sacred pair in Palestinian religion.[104]

The bark, and occasionally the leaf, of the holly form a part of some early remedies noted in the *Lacnunga* and the *Leechdoms*, used as a salve against toothache, leprosy and wounds or drunk in ale against a 'dry lung'. Taken in a hot infusion, holly leaves have a diaphoretic effect, causing sweating but helping to bring down fevers; the berries, however, are mildly poisonous.[105] As a timber, holly wood burns very hot and was used by smiths and weapon makers, used to make spear shafts and, later, cart and coach wheels; it is also dense, hard and heavy and has been used historically for carving and inlay work.

The lime

The lime played a part in the mythology of trees, for it was venerated as a holy tree by the ancient Germans and the Slavs. It was thought to ward off lightning and to possess the ability to absorb disease from those who touched it. It was seen as a 'feminine' tree, in contrast to the oak.[106] The flowers have a relaxant effect and have been used historically in infusions to relieve high blood pressure and promote sleep, while lime-flower tea has been used externally as a soothing lotion for the skin.[107]

The small-leaved lime or linden (to give its old vernacular name; it was also referred to as 'pry' in Essex and 'whitewood' in Worcestershire), *Tilia cordata* (OE *lind*), is a native species that has been described by Oliver Rackham as 'a living link with Mesolithic wildwood' and 'strongly associated with ancient woodland' and, hence, ancient countryside.[108] In early prehistoric times (*c.*4500 BC) lime was characteristic across south, south-eastern and midland England and in most pollen profiles comes out as the commonest tree.[109] Large-leaved lime, *Tilia platyphyllos*, also native, was always a much rarer species and usually found on limestone rocks. Numbers of lime fell drastically in many regions in the late Neolithic and Bronze Age, following the decline in elm, and it is thought that the tree was deliberately grubbed out and checked by grazing so that it became less common by Roman times. It is absent even from the charcoals of the Roman ironworks of the Weald[110] but this could be due to the fact that it was avoided as it had a tendency to reignite when the stacks were opened;[111] it is found in some early medieval Wealden place-names (see below). Earlier it had been one of the trees used to provide timber for the Sweet Track in the Somerset Levels.[112] Decline took place at different times and to differing degrees in different areas,[113] for elsewhere in some well-wooded regions such as Epping Forest, Essex, decline was apparently later, perhaps as late as the early medieval period.[114] Generally, in wood-pastures and medieval parks the lime gradually declined, according to Rackham, a trend that was irreversible, but from about 1,200 years ago woodland conservation and coppicing preserved it within many areas of ancient woodland. Rackham notes how in the New Forest lime was to give way in medieval times to oak and, subsequently, to beech, but he remarks upon the survival of 'great lime-trees and curious whitebeams' growing on the cliffs of the Avon Gorge at Bristol where they could not be reached by animals.[115]

The lime can tolerate poor soils and, like the oak and ash, can cope with damaging environmental conditions by reverting to a 'stag-head' condition, but the tree behaves like a relict in southern Britain: slow to re-establish itself and unlikely to colonise new ground. 'Successful establishment requires an unusual combination of circumstances in addition to a good seed year',[116] including freedom from competition, while coppicing might also reduce the chance of seed production. This tree can be either coppiced or pollarded, and in either case can be extremely long-lived. Amazingly, it is thought that the limes growing over the ramparts of Welshbury Iron Age hillfort in Westbury-on-Severn on the eastern margin of the Forest of Dean, Gloucestershire, come from root-stock which pre-dates the ramparts themselves or may even have been used to produce a coppiced palisade. Here, too, the lime appears to have escaped the taking of timber for the charcoal-burning operations carried out by Flaxley Abbey. Individual trees have suckered to give rise to groups of 'clones' now covering the ramparts and spreading over the interior of the fortified area.[117]

There are literary references to the use of the light wood of the lime for shields, so that *lind* was actually used to indicate 'shield': *Stod under linde, under leohtum scylde*, 'Stood he under the linden [shield], under the light shield'[118] and the linden shields are frequently mentioned in poems such as *Beowulf*, in one case described as 'yellow', in another 'white'. Thus in poetry *lindcroda* 'clash of shields' is a euphemism for battle,[119] *lindegecrod* or *lindwered* a 'troop armed with shields', *lindwiga* a 'warrior', *lindgestealla* a 'comrade in battle' (the last two in *Beowulf*). Historically, it was used in the wattle-work of medieval buildings: Rackham[120] illustrates lime rods taken at about seven years' growth, their bark removed for use as fibre, used for the rods in a house at Lavenham, Suffolk. The bark itself, referred to as bast, was used for making low-grade string and cordage. In Somerset, during lead-smelting operations, poles of lime were apparently thrown into molten lead in order to cause an explosion which would remove impurities. However, Amphlett and Rea, writing early in the twentieth century, considered that in a modern context 'the timber of the tree is comparatively worthless'.[121]

The tree has historically displayed scattered regional groupings,[122] and this also seems to be hinted at in the pre-Conquest record (Fig. 15). Not a conspicuous tree, the lime is not often found in charter boundary clauses, and is usually only mentioned because it was common in a particular location. These include hilly locations: the *lind oran* 'lime-tree bank' of Chalke, Wiltshire, or Pitminster, Somerset, the *lind hoh* 'lime-tree spur' of Bredon's Norton (on Bredon Hill), Worcestershire, and the *lind rycg* 'lime-tree ridge' of Powick, Worcestershire.[123] In valley locations, *lindescomeleighe* of Pilton, Somerset, is 'the wood of lime-tree coomb' and this tree must have been common, too, in the valleys of the *lindebourne* of the Brokenborough estate, Wiltshire, or the *lind broc* of Marchington, Staffordshire.[124] Where *lin* occurs with *lēah* 'wood' the reference is perhaps more likely to be to the *lind* tree than to OE *līn* 'flax', with the loss of the medial 'd'; this is found on the boundaries of Bishops Lydeard in Somerset and Horton in Dorset.[125] References to *lindune*

(Didlington, Dorset) could be either to 'lime-tree hill' or 'flax hill' and *lincumbe* (Ombersley, Worcestershire) could be 'coomb with lime-trees' or 'flax coomb' but in both cases association with the tree seems more likely.[126] But a 'great lime' is also recorded on the boundary of Pitminster, Somerset, of *Peadingtun*, Devon, and of both Powick and Tardebigge, Worcestershire, a *geapan linde* 'spreading lime-tree' on the boundary of *Hellerelege* (part of King's Norton, Birmingham), and a *gemearcodan lindan* 'mark linden', on the boundary of Horton in Dorset.[127] Given the problems of distinguishing OE *lind* from *līn*, the lime may form some 2.6% of the charter boundary trees, with apparent concentrations in east Dorset and Worcestershire, and only 2.9% of those in early place-names.

In the Worcestershire group, the two individual trees are recorded in the charters of the north-eastern part of the county, and in each case earlier or later recorded place-names suggest that the tree was common in both localities. 'The spreading linden' on the boundary of *Hellerelege* is found close to a settlement bearing the name Lindsworth in King's Norton, 'the enclosure/farm by the lime-trees', and 'the great linden' of Tardebigge is also noted again as the tree growing at the junction of the three boundaries of the parishes of Tardebigge, Alvechurch and Bromsgrove in a Cofton Hackett charter.[128] A later place-name, Linthurst, is recorded in the sixteenth century just over a mile away in Bromsgrove. Other linden names appear in the charters of the Malvern area, across the Severn on Bredon Hill and in Ombersley parish, and in north-west Worcestershire (Lindridge and a lost *Lindon* in Rock). Amphlett and Rea also record the presence of the tree in the Malvern, Lickey and Severn regions of the county in 1909.[129] The concentration of such names in Dorset and Worcestershire suggests that the tree was plentiful in these regions. Most of the early place-names lie in the Weald of south-eastern England, where it gave rise to a number of *lind* place-names close to the borders of Kent and Sussex, often the names of Wealden dens: in Kent, Lindridge and East Lindridge in Lamberhurst and Lindhurst in Edenbridge, and in Sussex, on the southern edge of the Weald, Lindfield (Fig. 12b). Interestingly, all these were wood-pasture regions despite Rackham's assertion that the lime tends to disappear from such an environment.[130]

Although the lime is rarely found in grazed parklands there are many small-leaved limes in the woods of Oakly Park, Shropshire, but one of the oldest surviving limes today is the Pitchford Lime in this county, which is an old large-leaved lime (*T. platyphyllos*) standing in the grounds of Pitchford Hall near Acton Burnell in the heart of the county. Holding a tree-house recorded by 1692 it has a girth of 741cm and is 14m tall; it must be over 400 years old. It is surpassed in size, however, by a specimen at Ancrum, Jedburgh (Scottish Borders), with a girth of 792cm, and by another in Moccas Park, Herefordshire (girth 776cm). Other, possibly older specimens of *Tilia cordata* are recorded at Dallam Park, Milnthorpe in Cumbria (girth 823cm at 0.5m; ht 16m), and at Worth, Crawley in West Sussex: girth 776cm; ht 23m). Another ancient lime pollard is found near Downton in northern Herefordshire. Many ornamental lime avenues were later planted in the period of landscaped parks, as at Hampton Court. The ornamental silver lime, *Tilia tomentosa*, from the Balkans and south-west Asia, was widely introduced in gardens at the end of the eighteenth century while the common lime, thought to be a hybrid between the small- and large-leaved limes, has also been frequently planted along city streets, the native small-leaved lime now mostly found within ancient woodland or old hedgerows.

ENDNOTES

[1] *CBDC*, pp. 46–8.

[2] S 255, B 1331, 1332 and 1333; *CBDC*, pp. 86–99.

[3] Rackham, *Trees and Woodland*, 2nd edn, p. 187.

[4] Aldhouse-Green, *Seeing the Wood for the Trees*, p. 20.

[5] Graves, *The White Goddess*, p. 171.

[6] Paterson, *Tree Wisdom*, pp. 176–7.

[7] Ibid., p. 178.

[8] *Life of St Boniface*: Talbot, *The Anglo-Saxon Missionaries in Germany*, pp. 45–6.

[9] Graves, *The White Goddess*, p. 173.

[10] For the earliest recordings of such rituals (twelfth century in France, thirteenth in England) see Hutton, *The Stations of the Sun*, p. 312; for the rather more imaginative interpretations of Robert Graves, see *The White Goddess*, p. 172.

[11] Grattan and Singer, *Anglo-Saxon Magic*, pp. 100–1.

[12] McIntyre, A., 'Tree culture', in A. Miles, *Silva. The Tree in Britain* (London, 1999), pp. 223–69.

[13] Halsall, *The Old English Rune Poem*, pp. 92–3, no. 25.

[14] D. Jenkins, ed. and trans., *Hywel Dda, the Law* (Llandysul, Dyfed, 1990), pp. 188–9.

[15] S 912, S 916, Crick, *Charters of St Albans*, nos 11 and 12 and p. 197.

[16] S 481, B 776; S 1004, K 772. The Old Englsih words will be given here as they appear in the actual documents, rather than in the nominative case, although this may be indicated.

[17] S 867, K 658; S 142, B 219.

[18] Attenborough, *The Laws of the Earliest English Kings*, pp. 50–1.

[19] S 1380, Dugdale, *Monasticum Anglicanum*, i.1443–6, no. 1 (sp); Hooke, *The Landscape of Anglo-Saxon Staffordshire*, pp. 78–81.

[20] S 1395, K 765, *WoASCB*, pp. 366–7.

[21] S 60, B 204 (sp), *WoASCB*, pp. 65–9; S 563, B 903; S 418, B 692, Miller, *Charters of the New Minster*, no. 10; S 567, Kelly, *Charters of Abingdon*, II, no. 51 (sp); Gelling, *Place-Names of Berkshire*, part III, pp. 732–3.

[22] S 1486, B 1289; S 473, B 751.

[23] S 377, B 625, B 626 (suspicious); S 878, Sawyer, *Charters of Burton*, n. 27; Hooke, *The Landscape of Anglo-Saxon Staffordshire*, pp. 88–90.

[24] Rackham, *Ancient Woodland*, revised edn, pp. 283–4.

[25] For example, S 412, B 674; S 364, B 588.

[26] A. H. Smith, *The Place-Names of the West Riding, Part IV*, English Place-Name Society 33 (Cambridge: 1961), p. 88; Anderson, *The English Hundred-Names*, pp. 13, 22–3.

[27] Anderson, *The English Hundred-Names, The South-Eastern Counties*, pp. 84–5.

[28] Mills, *A Dictionary of English Place-Names*, p. 24.

[29] Ibid., p. 132; A. Mawer and F. M. Stenton, *The Place-Names of Sussex, Part II* (Cambridge, 1986), English Place-Name Society 8 (Cambridge, 1986), pp. 359–60; *CDEPN*, p. 231 – Watts also cites another possible meaning for these names.

[30] Hooke, 'Medieval forests and parks'.

[31] Rackham, *Ancient Woodland*, revised edn, p. 293; Peterken, *Woodland Conservation*, pp. 15–17.

[32] S 359, B 594.

[33] J. Oliver and J. Davies, 'Savernake Forest oaks', *Wiltshire Archaeological and Natural History Magazine* 94 (2001), p. 26.

[34] J. Dryden, *Palamon and Arcite* III.i, line 1,058 (www.online-literature.com).

[35] A. Mitchell, *Trees of Britain* (London, 1996), pp. 312–13. Tree Register.

[36] Rackham, *Trees and Woodland*, 2nd edn, p. 14, citing W. Menzies, *The History of Windsor Great Park and Windsor Forest* (London, 1864).

[37] S 79, b 124, Hooke, *The Landscape of Anglo-Saxon England*, p. 22, pl. IV; *WaASCB*, pp. 30–6.

[38] Wilks, *Trees of the British Isles*, pp. 168–70.

[39] S 424, B 699 (sp).

[40] Oliver and Davies, 'Savernake Forest oaks', p. 33.

[41] Halsall, *The Old English Rune Poem*, pp. 92–3, no. 26.

[42] Ibid., p. 154.

[43] *The Battle of Maldon*, lines 43, 230, 310: Hamer, *A Choice of Anglo-Saxon Verse*, pp. 52–3, 64–5, 68–9.

[44] Cited by Bosworth and Toller, *An Anglo-Saxon Dictionary Based on the Manuscript Collections of the late Joseph Bosworth, D.D., F.R.S., Edited and Enlarged by T. Northcote Toller, M.A.* (Oxford, 1898), p. 19.

[45] S 766, Dugdale, *Monasticum Anglicanum*, ii.324–5 (no. 7); S 619, B 982; S 811, B 1319 (suspicious). However, it cannot always be possible to differentiate between the word used as a place of battle or, like the *acstede* of Hinton Ampner, Hants, and Calborne, Isle of Wight, and perhaps also the place-name Ashstead in Surrey (*Stede* in 1086), merely 'a stand of oak- or ash-trees'; see *CDEPN*, p. 22.

[46] R. Hutton, *The Pagan Religions of the Ancient British Isles. Their Nature and Legacy* (Oxford, 1991), p. 199.

[47] Aldhouse-Green, *Seeing the Wood for the Trees*, p. 20.

[48] Graves, *The White Goddess*, p. 163.

[49] Paterson, *Tree Wisdom*, p. 145.

[50] Ibid., p. 153.

[51] Graves, *The White Goddess*, p. 164.

[52] Lucas, 'The sacred trees of Ireland'.

[53] G. White, *The Natural History and Antiquities of Selborne* (London, 1789).

[54] Wilks, *Trees of the British Isles*, p. 139.

[55] J. Blair, 'A saint for every minster? Local cults in Anglo-Saxon England', in *Local Saints and Local Churches in the Early Medieval West*, ed. A. T. Thacker and R. Sharpe (Oxford, 2002), pp. 473, 483, 516, 530; Blair, *The Church in Anglo-Saxon Society*, pp. 476–7.

[56] Grattan and Singer, *Anglo-Saxon Magic*.

[57] Cockayne, *Leechdoms*, II.

[58] www.ancient-tree-hunt.org.uk; www.treeregister.org

[59] *Fraxinus*: Llandaff Charters 51: Evans, *The Text of the Book of Llandâv*, pp. 171–3; *onnen*: *Llandaff Charters*, 51: pp. 173–4; 59: pp. 201–2; 75: 249–5.

60 S 230, B 50, Kelly, *Charters of Selsey*, App. 2, p. 100; S 311, B 476 (sp).

61 S 1586, B 279a, Kelly, *Charters of Malmesbury*, no. 43.

62 S 219, B 552, Hooke *WoASCB*, pp. 129–34; S 308, B 469 (sp, possibly C11); S 290, M. A. O'Donovan, ed., *The Charters of Sherborne*, Anglo-Saxon Charters III (Oxford, 1988), no. 3; S 423, O'Donovan, op. cit., no. 8 (sp).

63 S 553, B 887 (sp); S 854, K 743 (sp).

64 S 1547, B 1323, *CBDC*, pp. 217–24; S 918, K 1305, *Charters of Abingdon*, II, no. 135 (suspicious).

65 S 766, Dugdale, *Monasticum Anglicanum*, ii.324–5 (no. 7); S 785, B 1287; S 606, B 959 and S 804, B 1313 (sp); S 740, E. H. Bates, ed., with notes by W. H. Stevenson, *Two Cartularies of the Benedictine Abbeys of Muchelney and Athelney in the County of Somerset* (Somerset Record Society, xiv, 1899) p. 48, no. 7; S 793, B 1291; S 1317, B 1236.

66 S 693, B 1077, B 1078; S 444, B 731.

67 Anderson, *The English Hundred-Names*, pp. 144, 167–8; *The English Hundred-Names, The South-Western Counties*, p. 36, 185; *The English Hundred-Names, The South-Eastern Counties*, p. 6.

68 For Berkshire see Hooke, 'Regional variation', pp. 141–6.

69 Rackham, *Trees and Woodland*, 2nd edn, p. 32.

70 Ibid., pp. 127–9.

71 Ibid., p. 50, table 2.

72 Rackham, *The History of the Countryside*, p. 211, table 10.1; 1990, 187, table 6.

73 Graves, *The White Goddess*, p. 189.

74 Elliott, 'Runes, yews, and magic', pp. 253–4.

75 Cited by Morton, *The Trees of Shropshire*, p. 28.

76 Ibid., pp. 31–2.

77 Mitchell, *Trees of Britain*, pp. 157–8.

78 A. Morton, *Tree Heritage of Britain and Ireland* (Shrewsbury, 1998), pp. 176–8. Long since split into separate parts, this tree is now unmeasurable.

79 Graves, *The White Goddess*, p. 189.

80 Ibid.

81 D. Stuart, *Dangerous Garden. The Quest for Plants to Change our Lives* (London, 2004), pp. 127, 130.

82 *Leechdoms* III.lxiii: Cockayne, II, pp. 350–1.

83 Halsall, *The Old English Rune Poem*, pp. 88–9.

84 Ibid., p. 183.

85 Ibid., p. 186.

86 Virgil, *Georgics* II, line 448: R. A. B. Mynors, *Virgil, Georgics, Edited with a Commentary* (Oxford 1969/1990), p. l: *Ituraeos taxi torquentur in arcus*; Mynors (p. 160) notes that the Itureans were inhabitants of part of Ceole-Syria, north-east of Palestine, famous as archers.

87 J. Lowe, *Yew-trees of Great Britain and Ireland* (London, 1897), p. 103; Bevan-Jones, *The Ancient Yew*, p. 44.

88 Mitchell, *Trees of Britain*, pp. 153–8.

89 S 857, K 652.

90 *Llandaff Charters* 49: Evans, *The Text of the Book of Llandâv*, p. 166.

91 S 218, B 551; S 610, B 927; S 912, K 672, Crick, *Charters of St Albans*, no.11; S 1300, B 1088, *WoASCB*, pp. 244–7.

92 S 255, B 1331, 1332 and 1333 (bounds added), *CBDC*, pp. 86–99; Ekwall, *English River-Names*, pp. 480–1, 268.

[93] Gelling, *Place-Names of Oxfordshire, Part II*, English Place-Name Society 24 (Cambridge, 1954), p. 488; S 584, B 967, Kelly, *Charters of Abingdon*, II, no. 68 (sp), based upon S 611, B 966.

[94] Peterken, *Woodland Conservation*, ch. 7, pp. 107–74.

[95] Wilks, *Trees of the British Isles*, p. 65.

[96] Rackham, *Trees and Woodland*, 2nd edn, p. 187, table 6.

[97] S 573, B 910, Kelly, *Charters of Shaftesbury*, no. 20 (sp – conflation of S 534 and S 632, forged shortly after the Conquest: Kelly, op. cit., pp. 82–3 and Electronic Sawyer).

[98] S 1185, B 1007, *WoASCB*, pp. 82–7; S 579, B 1023, S. E. Kelly, ed., *Charters of Bath and Wells*, Anglo-Saxon Charters XIII (Oxford, 2007) no. 30 (sp); *WoASCB*, pp. 162–7; S 298, B 451, *CBDC*, pp. 105–12.

[99] Ibid., p. 347.

[100] Morton, *The Trees of Shropshire*, pp. 74, 76.

[101] G. F. Peterken, 'Development of vegetation in Staverton Park, Suffolk', *Field Studies* 3 (1969), pp. 1–39. The Tree Register.

[102] Paterson, *Tree Wisdom*, pp. 34–8.

[103] Graves, *The White Goddess*, pp. 174–6.

[104] Ibid., p. 175.

[105] McIntyre, 'Tree culture', pp. 238–9.

[106] Becker, *The Continuum Encyclopedia*, pp. 178–9.

[107] McIntyre, 'Tree culture', p. 244.

[108] Rackham, *Trees and Woodland*, 2nd edn, pp. 132, 187.

[109] Ibid., pp. 28–33.

[110] J. Turner, 'The *Tilia* decline: an anthropogenic interpretation', *New Phytologist* 61 (1962); H. Cleere, 'Some operating parameters for Roman ironworks', *Bulletin of the Institute of Archaeology* 13 (1976).

[111] Rackham, *Ancient Woodland*, revised edn, p. 242 citing G. B. Hughes, *Living Crafts* (London, 1953).

[112] J. M. Coles, F. A. Hibbert and B. J. Orme, 'Prehistoric roads and tracks in Somerset: 3. The Sweet Track', *Proceedings of the Prehistorical Society* 39 (1973); B. Coles and J. Coles, *Sweet Track to Glastonbury: The Somerset Levels in Prehistory*, London, 1986).

[113] Rackham, *Ancient Woodland*, revised edn, p. 239.

[114] C. A. Baker, P. A. Moxey and P. M. Oxford, 'Woodland continuity and change in Epping Forest', *Field Studies* 4 (1978); but see Dark, *The Environment of Britain*, pp. 141–2.

[115] Rackham, *Trees and Woodland*, 2nd edn, pp. 150, 174.

[116] Rackham, *Ancient Woodland*, revised edn, p. 243.

[117] *Ex inf.* R Jarman; unpublished report Andre Berry.

[118] *Metrical Charms*, British Library, Harley 585: Dobbie, *The Anglo-Saxon Minor Poems*, p. 122.

[119] *Genesis* line 1998: Krapp, *The Junius Mansuscript*, p. 60.

[120] Rackham, *Trees and Woodland*, 2nd edn, pl. IX.

[121] J. Amphlett and C. Rea, *The Botany of Worcestershire* (Birmingham, 1909), p. 67.

[122] Rackham, *Ancient Woodland*, revised edn, p. 237.

[123] S 582, B 917 (bounds probably later: Kelly, *Charters of Shaftesbury*, p. 88 and Electronic Sawyer); S 440, B 729 and S 475, B 770; S 786, B 1282, *WoASCB*, pp. 177–90, 208–15.

[124] S 247, B 112 (?adapted from S 248 late C10); S 1577, B 922; S 557, B 890, Sawyer, *Charters of Burton*, no. 11; Hooke, *The Landscape of Anglo-Saxon Staffordshire*, pp. 103–6.

[125] S 380, B 610 (?suspicious); S 969, K 1318, O'Donovan, *Charters of Sherborne*, no. 20A.

[126] S 519, B 818; S 54, B 116 (sp) and S 1594, K 1355, *WoASCB*, pp. 36–40, 371–3.

[127] S 1006, K 774; S 786, B 1282 (suspect), *WoASCB*, pp. 208–15; S 1598, Hearne, *Heming*, p. 362; *WoASCB*, pp. 403–7; S 64, B 123, *WoASCB*, pp. 58–61 (uncertain location); S 969, K 1318, O'Donovan, *Charters of Sherborne*, no. 20A.

[128] S 1272, B 455 (1), *WoASCB*, pp. 135–42.

[129] Amphlett and Rea, *The Botany of Worcestershire*.

[130] Rackham, *Ancient Woodland*, revised edn, p. 253; *The History of the Countryside*, p. 140–1.

9

Trees of Wet Places in Early Medieval Records: Alder and Willow

There were large areas of undrained land in Anglo-Saxon England. The underground drains of later historical times were, of course, not available and arable land probably already relied heavily upon ridge and furrow ploughing to remove surplus rainwater. Undoubtedly there were also deliberately cut ditches to alleviate flooding but the many references to marsh and fen in charter boundary clauses clearly indicate the presence of scattered patches of ill-drained land throughout most of the countryside. Extensive fenlands such as those around the Wash in eastern England were not to be drained on a large scale for many centuries and the Somerset Levels were particularly extensive until reclamation was undertaken by ecclesiastical landowners in the thirteenth century; patches of marshland like the Weald Moors of Shropshire, previously used as seasonal pasture, only yielded to agricultural improvement after the mid-sixteenth century. Many ill-drained areas like Otmoor in Oxfordshire had to wait until the enclosure movement of the eighteenth and nineteenth centuries before they were drained for farmland. In Worcestershire, pre-Conquest charters reveal the presence of many areas of marshland, some extensive, some less so: *byligan fen* 'the ?bag-shaped fen', for instance, was a low-lying area of marshy land at the head of the Whitsun Brook in the heart of the county, and Longdon marsh was once much extensive on the low plain below the Malvern Hills.[1] In Cornwall the little estate of Lamorran at the head of an inlet near Truro on the south coast was almost completely bounded by streams and marshes.[2]

In addition, floodplains were valued for their hay crop, itself dependent upon the annual floodwaters that encouraged the growth of grass in the spring. Many species of tree flourished in damp conditions, most notably the alder and willow. Even today, alderwoods are a feature of stream and river banks in valleys and on damp spring-fed slopes – wherever water is running and not stagnant – and willows are distinctive features of the landscape, especially along water meadows.

THE ALDER

The alder, *Alnus glutinosa*, sometimes known as 'the aller' (OE *alor*) is not a long-lived tree, seldom surviving more than 150 years unless pollarded, but readily grows from seed carried along by flowing water. It may reach a height of about 19m. It is one of the commonest trees recorded in charter boundary clauses and in early place-names; Rackham places it sixth in his list of charter occurrences and in his list of settlement names;[3] in the present study it has been found to lie seventh in the list of charter occurrences (and just over 4% of all tree names, as noted in Table 3). It is often called the black alder, perhaps because once its seeds have spread the small blackish cones remain on the tree; this characteristic may be covered by the Old English name *fūla bēam*. Another native shrub, *Rhamnus fragula*, the alder buckthorn or 'the berry-bearing alder', also grows in swamps and damp places and may be the OE *spracen* of the herbals.[4] It is a smaller shrub, growing to little more than 5m, and is unlikely to have drawn attention as a suitable landmark tree. Alder occurs in the *Leechdoms*, its bark used against 'white spot of the eye', deafness, in a drink for 'pocks', for 'a milt-sick man' (illness of the spleen, ?wind), against 'dry lung', coughs, as an emetic and so forth.[5] Historically, it was used to stop bleeding because of its astringent properties.[6]

As a timber, alder is resistant to alternate wetting and drying, which made it useful in historical times for clogs, brooms and so forth. It was also used as early as *c.*3200 BC with oak, ash, lime, hazel and holly in the poles used for the Sweet Track in Somerset, with alder and hazel pegs holding the larger planks in place.[7] In Anglo-Saxon times it was the commonest wood used to produce turned drinking vessels. In historical times, it also produced high quality charcoal suitable for producing gunpowder.[8] These attributes may account for its role in legendary sources, especially the connection with fire and the fact that it yielded the best charcoal. In early Welsh literature, alder, *Fearn*, was, according to Graves, the tree of Bran. Bran's sister's son was said to have been burned in a bonfire and Graves notes that 'in country districts of Ireland the crime of felling a sacred alder is held to be visited with the burning down of one's house'.[9] Bran also bridged the River Linon by using alder piles, just as early European lake houses were built on alder piles at the edges of lakes. In Irish legend the first male was said to have been created from alder;[10] here it was regarded as a 'faerie tree' able to grant access to faerie realms. The alder has also been used to produce pipes for playing.

The sap of the tree flows readily when the bark is cut and this property has attracted attention in the realms of folklore, together with its burning qualities, although little of this appears in Old English literary sources. Indeed, the fact that it seems to bleed crimson sap, akin to blood, when felled, has given it a reputation of sanctity, and the green dye obtained from the flowers associated it with the clothes of fairy folk. Graves, in his interpretation of the 'Tree Alphabet', associates the alder

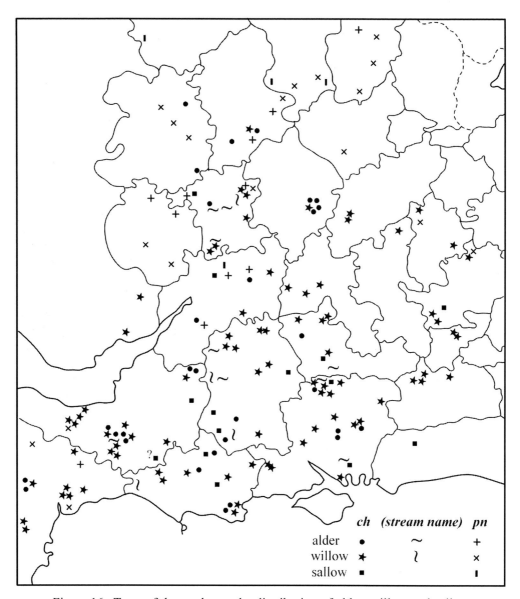

Figure 16. Trees of damp places: the distribution of alder, willow and sallow
in early medieval charters and place-names

with 'the fourth month' extending from 18 March, when the alder first blooms, to 14 April, marking the drying up of winter floods in the spring sun.[11] When first cut, the wood takes on a blood-orange tinge, as if bleeding, a characteristic that again gave rise in old German legend to the belief that the the tree was the embodiment of a malign spirit, the *Erlkönig*.[12] The bark, fruit and leaves of the alder have been used in dyes, its bark producing a fiery red colour, its flowers a shade of green and its twigs a shade of brown.

In the charters, the alder is found in association with the valley term *cumbe* on several occasions, but more often in stream names, either compounded with *burna*, *broc* or *rið(e)* as in the *alleburne*, *alorburna*, *alr broc*, *aler riðe*, and so forth, or alone, as in *alar* and *alr* (Fig. 16) (the *alorburnan*, now the Elborne, occurs six times in the charters of north Hampshire, but all refer to the same river). An *alre wyllan* 'alder spring' is recorded on the boundary of Withington, Gloucestershire, and several 'alder fords' are recorded.[13] There are few adjectives describing the charter alders, although the *ða greata alres* 'the great alders' are recorded close to marshy stream valleys on the boundary of Ogley Hay, Staffordshire, and a *wonalre* 'crooked alder' on the boundary of East Orchard, Dorset.[14] Reference to *hreod alras*, 'reed alders', suggests damp ground in Bishops Lydeard, Somerset, while *hafu-calras* 'hawk alders' occurs on the boundary of Taunton estates in Somerset (the only alders in charters to be associated with a plant or an animal).[15] The *ibihttan alr* of Creech, Somerset, may be 'ivy-covered' (OE *ī̆fihtan*).[16] Alder stubs are not usually found and those recorded on the boundary of Long Itchington in Warwickshire as *þone ælrenan stob* and *þæm ælrenan stobbe* may be a scribal error, for the first of these is described as *þam ællenstibbe* 'the elder stub' in a contiguous clause of Southam.[17] Some references indicate that the alders were often growing in small woods or thickets as when the name is compounded with shaw (OE *sceaga*), as in Upper Arley, Staffordshire; Crediton, Devon; and Bilston and Wednesfield, Staffordshire.[18] Other references include a *litlan alh rewe* 'little alder row' on the boundary of Meon and Privett, Hampshire, the *ælrbed* 'alder bed' of Hardwell, Berkshire, and the *alra ofesce* 'edge of the alders' at Grimley, Worcestershire.[19] The Cornish term *guern* appears in the boundary landmark *penn lidanuwern* 'head of the wide alder-swamp' in Tregony, Cornwall.[20]

The early alder place-names are similar: some are merely references to the alder alone (three in Devon); others associate the tree with streams (Arbrook Surrey; Alderbourne, Buckinghamshire) or marshy ground (Yorkshire North Riding), and with fords. A few indicate woods or small woods (e.g. Alderley, Gloucestershire) and a few associate the alder with a habitative name (Orleton, Worcestershire: *Ealretune* 1023, *Alretune* 1086; and Orleton, Herefordshire: *Alretun*(e) 1086; and four times in the Ridings of Yorkshire). The British name for alder swamp, **u̯erno-*, PrW **werned*, is found in the Cheshire name Werneth: *Warnet* 1086, and, as Welsh *guern*, in the Herefordshire place-name Llanwarne: *Lann Guern* eighth century, the latter indicating 'church by the alder-swamp'.[21] The Scandinavian form *elri* is found in Ellerburn, Thornton Dale, and Ellerbeck, Osmotherly, Yorkshire North Riding; Ellerton and Ellerker (with *kiarr* 'marsh'), Yorkshire East Riding. This tree occurs only in 4% of all the tree names recorded.

Alders are frequently pollarded; some of the oldest alder pollards are to be found in Scotland. Few alders are notable because of their size but a specimen at Coniston in Cumbria has a girth of 647cm and another in Chatsworth Park, Derbyshire, a girth of 609cm; the tallest specimen in England is an alder found at Luton, Bedfordshire, which is 31 metres tall.[22]

THE WILLOW

Willows have always been familiar trees along rivers and streams in England and there are no fewer than nineteen species of willow native to Britain, ranging in size from 30 metres tall to tiny ground-hugging shrubs. There are, however, fewer common varieties. Fine specimens of willow can be seen in many waterside locations: Wicken Fen in Cambridgeshire has notable examples of the great sallow, the goat willow or 'sally withy', *Salix caprea*, and the Lugg Meadows in Herefordshire fine white willows, *Salix alba*. The white willow, *Salix alba*, and the crack willow, *Salix fragilis*, are both relatively tall trees reaching 25m, which have long narrow leaves, and the male tree of both species bears similar yellow catkins; the silver hairs, denser on the underside of the leaf, characterise the former of these while the twigs of the crack willow are particularly brittle, snapping off easily. Both could be pollarded for small poles suitable for fencing, wattle, basketry or firewood and charcoal. Large speciman trees are found at Amberley Wild Brooks in West Sussex and Moreton-on-Lugg, Herefordshire. The goat willow or great sallow, on the other hand, *Salix caprea*, has more rounded leaves and bears the stubby grey catkins which give rise to its common name of 'pussy willow'. Like the grey sallow, *Salix cinerea*, it is a smaller tree reaching only 10m. The osier, *Salix viminalis*, another small willow with long leaves native to Britain, has been historically cultivated beside water but coppiced rather than pollarded to produce pliant withies suitable for the manufacture of baskets, fish-traps, chairs, and so forth. At Colwick in Nottinghamshire oak, holly and hawthorn posts were interlaced in a double row with hurdles of hazel and willow to make a fish weir across the River Trent in the ninth century. A later (eleventh-century) weir used hazel and alder for the interlacing.[23]

The willow had a role in Classical mythology, being associated with Persephone, queen of the Underworld, and Demeter, the Greek goddess of the earth, who had a sacred grove which is said to have contained black poplars and willows. Willows were said to have been used in water magic and witchcraft, and the sorceress of Greek legend, Circe, had a riverside cemetery planted with willows dedicated to

Hecate and her moon magic. Even in Christian literature, the 'weeping willows' dropped their branches in sympathy for the Jews in captivity. Used in folk custom as a funerary herb, it was advisable to 'plant a willow and allow it to grow, to ease the passage of your soul at death'. To 'wear the willow' was to grieve openly and garlands for mourning were traditionally woven from willow branches.[24] The wearing of the willow in a hat was also, however, to become the sign of the rejected lover. The willow has a place in healing. It appears in the *Lacnunga* where its bark, mixed with that of the ash, oak, crab apple and sallow taken from 'the nether part and from the eastward side of the trees', boiled together with the leaves of woodbine 'in holy water', was used to make a salve for a sore or a bone salve 'good for headache'.[25] The leaves of the 'red sallow' also formed part of a potion 'for any evil'.[26] In the *Leechdoms*, the bark of withy and sallow were part of a mixture against shingles and a salve for 'every wound'; willow was burnt, mixed with other ingredients, and applied against headaches and warts; its leaves pounded in oil as a smear against baldness.[27] In later folk medicine, the willow was thought to ease rheumatism and other conditions aggravated by damp weather. It is now known that its bark and leaves contain salicylic acid, a painkiller that was subsequently to be the source of aspirin.

The Anglo-Saxon names appear to differentiate clearly between these species, for the sallows are OE *sealh*, **sele*, ON *selja* 'sallow', the others *welig*, **wilig*, *wīðig* 'willow, withy', **wiligen*, **wiðigen* 'growing with willows', **wīðign* ('?willow copse'); with *wiliht* meaning 'full of willows', and *wiliga* meaning 'basket', indicating a common usage of these species.[28] The Scandinavian term *víðir* may be found in the place-name Withgill in Great Mitton, Yorkshire West Riding, while the Cornish term for willow is *heligen*, as in Halligey in St Martin in Meneage, Cornwall: *Heligin*, *Heligi* 1086. The *haran wiðig* may, however, have been the whitebeam, known as the 'hoar withy' or the 'whitten, whittenbeam' ('the tree that goes white') in Hampshire (see Chapter 11).[29] References to the *haran wiðig* occur in the boundary clauses of Pendock, Worcestershire, South Cerney, Gloucestershire; and Horton, Dorset.[30]

References to willows are particularly common in Anglo-Saxon boundary clauses – the third most common tree recorded (Table 3), and forming (with sallow) just over 9% of all the tree references noted, equally distributed across both ancient and planned landscapes. Charters and place-names naturally reveal concentrations in certain damp low-lying areas. Withiel Florey, which lies in a tributary valley of the Exe below the Brendon Hills in Somerset, is *Withiglea* in 737 and its charter-bounds note a *wiðig slede/slæde* (valley), *wiðig leagate* (gate to willow wood) and *wiðig mor* (marsh),[31] clearly indicating an abundance of willows in the vicinity. Withycombe 'valley where willows grow' is found on the northern side of the hills, and others abound in the Vale of Taunton (there are more willows recorded in Somerset boundary clauses than in any other county). However, single willows are also commonly found as boundary markers, as at Sevington in Wiltshire, Buckland Newton and Purbeck in Dorset and Ottery St Mary in Devon; that at Buckland, Berkshire, is described as 'the westernmost willow'.[32] It is a 'great withy' that is noted at Eastcourt, Wiltshire; Abingdon/Wootton and Sunningwell, Berkshire (now Oxfordshire); and Chertsey, Surrey,[33] while an 'old withy' occurs in the bounds of Moredon, Rodney Cheney and Ebbesborne/Combe Bassett, Wiltshire,[34] a willow stub at Fen Stanton, Huntingdonshire,[35] and at Buckland, Berkshire. Þene blake wiþge at Chersey and Thorpe/Egham, and þan blake wiþig at Egham, Surrey, may be 'the pale willow' (OE blāc, 'bright, shining, pale'), probably the white willow.[36] In the Llandaff Charters the willow is noted four times, twice as willow woods, either as Latin salix or Welsh helyg, pl. helygen (sometimes both in one clause as ad salices hir helicluin beticelli 'as far as the willows; the willow-wood as far as the Gelli' at Penn Celli Guenhuc), or irhelicluin 'the willow-wood'.[37]

Willows are often recorded as groups characterising a specific location and are, not surprisingly, frequently found in association with watery locations: especially with meres (around thirteen in charter bounds, once in a place-name), but also, less frequently, with pools, marshes, springs, brooks and other watercourses, and, in such a location, with fords or meadows. Others occur with healh 'corner, nook, small hollow', and with 'pit'. The numerous withy beds, recorded at Dauntsey, Rodbourne and Christian Malford in Wiltshire, Wootton and Sunningwell/Abingdon formerly in Berkshire, Corfe in Dorset and Long Itchington in Warwickshire, are likely to have been used for their produce. As valleys, several withy coombs and slades are noted (coombs in Pitminster, as well as Withycombe, Somerset, and With-ycombe Raleigh, Devon; slades in Pitminster, Withiel Florey and Creech, Somerset; Crediton, and Ayshford and Boehill, Devon) but also with a ridge in Witheridge, Devon, and a barrow in Willbury Hill in Stotfold, Bedfordshire. Willow thickets (þȳfel) are noted at Ecchinswell, Hampshire; Mapperton in Almer, Dorset; Clyst Wicon, Devon; and at Purbeck and Mapperton in Almer, Dorset; a row of willows also at Clyst Wicon, and a withighege 'willow hedge' at Halstock, Dorset.[38] A willow lēah is likely to have been a willow wood, as at Withiel Florey in Somerset, Willey in Shropshire and Widley Copse in Swinbrok and Widford, Oxfordshire; at Rimpton in Somerset the boundary ran to widig leas wyrttruman ' the roots (?wood bank) of willow wood',[39] while willow groves are recorded at Stoke by Hurstbourne and Highclere in Hampshire. Some settlements were also named as 'at the willows', places where willows grew (Wellow, Isle of Wight; Widey in Egg Buckland, Devon; Willey Hundred, Bedfordshire; Welwyn, Hertfordshire; Willian and Wilbury Farm in Norton, Hertfordshire; Widdington, Essex; Winnall in Allensmore, Herefordshire); with OE weorð ('farm/enclosure') in Wythall (wiððan weorðing) and Wythwood: Witeurde 1086, in King's Norton, both in north-east Worcestershire; with toft at a lost Willitoft in Patrington, Yorkshire East Riding, or with tūn (Wilton in Bridstow,

Herefordshire; Withington, Gloucestershire; Weeton, Little Wighton in Rowley, Yorkshire East Riding; Weeton in Harewood, Yorkshire West Riding).

References to the sallow in charters and place-names are similar but fewer: river-names include the *seleborne* which gave its name to Selborne, Hampshire (and the estate name Selborne), probably referring to sallows in the vicinity, and a landmark *on sele næticas* in Kingsbury, Hertfordshire, is probably to 'the sallow place where there are clumps of marsh grass' (OE *nættoc* associated with wet areas); a post-Conquest boundary clause of Cassio, Hertfordshire, also notes *hægþorn nætican* and *wiðig nætican* – i.e. this term with 'hawthorn' and 'willow'.[40] The great western woodland of Selwood, however, bordering the heartland of Wessex and recorded in the ninth century in the *Anglo-Saxon Chronicle*, seems to have been 'the sallow wood'.[41] The Old English term **sele* can be difficult to distinguish from the same term *sele* 'a dwelling, a house, a hall' and **sele* 'a bog' and, in charters, *þone sele* of Littleham, Devon, or *on ðac sele heal* 'to the ?sallow nook', of Meon, Hampshire, might be any of these, although reference to the tree is perhaps more likely, and a landmark *ðone ealdan sele* of Preston, Somerset, is certainly more likely to be 'the old sallow'.[42] Places named after sallows growing nearby are Selworthy, Somerset: *Selevrde* 1086; Selham, West Sussex: *Seleham* 1086; Silton, Dorset: *Seltone* 1086; and Salton, Yorkshire North Riding: *Saletun/Saleton* 1086. Selby, Yorkshire West Riding: *Seleby* c.1030, is also likely to derive from OE **sele*, ON *selja* 'a willow copse'. Selside in Ewcross, Yorkshire West Riding: *Selesat* 1086, is ON *selja* with *sætr* 'shieling near the willow(s)'.

It is unlikely that the Anglo-Saxons differentiated between the Great Sallow, *Salix caprea*, commonly referred to as the Pussy or Goat willow, and the Grey Sallow, *Salix cinerea*, both small trees native to Britain with similar silky catkins. Single trees are rarely recorded as boundary markers but *þane ealde seale* 'the old sallow' is a boundary marker in Winterborne Tomson, Dorset, *ða woche sæla*, 'the crooked sallow' occurs at Pensax, Worcestershire, and a sallow *stub* is another landmark at Droxford, Hampshire.[43] Sallows also grew close to a gate in Bedwyn, Wiltshire, and Colworth in Oving, West Sussex, and to a barrow in Knoyle, Wiltshire. Sometimes woods were characterised by the presence of sallows: a hanger (a wood on a slope), at West Chieveley and Beedon, Berkshire, a *hyrst* (a wooded hillock) at Exton, Hampshire, and Salehurst, East Sussex, and a *lēah* in the place-names Sawkley in Ripon and Sawley, Yorkshire West Riding. In other place-names the sallow is asso-ciated with a valley (lost *Salden* in Tewkesbury, Gloucestershire), a spur of high land (Salph End, Bedfordshire), a ford (Salford End in Renhold, Bedfordshire), and a bridge (Sawbridge in Wolfhampcote, Warwickshire). Associated adjectives are rare but the boundary of Ecchinswell, Hampshire, ran *to ðon hnottan seale on searleage stent* 'to the pollard (lit. 'close-cut') sallow standing at *sear* wood'.[44]

Today the lingering dark fruits of the alder and the golden pollen-covered catkins of the goat willow are especially distinctive in spring and the fine foliage of some willows, trees often traditionally pollarded, ensures that these trees remain an attractive feature of many water meadows today. In the Anglo-Saxon period, when there was more surface water around, these trees must also have been familiar features of the landscape.

ENDNOTES

1   S 786, B 1282 (suspect), *WoASCB*, pp. 190–3.
2   *CBDC*, pp. 41–2.
3   Rackham, *The History of the Countryside*, p. 211, table 10.1.
4   *Leechdoms* I.xv.4, fol. 21b; xxii 24b: Cockayne, II, pp. 58–9, 66–7.
5   Ibid. I.ii.15, fol. 12b; iii.9, fol. 15b; xl, fol. 40a; II.xxxix, fols 93a, b; li.3, fol. 100a; lii.1, fol. 101b: Cockayne, II, pp. 32–3, 42–3, 106–7, 248–9, 266–7, 270–1; Cameron, 'Anglo-Saxon medicine'.
6   McIntyre, 'Tree culture', p. 223.
7   J. Hillam, C. M. Groves, D. M. Brown, M. G. L. Baillie, J. M. Coles and B. J. Coles, 'Dendrochronolgy of the English Neolithic', *Antiquity* 64 (1990); B. Coles and J. Coles, *Sweet Track to Glastonbury: The Somerset Levels in Prehistory* (London, 1986), pp. 201–3.
8   Mitchell, *Trees of Britain*, pp. 201–3.
9   Graves, *The White Goddess*, pp. 164–5.
10 Paterson, *Tree Wisdom*, pp. 245–1.
11 Graves, *The White Goddess*, p. 167.
12 Reader's Digest, *Field Guide to the Trees and Shrubs of Britain* (London, 1981), p. 65.
13 S 1556, B 299; S 376, B 620 (suspicious); S 340, B 520.
14 S 1380, Dugdale, *Monasticon Anglicanum*, vi.1443–6 (no. 1) (sp); Hooke, *The Landscape of Anglo-Saxon Staffordshire*, pp. 76–9; S 710, B 1115, Kelly, *Charters of Shaftesbury*, no. 24.
15 S 380, B 610, Kelly, *Charters of Bath and Wells*, no. 28; S 311, B 476 (sp).
16 S 345, B 550.
17 S 898, K 705, *WaASCB*, pp. 110–13; S 892, Napier and Stevenson, *The Crawford Collection*, pp. 19–22, no. 8; *WaASCB*, pp. 71–4.
18 For example, S 1380, Dugdale, *Monasticum Anglicanum*, i.1443–6 (no. 1); Hooke, *The Landscape of Anglo-Saxon Staffordshire*, pp. 68–71, 72–5 and *WoASCB*, pp. 235–9; S 255, B 1331, 1332, 1333, *CBDC*, pp. 86–99.
19 S 811, B 1319 (suspicious); S 369, B 601, Kelly, *Charters of Abingdon*, I, no. 19; S 201, B 462, *WoASCB*, pp. 115–18 (sp) and S 1370, B 1139, *WoASCB*, p. 287.
20 S 1019, *CBDC*, pp. 64–5.
21 B. Coplestone-Crow, *Herefordshire Place-Names*, British Archaeological Reports, British Series 214 (Oxford, 1989), p. 136. *CDEPN*, p. 378.
22 Tree Register.
23 P. M. Losco-Bradley and C. R. Salisbury, 'A medieval fish weir at Colwick, Nottinghamshire', *Transactions of the Thoroton Society of Nottinghamshire* 83 (1979), pp. 15–22.
24 Paterson, *Tree Wisdom*, pp. 261–3.
25 *Lacnunga* XXXIa, fol. 139a: Grattan and Singer, *Anglo-Saxon Magic*, pp. 110–11.
26 Ibid., fol. 179b, 180a, pp. 180–1.

[27] *Leechdoms* I.xxxvi, fol. 33a, xxxviii, fol. 37a; I.lxxiv, fol. 56a; I.xxxvii, fol. 57b: Cockayne, II, pp. 86–7, 98–9, 148–51, 154–5.

[28] Many of these variants can be found in Smith, *English Place-Name Elements*, II.

[29] G. Grigson, *The Englishman's Flora* (St Albans, 1975), p. 191.

[30] S 1314, B 542, B 1208, *WoASCB*, pp. 264–8; S 896, K 703, Kelly, *Charters of Abingdon*, II, no. 128; S 969, K 1318.

[31] S 254, B 158 (sp).

[32] S 999, K 767, *Charters of Abingdon*, II, no. 142; S 474, B 768; S 534, B 868, Kelly, *Charters of Shaftesbury*, no. 16; S 721, B 1104; S 639, B 1005, Kelly, *Charters of Abingdon*, II, no. 75.

[33] S 1582, K iii. 467–8; S 605, B 924, Kelly, *Charters of Abingdon*, II, no. 52 (?sp) and S 590, B 932, Kelly, op. cit., no. 60; S 1165, B 34.

[34] S 486, B 788; S 763, B 1217; S 638, B 983; S 918, K 1305, Kelly, *Charters of Abingdon*, II, no. 135 (sp); S 696, B 1071.

[35] S 1562, Campbell, *Charters of Rochester*, no. 33.

[36] S 1165, B 34; S 353. B 563 (sp).

[37] *Llandaff Charters* 75, 80: Evans, *The Text of the Book of Llan Dâv* pp. 242, 379; 251, 381; 268, 384.

[38] The latter S 290, O'Donovan, *Charters of Sherborne*, no. 3; H. P. R. Finberg, *The Early Charters of Wessex* (Leicester, 1964), no. 567, pp. 160–4.

[39] S 441, B 730; S 571, B 931 (sp).

[40] S 912, Crick, *Charters of St Albans*, nos 11 and 1B, pp. 75, 114, 188; A. R. Rumble, 'The Wheathampstead (Herts.) charter-bounds, A.D. 1060': a corrected text and notes on the boundary-points', *Journal of English Place-Name Studies* 9 (1977), pp. 6–11.

[41] *Anglo-Saxon Chronicle* 878: Swanton, pp. 40, n. 5, 76–7, 87; J. E. B. Gover, A. Mawer and F. M. Stenton, *The Place-Names of Wiltshire*, English Place-Name Society 6 (Cambridge, 1939), p. 15.

[42] S 998, K 1332, O'Donovan, *Charters of Sherborne*, no. 21; *CBDC*, pp. 200–3; S 811, B 1319 (suspicious); S 414, B 670 (sp).

[43] S 485, B 775, Kelly, *Charters of Shaftesbury*, no. 13; S 276, B 393 (sp); S 446, B 742.

[44] S 412, B 674.

10

Trees of Open or Planned Countryside

While most trees recorded in pre-Conquest contexts were naturally found where ancient or relict woodland was plentiful, two species stand out as being referred to rather more often, at least in charters, in farmed landscapes: the thorn and the elder (Fig. 17). Species of thorns were common everywhere but both the blackthorn (the sloe) and the whitethorn (the hawthorn) readily colonise abandoned arable land, pasture fields and pockets of waste ground. In addition, both these species have been planted as hedgerow trees as they form a quick-growing and effective barrier. The elder, too, grows readily wherever there is a high nitrogen content in the soil, flourishing, therefore, near abandoned dwellings, animal setts and country church-yards.[1] Birds carry the seeds in their droppings and the tree colonises suitable land very quickly, growing rapidly and vigorously.

THE ELDER

The elder, *Sambucus nigra* (OE *ellen*), is the tree species that is especially noted in the early Christian edicts against tree-worship – the tree of witches. It is the tree singled out by Wulfstan in the *Canons of Edgar*, c.1005–8, noted in Chapter 2, as a place for the carrying out of 'devil's craft', although what practices this involved remain unspecified. Paterson notes the anthropomorphic nature of this tree, regarded as an abode of the 'Elder Mother', called Elle or Hyldemoer in Scandi-navian and Danish myth; it was she who worked strong earth magic and avenged all who harmed her host trees.[2] Because of this, the tree was, in popular folklore, traditionally treated with awesome respect. Witches were thought to have been able to turn themselves into elder trees, and one such 'elder witch' was involved in the legend of the Oxfordshire Rollright Stones, turning the king and his men to stone. People are said to have danced here in the past on Midsummer's Eve, with elder garlands in their hair, but Christian reaction to these activities led to other customs, which involved cutting the elder in order to 'bleed' the witch. The damaged witch returning to human form might be recognised by the marks on her person of the damage caused. Beliefs in witchcraft were particularly long-lived in this area. and there were also many local superstitions concerning divination at the site. Because

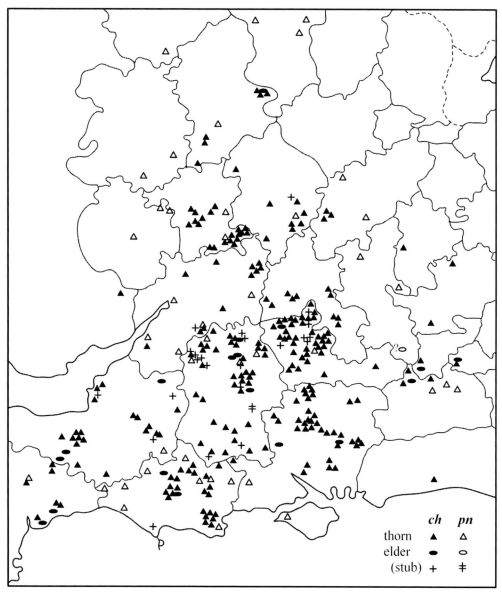

Figure 17. Trees of cultivated areas: the distribution of elder and thorn
in early medieval charters and place-names

of the elder's association with witchcraft, no baby's cradle would be made of its wood or the occupant would surely pine away or be pinched black and blue by the fairies. In Ireland, witches used elder sticks, rather than ashen ones, as magic horses.

The elder was also seen by many as the tree of doom and death, the thirteenth tree in the so-called 'Tree Alphabet'; thirteen, of course, is still regarded as an unlucky number, the number of Christ's thirteenth guest, Judas, at the Last Supper. Even the scent of an elder plantation, likened to that of the smell of corpses, was held to cause death and disease, and to sleep under an elder would bring certain death for the fragrance of the flowers would transport the unfortunate person to the Underworld. Because of its reputation, some make 'the cursed elder' the tree of Christ's crucifix (although elders do not grow in Palestine); Langland has Judas, in his *Piers Plowman*, hanging himself upon an elder tree; William Rufus was said to have been killed by an archer posted under an elder. It remained involved with magic, medicine and witchcraft. To bring elder logs into the house was believed, in English folklore, to 'bring the devil into the house' but its white flowers allied it, according to the interpretations of Graves, to the 'White Goddess'.[3] Indeed, the elder has healing properties denied by the early Christian priests who probably encouraged people to accept its association with witchcraft and, according to Paterson,[4] to regard its 'only proper use' as a means of seeking out the evil of witches. To do this, a baptised person was to dab the green juice of the elder on the eyelids, enabling them to recognise and see all the doings of witches in the community. In a mixture of superstitious belief, embodying possible pre-Christian beliefs strongly affected by Christian teaching, the elder in folklore remained, however, 'a feminine tree used for protection, healing, exorcism and prosperity'.[5]

While most superstitions therefore regarded the elder as deadly or, at best, dangerous, its healing properties are noted in early literary sources. In the *Leechdoms*, its leaves are included in a salve for 'foot ache' and wens, its blooms also as a salve or, mixed with honey, for 'the half-dead [disease]', its bark used with that of other plants against leprosy, shingles, and 'for a worm-eaten and mortified body', and the bark of its trunk or roots as an emetic drink. Even its ashes could be used against palsy. It appears in an ancient charm: 'Again for fellons [*sic*], take, to begin, a hazel or an elder stick or spoon, write thy name thereon, cut three scores on the place, fill the name with the blood, throw it over thy shoulder or between thy thighs into running water and stand over the man. Strike the scores, and do all that in silence'.[6] Yet the elder has strong medicinal qualities, and in the eighteenth century John Evelyn, referring specifically to the elder, remarked: 'If the medicinal properties of the leaves, bark, berries, etc. were thoroughly known, I cannot tell of what our country-men could ail, for which he might not fetch a remedy from every hedge'.[7] The bark, leaves and root of the elder have diuretic and strong purgative properties, as the *Leechdoms* noted; the young shoots, boiled, were said to clear the lungs and head of phlegm and the juice of freshly dried leaves or an infusion of the flowers, sniffed, helped to clear a blocked nose. The pith of the shoots was sleep-inducing. A type of fungus which grows on elder has been used to treat throat troubles. Elder flowers, helping to relieve fluid retention in the body, can be used to allay pain and infusions of the blossoms were used in the past to relieve many ailments from scarlet fever to measles and so forth. A volatile oil distilled from the flowers has been used in eye and skin lotions as elder flower water, historically a popular ingredient in a lady's toilette as 'Nature's gift to the complexion'. The berries, root and bark are powerful laxatives but 'hot elderberry wine, often made with spices, was sold on London streets on cold winter days and nights until about 100 years ago, to warm the body and cheer the soul'.[8] Dyes can also be made from different parts of the plant: black from the bark, green from the leaves, and blue or lilac from the flowers. Many ancient remedies, however, involved a degree of magic, indicating, perhaps, the antiquity of such 'cures': warts rubbed with a green elder stick were thought to disappear if the stick was buried in the ground and left to rot; fevers could be transferred to such a stick in the same way; toothache could be dissipated by holding an elder twig in the mouth and reciting 'Depart, thou evil spirit!'. Although the berries of the elder also have curative properties similar to the flowers, their most popular use today is in elderberry wine. Both the fruits and the flowers have traditionally been used to make wine and jams, the latter rich in Vitamin C.

The wood of the elder is hard and yellowish-white and has been used historically to make combs and wooden spoons while the hollowed-out stems have been used by children to make whistles and peashooters.

The elder, as noted in Chapter 7, stands out for the number of references to this tree being to 'stubs', with at least thirteen elder-stub references and three thorn-stub references in Wiltshire. Although none are recorded in Worcestershire, Warwickshire with its small number of charters has one elder and four other elder-/or alder-stubs on boundaries. Seven elder-stubs, one *elebēam*-stub and five or six thorn-stubs are recorded in Berkshire (at least one of the latter may be a repetition). Indeed, of the likely seventeen separate references to the elder in Wiltshire charter boundary clauses, no fewer than thirteen are to stubs; in Berkshire all but one of the eight elder references are to elder-stubs, in Somerset three of seven, and an elder-stub is the only reference to this tree as a boundary landmark in each of the counties of Warwickshire, Gloucestershire and Middlesex. These elder-stubs may conceivably have been a type of pollard – the production of a stub by removing tree branches was a recognised form of management in later times.[9] Because of its association with witchcraft, the elder may not have been generally liked – had the elders been deliberately cut down? It was this tree that was singled out in an edict issued by Wulfstan in 1005 x 1008 (see above). It was thus to be hacked down wherever it occurred in obvious locations (it may be significant that an elder stump was found in a churchyard in an eleventh- to twelfth-century context during excavations at

London Guildhall).[10] But this may be entirely fanciful: its flowers and fruits can of course be used and its leaves are eaten by sheep and cattle; it also grows readily in most situations and may have needed control. In southern Germany and Austria elders are still 'pollarded' and treated like vines to make the fruit easier to pick – the resulting trunk, about a metre high, grows thick like a stump.

In addition to the many elder-stubs recorded, an elder grove is recorded in Pewsey, Wiltshire, and elders characterised a coomb in Somerset, a *crundel* or quarry in Dorset, and grew close to a ford in Hinton Ampner, Kilmeston and Tichborne, Hampshire, and Ottery St Mary, Devon, a spring in Somerset and a pool in Wetmoor, Staffordshire. Only one habitative site is recorded associated with elders: *elewurðie*, a lost settlement site on the downs above the sea in Littleham, Devon.[11] No adjective is ever used to describe an elder appearing as a charter boundary landmark. One Somerset charter with the bounds given in Latin notes both the Latin and Old English names for the elder when the bounds of the estate, beside the Wellow Brook, run *usque sambucin quem uocitant ellentrow* 'to the *sambucus* which they call elder-tree'.[12]

It is also difficult to explain why the elder appears so frequently in south-central England, but this tree, as noted above, prefers nitrogen-rich soil which has been enriched by human and animal faeces and is often found near abandoned settlement sites – and much of south-central England was an area of farmed countryside consistently adapting to changing patterns of settlement location.[13] Although place-name references to the elder are rare, one hundred meeting-place is recorded as being at an elder stump – that of Elstub Hundred in Wiltshire, recorded in the 1084 Geld Roll.[14] It stood in the parish of Enford. This tree is the sixth commonest of those recorded in charter boundary clauses but, with only about four place-name occurrences, is only 3% of all the recorded tree names.

The Cornish name for the elder, *scawen*, occurs in the manorial place-name Trescowe in Breage, recorded as *Trescav* in 1086, associated with *tre* 'farmstead', and is not uncommon in later names[15] but elder is relatively rare in England in those counties covered here. Elwicks in Little Ouseburn, Yorkshire West Riding: *Eleuuic* in 1086, appears to be a recording of this term, coupled with OE *wīc* 'dairy farm, collection of buildings' (sometimes 'place of trade, place where a specialised activity was carried on'), and Elsted in West Sussex (*Halestede* 1086) is *ellen* with OE *stede* 'place' (in Surrey, a similar name is not recorded until 1128). It is again noteworthy that in all these cases the elder is probably associated with a settlement site.

THE THORN, INCLUDING THE SPINDLE AND SLOE

Several species were included in the generalised name *þorn* 'thorn'. Commonest by far were the *Cretaegus* species: the midland or woodland hawthorn, *Crataegus laevigata* (formerly *oxyacanthoides*), usually found as a tree rather than a hedgerow shrub, and the common hawthorn, *Crataegus monogyna*, the fast-growing shrub frequently planted in eighteenth- and nineteenth-century hedgerows. The thorn references are not all to the hawthorn, although this species is specified on a few occasions in charters as the *hægþorn, hegeþorn, haguþorn, haggeþorn, *hagu-þyrne* or **haca-þorn*. The unrelated blackthorn or sloe, *Prunus spinosa*, is occasionally specified, as on the boundary of Church Honeybourne, Worcestershire; *slahhyll* 'sloe hill' in Bishopton in Old Stratford, Warwickshire;[16] or in the place-names *Slacham*, a lost Domesday manor in Hampshire; and Slaugham, West Sussex. 'Black thorns' are noted in the boundary clauses of Brokenborough, Wiltshire (the *blakethorne*); Church Honeyboume, Worcestershire (*þa blacan þyrnan*); Ducklington, Oxford-shire, Cheselbourne, Dorset; and Aspley Guise, Bedfordshire.[17] The common hawthorn, *haguþorn* (and variants) is also recorded in charters, appearing as the *þære hegðorn* of Overton, Hampshire, or the *spinam que appellatur haythorne* 'the thorn called hawthorn' in a late boundary clause of *Swanhammes* meadow belonging to Dauntsey, Wiltshire.[18] It is recorded in the early place-names Hackthorn, Lincoln-shire: *Hagetorne* 1086; and Hathern, Leicestershire: *Avederne* 1086. In Hatherden, Hampshire: *Hetherdon* 1086, it characterises a valley (*denu*); in Hatherleigh, Devon: *Hadreleia* 1086, and Down and Up Hatherley, Gloucestershire: *Athelai* 1086, it refers to two woods or clearings (*lēah*); in Hatherton, Cheshire: *Haretone* 1086, it occurs with *tūn*; and in Hatherton, Staffordshire: *Hagenthorndun* 996, *Hargedone* 1086, with *dūn*.

The *sceddern þorn*, noted on the boundary of Pillaton, Staffordshire,[19] may be a reference to the bullace, *Prunus domestica*, still known as 'the scad-tree' in eastern and south-eastern England. Another 'thorn' referred to as the *lusþorn*, as in Eington, Wiltshire, or Stoulton, Worcestershire, is thought to be the spindle tree, *Euonymus europaeus*. Wallenberg suggests that the *crawan þorn* of Crowthorne Hundred, Gloucestershire, recorded in 1327, may have been the same as the Swedish *kråk-torn*, *Rhamnus catharticus*, commonly known as the 'purging buckthorn' or the 'crossthorn'.[20] This is a common shrub of hedgerows and woodland on chalky soils which bears black berries and has a sharp thorn at the end of each twig. Other thorny plants which may find their way into the literature include the holly, known as the *pric þorn* in Lincolnshire and possibly referred to as the *pric þorn* on the boundary of Denton, Cuddesdon and Wheatley in Oxfordshire.[21] Bramble briars may be meant by the *brembel þyrnan* or *brembel þorn*, of Abingdon and Harwell, Oxfordshire, or the *bremelwirnan* of Berrow, Somerset – and perhaps, too, by the *brer þurne* 'briar thorns' of Badsey, Worcestershire.[22] The *ellen þirnen* of Cheselbourne, Dorset,[23] might just be a confused reference to the alder buckthorn, *Frangula alnus*, because *alre* and *ellern* have also been confused elsewhere (in Warwickshire charters) but this tree is not thorny. The *appelthorn* (?crab-apple) of Brokenborough, Wiltshire,[24] is also difficult to explain while the *eorðnutena ðorn* of Overbury and Conderton,

Worcestershire, is probably a reference to a quite different kind of plant, the tuber *Conopodium majus*, 'the earth-nut' or 'pig-nut', found growing close to a thorn-tree.[25]

Generally considered an unlucky tree, the thorn appears in the Irish Brehon Laws as *sceith*, a name apparently connected with the Germanic root *sceath* or *sceth*, meaning 'harm'.[26] The hawthorn is also commonly referred to as the May-tree, for it flowers in this month. However, the month of May was considered an unlucky month in ancient Greece, and the thorn is also generally considered an unlucky tree. The Greek goddess Maia could be either a damsel 'ever fair and young' or a malevolent beldame: her name is derived from *maia* 'grandmother'. The destruction of an ancient hawthorn spelt 'the greatest peril' in Ireland, and was believed to cause the death of one's cattle and children and the loss of all one's money. In Derbyshire, a place-name Shuckstonefield in Crich: *Scochetorp* in 1086, was 'demon's or goblin's [OE *scucca*] thorn-bush'.[27] Yet hawthorns might also be associated with holy wells and shreds of torn garments would be hung on them as a sign of mourning and propitiation. It was at first the tree of 'enforced chastity' but became associated with female sexuality in the cult of the Goddess Flora. In the case of the Glastonbury thorn, the tree was sanctified by associating it with Joseph of Arimathea. According to Graves,[28] the blackthorn in folklore is also an unlucky tree, often associated with witches, and in monkish tradition with the thorn of Christ's crucifixion crown (in his interpretation of the *Beith-Luis-Nin* alphabet it shared a month with *saille* the willow but in another arrangement instead associates with the hazel).

The thorn does occur in the *Leechdoms*, and it is usually the sloe or blackthorn that is specified in cures. For 'white spot' the juice of an unripe sloe was put to the eye, but it was more often the bark or 'rind' of the blackthorn that was used: in a wound salve (the rind of 'the nethermost part'), in a 'smearing for a penetrating worm', against cancer, palsy, shingles and secretion of the joints, and for 'a dry lung'. For 'spider bite' it was the lichen from the blackthorn that was used, moistened with honey. The bark of the thorn (unspecified) was used against 'tooth wark', some parts drunk in a concoction against 'thigh ache'. The fruit is indeed an emetic while the powdered leaves and seeds were used in the past to sprinkle over animals and children to deter lice. A common Midlands name for the spindle, the *lusporn*, was 'louse-berry'.[29] Today it is thought that the hawthorn, traditionally used to treat nausea, may help patients with chronic heart failure. The berries may also stimulate the appetite and help to relieve the gut; they may also relax the nervous system and help to induce sleep.[30]

Although often seen today as a hedgerow shrub, the thorn-tree can reach sizeable proportions. The common hawthorn, *Cr. monogyna*, naturally reaches 18 metres in height, and the midland hawthorn, *Cr. laevigata*, reaches 10 metres, while both can be long lived. Cornish[31] shows a photograph of the enormous and ancient Hethel Thorn, known as 'the witch of Hethel', which grows in the churchyard at Hethel five

miles south-west of Caister near Norwich, now one of the smallest Sites of Special
Scientific Interest in the country. Herefordshire also had a number of historic thorn-
trees,[32] and veteran thorns survive today in this county, usually where they have
been coppiced, in parkland situations as at Croft Castle and Eastnor Park. Of the
Cr. monogyna listed in the Tree Register an English specimen in Crawley, West
Sussex, has a girth of 390cm and a height of 7m, while two large specimens of *Cr.
laevigata* are found in Greater London: one in Regent's Park, Greater London, with
a girth of 192cm, standing 9m high, and a second at Mortlake, Barnes, with a girth
of 163cm, standing 8m high (neither as big as the champion tree found at Gordon
Castle, Fochabers in Moray, Scotland, which stands 10m high with a girth of 39cm.
The sloe, too, is usually seen as a large shrub. Its twigs have viscous thorns and it
can form dense hedges. It readily suckers to dominate other shrubs; its blossoms
are earlier than those of the hawthorn, often appearing in the cold easterly winds
of March – a cold spring is traditionally known as 'a blackthorn winter' – and its
autumn berries provide fruit for birds but can also be used in wines and jams. The
wood is hard and tough, and polishes well, but is never available in large sizes; it has
been used for marquetry, the teeth of hay-rakes, walking-sticks and the Irish shil-
lelagh or cudgel. The spindle is so-named because its white, hard and dense wood
was much used for making spindles for spinning wool. It is most obvious when it
bears its pinkish-red four-lobed fruits in autumn.

  In most counties, the thorn was the most ubiquitous tree referred to in charters
and early place-names: twenty-five in Worcestershire, fifty-four in Wiltshire and
fifty-one in Hampshire. In Berkshire, with forty-three references, the thorn is noted
almost as often as all other tree types together (given problems of repetition and
uncertain name derivation, numbers given here may not be exact – attempts have
been made to discount repeated landmarks). It accounts for nearly 30% of all references to tree species recorded in charters and 25% of all trees recorded by the end of
the eleventh century (Table 3). It occurs so frequently along estate boundaries that
some once thought that thorns had been planted deliberately as boundary landmarks,
even as early as the Roman period.[33] This is unlikely to be true: the hawthorn is
just a very common tree that grows readily. Although present in ancient woodlands
and areas of secondary woodland, as well as in areas of wood-pasture, in the charters, where it is used as landmark feature, it is primarily a tree of cultivated land,
noted either as an individual tree or as a small group, perhaps noted because other
trees were few in such locations. It is readily dispersed by seed and ever ready to
regenerate if land is left unploughed or protected for even a short time from animal
pasture. Its invasive nature was clearly apparent after the rabbit populations had
been devastated by myxomatosis in the 1950s, and it grows rapidly if sheep grazing
declines on downlands. Its use as a hedgerow tree is well known but such hedges
soon become gappy and useless without management by layering. Although the
thorn in charters is not confined to cultivated regions, being one of the first shrubs

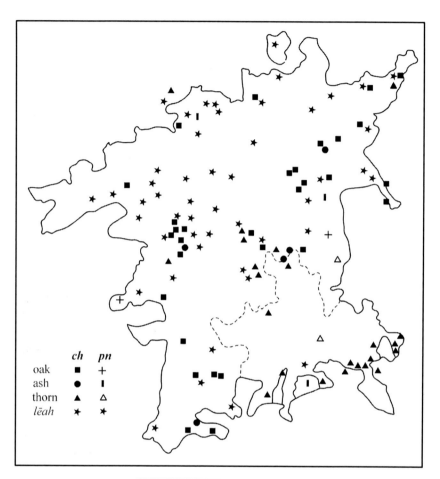

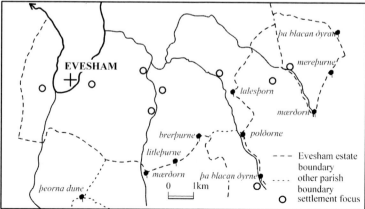

Figure 18. The trees of Worcestershire with, below, the boundary thorns
in the Vale of Evesham

to colonise abandoned arable or neglected corners of a heavily farmed landscape, it normally occurs in quite different locations to the oak and the ash.

In Worcestershire the thorn is most frequently noted in the heavily cultivated Vale of Evesham, a region which extends southwards into eastern Gloucestershire and southern Warwickshire. A series of thorns – nine in all – lay alongside the boundaries of the estates belonging to the abbey of Evesham (see Figs 18a and b). In Wiltshire it is again a tree found extensively but especially on the cultivated chalk soils and in Berkshire, too, thorns characterised the Vale of the White Horse, an area of known open field farming, and around Blewbury to the east: in Berkshire, Wiltshire and Hampshire it is frequently mentioned across the chalk downlands, heavily cultivated in Roman times but reverting to pasture in the early medieval period.[34] In the charters it is constantly found in association with features of cultivated ground such as headlands, lynchets and furrows.[35] It may also be significant that thorn place-names cluster in the North Riding of Yorkshire in the hinterland of the Roman centre of *Cataractonium* (Catterick) (Fig. 12a).

Perhaps surprisingly, the thorn attracted the widest variety of descriptive adjectives, especially when used in charter bounds. Some occurred in woods or as thickets (often referred to as 'groves'), or as hedgerows, or characterised topographical locations such as valleys and hills, or marshes, springs and pools; others were associated with the edges of cultivated ground: with headlands, lynchets and open land (*feld*). Sometimes thorns were associated with habitation sites, as in the case of *þornwic* in Havant, Hampshire,[36] Thornham (with *hām*) and Thurton in Norfolk (*þorn* or *þyrne* with *tūn*) or the three Thornton names (Thornton Curtis, Thornton by Horncastle and Thornton le Moor) in Lincolnshire. Some stood alongside man-made features such as a way, bridge or gate and three with fingerposts at road junctions (*stapol* thorns). Many of the thorns noted were clearly solitary trees, some referred to as an *anlipigan* 'solitary' thorn, as at Corston and at Weston in Somerset or at Handley, Dorset.[37] On the boundaries of the Blewbury estate in Berkshire, *þam langan cyrstel mæle æt hafurc/hafuc þorne* 'the tall crucifix at hawk thorn', stood on the eastern boundary of Aston Tirrold beside a branch of the Icknield Way (Fig. 13b).[38] The way is referred to in the charter bounds as a *herepað* route, which crossed the estate from west to east, and a 'tall thorn' stood beside the Way itself a little further to the south. A series of further thorn-trees marked the remaining stretch of the boundary, together with an *elebēam*, and other thorns stood on the southern boundary and on the western boundary of Aston Upthorpe.

Despite the associations of the thorn in folklore with misfortune it is a beautiful bush, especially when it is in full bloom in late spring scattered over fresh green pastures and it is not altogether surprising that the thorn offers what is only the third reference to a 'beautiful' tree: the *fegeran þorne* 'fair thorn' of Rodbourne in Wiltshire.[39] The commonest description, however, was *(ge)mǣr* 'boundary' thorn, noted on at least sixteen occasions, and the *wroht ðorne* of Pewsey, Wiltshire,[40] may have indicated a disputed boundary (OE *wrōht* 'dispute'). Many thorns were associated with named individuals, probably indicating local landownership, but several with beggars and felons (as in the case of the *lodder þorne* 'beggar's thorn' of Chilton, Berkshire, and the *Beggaresthorne* of Bleadon, Somerset).[41] Can any significance be given to the *setl þorn*, apparently on the western boundary of Ottery St Mary, Devon (a hundred boundary), in 1061?[42] One meaning of *setl* is 'judgement seat' and another *set* 'seat' thorn is noted on the boundary of Denton, Cuddesdon and Wheatley in Oxfordshire.[43] The *weawan þorn* of Meon and Privett in Hampshire[44] may be a 'felon's thorn' (see Chapter 7), perhaps marking a tree used as a gallows or one marking the grave of an executed criminal: *ðan þorne þer ða þeofes licgan* 'the thorn where the thieves lie', noted in a boundary clause of Rolleston, Staffordshire, in 1008,[45] as also noted in Chapter 7, marked the burial ground of an execution site close to a major crossing place of the River Trent at Burton-on-Trent. Fretherne in Gloucestershire, on the other hand, may have been 'sanctuary thorn' incorporating OE *frið* 'sanctuary'.[46]

The thorn was incorporated in hundred names surprisingly often: three times in Wiltshire and Gloucestershire (two post-Conquest recordings); twice in Hereford-shire, Somerset and Middlesex (Spelthorne Hundred is *Speletorne* 'speech thorn' in 1086); and once in Dorset, Berkshire, Surrey, Essex and Kent; also, in the Old Norse form *þyrnir*, in Aswardhurn Hundred, Lincolnshire/Lindsey. In Somerset it is the blackthorn that is specified in the lost *Blacheterne* Hundred while the hawthorn is specified in Eyhorne Hundred, Kent; *Haihorne hvnd'* in 1086. Thorns might be 'copped' or pollarded (see below), as in Copthorne Hundred, Surrey. Anderson notes a great thorn-tree growing from an enormous old stump in a hedgerow near Down House on the brow of Horethorne Down in Horethorne, Somerset, which might be related to the Horethorne Hundred: this tree may have been that standing in 1633.[47]

Thorn-trees are described variously as *lȳtel* 'little' or *scort* 'short', *lang* 'tall' or *grēat*, *micel* 'great', *brād* 'broad' or *smæl* 'small, slender', *pīc* 'pointed', *þicce* 'thick', *eald* 'old' or *hār* 'grey, ?lichen-covered', *rūh* 'rough'. Some adjectives, with corrupt or uncertain spellings, are difficult to translate or interpret (e.g. *hægla*, *hragra*, *grawas*, *writeles*). The *feden þorn* and the *spedig* thorn (the first possibly from OE *fēding* 'feeding', the second *spēdig* 'rich, plenteous, abundant') may have been nourishing and abundant thorns, referring to the haws. Does the description, the *red* thorn, at Muchelney, Somerset, also refer to the colour red of the haws? Certainly the propensity to attract birds is noted with references to crows, hawks, pigeons, herons, swallows and 'hens and cocks'. A *rægen* thorn may have been associated with the roe-deer (OE *rǣge*: Ottery St Mary, Devon), the *doggi þorn* (OE *docga*: Olveston, Gloucestershire) with a dog. However, the latter may be a refer-ence to the dogwood tree, sometimes a derogatory local name for the spindle-tree and, in some regions, also for the alder and elder, but none of these have thorns and the dog rose has also been suggested.[48] Thorns could be pollarded, as the 'copped' thorn noted earlier indicates: references include *þem coppedan þorne* of Altwalton, Huntingdonshire, Essex; the *coppenthorn* of Dameham and *þan coppedan þornæ* of Worthy, both in Hampshire, and *ðam coppede ðorne* of Battersea, Surrey,[49] together perhaps with the *loppede þorne* of Ducklington in Oxfordshire.[50] Again, a thorn has been described as *hnot* 'close-cut': *þone hnottan þorn* at Leckhampstead, Berkshire.[51] Two thorn-trees had been burnt (e.g. the *sænget þorn* of Polhampton in Overton, Hampshire) and many others were mere stumps.

The Cornish terms for thorns, *dreyn* or *spern*, are usually found in later place-names but *cruc drænoc* on the boundary of Traboe in St Keverne parish is 'the barrow at the thorns',[52] located on the moorland of Goonhilly where several boundaries converge – one of the relatively few references to trees marking boundaries on this windswept peninsula. The only other reference to a solitary tree in Cornish charters is to another thorn-tree on the boundary of Tregony.[53]

ENDNOTES

[1] Kelly, 'The Old English tree-list', p. 117.

[2] Paterson, *Tree Wisdom*, pp. 279–83.

[3] Graves, *The White Goddess*, pp. 180–3.

[4] Paterson, *Tree Wisdom*, p. 281.

[5] Ibid., p. 290.

[6] *Leechdoms* I.xxxix, fol. 39b: Cockayne, II, pp. 104–5.

[7] J. Evelyn, *Silva: or a Discourse of Forest-Trees, and the Propogation of Timber in His Majesty's Dominions* (London, 1664), as quoted by Paterson, *Tree Wisdom*, p. 284.

[8] McIntyre, 'Tree culture', p. 234.

[9] Rackham, *Trees and Woodland*, 2nd edn, p. 9, fig. 2.

[10] I. Howell, D. Bowsher, T. Dyson and N. Holder, *The London Guidhall: An Archaeological History of a Neighbourhood from Early Medieval to Modern Times*, MoLAS monograph 36 (London, 2007).

[11] S 998, K 1332, O'Donovan, *Charters of Sherborne*, no. 21.

[12] S 262, Kelly, *Charters of Bath and Wells*, no. 27, pp. 193, 198.

[13] F. Kelly, 'The Old English tree-list', *Celtica* 11 (1976), p. 117.

[14] O. S. Anderson, *The English Hundred-Names, The South-Western Counties*, p. 168.

[15] Padel, *Cornish Place-Name Elements*, pp. 205–6.

[16] S 1388, K 724, *WaASCB*, pp. 121–4.

[17] S 1577, B 922, Kelly, *Charters of Malmesbury*, no. 34; S 1599, K 1368, *WoASCB*, pp. 408–17; S 678, B 1036, Kelly, *Charters of Abingdon*, II, no. 82; S 485, B 775, Kelly, *Charters of Shaftesbury*, no. 13; S 772, B 1229.

[18] S 377, B 625 (suspicious); S 1580, B 458, Kelly, *Charters of Malmesbury*, no. 44.

[19] S 955, K 730, *Kelly, Charters of Shaftesbury*, no. 30.

[20] Wallenberg, 'Kentish place-names', p. 481; Smith, *Place-Names of Gloucestershire*, I, p. 48.

[21] S 587, B 945, Kelly, *Charters of Abingdon*, II, no. 70.

[22] S S 605, B 924, Kelly, *Charters of Abingdon*, II, no. 52; S 856, K 648; S 793, B 1291; S 80, B 125 (sp).

23 S 955, K 730, Kelly, *Charters of Shaftesbury*, no. 30.

24 S 1577, B 922.

25 S 216, B 541 (?sp), *WoASCB*, pp. 125–9.

26 Graves, *The White Goddess*, p. 169.

27 K. Cameron, *The Place-Names of Derbyshire, Part II*, English Place-Name Society 28 (Cambridge, 1959), pp. 437–8.

28 Ibid., pp. 238–9.

29 Grigson, *The Englishman's Flora*, pp. 129–30.

30 McIntyre, 'Tree culture', p. 238.

31 Cornish, *Historic Thorn Trees*, pl. 2; see too J. Stokes and D. Rodger, *The Heritage Trees* (London, 2004), p. 103 with photograph by A. Miles.

32 E. M. Leather, 1912. *The Folk-Lore of Herefordshire* (Hereford and London, 1912).

33 Cornish, *Historic Thorn Trees*, p. 28.

34 Hooke, 'Regional variation'.

35 For example, S 402, B 666 (sp).

36 S 754, B 1200.

37 S 476, B 767; S 508, K 408, iii. 423–4, Kelly, *Charters of Bath and Wells*, no. 7; S 630, B 970, Kelly, *Charters of Shaftesbury*, no. 21 (unreliable).

38 S 496, B 801, Kelly, *Charters of Abingdon*, I, no. 36.

39 S 1587, K 632, Kelly, *Charters of Malmesbury*, no. 35: bounds incorrectly attached to a different charter (S 841). However, a second charter of the neighbouring estate of Brinkworth refers to this (?) landmark as 'Fæger's tree' – here a personal name derived from OE *fæger* 'fair': Kelly, op. cit., pp. 262, 275.

40 S 470, B 748.

41 S 934, K 1255, K 1310, Kelly, *Charters of Abingdon*, II, no. 137; S 804, B 1313 (sp).

42 S 1033, K 810, *CBDC*, pp. 168–72.

43 S 587, B 945.

44 S 754.

45 S 920, Sawyer, *Charters of Burton*, no. 31; Hooke, *The Landscape of Anglo-Saxon Staffordshire*, pp. 93–7.

46 Smith, *Place-Names of Gloucestershire*, II, p. 178.

47 Anderson, *The English Hundred-Names, The South-Western Counties*, pp. 56–8, citing T. Gerard, *The Particular Description of Somerset*, Somerset Record Society 15 (1633), p. 154.

48 For the roe-deer thorn see S 1033, K 810, *CBDC*, pp. 207–12; for the 'dog thorn' see S 664, B 936, Kelly, *Charters of Bath and Wells*, no. 12 and p. 109.

49 S 566, B 909; S 513, B 817; S 351, B 740 (sp); S 645; B 994.

50 S 678, B 1036, Kelly, *Charters of Abingdon*, II, no. 82.

51 S 491, B 789.

52 S 832, *CBDC*, pp. 46–8, 68–9.

53 S 1019, *CBDC*, pp. 64–5.

11

Other Trees Noted in Charters
and Early Place-Names

FRUIT AND NUT TREES

Fruit trees frequently appear as boundary landmarks in pre-Conquest charters, although it is not always the improved varieties that may be being referred to. Apples and pears are frequently referred to in charter boundary clauses as well as in early place-names but references to the cherry are much rarer and this can, of course, be to the wild variety. Even rarer is a reference which may be to the *Mespilus germanica*, the medlar, in the name of Kirby Misperton: *Mispeton* 1086, Yorkshire North Riding. It may be significant that at least part of this estate was Church land, as the name implies, held by the abbot of York from Robert de Tosny in Domesday Book, and the Church was instrumental in maintaining orchards.[1]

There is little doubt that orchards were being deliberately planted and maintained throughout the early medieval period. Many of our common orchard fruit trees are thought to have been introduced by the Romans and orchards were planted by both them and the Anglo-Saxons. Many monasteries were reorganised shortly before the Norman Conquest to a revised Benedictine rule and the monks of that order had long been instructed to maintain water mills, orchards and kilns within the monastic precincts,[2] although the term 'orchard' at first could be used to apply to a garden which was not confined to fruit trees. Plantings are said to have been carried out at Ely under the guidance of the first abbot, Byrhtnoth, of the new Benedictine monastery established in 970: *hortos quoque et pomeria circa ecclesiam late plantavit nascentium* 'he also planted gardens and orchards of newly propagated stock over a wide area around the church'[3] and similar claims are made for the monastery at Thorney in Cambridgeshire.[4] The duties of an estate reeve described in the tenth or eleventh century also specify that winter tasks included *timber cleofan. orcerd ræran* 'cleave timber, establish an orchard'.[5] Domesday Book confirms the presence of orchards in many places by that date, especially on monastic estates: a *virgultum* 'orchard' noted at Exeter, Devon, and another at Orchard in Church Knowle, Dorset, are examples in south-western England while at Nottingham an orchard (*pomerium*) was about to be planted.[6]

Orchards are themselves referred to both in place-names and charters[7] and even vineyards were present by Roman times, in spite of the difficulties experienced in ripening the grapes in Britain noted by Tacitus, due, he explains, to the moist soil and atmosphere.[8] Place-name references include Orchardleigh: *Orcerdleag* ?C10, and Orchard Portman: *Orceard* 854, in Somerset; Orcheton: *Orcartona* 1086, in Devon; and Orchard in Church Knowle: *Horcerd* 1086, Dorset. In Wiltshire in 940 King Edward granted an estate at Liddington whose boundary ran 'through the orchard' and an 'old orchard', which seems to have been hedged, lay on the boundary of Abbotstone, an estate identifiable as Tichborne Farm in Whitparish in the south of the county which was granted by King Edgar to Wilton Abbey in 968.[9] The Church of Worcester appears to have held an orchard in the Vale of Evesham in Worcestershire at Cropthorne, and another was leased with an estate at Bentley, Holt, in the mid-eleventh century, together with an urban messuage at Worcester in the Severn valley, which comprised 'the orchard at the boundary dyke', perhaps an orchard in Worcester itself near the River Severn.[10] These again betray an ecclesiastical interest in the planting of orchards. Another orchard appears in a boundary clause of South Stoneham, Hampshire, in 1045, while 'orchard coomb' is recorded on the boundary of the Taunton manor estates in the bounds of Ruishton and Orchard Portman in Somerset in 854, and in the bounds of Nynehead, Stoke St Mary, Ruishton and Hestercombe *c*.900; an *orcerd ford* 'orchard ford' is found at Creech St Michael in the same county in 882.[11] The Welsh Laws attributed to Hywel Dda refer to the grafting of cultivated fruit onto wild stock, raising the value of a fruit tree from four pence to sixty pence ('by two pence each season until it bear fruit') but this is not necessarily from the tenth-century core of the material.[12]

The apple, pear and plum

The commonest fruit-bearing tree to be mentioned in Old English sources is undoubtedly the apple. The native apple, *Malus sylvestris*, is inedible and genetically distinct from the introduced variety, *Malus domestica*. The long-held belief that the domestic apple was a hybrid of crosses between wild species has now been shown to be unfounded. DNA analysis suggests that the edible form originates from the Ili Valley region of western China, close to the borders of the former USSR, and was carried by migrating tribes after the end of the last Ice Age some 10,000 years ago, but particularly by Caucasian or Indo-European tribes moving eastwards and westwards some 6,000 years ago. This big, sweet apple was to be cultivated in Mesopotamia and around the Mediterranean and was probably grown from seed before the Romans perfected the art of grafting and carried it with them to Britain.[13]

While literature based upon Classical texts, such as the *Lacnunga* and the *Leechdoms*, may include remedies which contain items from Mediterranean fruit trees, such as peach leaves or the fruit of the medlar, which are less likely to have been found in England, the apple is particularly common (see Chapter 3). This fruit had, of course, a mythological role in Christianity, as the forbidden fruit of the Garden of Eden, and in Old English lore, where in *The Lay of the Nine Twigs of Woden*, Wōden is said to have smitten the adder so that it fell into nine parts:

> þær geændode   æppel ꝺ attor,
> þæt heo næfre ne wolde   on hus bugan.

> 'There did apple and venom bring it about
> That she never would turn in to the house'[14]

Graves describes the wild apple, *quert*, as one of the most sacred of trees in mythology, in the early Irish tradition of the *Triads of Ireland* 'one of the only two sacred trees for the wanton felling of which death is exacted' (along with *coll* hazel).[15]

> Three unbreathing things paid for only with breathing things:
> An apple tree, a hazel bush, a sacred grove.[16]

It was the noblest tree of all, the tree of immortality or of eternal youth. If, in north-western Europe, the apple became the fruit taken by Adam in the Garden of Eden, a symbol of the temptations of this world, images of Christ holding an apple were also to symbolise salvation from original sin. It was the fruit of the sacred thicket of Celtic literature that harboured the white roe or unicorn, the talisman to be carried by Bran when summoned by the White Goddess to enter the Land of Youth: 'a silver white-blossomed apple branch from Emain in which the bloom and the branch were one'.[17] The bright-plumaged birds of the Irish goddess Clíodna ate fruit from a sacred apple tree. Several Irish literary sources refer to the golden apple: in the *Echtrae Cormaic* it was a warrior carrying a branch with three golden apples that approached Cormac king of Tara at sunrise one day in May; the branch gave out delightful music when shaken and would cause wounded men to fall asleep.[18] Apples also characterised the legendary island known as the Isle of Avalon, 'island of apple-trees' (probably incorporating the British *aval/afal*, Cornish *auallen* 'apple-tree')[19] to which the body of King Arthur was carried after his death.

Graves explores such legendary associations much further. He finds the apple again in the grove of *The Song of Solomon*, a collection of village love-songs which were incorporated into the Bible as 'the mystical essence of King Solomon's wisdom, and as referring to the love of Jehovah for Israel', which Graves believes show a strong Hellenistic influence. The apple stands again above all other trees: 'As the apple tree among the trees of the grove, so is my beloved among the sons. I sat down under his shadow with great delight and his fruit was sweet to my taste.'[20] This apple Graves identifies as the Sidonian (Cretan) apple or quince, sacred to

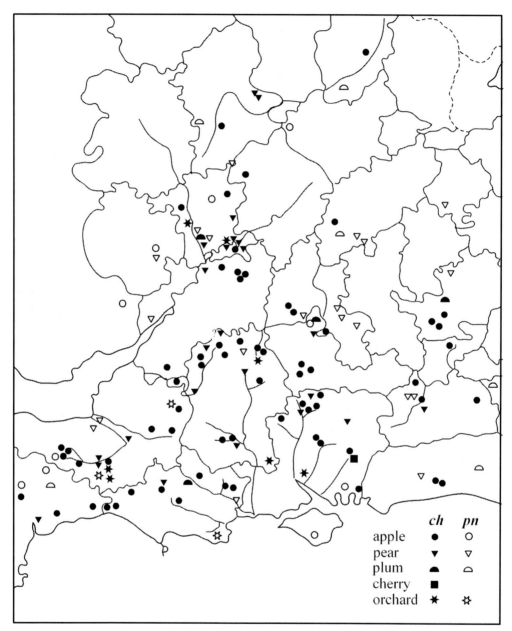

Figure 19. The distribution of fruit trees recorded in early
medieval charters and place-names

Aphrodite the love-goddess, which was the apple which grew wild in ancient times on the southern shores of the Black Sea and in Macedonia. (In the *Song of Solomon*, too, is the wild hart, a striking analogy perhaps with the unicorn or roe which, in mythology, could only be captured by a pure virgin – wisdom herself.)[21] Graves's reason for the outstanding mythic importance of the apple is that 'if an apple is halved cross-wise each half shows a five-pointed star in the centre, emblem of immortality, which represents the Goddess in her five stations from birth to death and back to birth again'.[22]

In the Old English *Lacnunga*, the bark or the juice of the wild crab-apple, *wudu-suræppel*, was included with other herbs in a salve over which charms had to be sung to be effective in healing a wound.[23] In the *Leechdoms*, apple was included in potions and salves for easing thigh ache; its bark was used in a salve for shingles, 'every wound', 'dry lung' (the sour or crab apple specified) and cancer, and in a fomentation for palsy; its juice and roasted fruits (again a sour apple) could be used for other wounds. Peeled apples or apples seethed in wine or water could be eaten to help heart disease and digestive problems; mild apples are specified for 'the overcold' (but green apples were to be avoided); but several remedies note how apples could also cause 'windy distention of the milt'.[24] However, apples can help the digestion of heavy, fatty foods and are rich in vitamins, minerals and trace elements.[25] Pears occur only once in the Anglo-Saxon sources, eaten with apples, medlars, peas moistened and sodden in vinegar, water and 'pretty sharp' wine, and 'the [roasted] flesh . . . of little creatures', such as small fowls, 'if the maw be swollen or distended'.[26] They can, indeed, help against inflammatory conditions of the digestive tract and are also rich in fibre, vitamins and trace elements.[27] In Irish law, the apple was noted for its fruit and its bark, the latter suitable for tanning.[28] Its wood, however, has been found used for fine woodwork, as in the carved applewood and hawthorn flute from the Danish levels at York.[29]

The apple-tree, OE *æppeltrēow*, *apuldre*, *apulder*, is by far the commonest fruit tree to be recorded in early place-names and charters, occurring seventy-one times in the latter source and some twenty-three times in place-names (Fig. 19). The crab-apple is sometimes referred to as the *æppelþorn*, as on the boundary of the Brokenborough estate in Wiltshire, or, more commonly, as the *sur æppel*; only rarely is a 'sweet apple' referred to, as on the boundary of an estate beside the River Nadder in Wiltshire.[30] 'Sour' apples are, however, noted twice in Somerset, once in Dorset, twice in Devon and once in Staffordshire. The commonest adjective for the apple in charter boundary clauses is *hār*, 'grey', found three times in Wiltshire, twice in Berkshire, five times in Hampshire, four times in Somerset, three times in Dorset and twice in Worcestershire. The apple is the commonest tree of all to be described in this way, and Biggam[31] suggests that this may be an indication of age in the case of trees acting as boundary markers – certainly old apple trees do have barks that become scarred with lichen and disease as they age. While the apple is rarely a large tree, one described as *lang* or 'tall' occurs on the boundary of Bricklehampton, Worcestershire, and *miclan* 'great' apple-trees are noted on the boundaries of Meon with Privett and Ecchinswell, Hampshire, 'broad' apple-trees on the boundary of Manworthy in Milverton, Somerset, and Yardley, Worcestershire, while the place-name *Fickenappletree* (lost) in Hampton Lovett, Worcestershire: *Thiccan apel treo* C11 may be 'thick apple-tree'.[32] On the boundary of the wooded part of Hawling in Gloucestershire no fewer than three of the landmarks are apples: *þære wohgan apeldran* 'the twisted or crooked apple-tree', *þære haran apeldran* 'the hoar apple-tree', and the *mær apeldran* 'boundary apple-tree'.[33] A crooked apple (*wōh*) is noted in Wanborough, Wiltshire, and an apple stump on the boundary of Dauntsey, Wiltshire. Veteran specimans of the wild apple surviving today reach 17 metres in height at Eridge Park in East Sussex and The Mens Nature Reserve in West Sussex, although usually the tree rarely grows higher than 9m.

The crab apple has also given rise to a place-name Appledore (in Burlescombe), in Devon: *Svrapla* 1086, but it is not usually possible to distinguish between the wild crab and improved varieties, as with Appledore, Kent: *Apuldre* 839. Certainly the cultivated variety seems to be indicated in the *æppel-tūn* names which mean 'farmstead where apples grow or apple orchard', which are found in Cheshire, Yorkshire and Oxfordshire (in what was formerly Berkshire). They are surprisingly common in early Yorkshire names, including East Appleton, Appleton-le-Moors, Appleton-le-Street, Appleton Roebuck and Appleton Wiske (Fig. 12a). Apple is also found with other habitative terms: with *wīc* in Appletreewick, Yorkshire West Riding, and with *bȳ* in Appleby Magna and Parva, Leicestershire, Appleby, Lincolnshire, and Eppleby, Yorkshire North Riding. Here the apple acquires its Scandinavian form *epli* and one wonders if the frequency of references to apple orchards in the north of England might reflect Danish influence. Apple is, however, common in place-names across England and is found with *lēah* in Appley, Somerset; with *stede*, in *Aplestede*, Hampshire, and with 'ford' in the Isle of White and Berkshire. The Cornish term for the apple-tree, *auallen*, may be found in several later Cornish place-names and perhaps in the name Worthyvale, Minster, Cornwall: *Guerdevalan/Gerdavalan* 1086.

Fruit trees are also mentioned in several early hundred names, presumably marking the site of a hundred meeting place or referring to the name of the estate where the hundred met. In Derbyshire, the apple is referred to in Appletree Hundred, in the south-west of the county, so-named in Domesday Book, the pear in Pyrton, Oxfordshire, and Parham (half-hundred), Suffolk, both named from nearby settlements, and the plum in Plomesgate, Suffolk, and Plympton, Devon.

In both place-names and charter boundary clauses references to most fruit trees, including the apple, tend to occur in valley areas, often those that were to become favoured places for later orchards (Fig. 19). This is particularly pronounced in the counties of south-central England. In Worcestershire, too, where charter coverage is good for almost the whole county area, they are concentrated in the Vale of

Evesham, an area open to warm south-westerly winds but sheltered from the north and already in Roman times a prime area for farming, likely to include orchards.

A form of wild pear may be native to Britain – *Pyrus pyraster* is occasionally found in ancient woodland in southern and eastern England – but the common pear, *Pyrus communis*, originally from western Asia, appears to be either a hybrid between this and an introduced orchard species, again probably brought in by the Romans, or, where growing wild, a degenerate form of that species. The pear-tree, OE *pirie*, *pirige*, *peru*, is found in both place-names and charter boundary clauses (seven together on the boundary of Bradford-on-Avon, Wiltshire).[34] The pear is mentioned at least twenty-seven times in charter boundary clauses and at least twenty-nine times in early place-names, making this the second commonest fruit tree recorded (Table 3). The boundary of an estate north of the River Parrett in Somerset runs *per summitatem loci in arborem fructosum, id est, Perie* 'by the summit/extremity of the place to the fruit tree, that is the pear',[35] which seems to indicate a cultivated variety, and the term *pir graf*, literally 'pear grove', recorded on the boundary of Burghclere, Hampshire, has also been taken to refer to a 'pear-orchard'.[36] But *peru* also occurs with *lēah*, more usually 'wood', in the place-name West Parley in Devon, Parley in Dorset and Parley farm in Horsell, Norfolk, and with *hangra* 'hanging wood, i.e. wood on a slope' on the boundary of Abingdon estates in Oxfordshire.[37] *Pirige* with *tūn*, 'pear orchard' or 'farmstead where pear-trees grow', is seemingly more likely to refer to the cultivated variety; it is found in the names Pirton, Worcestershire; Pirton, Hertfordshire; Puriton, Somerset; Pirton in Lydney, Gloucestershire; Purton, Wiltshire; and Pyrton, Oxfordshire. *Perhamstede/Perstede*, a single-hide land unit at Higham Upshire in Kent, granted *c.*767, perhaps Palmstead, may be 'pear homestead', and other possible pear names occur in corrupt form in Perry (*wirigenn*) and a the name of a swine-pasture belonging to Nackington (*wirege/wireding æcras*), both in Kent.[38]

Many pears seem to have been growing in riverine locations, actually beside rivers or streams: a river-name, *periride/pergeride*, a tributary of the River Avon in the Vale of Evesham which is followed by the boundary of Bengeworth, Worcestershire, seems to refer to the pear, and *peru* or *pirie* is found compounded with *hamm* 'meadow' in *Pyrihomme*, a meadow again beside the River Avon of which 8 acres belonged to Bengeworth; in the same area a charter landmark *piriforda* 'perry ford' again lay across the River Avon at Bricklehampton, on the boundary of the estates of Pershore Abbey (this is followed by a pear-tree and then a tall apple-tree as the following landmarks).[39] Another pear beside a ford appears to be recorded in the place-name Pyrford in Surrey and pear-tree with *hamm* is Parham in West Sussex. A boundary clause of land in and to the north of Rochester, Kent, names one landmark as *Pirigfliat* which may be 'pear channel' in an area of marshes and meadows close to the River Medway.[40] However, other pear-trees are associated with higher land for a lost *Piriho Wood*: *?Pereio* 1086, in Stanton Harcourt, Oxfordshire, may be *pirige* with *hōh* 'hill-spur', and Great Parndon, Essex: *Perenduna* 1086, is **pirigen* with *dūn* 'hill where pears grow'. Only one pear stump is noted, in *þan pyrigean styb* on the boundary of Winterbourne Bassett, Wiltshire,[41] and a pear-tree associated with a named individual is found only once, as *puntes pirian* 'Punt's pear-tree' on the boundary of Deerhurst estates in Gloucestershire.[42]

Prunus varieties include both the plum and the cherry and the cultivated varieties are again introductions. There are several native *Prunus* species: *Prunus avium*, the gean, wild cherry or mazzard (commonly, the 'merry'-tree), in spring a mass of white blossom, has rather bitter fruits, although its wood can be used for fine furniture, pipes and musical instruments. It has been found in archaeological contexts since the Neolithic but has a patchy distribution, mainly found in south-eastern England.[43] *Prunus padus*, the bird cherry, is a larger tree, now more common to regions north of the Midlands and in Ireland, which bears black, bitter fruits which can, however, be used to flavour wines. *Prunus spinosa* is the wild plum, sloe or blackthorn, whose dark fruit has a strongly astringent taste and can also be used for jam, wine or flavouring – this variety may be one of the parents of the damson and other domestic plums. Most edible varieties are introductions: *Prunus cerasifera*, the cherry plum or myrobalan plum, derives from the region extending from the Balkans to central Asia and *Prunus domestica*, the damson, appears to have come from the Middle East. Both varieties were widely grown for their fruit before they were replaced by more productive larger fruited varieties. *Prunus cerasus* is the sour cherry of south-eastern Europe and south-west Asia which is the parent of the morello cherry. The small wild plum, the sloe, *Prunus spinosa*, appears in glossaries as the *plūmslā* glossed with L. *pruniculus*. It may, however, be an improved variety that is indicated by the OE *plūme*, *plūmtrēow*, which occurs sporadically but infrequently in place-names across southern and central England, although it is not common as a boundary landmark in charters, occurring only three times as a boundary landmark and approximately fifteen times in early place-names. In boundary clauses, a plum-tree ridge is found in Whittington near Worcester, Worcestershire, a *plumleage* 'plum *lēah* or wood' to the north of Abingdon (now Oxfordshire), and a *plumstigele* 'plum (uphill) path' in Wheathampstead, Hertfordshire,[44] but in place-names the tree occurs several times in counties as far apart as Norfolk (Great and Little Plumstead and Plumstead near Holt) and Devon (Plympton, Plymtree and Plymstock).

Rackham[45] notes rare references to *ciris* (*cirisbēam*) or *cyrs* (*cyrstrēow*), which may be to the wild cherry, *Prunus avium*, a tree recorded from the Neolithic period onwards, but its rarity in these sources suggests that this tree was much less common in Anglo-Saxon times than it is now. The name appears in glossaries, including those of Ælfric, glossed with the Latin form *cerasus*. The cherry may occur in the charters in the reference to a *circumbe lace* 'cherry-combe stream', a coomb in the chalk downs of Meon, Hampshire, recorded in the tenth century, but does not appear in early place-names.[46]

The hazel, nut-tree

Several kinds of nut-trees not regularly found in Britain played a role in religious iconography. The almond became a symbol of Christ, its protected, hidden kernel representing his divine nature hidden within a worldly body. However, in earlier mythology the nut had been a symbol of pregnancy and fertility, its oil thought to be of phallic significance as the seed of Zeus (sometimes transferred in Christian iconography to fertility associated with the Madonna). But St Augustine regarded the walnut as a symbol of man – the green covering the flesh, the hard shell the bones and the sweet kernel the soul. As a symbol of Christ the bitter covering also represented the flesh that suffered the bitter Passion, the shell the wood of the cross and the kernel Christ's divine nature (as with the almond).[47]

In Celtic legend, the nut was an emblem of concentrated wisdom (Chapter 4). All the knowledge of the arts and sciences was bound up with the eating of the nuts, as in the story of Fionn son of Mairne who tasted the salmon which had fed on nuts falling into the River Boyne, as he was preparing the dish for the druid priest. Such wisdom could, however, be put to destructive uses too, for in the Fenian legend of the Ancient Dripping Hazel, the tree dripped poisonous milk, had no leaves and was the abode of vultures and ravens, birds of divination.[48] In a fifteenth-century edition of the *Book of St Albans*, a recipe is given for making oneself invisible merely by carrying a hazel rod, a fathom and a half long, with a green hazel-twig inserted in it; forked hazel rods continued to be used until the seventeenth century for divining, not only buried treasure and hidden water, but persons guilty of murder and theft.[49] It may be significant that one of the Lindow bog-men, apparently sacrificial victims, had eaten a last meal of crushed hazel-nuts immediately prior to his death.[50] In the *Leechdoms*, the lichen which grew on hazel was recognised as an effective wound salve; a fine meal made of hazel or alder could be taken with other ingredients in ale as an emetic; and hazel also played a part in magic charms, while in the (?)earlier *Lacnunga*, it is included in several recipes for salves.[51] There is little indication of its 'magical' connections here except in two charms in the *Leechdoms*: one 'for felons' where hazel or elder sticks are used and one in which a green spoon of hazel wood is used to catch the blood drawn after 'a hunting spider bite'.[52]

The hazel, *Corylus avellana*, is a native tree found throughout Britain and is tolerant of most kinds of soils. It had, with pine, recolonised these islands by 8500 BC but its pollen only becomes well represented when the tree escapes from woodland cover, allowing it to flower and fruit adequately. Throughout prehistoric and later times it was exceedingly common. The Welsh laws attributed to Hywel Dda allot a hazel grove the value of 'twenty-four pence', but one hazel as 'four pence'.[53]

Given the bias of pre-Conquest charter distribution, it may not be surprising to find this tree most commonly referred to in south-central England but it is nevertheless interesting to find it virtually confined to this region in its use as a charter boundary landmark.

References to nut-trees (OE *hnutu*, *hnutbēam*) are probably also to hazel, although Richard Coates (pers. comm.) has suggested that some may be to the walnut, *Juglans regia*. This tree had also been introduced by the Romans but had found its way into the wooodland mix by early medieval times. These nut/nutbeam references extend the coverage a little to Somerset and, on one occasion, to Suffolk. The hazel occurs thirty-two times as a boundary landmark, the nut-tree a further seven times and in early place-names the numbers recorded are twenty-eight and eight respectively (not illustrated but see Table 3). Place-name references are rather more widespread but still concentrated in the same general area. In pre-Conquest or Domesday record-ings they are found as far west as Herefordshire where Hazeltree Hundred, in the far north of the county, recorded as *Hezetre* in 1086, is **hæsltrēow* 'hazel-bush', and in the other Midlands counties of Warwickshire, Gloucestershire, Oxfordshire, North-amptonshire and Buckinghamshire. A second group of hazel place-names run from Somerset through Dorset (where Hasilor Hundred is recorded in 1084), Hampshire and the Isle of Wight, with occasional occurrences in Sussex and Kent. A 'well of the hazel' (Welsh *finnaun he collen*) is also mentioned in a Llandaff charter of Rock-field, Monmouthshire.[54] There are a few additional hazel place-names in Yorkshire where *hesli* is the Old Norse form of the word (Fig. 12a). Again, 'nut' place-names extend this coverage to Devon, Essex and Surrey but are few in number. Neither the Cornish term for hazel, **collwyth*, or the associated term **cnow* 'nuts, hazels', are found in an early context.

It is clear from the early medieval references that the hazels noted as charter boundary landmarks were frequently noted as clusters of trees, often growing in wooded situations, rather than as single trees, for the hazel is most often found compounded with terms for wood such as *lēah*, *holt*, *wrid* (?thicket) and *hurst*, and in place-names with *bearu*, *lēah* and *wudu*, or *den/denn* 'wood-pasture'. Among the latter, swine-pastures at *Haeseldenne/Haeseldaen*, in Kent, lay in 'the common woodland' that belonged to the Church of Rochester.[55] On other occasions they seem to have been plentiful on certain hills and slopes (e.g. Haselor, Warwick-shire; Hasilor Hundred, Dorset), in particular valleys and coombs, alongside some brooks and close to a few springs, fords, fortifications or dykes, and one settlement (*hæslwic* in Washington, West Sussex). Only rarely does a single tree seem to be depicted but the *hwitan hæsl* 'white hazel' of Havant, Hampshire, seems to be one such tree and in Wiltshire the *haran hæsel* of Fovant is the 'grey hazel'.[56] The occur-rences of the 'nut-tree' are similar, again found in charters and place-names with the woodland terms *lēah*, *hurst*, *holt* and *wald* and with topographical features such as coombs, a fen, a hill and a cliff. Hazel in place-names is also found compounded with woodland terms (most commonly with *lēah* as in Haseley, Warwickshire, or Hazle Farm, Ledbury, Herefordshire, but also with *wudu* and *bearu*); with one *feld* name indicating more open land: Hasfield, Gloucestershire; and in topographical locations which include valleys and slopes. Names including habitative terms include East and West Heslerton in Yorkshire West Riding (the latter **hæsling* with *tūn* 'farmstead where hazels grow')[57] and, perhaps, Helsington: *Helsingetune* 1086, in Westmorland, which may be derived from *tūn* with *hæsling* 'hazel copse' (see Chapter 7). While present across all types of countryside, the hazel is slightly more often referred to in 'ancient countryside' and is most frequent in the charters of southern and south-eastern England (Table 1).

Admittedly, the tree does not have an impressive presence as an individual specimen (although some veteran hazels are noted in the Tree Register, with 'champion' specimens found at Ashcombe Bottom Barlavington, Lewes in East Sussex, Kentchurch Court Park, Ewyas Harold in Herefordshire, and Stourhead in Wiltshire) but the tree makes up for this by its usefulness: its nuts can be eaten and were thought to ward off rheumatism or lumbago. Because of its pliability it was commonly used instead of sallow for wattle-work such as hurdles, wattle-and-daub in buildings and woven fences, and for thatching. It was the commonest small wood used in the wattle and post buildings, fences, hurdles and pit linings, especially from the ninth century onwards, that were recovered from the excavations at Coppergate, York.[58] Its rods could be split and it was often coppiced, sometimes alongside ash, to produce the type of timber required. Walnut burrwood, on the other hand, was used for more luxury items; it had been turned to make the small cups found in the Sutton Hoo Mound 1 burial, which perhaps held fruit juice and honey drunk as part of the burial ritual.[59]

OTHER BROAD-LEAFED TREES IN EARLY MEDIEVAL RECORDS

There are several other trees that have not been covered so far in this discussion. There are also a number of tree species that do not play a notable role as charter landmarks or as features that have given rise to many place-names. In general, these are trees that are often less visually distinctive or have a limited distribution. The latter include the beech and the box.

The maple, hlyn

The native maple, *Acer campestre*, often referred to as the field maple, prefers lime-rich soils but is found widely scattered across southern and central England. It is not uncommon in early medieval charters and early place-names and is found in both ancient and planned landscapes (Table 1, Fig. 20). This tree is often common in

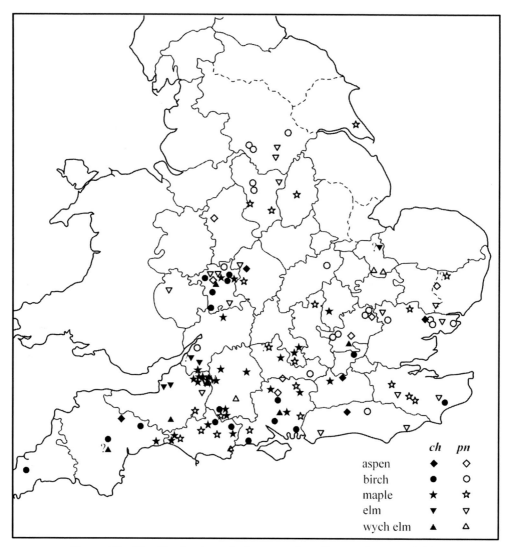

Figure 20. The distribution of other trees less frequently recorded in
early medieval charters and place-names

woodland mixed with ash and hazel, and these three trees are the dominant under-wood of some 40% of the native woodland area of eastern England, although it is missing from the pollen record of northern and western regions – not necessarily a reliable record, although in Britain the tree is near its climatic limit.[60] It grows today within woodland and in ancient hedges. The sycamore, *Acer pseudoplatanus*, England's largest maple, is thought to have been introduced in the sixteenth century, although some botanists believe there may have been earlier introductions during the Roman period.[61]

In charters, the maple is most frequently referred to in south-central counties, seemingly preferring, but not restricted to, lime-rich soils. The tree is common, for instance, across Worcestershire, although it only appears in charters in the north-east of the county. It is recorded in boundary landmarks some thirty times, with twenty occurrences in early place-names. Historically, its wood has been favoured, even in Anglo-Saxon times, for the manufacture of musical instruments. It was also turned to make drinking vessels and in the Sutton Hoo ship burial referred to above field maple had been used for the six flasks which may have held mead and ale.[62] The tree could be either coppiced or pollarded.

Maple woods appear in place-names with OE *lēah*, as in the charter-bounds of East Overton, Wiltshire; Priston, Somerset; Horton, Dorset; and Cold Ashton, Gloucestershire; and with *hurst* 'wooded hill' in Maplehurst: *Mapol der hest* 850, a swine-pasture belonging to Lenham in Kent.[63] The tree is usually referred to by the Old English term *mapuldor* but *hlyn* is an alternative term found in the place-name Great Linford in Buckinghamshire and perhaps in Linstead Magna and Parva in Suffolk in 1086 – the term is sometimes difficult to distinguish in place-names from *līn* 'flax' or *lind* 'lime-tree'.[64] The trees were presumably a feature in the coombs at Easton Bassett/Berwick St John, Wiltshire, and Maplecombe, Kent, but probably prominent landmarks on a hill at Steeple Ashton, Wiltshire (?*hapuldure*), Mapple-borough in Studley, Warwickshire (*beorg*, possibly here a 'barrow-shaped hill'), and where compounded with OE *cnæpp* in Lyme, Dorset, and Uplyme, Devon. Maples must have grown close to the settlements of Mapledurham, Hampshire; a lost *Mapleham* in the New Forest, Hampshire, and Mapledurham, Oxfordshire (all OE *hām*); Maperton, Somerset, Mapperton in Almer near Winterborne Zelstone and Mapperton near Beaminster, Dorset, and Mappleton, Yorkshire East Riding (OE *tūn*). There are other associations with gates (or natural cols) (three) and a spring. Individual trees could be chosen as boundary markers, often not distinguished by any adjective (six), but an 'old' maple grew on the boundary of Frustfield, Wiltshire, and a 'great' (*mycelan*) maple on the boundary of Abbots Wootton, Dorset;[65] others were 'little', 'rough' or, in one instance, 'red-leaved': *þon read leafan mapuldre*; the latter stood on the boundary of Blewbury, Berkshire.[66] Yet another, *þene hare mapeldure* of Chertsey/Egham, Surrey, was described as *hār* or grey.[67] At Avington, Hampshire, the tree was no more than a *stocc* or stump. Perhaps the most evocative picture is that of the Bishops Cleeve, Gloucestershire, charter, also referred to elsewhere, where on the edge of the north Cotswolds, the bounds run to *wata cumb. þer stondað apel treo & mapeltro togædere gewæxen* 'Wat's coomb, where stand the apple and maple grown together'.[68]

The field maple is often an unassuming tree but notable specimens are recorded in some Kentish and Suffolk parklands, with one 15m high tree with a girth of 520cm at Frittenden House, Cranbrook in Kent.

The birch

The birch was, with aspen and sallow, one of the first trees to recolonise Britain after the withdrawal of the ice *c.*11000 BC, but in the prehistoric period it was most abundant in northern Britain. It has increased in southern Britain in the last hundred years. It remains one of the first trees to colonise bare ground, although it is quickly replaced by other species as woodland shade increases. It is, in any case, the shortest-lived common tree after aspen, readily succumbing to drought and parasitic disease.[69] Preferring open ground, in south-eastern England it is a tree of sandy soils and areas of heathland, often found in association with oak, pine, and beech woodland, and is currently invading open heathland. In northern England the tree prefers the shallow soils found on older siliceous rocks, either alone or mixed with oak, ash and pine.[70] There are two native British species, *Betula pendula*, the 'silver' birch, and *Betula pubescens*, the cylindrical trunk of the former more useful as a timber, the stiffer twigs of the latter useful for besoms. Although a graceful and beautiful tree, especially when white-barked, it occurs only sporadically in charters with particular frequency limited to Worcestershire. Place-name occurrences, on the other hand, are more frequent in eastern England (Fig. 20). Obviously the local terrain requires detailed scrutiny if the location of such names is to be understood. Northern regions are not generally covered in this book but it is worth noting that birchwoods are the commonest native woodland of Scotland, often adjoining moorland, and such woods often also include rowan. Scotland and northern England once had a birch economy like that of Sweden, using the timber in buildings, fences, farm implements, reels and bobbins, and so forth; its bark was used for tannin.[71]

In charters and place-names, it is birchwoods that are most commonly recorded, for birch, in its variants, OE *beorc(e)*, *birce* (and in place-names Norse *birki*), occurs frequently with wood terms: with *lēah* in the *byrce leage* of Redmarley D'Abitot, the *beorclege* of Oxhey and Batchworth, Hertfordshire, and the *ruge beorclege* 'rough birchwood' of Barnet, Middlesex, or the place-name Berkeley, Gloucestershire, and Bartley Green in Northfield, Worcestershire;[72] with *hangra* in the *byrich hangran* on the boundary of Culmstock, Devon, and in the place-name Birchanger in Essex; and with *holt* in the *biricholte* of a charter of Evegate, Kent.[73] Others are recorded as characterising particular hill slopes or valleys (with *slæd, denu* and *cumb*) but distinguishing settlements at Little and Great Berhamstead (with *hām-stede*) in Hertfordshire and Ingbirchworth and Roughbirchworth in the East Riding of Yorkshire. References to single trees are rare, although *þa langan byrce* of Durley in Hampshire appears to refer to a single tall tree marking the boundary of this estate, and both *ða hwitan biricean* 'the white birch' and *ða twislihtran biricean be suðan Coenberhtes græfe* 'the forked birch-tree south of Coenberht's grove' occur as single trees in Worcestershire boundary clauses, the first in Stoke Prior and the second in Alvechurch.[74] The Worcestershire birches are all found on light soils often in areas still later supporting heathland: the first noted above, the white birch of Stoke Prior, must have stood on the fringes of Stoke Heath close to the edge of an outcrop of Keuper sandstone but the 'forked' birch of the Cofton Hacket charter, its location not positively identified, must have stood on drift soils close to Weatheroak Hill. Of the other birch locations, Bartley Green occupies a marlstone ridge which is overlain by glacial boulder clay; the birches of Pensax stood on the Upper Carboniferous sandstone uplands which lie in the north of that estate and in the early medieval period Redmarly D'Abitot was also part of Worcestershire in an area of Palaeozoic rocks and sandstones. The other concentration of birch names occurs in the place-names of Hertfordshire. In the north of the county, Berkenden Green in Aspenden and Barkway lie in a region where boulder clay is widespread over chalk, and in the west of the county Great and Little Berkhamstead are situated where the chalk is overlain by pebbly clays and sands or clay-with-flints, with valley gravels along the River Thames. Another group of charter occurrences is found in southern Wiltshire and north Dorset – again on chalk soils. It is clearly local soil types, with the emphasis upon lightness rather than pH values, which affect the distribution of this species that is reflected in the associated place-names of midland and southern England. Rackham notes its localised occurrence in eastern England before 1100.[75] In charter bounds the birch is referred to some seventeen times and it also occurs in seventeen early place-names (Table 3). The Cornish tern for birches, **beðow*, appears in one charter landmark in Trenowth.[76]

The birch does not play a large role in early herbal 'cures'. In the *Leechdoms*, its bark is used with that of many other trees against shingles and as a 'smearing for a penetrating worm', but it occupies a greater role in folklore.[77] The birch in folklore and literature 'is the tree of inception. It is the indeed the earliest forest tree, with the exception of the mysterious elder, to put out new leaves . . . and in Scandinavia its leafing marks the beginning of the agricultural year, because farmers use it as a directory for sowing their Spring wheat'.[78] It was dedicated to the Norse goddess Frigg, who became the wife of Óðinn, and the tree figures in many northern ballads, usually in joyous situations. Thus Väinämöinen, in the Finnish bardic epic the *Kalevala*, when he loses his *kantele* (harp) in a lake, makes a new one from a weeping birch threaded with the hair of a maiden (the goddess), enabling a tree that formerly had no joy in its life to bring great joy to the world with its music. It was probably the whiteness of the tree that led to a belief in its protective qualities: it was the traditional wood used for babies' cradles, thought to drive away evil spirits. For this reason, too, it was used for beating the bounds of a parish and for beating evil spirits out of lunatics. Its pendulous form was also seen to be in sympathy with weeping for the dead. The gracefulness of the birch led to it becoming known traditionally as the 'Lady of the Woods', a tree of fairy enchantment, strongly associated with love and fertility.[79]

Those wishing to seek out 'champion' specimens today in England will find fine specimens of *B. pendula* at Leith Hill in Surrey and Parham Park in West Sussex, and of *B. pubescens* at Priory Park in Reigate and Grayswood Hill in Surrey or Westonbirt Arboretum in Gloucestershire. The birch is a delicate tree, particularly when, in fresh leaf in spring, in woodlands it may be underlain by a carpet of bluebells.

The beech

The beech, *Fagus sylvatica*, also prefers light soils but the typical habitat of the native beech was poor acid soil conditions; since its numbers have been increased by deliberate planting it has thrived on more calcareous soils. This species was a late arrival in Britain, increasing only during the Bronze Age. Rackham[80] does not include it in his table of trees noted in charters and Domesday Book but notes that this tree was valued as equal to the oak: for compensation purposes at 'six score pence' – more than any other ordinary tree – in the Welsh laws.[81]

The beech does occur, however, in both charters and early place-names. In these sources, it has a restricted distribution, found, like the box, mostly in southern England (Fig. 21). The beech (OE *bōc*, *bēce*) occurs in the early recorded place-names of Kent, Sussex, Surrey and Hampshire (and once in Worcestershire) and is found as a charter landmark in Hampshire (seven times) and perhaps, rarely, in Wiltshire (?3), Gloucestershire (?1), Berkshire (?2), Hertfordshire (2) and Sussex (?4) (the form *bēce²* 'a beech-tree', is difficult to distinguish from *bece* 'a stream, valley' or even *bæc* 'a back'). A reference to *ðan ealdan beche* 'the old beech' in Chilton, Berkshire, may be to a tree rather than a topographical feature and another, *þare ealdan bec*, is noted at Olveston and Cold Ashton in Gloucestershire. One Hampshire reference, again at Meon, is *ꝺlang mearce to read lefan becan*, 'along the boundary to the red-leafed beech',[82] probably referring to its bright autumn colouring in comparison with other trees. There are also several references to a *boc haga* in this county, one of them at Meon where the bounds run to *þam sieran boc hagan* 'the dry beech *haga*'.[83] The latter was a kind of boundary which probably included an earthen wood bank. Some *haga* boundaries in the Kennet valley of Berkshire are still marked today by exactly such a feature, often with trees growing on it, and it is noteworthy that beech planted on banks was a characteristic form of boundary in Somerset and the southern counties as late as the eighteenth century. Other beeches in charters were associated with routeways, pathways, gates and fords and also with pools. In Kingsbury, Hertfordshire, a *boc spreg* may be 'beech spray' (OE *spræg* 'fine brushwood') and another beech in the same boundary clause is decribed as *þa rugan beca* 'the rough beech-tree'.[84]

Among 'beech' place-names, with a total of some eighteen noted, Buckholt was the name of a wooded region to the east of the Weald: *boc holte/Bocholt*,[85] and another Buckholt lay in the New Forest, Hampshire: *Bocolt* 1086. These names combine *bēce* with *holt*, perhaps to be interpreted as a managed beech wood, and Buckholt became a Forest name by 1086 in the latter county. Another wood outlier is Beckwith, Pannal, in N Yorkshire (Yorkshire West Riding): *bec wudu c.*972, *Becvi* 1086. The various Boughton names found in Kent (Boughton or Bockton Aluph, Boughton under Blean, Boughton Malherbe and Boughton Monchelsea) contain OE *bōc* compounded with the habitative term *tūn*, and outliers of this type are Baughton in Hill Croome, Worcestershire: *Bocctun* 1038, and Great Baughton near Chester, Chesh: *Bocstone* 1086. Great and Little Bookham in Surrey are *bōc* with *hām* 'village'; Buxshalls in Lindfield, West Sussex, is *bōc* with *geselle* (cognate of OE *sele*) 'buildings'; Boxsted, Essex, with *stede* 'place'. Hundred names only rarely contain references to the beech: Burbeach Hundred in Sussex: *Burbeca* 1086, may be 'beeches by a *burh/burg* or earthwork' but a derivation from *bece* 'valley' is also possible.[86] The Cornish term for beeches is **faw*, found in the name of the River Fowey (C13) 'beech-tree river', which gave its name to Fawton, St Neot: *Fauuitona* 1086; and possibly in Penfound, Poundstock: *Penfov* 1086.[87]

The tree could be coppiced and pollarded (a pollard beech is noted in the Sussex place-name Cowbeach: *Coppetbeche* in 1261) and the wood of the beech can be turned easily; historically it has been much used for furniture making. In wood-pasture, it was valued for its mast, foraged by herds of swine, and its Latin name may be derived from Greek *phagein* 'to eat'.[88] Today it is the third most common tree in British woodlands, and beechwoods can be classified by the combination of this species with other trees, most frequently holly and oak (*Quercus robur*) but variants include woods with sessile oak, ash, lime, wych-elm or maple, all commonest in southern England and south Wales. Some fine pollards are known, as at Burnham Beeches, Buckinghamshire, and other ancient pollards suspected to be about 400 years old are found in Epping Forest, Felbrigg Beeches, Norfolk, and Frithsden Beeches at Berkhamsted, Hertfordshire, all groves of old pollards on acid soils, the native habitat. The largest specimens recorded in the Tree Register are found in Windsor Great Park in Surrey (girth 1100cm) and Knole Park, Sevenoaks in Kent (girth 974cm).

The elm

Although there are some thirty species of elm, only a few of these can be regarded
as native . *Ulmus glabra*, the wych-elm, OE *wice*,[89] is a native hardy and non-suck-
ering species that can grow further north than other varieties, and is mainly a tree of
northern England and along the Welsh border. It is thought that the elm, presumably
the native wych-elm, was widespread at the onset of prehistoric times, declining
rapidly during the Neolithic period. Its young shoots were used as fodder, reducing
their pollen output, but this appears to be only one of the factors involved: increasingly damp conditions are another possible factor.[90] The wych-elm is a compo-
nent of ash and oak woods on a variety of soils across England and Scotland. The
'English' elm, *Ulmus procera (U. minor* var. *vulgaris)*, OE *elm, ulm*, long regarded
as native, has now been shown by DNA studies to be an introduction. These were
carried out at Madrid's City University and seem to show that the 'English' elm was
probably introduced into Britain via Spain by the Romans and that all trees living
today originated as a clone from a single tree – an Atinian elm found in central
Italy – 2,000 years ago.[91] This was widely used in Roman agriculture to support
and train vines (possibly a practice of Etruscan origin), as recommended around AD
50 by the Roman agronomist Columella in his treatise *De arboribus*, 'On Trees',
and was still a traditional practice, known as *vite maritata*, in northern Italy in the
nineteenth century. Columella noted the use of the (?black) poplar, the elm and the
(mountain) ash (the latter in more barren locations) for this purpose, although the
chestnut might also be used.[92] Virgil and Pliny, too, commented upon the practice,
particularly noting the use of the elm.[93] The species tree, normally pollarded (the
hautain), used to support the vine might vary – field maples were commonly used
– and vestiges of this practice can still be found in parts of France, Portugal and
Italy today. The so-called 'English' elm (its DNA indistinguishable from those of
Spain and Italy) may have been introduced into southern England for exactly this
purpose.[94] In this way, the vine was led to produce its fruit above the level of any
early autumn mists.[95] Today the English elm, a taller tree than the wych-elm and
formerly so characteristic of the Midlands and of southern England, has suffered
seriously from disease, the spread of which has no doubt been facilitated by its
narrow genetic make-up; full-grown trees have virtually disappeared from the landscape.

Other elms include *Ulmus minor* (this group includes *U. carpinifolia*), the
'smooth-leaved elm', found in warmer areas in southern and eastern counties. There
are today, however, many hybrids and innumerable forms of *minor* elms, such as
var. *cornubiensis*, 'the Cornish elm', which is the principle elm of Cornwall and
western Devon, and several other varieties of Field elm: *U. minor* var *minor*, the
'narrow-leaved elm', which is characteristic of East Anglia, northern Essex, parts
of the East Midlands and eastern Kent.[96]

The timber of both the English and wych-elm has been used historically: wych-elm for furniture, shafts of carts and wagons while English elm has been one of the three most important building materials in the past, used as a substitute for the more expensive oak for beams, rafters and floors. Its ability to withstand water without decay led to its use for pipes, ships' keels and bridge piers; it has also been widely used for coffins. Elm formed a major constituent of hedgerows, most varieties increasing by suckering, until decimated by disease – young trees are still present but die before reaching maturity.

The elm, as opposed to the wych-elm, is rarely found in pre-Conquest charters, perhaps because it was a relatively recent introduction: *schirebourne elm* and *elmedditch* were features upon the boundaries of Wrington and Bleadon, Somerset, but this tree can only be identified on four occasions. In place-names, however, it appears some fifteen times (Fig. 20). Among these, the *elmanstede* referred to in a charter of Kent is a place-name Elmsted (elm with *stede* 'place'), as is a Cambridgeshire bound *ad agistram/magistram aquam quae ducit ad Elm* 'to the great/dyked/flowing water which leads to Elm' on the boundary of an estate near Peterborough, a charter which is, in any case, a post-Conquest forgery.[97] Elm occurs in other recorded place-names including Great and Little Elm, Somerset: *Telma* 1086; Elmbridge, Elmley Castle, Worcestershire: *Elmlege* pre-Conquest / *Elmlæh* 1086, and Elmley Lovett, Worcestershire: *Ælmeleia* 1086, the latter two 'elm woods'; Elmdon, Warwickshire (with *dūn* 'hill'); Almeley, Herefordshire (again with *lēah*); another possible Kent occurrence in Elmhurst, Brenchley (with *hyrst* 'wooded hill'); Elmstead, Essex, 'elm-tree place' and Elmsett, Suffolk 'the dwellers or the houses at the elm-tree copse'. In the north of England, North and South Elmsall, Yorkshire East Riding, are both *elm* with *halh* 'nook, hollow'. Cornish *elow, 'elms', occurs only in later place-names. In the past, it has been thought that it was the elm that gave its name to an extensive wooded area in the north-west Midlands, close to the boundaries of the new counties of Staffordshire, Shropshire and Cheshire: the woodland of Lyme, interpreting this as 'elm-tree region'. Burslem in Staffordshire was recorded as *Barcardeslim* in 1086, 'estate in Lyme belonging to the fort-keeper, or to a man called Burgweard', while Newcastle-under-Lyme: *Novum castellum subtus Lymam* in 1173, and Audlem in Cheshire: *Aldelime* in 1086, seems to refer to the same district name, a British name thought to be derived from *lemo-, *lēmano 'at the elms'. This has, however, now been questioned and an alternative derivation from Latin *līmen* 'threshold', used in a metaphorical sense, or possibly *līmes*, used loosely as a 'boundary zone', has been suggested.[98] However, the region is largely underlain by Mercia mudstone and a concentration of *lēah* type names confirms its early wooded nature, although it was never to become a Norman forest.

The wych-elm, the hardiest of the native elms, may be referred to in two Cambridgeshire names: Witchford Hundred, one of the two hundred divisions in the Isle of Ely recorded in Domesday Book, which met at *Wiceforde*,[99] and Witcham:

Wichamme 970, *Wyceham* 1086 (OE *hamm*). In Worcestershire, Wichenford: *Wiceneford* C11, is now thought to mean 'ford by the wych-elms' rather than to be a reference to the Hwicce.[100] The wych-elm may also be represented in several charters such as that of Ruishton in Stoke St Mary and Orchard Portman, Somerset, where the reference is to *wice hrycg*, or *þam wicce* and *up to þam twam wycan standað on gerewe* 'up to the two wych-elms [which] stand in a row' at Weston near Bath in the same county,[101] but is difficult to distinguish from OE *wīc*, usually a dairying settlement, sometimes used seasonally. One 'rough' wych-elm, *þa rugan wican*, is noted in Burston, Hertfordshire, where the bounds also note a *wifeling wicon* (possibly a wych-elm associated with OE *wifel* 'weevil').[102] Today some of the largest surviving wych-elms are to be found in Scotland, as at Brahan and Tarbat House in Tain, both in the Highland Region.

Elm bark or 'rind' is a frequent ingredient in some of the *Leechdoms*, burnt to relieve toothache, used in a salve for a broken limb or any other wound, smeared on a burn, boiled in urine for leprosy and drunk in ale or water with other ingredients for 'dry' disease and palsy.[103] Wych-elm was specified as one of the ingredients for shingles.[104] It is recognised today that the elm has astringent properties.

TREES OF LIMITED DISTRIBUTION IN CHARTERS AND PLACE-NAMES

Other trees favouring light soils tend to have limited representation in charters and place-names (Fig. 21). The box, *Buxus sempervirens* (OE *box*, **byxe*), for instance, is a small tree of limestone and chalk soils in the south of England, today usually associated with beech. While not prominent as a tree its valuable wood would have drawn it to people's attention. In historical times, the box has become recognised as a heavy, even-textured wood suitable for high-class wood carving.

In the charters it occurs only twice. Both of these occurrences are in Hampshire, where at Meon it is described as the *readen bexean* 'red box'.[105] In Berkshire, Gloucestershire, Oxfordshire and Hertfordshire it occurs only once in the early place-names of each county: Boxford, Berkshire: *Boxoran* 960 (with 'ridge'); Boxwell, Gloucestershire: *Box(e)wella* 1086 (with 'spring'); Bix, Oxfordshire: *Bixa* 1086; Boxbury and Boxfield Farm, Walkern, Hertfordshire (from *Boxe* 1086) (and probably in Bixley, Norfolk: *Bischeleah* 1086); but in the early place-names of south-east England (Kent, East and West Sussex) it occurs eight times, twice in Kent in the the names Bexley: *Bixle* C8, and Boxley: *Boselau* 1086; four times in Sussex in the names Boxgrove, West Sussex: *Bosgrave* 1086 and Bexhill, East Sussex: *Bexelei* 1086 (twice repeated as a hundred name: *Bocse hvnd'* 1086 was a rape of Chichester in Sussex, the ancient hundred of Box or Boxgrove, probably named after the settlement name where the hundred would have met, while Bexhill in the same county was a rape of Hastings: *Bexelei hvnd'* 1086, limited to the parish of that name).[106] In three of these names the box seems to have been a constituent of a *lēah* feature, whether in a wood or on a piece of regenerating ground, and once of a grove. Some of the most ancient and interesting specimens to be found today include those at North Cerney House, Gloucestershire; the Bishop's Palace, Chichester, West Sussex; and Gunnersbury Park, Greater London (the largest and possibly oldest specimen, found at White Notley, Braintree in Essex, is 7m high with a girth of 145cm). As a landscape feature the box is prominent over parts of the chalk downlands, especially at its namesake Box Hill in Surrey.

The aspen

The aspen, *Populus tremula*, OE *æspe, æpse*, is infrequent in charter boundary clauses but certainly occurs (probably four times) (Fig. 20). This species was probably the commonest of the *Populus* species and that most likely to have been referred to in the early references (for the black poplar, see Chapter 12). The aspen was commonly used, surprisingly, for building.[107] An *æsphanhangran* appears to have been a wood on a slope in Whitchurch, Hampshire, but the other references to this tree as a boundary landmark are found in the West Midlands: *þ gratan æspan* 'the great aspen' was a feature on the boundary of *Wican*, Worcestershire, in the west of the county and another stood on the boundary of Arley, Warwickshire.[108] A landmark in a charter of Ecchinswell, Hampshire, is *to ðere gemearcoðan æfsan, of ðere gemearcodan æfsan* 'to the marked aspen, from the marked aspen',[109] but the significance of this is not clear and it may have been just an aspen marking a boundary ('marked' oaks are also known). The aspen is rather more frequent in early place-names (recorded ten times), mostly in south and central England: these include East and West Tapps, Devon: *Ausa* 1086; Apps Court, Walton-on-Thames, Surrey: *Epse* 675; Hapsbury Mill, St Peters, Hertfordshire: *Absa* 1086; and Aspenden, Hertfordshire: *Absedene* 1086 (with *denu* 'valley'); together with several in which *æspe* is compounded with *lēah*, 'aspen wood': Apsley Heath in Tanworth-in-Arden, Warwickshire: *Æpsleage* 963; Apsley Farm, Thakeham, West Sussex: *Abseleia* 1073; Apsley Guise, Bedfordshire: *Aspleia* 1086. In Cornwall, Idless in Kenwyn: *Edelet* 1086, may contain the Cornish term for aspen, *aidlen*.[110] The aspen today is found in woods where other species are usually dominant, such as the ash, maple, lime, oak or beech. It has been hybridised with many introduced varieties to produce a quick-growing source of timber which is light and useful for veneer or plywood, matches fruit boxes. At present, an impressive aspen some 31m tall can be seen at North Cerney House, Gloucestershire.[111]

 The Latin name of the aspen, *Populus tremula*, derives from the fact that the leaves of this tree appear constantly to tremble. In legend, Christianity associated this with guilt and suggested that it was the tree upon which Christ was crucified (a role also assigned in legend to the elder); it therefore remained unpopular in folklore. Graves regards the aspen as 'the tree of the autumn equinox and of old age'. He notes that golden head-dresses of aspen leaves are found in Mesopotamian burials of 3000 BC and that the measuring-rod or *fé* used by coffin-makers on corpses in ancient Ireland was of aspen, 'a reminder to the souls of the dead that this was not the end'.[112] Hercules is said to have bound his head in triumph with poplar after killing the evil giant Cacus, conquering death. In the *Leechdoms*, the 'rind' of aspen is only used with other barks, for, among other things, shingles but one constituent of this tree is salicin with properties similar to aspirin, making it a remedy for headaches, pains and fevers.[113]

Sorbus species

The wild service tree, *Sorbus torminalis*, is a medium-sized tree with leaves like the maple, widespread but uncommon and usually found in areas of ancient woodland or wood-pasture. Charcoal from this tree has been identified on late Iron Age sites in Dorset.[114] A *syrf treow* on the boundary of Stoke Prior, Worcestershire, seems to be a reference to this tree, and others are recorded as landmarks upon the boundaries of White Waltham/Waltham St Lawrence and West Chieveley and Beedon, Berkshire.[115] Some of the oldest recorded service trees surviving today are found at Parsonage Farm, Udimore, in East Sussex, and at Hall Place, Leigh in Kent. There is no obvious reference in place-names or charters to the rowan, *Sorbus aucuparia*, but this tree may be the *cwicbēam* discussed further in Chapter 12.

Even more intriguing is a single reference in a tenth-century boundary clause of Pendock, Worcestershire, to *æsc apaldre leage* 'ash-apple *lēah* (wood)'.[116] The leaves of the true service tree, *Sorbus domestica*, resemble those of the rowan or mountain ash and its fruits look similar to small crab apples so it is just possible that this is a reference to the 'Whitty pear', a variety found only on one occasion in the Forest of Wyre in the same county and first recorded in 1678. Yet Nennius in the ninth century also referred to 'the ash-tree that bears apples, by the River Wye', recounted among 'The Wonders of Britain' in the *History of the British*.[117] The true service tree, *Sorbus domestica*, may be native, although some believe it to have been introduced by the Romans from Mediterranean regions, possibly for its fruit that could be made into an alcoholic drink.[118] Rackham considers this unlikely – although it is a tree of southern Europe it is also found in Brittany. It remains, however, 'the rarest wild tree in Britain'.[119]

There is, however, another *Sorbus* species, *S. aria*, the whitebeam, which was known in Hampshire as the whitten or whittenbeam (see above), OE *hwītingtrēow*, or the hoar withy, perhaps the *har wiði* discussed above;[120] OE *hwītian* means 'to become white', probably referring to the white felt of silky thick hairs on the underside of the leaf which make the tree distinctive, the white down decking the tree in silver from spring onwards until the leaves turn golden in the autumn. (But in the

Midlands and south-west the whitten-tree is another name for the wayfaring tree, *Viburnum lantana*, a much smaller shrub with similar flowers, leaves and fruit, again with dense, white hairs on the underside of the leaf.) The whitebeam bears red berries but its leaves in no way resemble those of the rowan, being more like those of the wych-elm. It is a tree of dry limestone, chalk soils or sandy soils,[121] native to southern England and Co. Galway. In England, fine specimens can be found in St Clere Pinetum, Sevenoaks in Kent, including the largest on the Tree Register), and on the Rushmore Estate, Tollard Royal in Wiltshire. The hoar withy, dialect for whitebeam in Hampshire, occurs six times in charter boundaries (three of Biggam's nine are probably repeated landmarks).[122] In southern England *þone haran wiðig* is recorded on the boundary of Ringwood and Harbridge, Hampshire, on the boundary of Horton, Dorset, and of a wood belonging to Thames Ditton, Surrey;[123] in midland England, it is noted upon the boundary of Pendock, Worcester-shire; South Cerney, Gloucestershire; and Pelsall, Staffordshire.[124] In place-names, the hoar withy is recorded only in post-Conquest names, as at Hoarwithy, Hereford-shire,[125] or Harrowins in Halifax Chapelry.[126] *Hār* 'grey' as an adjective is found in combination with many other kinds of trees including the apple, hawthorn, maple and hazel.[127]

SHRUBS

While lesser shrubs are hardly likely to appear as single specimens in charter boundary clauses their presence often characterises a location. Broom and gorse or furze is frequently found in both charters and place-names, both preferring acidic sands and gravels, with the latter particularly resilient in exposed windy situations. Both were much used on farms in the past: broom provided early fodder for domestic stock and was thought to protect sheep against rot.

Broom, *Sarothamnus scoparius*, OE *brōm*, was formerly much more abundant on lowland heaths and is found frequently in pre-Conquest charters and many early place-names (at least twenty-one times in charters, once as Welsh *banadl* in the bounds of Merthyr Mawr,[128] and over fifty-seven times in place-names; sixth in the frequency of all names listed in Table 3). The plants could characterise certain coombs and valleys, as in the charter-bounds of Abingdon, Berkshire (now Oxford-shire); Meon, Hampshire; Upper Arley, Staffordshire; or the place-name Bramhope, Yorkshire West Riding; or a hill in a charter landmark of Ottery St Mary and a place-name Brendon in Devon. It is noted ten times (perhaps on six different occasions) in Hampshire charter-bounds, giving its name to the *bromburna* stream and a bridge; a valley *bromdene/-dæne* in Bramdean and Hinton Ampner; areas of open land (*feld*), including *þa twægen bromfeldas* 'the two broomfields' in Droxford; a shrub or wood-covered hill, *bromhyrste/bromhurst* in Crondall; and an enclosed area of land

(OE *(ge)hæg*), the *bromhæg* of Ossenley in Milton (as also at Bromhey in Frinsbury, Kent; also with *geard* in Bromyard, Herefordshire).[128] It is sometimes difficult to distinguish *brōm* from *brēmel* 'brambles' in place-names and, as with every place-name recording, it is essential to check the earliest spelling: thus Bromley, Greater London, derives from *Bræmbelege c.*1000.[129] In Hampshire, there are also four other broom place-names, including *brōm* with *denu*, *hyll* and *mōr*, but also with *lēah* in Bramley (a name also recorded by 1086 in Yorkshire and Surrey). Broom within a wooded region, probably growing on sandy areas cleared by grazing, occurs in the many 'Bromley' names. These include *bromleage* in Sandford in Devon, and the place-names Bromley in Kent (which became a hundred name), Hertfordshire, and Essex (twice); Kings and Abbotts Bromley, Staffordshire; Bramley in Yorks (three early names) and Surrey, while *brōm* with *feld* occurs further in Bramfield, Suffolk; Brimfield, Herefordshire; Bromfield, Shropshire. On the boundary of Ruin Clifford, Warwickshire, a steep slope on the edge of arable fields was referred to as the *brom hlinc*. Brampton or Brompton names, *brōm* with *tūn*, are fairly common, found in Cambridgeshire, Northamptonshire and Shropshire, four times in Herefordshire (Brampton Abbotts and Brampton Bryan, Great and Little Brampton) and even more times in parts of Yorkshire (eight out of sixteen early 'broom' place-names); the royal manor of Braunton in Devon, *Brantona* in 1086, gave its name to a hundred while *brōm* with *wīc* occurs in West Bromwich, West Midlands. Broom also occurs alone in early place-names in Warwickshire, Suffolk and Shropshire.

Gorse or furze, *Ulex europaeus*, OE *furs*, *fyrs* (OE *gors(t)* occurs mainly in literary sources and later place-names) occurs on the boundary of Idmiston, Wiltshire, with OE *ēg* in Brimpton, Berkshire (*?fyrs ige*), but is most common as a boundary land-mark in the south-west of Britain. Another Old English name for gorse appears to be **ceacga*, possibly found in the place-name Chagford in Devon (*Cagefort* 1086) and in a few later names in that county, and perhaps, too, in Chailey East Sussex (*Cheagele*, *Chaglegh* 1086–1100); however this term may also have covered 'broom' and 'brushwood'.[130] In charter-bounds it occurs as *on ceaggan heal* (with 'nook') in Waltham St Lawrence, Berkshire; *on ceacgan seað* (with 'pit') in Burgh-clere, Hampshire; *ceacgabroc* (with 'brook') in Monkton in Shobrooke, Devon; and on *ceaggancum* (with 'coomb') in Stoke Canon, Devon.[131] The more usual *furs*, *fyrs* occurs with *lēah* in Pitminster and Taunton, Somerset, with ford and gore in Cors-comb and Cheselborne in Dorset, and with *pen* (possibly Cornish *pen* 'top, head') in *Peadingtun* in Devon. *Peadingtun* was an estate which extended onto the granite moorlands of Dartmoor,[132] and two other Devon place-names containing *furs, fyrs* are also found on the edges of the moor at Furze in West Buckland and Fursham in Drewsteignton. The Cornish term for gorse is *eithin*, possibly found in the names Tredinnick in Morval and Probus combined with the habitative term *tre*, and is also common in later place-names.[133] In the Llandaff charters, too, it occurs in the Welsh form *eithin* in a name of a parcel of land known as *Rhos yr Eithin* 'the gorse moor' in *Lann Vedeui* (Penterry).[134] In Yorkshire, it is found with *lēah* in the name Farsley in Calverley, Yorkshire West Riding. A Norse term for gorse, *hvin*, occurs in a few later minor names in Yorkshire, and whin has remained a name for gorse in eastern and northern counties, Scotland and Ireland. Similar plants include the petty whin, *Genista anglica*, which is another spiny plant of barren ground which also bears yellow flowers, and the dwarf furze, *Ulex galli*, known in Cumbria as the cat-whin, which forms a low prickly cushion on moorland.

None of the places with furze names became parishes and, as the term implies, they seem always to have been minor places in marginal locations; references to gorse become much more common in later recorded minor names. The exception is the twelfth-century hundred name *Gosefeld* in Berkshire, **gorsiht* with *feld* 'furzy open land', a name that replaced an earlier name *Taceham* (Thatcham).[135] Gorse, however, had its uses and was of great value as a fuel, cut and faggotted for home cooking and industrial use – and used by bakers, brickmakers and lime-burners. It could be fed to livestock in winter if the spines were first crushed (often done in cider mills). Sprigs of furze blossom were thought to bring luck in Ireland and Anglesey.

The native privet, *Ligustrum vulgare*, is a common shrub in hedgerows and wood-lands (a different variety to the larger-leafed garden variety) but rarely attracted sufficient attention to find its way into charters and place-names. An exception is Privett, Hampshire, *pryfetes flodan* C9, OE *pryfet* with *flōde* 'channel, gutter',[136] and in this same county a charter boundary landmark, *swa þurh ðone pryet* 'thus through the privet', is recorded in Hoddington.[137]

The bramble, *Rubus fruticosus*, is another shrubby plant of abandoned places and is common in place-names (not included in the charter list given here); its fruit, the blackberry, has been eaten since prehistoric times. OE *brēmer*, 'bramble thicket', occurs in the place-names Bramber in West Sussex and with *tūn* in Bramerton in Norfolk, and in the form *brǣmel, brēmel* 'brambles' with *tēag* 'enclosure', in Brambletye in Forest Row, East Sussex, with *feld* in Brimpsfield, Gloucestershire, and, associated with woodland terms, with *sceaga* 'copse' in Bramshaw, Hampshire, and with *lēah* in Bromley, Kent (now Greater London) (*Brǣmbelege c.*1000). On occasions, the bramble might be referred to as *brembel þorn/ðyrnan*, as in tenth-century charters of Abingdon and Harwell in Oxfordshire.[138] Brambles were appar-ently plentiful in Devon in a coomb, Brambelcombe in Bulkworthy. The Cornish word for bramble is *dreys* and is found only in later minor place-names. Briars, OE *brēr*, could be either wild roses or brambles; they are referred to in the place-names Brereton, Cheshire, and Brereton, Staffordshire.

Ivy, *Hedera helix*, cannot really be described as either a tree or a shrub but occurs as an adjective in a few charters and place-names, especially when it caused a tree upon a boundary to be a readily distinguishable landmark. Thus *þa ifihtan ac* 'the ivy-covered oak' was a landmark on the boundary of Stoke Prior, Worcestershire, and *þæm ifihtan æsce* 'the ivy-covered ash' another on the boundary of Winchester, Hampshire, while the *ifihtan stocc* 'ivy-covered stump' stood close to a ridgeway in Havant, Hampshire.[139] In Devon an *ifigbearo* on the boundary of Crediton estates may have been an 'ivy grove', as may also have been *iffingknap* '?ivy-grove summit' and *iffingberlake*, the same name combined with *lacu* (the name of the stream flowing away from the former landmark) on the Ottery St Mary boundary.[140] In early place-names Ivychurch in Kent, recorded in the eleventh century, is 'ivy-covered church'.

ENDNOTES

1 Domesday Book fol. 314.
2 H. Logeman, 1888. *The Rule of S. Benet*, EETS, OS 90 (London, 1888), p. 66.
3 *Lieber Eliensis* II.54: J. Fairweather, trans., *Liber Eliensis. A History of the Isle of Ely from the Seventh Century to the Twelfth* (Woodbridge, 2005), p. 150.
4 J. Harvey, *Medieval Gardens* (London, 1981), pp. 35–6.
5 Liebermann, *Die Gesetze*, p. 454.
6 D. Bk., *Exeter Text*: fols 104v, *222b*; fol. 84a, *61b*; fol. 280: A. Williams and G. H. Martin, eds, *Domeday Book. A Complete Translation* (London, 1992), pp. 292, 225, 757.
7 D. Hooke, 'A note on the evidence for vineyards and orchards in Anglo-Saxon England', *Journal of Wine Research*, 1 (1990).
8 Tacitus, *Agricola* 12: Mattingley, p. 63.
9 S 459, B 754, *Charters of Shaftesbury*, no. 11; S 766, Dugdale, *Monasticum Anglicanum*, ii.323–4 (no. 6); C. C. Taylor, 'The Saxon boundaries of Frustfield', *Wiltshire Archaeological Magazine* 59 (1964).
10 S 1590, K 1358, *WoASCB*, p. 373; S 1395, K 765, *WoASCB*, pp. 366–7.
11 S 1012, K 776; S 310, B 475 (sp); S 1819, Turner, 'Some Old English passages', p. 119; S 345, B 550.
12 Jenkins, *Hywel Dda*, p. 188.
13 E. Price, 'East of Dean', *The Garden*, Journal of the Royal Horticultural Society 126, part 6 (2001), citing work of Dr Barrie Juniper.
14 *Lacnunga* LXXXb: Grattan and Singer, *Anglo-Saxon Magic*, pp. 152–5.
15 Graves, *The White Goddess*, p. 246.
16 Ibid., p. 198.
17 Ibid., p. 246, citing the *Câd Goddeu*, 'Battle of the Trees'.
18 Dillon, *Early Irish Literature*, p. 110.
19 Padel, *Cornish Place-Name Elements*, p. 13.
20 Graves, *The White Goddess*, p. 253, quoting *The Song of Solomon*, 2, 3.
21 Ibid., pp. 248, 253.
22 Ibid., p. 250.
23 *Lacnunga* XV, fol. 133a; LXXXIIb, fols 162b, 163a: Grattan and Singer, *Anglo-Saxon Magic*, pp. 100–1, 156–7.
24 *Leechdoms*: Cockayne. For apple as a cure see especially *Leechdoms* I.xxiii, fol. 24b; xxxvi, fol. 33a; xxxviii, fol. 37a; xliv, fol. 41a; lxi (1), fols 49b, 50a: Cockayne, II, pp. 66–7, 86–7, 98–9, 108–9, 132–3; *Leechdoms* II.i (1), fols 66a; iii (2), fol. 67a; iv, fol. 68a; xii, fol. 70b;

xvi (1), fol. 72a; li. (3), fol. 100a: Cockayne, II, pp. 176–9, 180–1, 182–3, 190–1, 194–5, 266–7; *Leechdoms* III.xlvii, fol. 121b: Cockayne, II, xlvii, fol. 121b, pp. 338–9; as a cause of discomfort, *Leechdoms* I.xxxix, fol. 62a; II.iv, fol. 68a: Cockayne, II, pp. 166–7, 182–3.

25 McIntyre, 'Tree culture', p. 224.

26 *Leechdoms* II.ii (2), fol. 67a: Cockayne, II, pp. 180–1.

27 McIntyre, 'Tree culture', p. 254.

28 Brehon Law: Graves, *The White Goddess*, p. 198.

29 Wilson, 'Craft and industry', p. 253; K. M. Richardson, 'Excavations in Hungate, York', *Archaeological Journal* 116 (1959), fig. 19.

30 S 1577, B 922, Kelly, *Charters of Malmesbury*, no. 34; D. Hooke, 'The administrative and settlement framework of early medieval Wessex', in *The Medieval Landscape of Wessex*, ed. M. Aston and C. Lewis (Oxford, 1994), pp. 93–4; S 586, B 1030.

31 Biggam, *Grey in Old English*, pp. 225–30.

32 S 786, B 1282, *WoASCB*, p. 182; S 811, B 1319 (?sp); S 412, B 674; S 709, B 1116, B 1117; S 786, B 1282, *WoASCB*, pp. 222–5.

33 S 179, B 356 (C11 fabrication).

34 S 899, K 706, Kelly, *Charters of Shaftesbury*, no. 29.

35 S 267, Bates, *Two Cartularies* (*Athelney Register*), pp. 144–5; Finberg, *The Early Charters of Wessex*, no. 398, 118–20, querying whether *Perie* might be Perry Green in Wembdon.

36 S 487, B 787; J. R. Clark Hall and H. D. Merrit, *A Concise Anglo-Saxon Dictionary*, 4th edn (Cambridge, 1960), p. 273.

37 S 605, B 924, Kelly, *Charters of Abingdon*, II, no. 52 (?sp) (formerly Berkshire).

38 S 31, B 176, B 199; S 1614, B 263; S 877, E. Edwards, ed., *Liber Monasterii de Hyda*, Rolls Series (London, 1886), pp. 242–53; Miller, *Charters of the New Minster*, Appendix, pp. 207–10; Wallenberg, *Kentish Place-Names*, pp. 41, 51, 61–9, 336–51.

39 S 1590, K 1358, *WoASCB*, pp. 373–5; S 786, B 1282, *WoASCB*, pp. 177–90;

40 S 339, Campbell, *Charters of Rochester*, no. 26, p. 31 n.1.

41 S 668, B 1145.

42 S 1551, Finberg, *The Early Charters of the West Midlands*, no. 187, pp. 80–5.

43 Rackham, *Ancient Woodland*, revised edn, p. 349.

44 S 1361, K 670, *WoASCB*, pp. 315–18; S 663, B 1002, Kelly, *Charters of Abingdon*, II, no. 59; Gelling, *Place-Names of Berkshire*, part III, pp. 729–30; S1031, J. E. B. Gover, A. Mawer and F. M. Stenton, *The Place-Names of Hertfordshire*, English Place-Name Society 15 (Cambridge, 1970), p. 313.

45 Rackham, *Ancient Woodland*, revised edn, pp. 349–50.

46 S 619, B 982; S 811, B 1319 (suspicious).

47 Becker, *The Continuum Encyclopedia*, pp. 13, 213.

48 Graves, *The White Goddess*, pp. 71, 176–7.

49 Ibid., pp. 176–7.

50 T. G. Holden, 'The last meals of the Lindow Bog Men', in *Bog Bodies: New Discoveries and New Perspectives*, ed. R. C. Turner and R. G. Scaife (London, 1995), pp. 6–82.

51 *Leechdoms* I.xxxviii, 8, fol. 36b: II.lii, 1, fol. 101b, 102a: Cockayne, II, pp. 96–7, 270–1; *Lacnunga* XVa, fol. 133a, b, XXXIa, fol. 138a, b; XXIIIa, fol. 141a: Grattan and Singer, *Anglo-Saxon Magic*, pp. 100–1, 110–13, 114–15.

52 *Leechdoms* I.xxxix, fol. 39b; lxviii, 1.4, fol. 54a: Cockayne, II, pp. 104–5, 142–5.

53 Jenkins, *Hywel Dda*, p. 188.

54 Davies, *An Early Welsh Microcosm*, p. 30; Evans, *The Text of the Book of Llan Dâv*, pp. 246–7.

[55] S 157, B 303, Campbell, *Charters of Rochester*, no. 16; S 165, B 339, Campbell, op. cit., no. 17 (swine pastures added later to the grant).

[56] S 837, K 624; S 430, B 707; S 881, K 687.

[57] A. H. Smith, *The Place-Names of Westmorland, Part I*, English Place-Name Society 42 (Cambridge, 1967), p. 108.

[58] Kernnard and Hall, *Biological Evidence from 16–22 Coppergate*, p. 722.

[59] Comey, 'The wooden drinking vessels'.

[60] Rackham, *Ancient Woodland*, revised edn, pp. 203, 204–5, 208–9.

[61] A. Mitchell, *A Field Guide to the Trees of Britain* (London, 1978), p. 331.

[62] Comey, 'The wooden drinking vessels'.

[63] S 300, B 459, Kelly, *Charters of St Augustine's*, no. 21.

[64] Mills, *A Dictionary of Place-Names*, p. 212.

[65] S 766, Dugdale, *Monasticum Anglicanum* ii. 323–4 (no. 6); S 1004, K 772, *Ordnance Survey Facsimiles*, vol. II, ed. W. B. Sanders (Southampton, 1878–84), no. 3.

[66] S 496, B 801, Kelly, *Charters of Abingdon*, I, no. 36.

[67] S 1165, B 34.

[68] S 1549, *Heming*: Hearne, pp. 245–6.

[69] Rackham, *Ancient Woodland*, revised edn, p. 311.

[70] Peterken, *Woodland Conservation*, p. 108.

[71] Rackham, *Ancient Woodland*, revised edn, p. 312.

[72] S 1338, K 619; S 916, K 1304, Crick, *Charters of St Albans*, no. 12; S 912, K 672, Crick, op. cit., no. 11.

[73] S 386, B 724, *CBDC*, pp. 137–41; S 877, Miller, *Charters of the New Minster*, no 31.

[74] S 360, B 596, Miller, *Charters of the New Minster*, Appendix, pp. 178–83 (sp); S 60, B 204, *WoASCB*, pp. 65–9 (sp); S 1272, B 455 (1), *WoASCB*, pp. 135–42.

[75] Ibid., p. 314, fig. 19.1.

[76] S 770, B 1231, *CBDC*, pp. 42–3.

[77] *Leechdoms* I.xxxvi, fol. 33a; III.xxxix, fol. 119b: Cockayne, II, pp. 86–7, 332–3.

[78] Graves, *The White Goddess*, p. 161.

[79] Paterson, *Tree Wisdom*, pp. 94–7, 101.

[80] Rackham, *Trees and Woodland*, 2nd edn, p. 187, table 6; *Ancient Woodland*, revised edn, p. 319.

[81] Jenkins, *Hywel Dda*, p. 189.

[82] S 754, B 1200.

[83] S 283, B 377 (sp).

[84] S 912, K 672, Crick, *Charters of St Albans*, no. 11, pp. 180–1, 188.

[85] S 40, B 322; S 123, B 247; S 125, B 248 (fabricated from S 123 and S 89); S 1615, B 323.

[86] A. Mawer, F. M. Stenton, with J. E. B. Gover, *The Place-Names of Sussex, Part I*, English Place-Name Society 6 (Cambridge, 1929), p. 203.

[87] *CDEPN*, p. 238; Padel, *Cornish Place-Name Elements*, p. 96.

[88] Milner, *The Tree Book*, p. 17.

[89] *Wice* is translated in the Toronto *Dictionary of Old English* 1210 (Dictionary of Old English Project, University of Toronto Centre for Medieval Studies, Pontifical Institute of Medieval Studies: http://www.doe.utoronto.ca/) as 'witch-hazel, mountain-elm', but witch-hazel is *Hamamelis*, not introduced into Britain until the nineteenth century; wych hazel is, however, also a dialect term for the wych-elm or hornbeam.

[90] Evans, *Land and Archaeology*, pp. 83–6, 105–7.

[91] L. Gil, P. Fientes-Utrilla, A. Soto, M. T. Cervera and C. Collada, 'Phylogeography: English elm is a 2,000-year-old Roman clone', *Nature* 431 (28 October, 2004), pp. 1053–4.

[92] Columella, *De arboribus*, xvi: trans. E. S. Forster and E. H. E. H. Heffner, *Lucius Junius Moderatus Columella on Agriculture and Trees: On Trees* (Cambridge, Mass., 1968), p. 381. Columella, *De re rustica*, IV.xxxiii; trans. H. B. Ash, *On Agriculture by Lucius Junius Columella* (London, 1941), pp. 456–7.

[93] Virgil, *Georgics* II, lines 362, 367: Mynors, Virgil, *Georgics*, p. 92.

[94] Luis Gil: *Nature* 27/28 Oct 2004; reported by Mark Henderson, Science Correspondent, in *The Times*, 28 Oct; http://news.bbc.co.uk/1/hi/sci/tech/3959561.stm.

[95] P. Pointereau, 'La diversité des systèmes arborés et des pratiques de gestion dans le sud de l'Europe: les dehesas ibériques et les hautains méditerranéens', 1ʳ colloque européen sur les trognes, Vendome 26–28 octobre 2006. Vendome: Maison Botanique, 2006; www.maison-botanique.com.

[96] R. H. Richens, *Elm* (Cambridge, 1983), pp. 1–5; Rackham, *Trees and Woodland*, 2nd edn, pp. 255–7.

[97] S 168, B 335; S 68, B 22A.

[98] R. Coates, '"The Lyme"', *English Place-Name Society Journal* 36 (2004), pp. 39–50. The term is also discussed by D. Horovitz, *The Place-Names of Staffordshire* (Brewood, Stafford, 2005), p. 337.

[99] Anderson, *The English Hundred-Names*, p. 108.

[100] Mills, *A Dictionary of English Place-Names*, p. 358; *CDEPN*, p. 676; *WoASCB*, p. 358.

[101] S 310, B 475 (sp); S 508, B 814.

[102] S 888, K 696, Crick, *Charters of St Albans*, no. 9, pp. 168, 174.

[103] *Leechdoms* I.vi, fol. 19b; xxiv, fol. 25a; xxvi, fol. 26a, b; xxxii, fol. 29a, 3; xxxvi, fol. 33a; xxxviii, fol. 37a; xlvii, fol. 44a; III.xxix, fol. 117a; xlvii, fol. 121b: Cockayne, II, pp. 52–3, 66–7, 78–9, 86–7, 98–9, 116–17, 126–7, 324–5, 338–9.

[104] *Leechdoms* I.xxxvi, fol. 33a: Cockayne, II, pp. 86–7.

[105] S 283, B 777 (sp but C9).

[106] Anderson, *The English Hundred-Names, The South-Eastern Counties*, pp. 71–2, 103.

[107] Rackham, *Trees and Woodland*, 2nd edn, p. 67.

[108] S 142, B 219, *WoASCB*, pp. 69–78.

[109] S 412, B 674.

[110] Padel, *Cornish Place-Name Elements*, p. 3.

[111] Tree Register.

[112] Graves, *The White Goddess*, p. 188.

[113] *Leechdoms*, fol. 33a: Cockayne, II, pp. 86–7; MacIntyre, 'Tree culture', p. 227.

[114] Rackham, *Ancient Woodland*, revised edn, p. 358.

[115] S 60, B 204 (sp), *WoASCB*, pp. 65–9; S 461, B 762; S 558, B 892, Kelly, *Charters of Abingdon*, I, no. 45.

[116] S 1314, B 1208, *WoASCB*, pp. 264–8.

[117] Nennius 70: J. Morris, ed. and trans., *Nennius. British History and The Welsh Annals* (London and Chichester, 1980), p. 41; Hooke, *Anglo-Saxon England*, p. 95.

[118] N. E. Hickin, *The Natural History of an English Forest* (Newton Abbot, 1972), pp. 14–20.

[119] Rackham, *Ancient Woodland*, revised edn, p. 359.

[120] Bosworth and Toller, *An Anglo-Saxon Dictionary*, p. 577; B. O. E. Ekwall, ed., *The Concise Dictionary of English Place-Names*, 4th edn (Oxford, 1960), p. 243; Grigson, *The Englishman's Flora*, p. 191.

[121] It is not noted separately in Rackham, *The History of the Countryside*.

[122] A. H. Smith, *The Place-Names of the West Riding, Part III*, English Place-Name Society 32 (Cambridge, 1961), p. 87; Grigson, *The Englishman's Flora*, p. 191; Biggam, *Grey in Old English*, pp. 140–2.

[123] S 690, B 1066, Kelly, *Charters of Abingdon*, II, no. 87; S 969, K 1318, O'Donovan, *Charters of Sherborne*, nos 20 and 20A; S 847, C. Hart, *The Early Charters of Eastern England* (Leicester, 1966), pp. 186–7.

[124] S 1314, B 1208, *WoASCB*, pp. 264–8; S 896, K 703, Kelly, *Charters of Abingdon*, II, no. 128; S 1380, Dugdale, *Monasticum Anglicanum*, i.143–6 (no. 1) (sp); Hooke, *The Landscape of Anglo-Saxon Staffordshire*, p. 76.

[125] Thirteenth century; Mills, *A Dictionary of English Place-Names*, p. 173.

[126] Smith, *Place-Names of the West Riding*, III, p. 87.

[127] Biggam, *Grey in Old English*, p. 225.

[128] Llandaff Charters 63: Evans, *The Text of the Book of Llandâv*, p. 214.

[129] For *bromburnan* see S 276, B 393 (sp); S 446, B 742; S 360, B 596, Miller, *Charters of the New Minster*, Appendix, pp. 178–83 (sp); *brom* with *denu* S 283, B 377 (sp); S 1007, K 780; with *feld* S 276, B 393 (sp); S 446, B 742; S 376, B 620, B 621 (sp); with *hurst* S 820, B 1307 (sp); S 1558, F. J. Baigent, *A Collection of Records and Documents relating to the Hundred and Manor of Crondal*, pt 1 (Hampshire Record Society, 1891), p. 9; with *(ge)hæg* S 852, K 1281, Kelly, *Charters of Abingdon*, II, no. 121; with *bricge* S 376, B 620, B 621 (sp).

[130] Mills, *A Dictionary of English Place-Names*, p. 54. See Mills and *CDEPN* for the latest thoughts on many of these names.

[131] A. Mawer and F. M. Stenton, with J. E. B. Gover, *The Place-Names of Sussex, Part II* (Cambridge, 1986), English Place-Name Society 8 (Cambridge, 1986), p. 296; Smith, *English Place-Name Elements*, I, p. 82.

[132] S 915, K 1303, Kelly, *Charters of Abingdon*, II, no. 134 and S 461, B 762, Kelly, *Charters of Abingdon*, I, no. 32; S 487, B 787; S 387, B 726, *CBDC*, pp. 141–4; S 389, B 723, *CBDC*, pp. 134–7 (sp) (also S 971), *CBDC*, p. 196.

[133] *CBDC*, pp. 217–24.

[134] Padel, *Cornish Place-Name Elements*, p. 92.

[135] *Llan Dâv* 66: Evans, p. 221.

[136] Gelling, *The Place-Names of Berkshire, Part I*, pp. 231–2.

[137] Mills, *A Dictionary of English Place-Names*, p. 264.

[138] S 1013, K 783.

[139] S 605, B 924, Kelly, *Charters of Abingdon*, II, no. 52; S 856, K 648.

[140] S 60, B 204, *WoASCB*, pp. 65–9 (sp); S 1560, B 630; S 430, B 707.

[141] S 255, B 1331, 1332 and 1333 (bounds added), *CBDC*, pp. 86–99; S 721, B 1104, *CBDC*, pp. 168–72.

12

Trees not Readily Apparent
in the Early Medieval Written Record

THE MISSING TREES

There are no references to pine, fir trees or other conifers in pre-Conquest charters. Certainly this tree appears in Old English literature but not in an English context: it was a pine-tree that St Martin encountered close to a temple 'protected and accounted very holy in heathen wise'.[1] The Scots Pine, *Pinus sylvestris*, re-entered Britain after the last Ice age but retreated to Scotland and some mountains of Ireland in the Atlantic period (6200–3800 BC), with only localised stands elsewhere, mainly in the Lake District and the Fens. Both pine and yew colonised raised peat bogs in these areas during prehistoric times (the yew, *Taxus baccata*, produces berries rather than cones). Spruce (*Picea*) and silver-fir (*Abies*) are rarely self-perpetuating in Britain and the spruce is naturally a tree of inland Europe.[2]

There are broad-leaved trees, too, which are missing from the early medieval written records or which appear only in restricted sources such as glossaries referring to translations of Classical literature. The sweet chestnut, *Castanea sativa*, OE *cystbēam*, *cistenbēam* or *cystel*, is a native of Mediterranean lands which does not germinate freely in Britain. It is not reliably found in the prehistoric pollen record and seems to have been an introduced species which was present by the Roman period. It is absent from the Anglo-Saxon charter and place-name evidence, although it appears in glossaries of the period. The nuts and husks of the sweet chestnut that have been found in a Roman context may represent imported chestnuts but its wood and charcoal have also been found on Roman sites in southern England.[3] Chestnut place-names are medieval recordings at the earliest (beginning in the thirteenth century). However, the tithe of chestnuts granted to Flaxley Abbey at Westbury-on-Severn, Gloucestershire, by Henry II came from a chestnut wood established in a remote location on the eastern margins of the Forest of Dean close to an earlier Roman villa. It is just possible that the tree was an early introduction that survived in this location; a chestnut wood is still found on the spot today. Other 'quasi-native' chestnuts are concentrated in south-east England and Essex, although the tree occurs in parks and plantations throughout Britain. The horse chestnut, *Aesculus hippocastanum*, was a late introduction, brought to Britain from the Balkans in the late sixteenth century.

There is also no certain reference to the hornbeam, *Carpinus betulus*, introduced to Britain only about 5,000 years ago and mostly confined to the south-east. It is a tree native to Britain but confined to particular areas of southern and eastern England, abundant in wood-pasture regions, especially in Essex, Hertfordshire and Middlesex but with outliers in Kent and Sussex. It is so-named because its wood is tough like horn and in some dialects it is known as the hardbeam or 'horse-beech' – superficially it resembles the beech, its leaves similar to those of the beech and the elm, and it may, therefore, have been included in references to either of these species. The wych-elm itself was also regularly called 'hornbeam' in Somerset and in historical times the hornbeam was sometimes not differentiated from this tree, both, to confuse the matter further, referred to as 'wych-hazel'.[4] Hornbeam pollen, charcoal or wood has been recognised in prehistoric deposits from areas as far north as Norfolk and possibly Lancashire and as far west as Somerset but it is a poor timber tree and produces no nuts or fibre, no herbal cures.[5] Rackham was only able to find one doubtful Anglo-Saxon citation and also noted a small number of later place-names, as in *Herinbemegatestret* in Essendon, Hertfordshire, recorded in 1367, and a few others in the later place-names of Hertfordshire and Middlesex.[6]

The black poplar

There is no direct recognisable reference to the black poplar, *Populus nigra*, but this may be another native tree that has not been recognised because of linguistic problems, perhaps being grouped with the aspen, OE *æspe*.[7] A boundary clause of Mickelmersh, Hampshire, which refers to a landmark *populfinige* does not seem to be to this tree, despite the entries for *popul* in the dictionaries of Clark Hall and Bosworth and Toller.[8] The boundary of the estate runs *of ðam ellene to populfinige. of populfinige to Lambhyrste* 'from the elder to *Popul finige* to Lambhurst'. Although *popylle* is glossed with *lolium* 'cockle, tares' in Wright's *Vocabularies*, Biggam suggests that this has nothing to do with the poplar at all and refers to *popel*, 'pebble', with OE *fīn* 'heap, pile', hence 'a heap, pile of pebbles'.[9] However, Rackham interprets the *popeler/popular* of medieval documents as the black poplar; a fourteenth-century document obviously refers to a poplar tree of immense size from Writtle, Essex, as its branches alone were sold for 12*d*.[10] The problems surrounding the interpretation of *Populus* species outline some of the difficulties that face interpretation of the Old English sources. The black poplar is probably also native to Britain and is a more distinctive tree than the aspen, its spreading crown forming a large dome; Rackham comments that 'No other native tree can compete with its rugged grandeur. It is recognizable a mile off by its outline . . . with a vast, straight, usually leaning trunk and heavy branches with [*sic* for 'which'?] arch and sweep down. The trunk and boughs are covered with great bosses; the bark is very deeply ridged and appears black from a distance.'[11] The arching branches of the black poplar have been used for cruck building in medieval buildings.[12] It is often a solitary tree and once characterised the gravels of floodplains. Although its numbers have diminished since about 1800, fine examples still exist, especially in the Welsh Borders in Herefordshire and Shropshire, often growing over 30m tall – two of England's tallest and widest (subsp. *betulifolia*) are found at Christ's College, Brecon, a specimen 31cm high with a girth of 685cm, and another in the grounds of Longnor Hall, Shropshire, a specimen 38m high with a girth of 631cm.[13] Ancient and younger pollarded black poplars abound on Castlemorton Common in the Malvern area of Worcestershire. According to Graves, the black poplar was, in mythological sources, a funereal tree sacred to Mother Earth in pre-Hellenic Greece and a sign of 'loss of hope'.[14]

Rackham also notes that the *abel* or *abele*, found in medieval but not earlier sources, may be another form of poplar, possibly the white (*P. alba*), but more probably the grey, poplar (*P. canescens*), which may be a hybrid between the native aspen and the introduced white poplar.[15] Neither the white nor the grey poplar is definitely native to Britain, but the date of introduction remains uncertain.

THE TREES OF UNCERTAIN IDENTITY

The elebēam

Bēam in Old English was a term for tree and was certainly not confined to a single species, although the *hnutbēam* was perhaps a hazel and *þan ellenebeam* at Damerham and Martin, Hampshire, may be either an elder tree or a corrupt reference to the *elebēam*.[16] The unidentified *elebēam* occurs several times (?ten) in the charters of southern England (Fig. 21). This was literally the 'oil-tree' and normally referred to the olive, as indeed it does in biblical and literary sources, including the Old English herbals. However, the olive is not native to England and although the Romans may have attempted to introduce it into their gardens botanists are reluctant to accept that it could have grown easily enough in England to have been found scattered in the boundary locations implied by pre-Conquest charters. With one exception it is only recorded in the south of England in charter boundary clauses emanating from the royal house of Wessex, where the scribes may have been more familiar with biblical and literary sources and more inclined to use a term found in these rather than an English vernacular term. It occurs three times in Berkshire, five times in Hampshire and once on the Isle of Wight. One reference in Hampshire is indeed to an *ellenebēam*, a form which led Rackham to interpret this tree as the elder.[17] However, the latter is a relatively small tree whereas the *elebēam* is once referred to as 'great' and twice as 'old'.[18] The only thing the *elebēam* has in

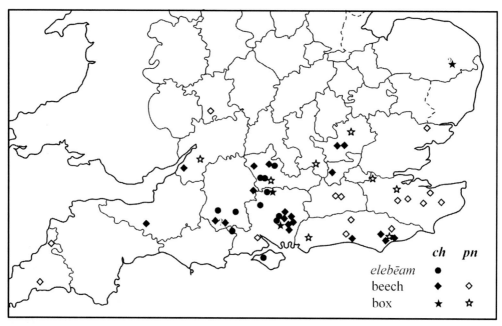

Figure 21. Trees of limited distribution recorded in early
medieval charters and place-names

common with the elder is that one reference is to a stump: the boundary of Welford
in Berkshire ran from *deoran treowe to þone elebeam styb*.[19] The term does not
appear in any early place-names. If one looks for species that may have resembled
the olive, there are several contenders: another tree with a *bēam* name, the whitebeam, has leaves which are hairy on the underside, like those of the olive, but are
closer in shape to those of the elm, and this seems to have been the *haran wiðig*
already discussed in Chapter 9. The English elm, *Ulmus procera*, or, more likely, the
wych-elm, *Ulmus glabra* (sometimes known locally in Somerset as hornbeam), are
other possible contenders but also have their own Old English names (*elm*, *wice*).
The white willow, *Salix alba*, also has silvery hairs on the underside but is likely
have been included with other willow species. The berries of the common juniper,
Juniper communis, can be distilled to produce oil but this is normally a small shrub.
One other possible tree which night be suggested is *Hippophae rhamnoides*, the sea
buckthorn, a tree now mostly restricted to coastal locations but once much more
widespread.[20] Although usually a relatively small tree normally reaching only 2.5
metres in height it can grow much taller (one specimen reaches 11m in the Kew
Royal Botanic Gardens). It resembles the olive closely and its fruit also produces
an oil, long noted for its vitamin content and curative properties. However, the true
identification of the *elebēam* remains uncertain.

The cwicbēam *and the rowan*

A tree that is named in the Metrical Charms and the *Leechdoms* is the *cwicbēam* and *cwictrēo*, its name incorporating OE *cwic* 'alive'; its bark appears as *cwic-rind* or *cwicbēamrind*. *Cwicbēam* has been glossed with, among others species, the juniper, *Juniperus communis*; with *wice*, the 'wych-elm', *Ulmus glabra* (but here it may be a corrupt word or a mis-spelling of *cwice*); with an unidentified *cariscus*, perhaps related to *carica* 'fig', or an error for *tamariscus* (neither native to England), and with *ficbēam* itself; and with the aspen, *Populus tremula*, the rowan, *Sorbus aucuparia*, the wild service tree, *Sorbus torminalis*, and even the gorse, but some such interpretations are very doubtful.[21] An interpretation as aspen, despite the fact that its trembling leaves may evoke a tree that is 'alive', also seems unlikely. It is the most recent interpretation, in the Toronto *Dictionary of Old English*, which gives one meaning as 'quickbeam (mountain-ash or wild service)' (the glossary entries for *wice* and *juniperus* are also noted).[22] The most likely interpretation is that this tree is indeed the rowan or mountain-ash, *Sorbus aucuparia*, a tree otherwise missing from the literary record. Quicken or quickbeam is still its local name throughout England.[23] For *cwictrēo* the Toronto *Dictionary of Old English* gives the same meanings as for *cwicbēam*, i.e. 'mountain-ash or wild service', noting, however, that it is also glossed with *P. tremulus* 'aspen'.[24]

It is interesting that the identification of the quickbeam as the rowan or mountain ash is the same conclusion reached by Robert Graves in his discussion of the Irish Tree Alphabet, where it is *Luis*, L, 'the tree of life'.[25] Graves claims that its round wattles were used by the druids as a last extremity to compel demons to answer difficult questions, and it was apparently used throughout the British Isles against lightning and witches' charms of all sorts – bewitched horses could only be controlled with a rowan whip. He notes how, in the Irish romance of Fraoth, the berries of the magical rowan, guarded by a dragon, were capable of healing the wounded and adding a year to a man's life. In the romance of Diarmaid and Gráinne (*Tóraighheacht Dhiarmada agus Ghráinne*), one version of which existed as early as the tenth century,[26] they are described as 'the food of the gods' and hence taboo, perhaps because of their colour, as red foods were forbidden in ancient Greece except in feasts to honour the dead. The way in which Gráinne urges Diarmaid to obtain the berries is in some ways reminiscent of Eve's role in the Garden of Eden and in both tales one attribute of the fruit is to confer near-immortality. It was the tree of quickening used in divinations, for the witch-wand used for metal divining, but could also be hammered through a corpse to immobilise its ghost. On Rügen and the Baltic amber islands, Graves notes 'the unexpected presence of great rowan thickets', grown for their oracular use, and associates the tree with the Celtic feast of Candlemas on 2 February, which marked the quickening of the year and one of the tenth-century Irish fire-feasts, and was the day of St Brigid (his 'White Goddess').[27]

In Ireland, Lucas notes how this tree was 'regarded as the sovereign protector of milk and its products against supernatural evils', kept in the byre to protect the cows and put in the pail and around the churn to ensure that the milk was not stolen – beliefs perhaps arising from the long use of its bark shavings as a winter feed for cattle in Norway (but not in Ireland). Thus a magical connection sprang up between the rowan and the animals, possibly brought in by Norse settlers, one old term for the rowan being *fid na ndruad* 'the wizards' tree'.[28] The rowan continues to be referred to as the 'quicken-tree' in dozens of later folk tales, offering protection against harm and witchcraft.[29]

References to the bark, the *rind*, of the *cwicbēam* occur in the *Lacnunga* and the *Leechdoms*. In the *Leechdoms*, the bark of the *cwicbēam* was mixed with that of other trees in a bath for lepers, for shingles or drunk against 'dry' diseases, 'yellow' disease (?jaundice) and *þeoh* (thigh ache) One reason the *cwicbēam* cannot be equated with the aspen, as suggested in some glossaries, is that both appear in the same remedies such as:

> Wiþ þære adle þe mon hæt circul adl genim cwicbeam rinde. ๅ æpsan. ๅ apuldor. mapuldor. ellen. wiþig. sealh. wir. wice. āc. slahþorn. bircean. elebeam. gatetreow. æsces sceal mæst. ๅ ælces treowes dæl þe man begitan mæg. butan hægþorne ๅ alore þara treowa mæst þe her awriten synd . . .

> 'Against the disease which is hight circle addle or shingles, take quickbeam rind, and aspen and apple tree, maple tree, elder, withy, sallow, myrtle, wich elm, oak, sloe thorn, birch, olive tree, the lotus tree [?for hornbeam], of ash there shall be most, and a part of each tree which a man can get at (except hawthorn and alder), the largest quantity of the trees which are here written . . .'.[30]

or again,

> Læcedomas wið þeoradlum. æscrind. æspan rind. elm rind. cwicrind . . .

> 'Leechdoms for "dry" diseases; ash rind, aspen rind, elm rind, quickbeam rind . . .'[31]

> Wið smeawyrme smiring. . . . Wyrc beþinge to þon ilcan nim æps rinde. ๅ wir rinde. cwic rinde. slah þorn rinde. wirrinde. berc rinde. cnua ealle þa rinde wyl on cyse hwæge þweah mid ๅ beþe þ lím þe se wyrm on sie . . .

> 'A smearing for a penetrating worm; . . . Work up a fomentation for that ilk; take aspen rind, and myrtle rind, quickbeam rind, sloethorn rind, birch rind; pound all the rinds together, boil them in cheese whey, wash therewith and foment the limb on which the wound is . . .'[32]

The quickbeam also appears in the *Metrical Charms*, in a Christianised pagan charm for infertile land. After sods from the land have been blessed on the altar, the instruction is: *And hæbbe him gæworht of cwicbeame feower Cristes mælo and awrite on ælcon ende: Matheus and Marcus, Lucas and Iohannes*, 'And let him have made four crosses of aspen wood and write on each end Matthew and Mark, Luke and John', but Gordon's translation of the *cwicbēam* as the aspen is open to question in the light of the *Leechdoms*.[33] If *cwicbēam* is indeed the rowan, as seems likely, all parts of this tree are rich in tannins that have an astringent action on the body – the bark used as a lotion to stem bleeding and as a mouthwash for bleeding gums, mouth ulcers and sore throats, the berries also as an astringent and an antiseptic.[34]

The rowan rarely appears in charters and place-names, nor is the Cornish name for these trees, *kerdan*, found in early place-names. This tree was, however, probably of limited distribution in early medieval times, possibly more frequent in Scotland and northern England.[35] In any case, it is hardly significant as a landmark tree. Where *cwic* occurs in early place-names, as in Quick in Rochdale: *Tohac, Thoac* in 1086, or Cookridge in Adel: *Cucheric* 1086, both in Yorkshire West Riding, is probably a reference to *cwic* 'a quickset hedge', although Smith recognises a derivation of *cwicen* 'mountain-ash' as a possibility for Cookridge.[36] *Raun, ranum*, ON *raunum*, occurs only later, as in a thirteenth-century name in Ribblesdale in Yorshire West Riding.[37] The tree generally rarely grows above a height of 20 metres but can attain impressive proportions when old: at Bolderwood Holms, Lyndhurst in Hampshire, the Tree Register notes an 8m high tree with a girth of 499cm, while in Bellingdon Wood, Chesham in Buckinghamshire, a specimen reaches 28m in height.

ENDNOTES

1 *Ælfric's Lives of the Saints II*, XXXI, 'St Martin, Bishop and Confessor': Skeat, pp. 244–5.
2 Rackham, *Ancient Woodland*, revised edn, pp. 103, 105; Rackham, *Trees and Woodland*, 2nd edn, p. 29, fig. 8.
3 Ibid., p. 330; H. Godwin, *History of the British Flora*, 2nd edn (Cambridge, 1975).
4 Grigson, *The Englishman's Flora*, pp. 259, 264.
5 Rackham, *Ancient Woodland*, revised edn, p. 221.
6 Ibid.
7 C. P. Biggam, ed., *From Earth to Art* (Amsterdam and New York, 2003).
8 S 857, K 652; Clark Hall, *A Concise Anglo-Saxon Dictionary*, p. 274; Bosworth and Toller, *An Anglo-Saxon Dictionary*, p. 776.
9 T. Wright, ed., *A Volume of Vocabularies* (London, 1857), I, p. 234; Biggam, *From Earth to Art*.
10 Rackham, *The History of the Countryside*, p. 207, ERO: D/DP M201.
11 Rackham, *Trees and Woodland*, 2nd edn, pp. 21–2.
12 Rackham, *Ancient Woodland*, 2nd edn, p. 463; R. Harris, 'Poplar crucks in Worcestershire and Herefordshire', *Vernacular Architecture* 5 (1974).
13 Morton, *The Trees of Shropshire*, p. 102.

14 Graves, *The White Goddess*, p. 188.

15 Morton, *The Trees of Shropshire*, pp. 22–3; Biggam, *From Earth to Art*, pp. 208–13.

16 S 513, B 817.

17 Rackham, *The History of the Countryside*, p. 211, table 10.1.

18 'Great': Meon and Privett, S 811, B 1319 (suspicious); 'old': Ecchinswell, S 412, B 674 and S 766, Dugdale, *Monasticum Anglicanum*, ii.323–4 (no. 6).

19 S 552, B 877, Kelly, *Charters of Abingdon*, I, no. 44.

20 D. Hooke, 'Trees in Anglo-Saxon charters', pp. 86–8.

21 See Bosworth and Toller, *Dictionary*, pp. 179, 2932; Clark Hall, *A Concise Anglo-Saxon Dictionary*, p. 79; Cockayne, *Leechdoms*, II, Glossary, p. 378.

22 Toronto *Dictionary of Old English*, 1210.

23 Grigson, *The Englishman's Flora*, pp. 186–8.

24 Toronto *Dictionary of Old English*, 1222–3. A suggested OE *cwice* 'couch-grass' clearly has no relevance here.

25 Graves, *The White Goddess*, pp. 162–3.

26 Dillon, *Early Irish Literature*, p. 42.

27 Graves, *The White Goddess*, pp. 162–3.

28 Lucas, 'The Sacred trees of Ireland', pp. 44–5.

29 Hooke, 'Trees in Anglo-Saxon charters: some uncertainties'.

30 *Leechdoms* I.xxxvi, fol. 32b: Cockayne, II, pp. 86–7. 'Lotus' may result from a misreading of *Carpinus* (*-betulus*) 'hornbeam' as *Caprinus*.

31 Ibid., I.xlvii, 1, fol. 44a: Cockayne, II, pp. 116–17.

32 Ibid., III.xxxix, fol. 119b: Cockayne, II, pp. 332–3.

33 Dobbie, *The Anglo-Saxon Minor Poems*, pp. 116–17, trans. Gordon, *Anglo-Saxon Poetry*, p. 89.

34 McIntyre, 'Tree culture', p. 261.

35 Rackham, *Ancient Woodland*, revised edn, p. 356.

36 Smith, *Place-Names of the West Riding*, II, p. 312; Smith, *Place-Names of the West Riding*, IV, pp. 189–90; A. H. Smith, *English Place-Name Elements, Part I*, English Place-Name Society 25 (Cambridge, 1956), p. 122.

37 A. H. Smith, *The Place-Names of the West Riding, Part VI*, English Place-Name Society 35 (Cambridge, 1961), pp. 329–30.

EPILOGUE: TREES IN ANGLO-SAXON ENGLAND

The trees of early medieval England offer us glimpses of a lost landscape. But our familiarity with their modern counterparts allows us to reconstruct these landscapes in our mind's eye. We can understand our ancestors' interest in trees as a valuable resource and something of the awe imposed by a great wood, often remote from the world of their everyday existence. They, too, cannot have been immune to the beauty of individual trees. The different species then bore, for the most part, the same names by which we know them today and each species, had, or was believed to have, its own special attributes.

In the above pages the role of these trees has been explored, especially as boundary markers or features that gave rise to local place-names. Attempts have been made to explain why particular species of trees became docmented in this way. The distribution of species can, however, reveal other aspects of the early medieval countryside, especially the regional variation which lends so much richness to the landscape of Britain. Through charters and place-names one is able to envisage the moorland landscapes of the south-west peninsula, where trees are only prolific in sheltered valleys, the open pastures of much of the southern chalk downlands (excluding Hampshire) where woods were often sporadic, to the wood-pasture habitats found across the country where heathland formed a landscape mosaic with patches of denser woodland or scattered trees. Of the latter regions, Hampshire and Worcestershire stand out – and in both counties, extensive areas were to be put into royal forests by the Norman kings. Some species introduced by the Romans had now found their way into the natural envrionment or were being deliberately cultivated; some species were apparently more at home in southern Britain – among them the beech, box and enigmatic *elebēam*.

Woodlands are likely to have been a managed resource and archaeology has been able to attest the enormous importance of wood in the Anglo-Saxon economy – both for building material and for making domestic utensils and luxury items. A valued environment for the pasture of domestic stock, the distribution of woodland and wood-pasture has influenced kingdom and district boundaries and the demarcation of early medieval estate structure. The exchange of commodities between complementary regions was influential in maintaining estate and manorial linkages (and, hence, ecclesiastical ones as well) and was to influence the location of markets as centres of exchange.

A long-established iconography of trees and woodlands was only to a limited extent undermined by changing religion (although trees as 'sacred' features was indeed to be abolished), with new roles replacing the old. However, individual trees, tree species and woodland continued to occupy a prominent position in legend and folklore through historical times. Veteran trees, in particular, hold a special place in folklore and are features that occupy a special place in maintaining countryside character and regional interest.

Today, the utilitarian value of trees is still important, as sources of fodder, fruit, timber, fuel, and so forth, but they are also increasingly recognised as the source of enormous environmental benefit. They provide rich wildlife habitats, supporting thousands of wild species of insects, birds and animals; they help to reduce pollution in the atmosphere, absorbing fumes and carbon emissions. Moreover, contact with trees as part of nature can promote a sense of spiritual wellbeing, an essential function given the pace and pressure of life today. Most of us today can appreciate the tree as a thing of beauty, a consoling feature in a rapidly changing world.

BIBLIOGRAPHY

Adams, I. H., *Agrarian Landscape Terms: A Glossary for Historical Geography*, Institute of British Geographers Special Publication 9 (London, 1976)

Aldhouse-Green, M., *Seeing the Wood for the Trees: The Symbolism of Trees and Wood in Ancient Gaul and Britain* (Aberystwyth, 2000)

Allegro, J., *Lost Gods* (London, 1977)

Amphlett, J., and C. Rea, *The Botany of Worcestershire* (Birmingham, 1909; repr. Wakefield, 1978)

Anderson, O. S., *The English Hundred-Names*, Lunds Universitets Årsskift 30 (Lund, 1934)

Anderson, O. S. *The English Hundred-Names, The South-Eastern Counties*, Lunds Universitets Årsskift 37 (Lund and Leipzig, 1939)

Anderson, O. S. *The English Hundred-Names, The South-Western Counties*, Lunds Universitets Årsskift 35 (Lund and Leipzig, 1939)

Assmann, B., *Angelsächsische Homilien und Heiligenleben* (Kassel, 1889; repr. Darmstadt, 1964)

Atkin, M., 'Excavations in Gloucester 1989: an interim report', *Glevensis* 24 (1990), pp. 1–13

Attenborough, F. L., *The Laws of the Earliest English Kings* (Cambridge, 1922)

Backhouse, J., The *Lindisfarne Gospels* (London, 1981)

Bæksted, A., *Målruner og troldruner: runemagiske studier*, Nationalmuseets skrifter 4 (Copenhagen, 1952)

Baigent, F. J., *A Collection of Records and Documents relating to the Hundred and Manor of Crondal*, pt 1 (Hampshire Record Society, 1891)

Baines, A. H. J., 'Wyrtruma and wyrtwala', *South Midlands Archaeology* 12 (1987), pp. 102–10

Baker, C. A., P. A. Moxey and P. M. Oxford, 'Woodland continuity and change in Epping Forest', *Field Studies* 4 (1978), pp. 645–69

Barnwell, P. S., 'Anglian Yeavering: a continental perspective?', in *Yeavering. People, Power and Place*, ed. P. Frodsham and C. O'Brien (Stroud, 2005), pp. 174–84

Bartlett, R. ed. and trans., *Geoffrey of Burton, Life and Miracles of St Modwenna* (Oxford, 2002)

Basford, K., *The Green Man* (Ipswich, 1978; repr. Cambridge, 1998)

Bates, E. H., ed., *Two Cartularies of the Benedictine Abbeys of Muchelney and Athelney in the County of Somerset*, with notes by W. H. Stevenson, Somerset Record Society 14 (London, 1899)

Baum, P. F. trans, *Anglo-Saxon Riddles of the Exeter Book* (Durham, N. Carolina, 1963)

Bauschatz, P. C., *The Well and the Tree* (Ann Arbor, 1982)

Becker, U., *The Continuum Encyclopedia of Symbols* (New York and London, 1992)

Bede, *Historia gentis Anglorum ecclesiastica: A History of the English Church and People*, trans. L. Sherley-Price, rev. R. E. Latham (Harmondsworth, 1968)

Bede, *Bede's Ecclesiastcal History of the English People*, ed. and trans. B. Colgrave and R. A. B. Mynors (Oxford, 1969)

Belfour, A. O., ed., *Twelfth Century Homilies in MS Bodley MS 343*, EETS, OS 137 (London, 1909, repr. 1999)

Bennett, J. A. W., and G. V. Smithers, eds, *Early Middle English Verse and Prose* (Oxford, 1968)

Bethurum, D., ed., *The Homilies of Wulfstan* (Oxford, 1957)

Bevan-Jones, R., *The Ancient Yew* (Bollington, Macclesfield, 2002)

Biddle, M., and R. N. Quirk, 'Excavations near Winchester Cathedral 1961', *Archaeological Journal* 119 (1962), pp. 150–94

Biggam, C. P., *Grey in Old English* (London, 1998)

Biggam, C. P., ed., *From Earth to Art* (Amsterdam and New York, 2003)

Bintley, M., 'The south Sandbach Cross "Ancestors of Christ" panel in its cultural contexts', paper presented at University College of London conference 'Woodlands, Trees, and Timber in the Anglo-Saxon World', 13–15 November, 2009

Birch, W de Gray, *Cartularium Saxonicum*, 3 vols (London, 1885–99)

Birmingham and Warwickshire Archaeological Society Newsletter, June 2005

Blair, J., 'A saint for every minster? Local cults in Anglo-Saxon England', in *Local Saints and Local Churches in the Early Medieval West*, ed. A.T. Thacker and R. Sharpe (Oxford, 2002), pp. 455–565

Blair, J., *The Church in Anglo-Saxon Society* (Oxford, 2005)

Bolandus, J., *Acta Sanctorum quotquot toto orbe coluntur. . .* (Antwerp, 1643)

Bord, J., and C. Bord, *Earth Rites* (St Albans, 1982)

Bord, J., and C. Bord, *Sacred Waters* (London, 1985–6)

Boretius, A. ed., *Capitularia Regum Francorum*, Monumenta Germaniae Historica 77 (Hanover, 1883)

Bosworth, J., and T. N. Toller, *An Anglo-Saxon Dictionary Based on the Manuscript Collections of the Late Joseph Bosworth, D.D., F.R.S., Edited and Enlarged by T. Northcote Toller, M.A.* (Oxford, 1898–1921)

Breeze, A., 'Plastered walls at Rudchester? The Roman place-names Vindovalva and Nemetovala', *Archaeologia Aeliana*, 5th series 30 (2002), pp. 49–51

Brodribb, A. C. C., A. R. Hands and D. R. Walker, *Excavations at Shakenoak Farm, near Wilcote, Oxfordshire* (Oxford, 1968–73)

Brookes, N., *The Early History of the Church of Canterbury: Christ Church from 597 to 1066* (Leicester, 1984)

Brooks, N., 'The creation and early structure of the kingdom of Kent', in *The Origins of Anglo-Saxon Kingdoms*, ed. S. Bassett (Leicester, 1989), pp. 5–74

Brown, M. P., *Pagans and Priests* (Oxford, 2006)

Bruce-Mitford, R. L. S., *The Sutton Hoo Ship Burial: A Handbook*, 2nd edn (London, 1972)

Caesarius of Arles, *Sermons. Vol. I (1–80)*, trans. M. M. Mueller (Washington, 1956)

Cameron, K., *The Place-Names of Derbyshire, Part II*, English Place-Name Society 28 (Cambridge, 1959)

Cameron, M. L., 'Anglo-Saxon medicine and magic', *Anglo-Saxon England* 17, ed. P. Clemoes (Cambridge, 1988), pp. 191–215

Campbell, A. ed., *Æthelwulf, 'De Abbaticus'* (Oxford, 1967)

Campbell, A. ed., *Charters of Rochester*, Anglo-Saxon Charters I (London, 1973)

Campbell, J., *The Masks of God: Primitive Mythology* (New York, 1959, London, 1973)

Cardale, J. S., trans., *King Alfred's Version of Boethius de Consolatione Philosophiae* (London, 1829)

Casey, P. J., and B. Hoffman, 'Excavations at the Roman temple in Lydney Park, Gloucestershire in 1980 and 1981', *Antiquaries Journal* 79 (1999), pp. 81–143

Chambers, F., *A Reconstruction of the Postglacial Environmental History of Tatton Park, Cheshire, from Valley Mire Sediments*, University of Keele Department of Geography Occasional Paper 17 (Keele, 1991)

Clark Hall, J. R., and H. D. Merrit, *A Concise Anglo-Saxon Dictionary*, 4th edn (Cambridge, 1960)

Clarke, C. A. M., *Literary Landscapes and the Idea of England, 700–1400* (Cambridge, 2006)

Cleere, H., 'Some operating parameters for Roman ironworks', *Bulletin of the Institute of Archaeology* 13 (1976), pp. 233–46

Cleere, H., and D. Crossley, *The Iron Industry of the Weald* (Leicester, 1985)

Clemoes, P. ed., *Aelfric's Catholic Homilies. The First Series. Text*, EETS, SS 17 (Oxford, 1997)

Coates, R., '"The Lyme"', *English Place-Name Society Journal* 36 (2004), pp. 39–50

Cockayne, T. O., ed., *Leechdoms, Wortcunning and Starcraft of Early England*, 3 vols, Rolls Series (London, 1865)

Coles, B., 'Wood species for wooden figures: a glimpse of a pattern', in *Prehistoric Ritual and Religion*, ed. A., Gibson and D. Simpson (Stroud, 1998), pp. 163–73

Coles, B., and J. Coles, *Sweet Track to Glastonbury: The Somerset Levels in Prehistory* (London, 1986)

Coles, J. M., F. A. Hibbert and B. J. Orme, 'Prehistoric roads and tracks in Somerset: 3. The Sweet Track', *Proceedings of the Prehistoric Society* 39 (1973), pp. 256–93

Columella, Lucius Junius Moderatus, *De arboribus*, ed. and trans. E. S. Forster and E. H. Heffner, *Lucius Junius Moderatus Columella on Agriculture and Trees: On Trees* (Cambridge, Mass., 1968)

Columella, Lucius Junius Moderatus, *De re rustica*, ed. and trans. H. B. Ash, *Lucius Junius Moderatus Columella on Agriculture* (London, 1941)

Comey, M., 'The wooden drinking vessels in the Sutton Hoo ship burial: materials, morphology and usage', University College of London conference, Woodlands, trees, and timber in the Anglo-Saxon world, 13–15 November, 2009

Coplestone-Crow, B., *Herefordshire Place-Names*, British Archaeological Reports, British Series 214 (Oxford, 1989)

Cornish, V., *Historic Thorn Trees in the British Isles* (London, 1941)

Cox, B., *The Place-Names of Leicestershire, Part 4: Gartree Hundred* (Nottingham, 2009)

Cramp, R., and R. N. Bailey, *Corpus of Anglo-Saxon Stone Sculpture* (Oxford, 1984–)

Crawford, S. J., ed., *The Old English Version of the Heptateuch*, EETS, OS 160 (London, 1922; repr. with addition by N. R. Ker 1969)

Crawford, S. J., ed., *Byrhtferth's Manual*, EETS, OS 177 (London, 1929; repr. 1966)

Crick, J., ed., *Charters of St Albans*, Anglo-Saxon Charters XII (Oxford, 2007)

Crossley-Holland, K., *The Anglo-Saxon World: Writings* (Woodbridge, 1982)

Cunliffe, B., *The Celts* (Oxford, 2003)

Darby, H. C., *Domesday England* (Cambridge, 1977)

Dark, P., *The Environment of Britain in the First Millennium A.D.* (London, 2000)

Darlington, R. R. ed., *Vita Wulfstani, The Vita Wulfstani of William of Malmesbury*, Royal Historical Society, Camden Society, 3rd series 30 (London, 1928)

Davidson, H. E., *The Lost Beliefs of Northern Europe* (London, 1993)

Davies, D., 'The evocative symbolism of trees', in *The Iconography of Landscape*, ed. D. Cosgrove and S. Daniels (Cambridge, 1988), pp. 32–42

Davies, W., *An Early Welsh Microcosm. Studies of the Llandaff Charters* (London, 1978)

Day, S. P., 'Post-glacial vegetational history of the Oxford region', *New Phytologist* 119 (1991), pp. 445–70

Day, S. P., 'Woodland origin and "ancient woodland indicators": a case-study from Sidlings Copse, Oxfordshire, UK', *The Holocene* 3 (1993), pp. 45–53

Dickins, B., *Runic and Heroic Poems of the Old Teutonic Peoples* (Cambridge, 1915)

Dictionary of Old English, Dictionary of Old English Project, University of Toronto Centre for Medieval Studies, Toronto, Pontifical Institute of Medieval Studies

Dillon, M., *Early Irish Literature* (Chicago, Illinois, 1948)

Dobbie, E. van K., ed., *The Anglo-Saxon Minor Poems*, Anglo-Saxon Poetic Records VI (New York, 1942)

Doel, F., and G. Doel, *The Green Man in Britain* (Stroud, 2002)

Dopolnenie k aktam istoricheskim I (St Petersburg, 1846)

Duczko, W., *Arkeologi och miljöarkeologi i Gamla Uppsala*, vol. II (Uppsala, 1993)

Dugdale, Sir W., *Monasticon Anglicanum*, ed. B. Bandinel, J. Caley and H. Ellis, 6 vols (London, 1846)

Edwards, E., ed., *Liber Monasterii de Hyda*, Rolls Series (London, 1886)

Edwards, N., *The Archaeology of Early Medieval Ireland* (London, 1990, 1996: repr. London, 1999)

Ekwall, B. O. E., *English River-Names* (Oxford, 1928)

Ekwall, B. O. E. ed., *The Concise Dictionary of English Place-Names*, 4th edn (Oxford, 1960)

Electronic Sawyer, *Revised Catalogue of Anglo-Saxon Charters*, http://www.esawyer.org.uk/content/charter/199.html

Eliade, M., *Patterns in Comparative Religion* (London, 1958)

Eliade, M., *The Sacred and the Profane: The Nature of Religion*, trans. W. R. Trask (New York, 1959)

Eliade, M., *Shamanism*, trans. W. R. Trask (London, 1964)

Elliott, R. W. V., 'Runes, yews, and magic', *Speculum* 32 (1957), pp. 250–61

Elliott, R. W. V., *Runes, an Introduction* (New York and Manchester, 1959)

Endter, W., *König Alfreds des Grossen Bearbeitung der Soliloquien des Augustinus*, Prosa 11 (Hamburg, 1922; repr. Darmstadt, 1964)

English14, 'Old Trees in The Netherlands and Western Europe' (English version), http://82.94.219.20/~jpa/english14.htm.

Evans, J. G., with J. Rhys, *The Text of the Book of Llan Dâv reproduced from the Gwysaney Manuscript* (Oxford, 1893, facsimile repr. 1979)

Evans, J. G., *Land and Archaeology: Histories of the Human Environment in the British Isles* (Stroud, 1999)

Evelyn, J., *Silva: or a Discourse of Forest-Trees, and the Propogation of Timber in His Majesty's Dominions* (London, 1664)

Everitt, A., *Continuity and Colonization: The Evolution of Kentish Settlement* (Leicester, 1986)

Fairbrother, J. R., 'Faccombe Netherton', *Archaeology and Historical Research* 1, City of London Archaeological Society (London, 1984)

Fairweather, J., trans., *Liber Eliensis. A History of the Isle of Ely from the Seventh Century to the Twelfth* (Woodbridge, 2005)

Feasey, H. J., *Ancient English Holy Week Ceremonial* (London, 1897)

Finberg, H. P. R., *The Early Charters of Wessex* (Leicester, 1964)

Finberg, H. P. R., *The Early Charters of the West Midlands*, 2nd edn (Leicester, 1972)

Flint, V. I. J., *The Rise of Magic in Early Medieval Europe* (Princeton, NJ, 1991)

Flood, G., *An Introduction to Hinduism* (Cambridge, 1996)

Fontaine, J., ed. and trans., *Sulpice Sévère, Vie de Saint Martin i* (Paris, 1967), ch. 13

Ford, W. J., 'Settlement patterns in the central region of the Warwickshire Avon', in *Medieval Settlement, Continuity and Change*, ed. P. H. Sawyer (London, 1976), pp. 274–94

Forester, T., trans. and ed., revised T. Wright, *The Historical Works of Giraldus Cambrensis* (London, 1891)

Fowler, R., ed., *Wulfstan's Canons of Edgar*, EETS, OS 266 (London, 1972)

Fox, H. S. A., 'The people of the wolds', in *The Rural Settlements of Medieval England*, ed. M. Aston, D. Austin and C. Dyer (Oxford, 1989), pp. 77–101

Frazer, Sir J. G., *The Golden Bough*, 13 vols; *The Illustrated Golden Bough* (1890 ff). *Illustrated Abridgement* by S. MacCormack (London, 1978)

Frontin, *L'œuvre gromatique*, *Corpus agrimensorum Romanorum IV Iulius Frontinus*, Cost Action G2 (Luxembourg, 2000)

Gardiner, M., 'The colonisation of the weald of south-east England', *Medieval Settlement Group Annual Report* 12 (1997), pp. 6–8

Garmonsway, G. N., ed., *Ælfric's Colloquy*, revised edn (Exeter, 1991)

Gaskell, G. A., *Dictionary of Scripture and Myth* (New York, 1988)

Gelling, M., 'Further thoughts on pagan place-names', *Otium et Negotium. Studies in Onomatology and Library Science presented to Olof von Feilitzen*, Acta Bibliothecae Regiae Stockholmiensis 16 (Stockholm, 1973), pp. 109–28

Gelling, M., *The Place-Names of Berkshire, Parts I–III*, English Place-Name Society 49–51 (Cambridge, 1973–6)

Gelling, M., *Signposts to the Past. Place-Names and the History of England* (London, 1978)

Gelling, M., and A. Cole, *The Landscape of Place-Names* (Stamford, 2000)

Gerard, T., *The Particular Description of Somerset*, Somerset Record Society 15 (1633), p. 154

Gil, L., Fientes-Utrilla, P., Soto, A., Cervera, M. T., and Collada, C., 'Phylogeography: English elm is a 2,000-year-old Roman clone', *Nature* 431 (28 October, 2004), pp. 1053–4

Godden. M., ed., *Ælfric's Catholic Homilies. The Second Series, Text*, EETS, SS 5 (Oxford, 1979)

Godwin, H., *History of the British Flora*, 2nd edn (Cambridge, 1975)

Gollancz, I., ed, *The Exeter Book, An Anthology of Anglo-Saxon Poetry, Part I*, EETS, OS 104 (London, 1895)

Goodburn, D. M., 'Fragments of a 10th-century timber arcade from Vintner's Place on the London waterfront', *Medieval Archaeology* 37 (1993), pp. 78–92.

Goodburn, D. M., 'London's early medieval timber buildings: little known traditions of construction', in *Urbanism in Medieval Europe: Papers of the 'Medieval Europe Brugge 1997' Conference*, ed. G. de Boe and F. Verhaeghe, Instituut voor het Archeologisch Patrimomium Rapporten 1 (Zellik, 1997), pp. 249–57

Gordon, R. K., trans., *Anglo-Saxon Poetry* (London: 1954)

Gover, J. E. B., A. Mawer and F. M. Stenton, *The Place-Names of Wiltshire*, English Place-Name Society 6 (Cambridge, 1939)

Gover, J. E. B., A. Mawer and F. M. Stenton, *The Place-Names of Hertfordshire*, English Place-Name Society 15 (Cambridge, 1970)

Grattan, J. H. G., and C. Singer, *Anglo-Saxon Magic and Medicine, Illustrated Especially from the Semi-Pagan Text 'Lacnunga' by J. H. G. Grattan and Charles Singer* (London, 1952)

Graves, R., *The White Goddess, A Historical Grammar of Poetic Myth*, ed. G. Lindop (Manchester, 1997)

Green, M. J., *Celtic Myths* (London, 1993)

Greig, J., 'Pollen and waterlogged seeds', in A. Jones, 'Roman Birmingham 2 Excavations at Metchley Roman Forts 1998–2000 and 2002', *Transactions of the Birmingham and Warwickhire Archaeological Society* 108 (2005), pp. 76–81

Grendon, F., *Anglo-Saxon Charms* (New York, 1909)

Grieve, M., *A Modern Herbal* (Darien, Conn., 1970)

Grigson, G., *The Englishman's Flora* (St Albans, 1975)

Grundy, G. B., 'The Saxon land charters of Hampshire with notes on place and field names', *Archaeological Journal*, 2nd series 33 (1926), pp. 91–253

Grundy, G. B., 'Saxon charters of Worcestershire', *Birmingham Archaeological Society Transactions and Proceedings* 52 (1927), pp. 1–183

Grundy, G. B., 'The Saxon land charters of Hampshire with notes on place and field names', *Archaeological Journal*, 2nd series 33 (1926), pp. 91–253.

Hagender, F., *The Heritage of Trees. History, Culture and Symbolism* (Edinburgh, 2001)

Halsall, M., *The Old English Rune Poem: A Critical Edition* (Toronto, 1981)

Hamer, R., *A Choice of Anglo-Saxon Verse* (London, 1970)

Hampshire County Council, *Hampshire's Countryside Heritage 2: Ancient Woodland* (Winchester, 1983)

Hardy, P. D., *The Holy Wells of Ireland* (Dublin, 1836)

Harmer, F. E., *Anglo-Saxon Writs* (Manchester, 1952)

Harmer, F. E., *Select English Historical Documents of the Ninth and Tenth Centuries* (Cambridge, 1914)

Harris, R., 'Poplar crucks in Worcestershire and Herefordshire', *Vernacular Architecture* 5 (1974), p. 25

Hart, C., *The Early Charters of Eastern England* (Leicester, 1966)

Harvey, J., *Medieval Gardens* (London, 1981)

Hawkes, J., 'The plant-life of early Christian Anglo-Saxon art', in *From Earth to Art*, ed. C. P. Biggam (Amsterdam and New York, 2003), pp. 263–6

Hayman, R., *Trees, Woodlands and Western Civilization* (London and New York, 2003)

Hearne, T., ed., *Heming. Hemingi chartularium ecclesiae Wigorniensis* (Oxford, 1723)

Heffernan, C. F., *The Phoenix at the Fountain* (Newark and London, 1988)

Heist, W. W., ed., *Vitae sanctorum Hiberniae ex codice olim Salmanticensi nunc Bruxellensi* (Brussels, 1965)

Hennessy, W. M., ed., *The Annals of Ulster* (Dublin, 1887)

Hickin, N. E., *The Natural History of an English Forest* (Newton Abbot, 1972)

Higham, N., *Rome, Britain and the Anglo-Saxons* (London, 1992)

Hill, D., *An Atlas of Anglo-Saxon England* (Oxford, 1981)

Hillam, J., C. M. Groves, D. M. Brown, M. G. L. Baillie, J. M. Coles and B. J. Coles, 'Dendrochronology of the English Neolithic', *Antiquity* 64 (1990), pp. 210–21

Hillgarth, J. N., ed., *Christianity and Paganism* (Philadelphia, 1986)

Holden, T. G., 'The last meals of the Lindow Bog men', in *Bog Bodies: New Discoveries and New Perspectives*, ed. R. C. Turner and R. G. Scaife (London, 1995), pp. 76–82

Hooke, D., 'Early Cotswold woodland', *Journal of Historical Geography* 4 (1978), pp. 333–41

Hooke, D., 'Anglo-Saxon landscapes of the West Midlands', *Journal of the English Place-Name Society* 11 (1978–9), pp. 3–23

Hooke, D., 'The Droitwich salt industry: an examination of the West Midland charter evidence', in *Anglo-Saxon Studies in Archaeology and History* 2, ed. J. Campbell, D. Brown and S. Hawkes, British Archaeological Reports, British Series 92 (Oxford, 1981), pp. 123–69

Hooke, D., *The Landscape of Anglo-Saxon Staffordshire: The Charter Evidence* (Keele, Staffs, 1983)

Hooke, D., *The Anglo-Saxon Landscape, The Kingdom of the Hwicce* (Manchester, 1985; repr. 2009)

Hooke, D., 'Regional variation in southern and central England in the Anglo-Saxon period and its relationship to land units and settlement', in *Anglo-Saxon Settlements*, ed. D. Hooke (Oxford, 1988), pp. 123–51

Hooke, D., 'Pre-Conquest woodland: its distribution and usage', *Agricultural History Review* 37 (1989), pp. 113–29

Hooke, D., *Worcestershire Anglo-Saxon Charter-Bounds* (Woodbridge, 1990)

Hooke, D., 'A note on the evidence for vineyards and orchards in Anglo-Saxon England', *Journal of Wine Research*, 1 (1990), pp. 77–80

Hooke, D., 'Early units of government in Herefordshire and Shropshire', *Anglo-Saxon Studies in Archaeology and History* 5, ed. W. Filmer-Sankey (Oxford, 1992), pp. 47–64

Hooke, D., 'Historical Landscapes Project: pilot study in methodologies: Oxfordshire', unpublished report for English Heritage (1993)

Hooke, D., *Pre-Conquest Charter-Bounds of Devon and Cornwall* (Woodbridge, 1994)

Hooke, D., 'The Early Charters of Kent', unpublished manuscript (1994)

Hooke, D., 'The administrative and settlement framework of early medieval Wessex', in *The Medieval Landscape of Wessex*, ed. M. Aston and C. Lewis (Oxford, 1994), pp. 83–95

Hooke, D., *The Landscape of Anglo-Saxon England* (London and New York, 1998)

Hooke, D., 'Medieval forests and parks in southern and central England', in *European Woods and Forests, Studies in Cultural History*, ed. C. Watkins (New York, 1998), pp. 19–32

Hooke, D., *Warwickshire Anglo-Saxon Charter Bounds* (Woodbridge, 1999)

Hooke, D., *England's Landscape. The West Midlands* (London, 2006)

Hooke, D., 'Early medieval woodland and the place-name term *lēah*', in *A Commodity of Good Names. Essays in Honour of Margaret Gelling*, ed. O. J. Padel and D. N. Parsons (Donington, 2008), pp. 365–76

Hooke, D., 'Recent views on the Worcestershire landscape', *Transactions of the Worcestershire Archaeological Society*, 3rd series 21 (2008), pp. 91–106

Hooke, D., 'Trees in Anglo-Saxon charters: some comments and some uncertainties', in *Old Names – New Growth. Proceedings of the 2nd ASPNS Conference, University of Graz, Austria, 6–10 June 2007, and Related Essays*, ed. P. Bierbaumer and H. W. Klug (Frankfurt am Main, 2009), pp. 90–3

Hooke, D., 'The woodland landscape of early medieval England', in *Anglo-Saxon Landscapes, II: Written Landscapes*, ed. N. Higham and M. Ryan (Woodbridge, forthcoming)

Hope, R. C., *Legendary Lore of the Holy Wells of England including Rivers, Lakes, Fountains and Springs* (London, 1893)

Hope-Taylor, B., *Yeavering: An Anglo-British Centre of Early Northumbria* (London, 1977)

Horovitz, D., *The Place-Names of Staffordshire* (Brewood, Staffordshire, 2005)

Howell, I., D. Bowsher, T. Dyson and N. Holder, *The London Guidhall: An Archaeological History of a Neighbourhood from Early Medieval to Modern Times*, MoLAS monograph 36 (London, 2007)

Howlett, D. R., *The Book of Letters of St Patrick the Bishop* (Dublin, 1994)

Hughes, G. B., *Living Crafts* (London, 1953)

Hughes, J. D., *Pan's Travail. Environmental Problems of the Ancient Greeks and Romans* (Baltimore, Mass., and London, 1994)

Hughes, J. D., 'Sacred groves of the ancient Mediterranean area: early conservation of biological diversity', in *Conserving the Sacred*, ed. P. S. Ramakrishnan, K. G. Saxena and U. M. Chandrashekara (1998), pp. 101–21

Hughes, J. D., and M. D. S. Chandran, 'Sacred groves around the earth: an overview', in *Conserving the Sacred*, ed. Ramakrishnan, Saxena and Chandrashekara (1998), pp. 71–86

Hutton, R., *The Pagan Religions of the Ancient British Isles. Their Nature and Legacy* (Oxford, 1991)

Hutton, R., *The Rise and Fall of Merry England: The Ritual Year, 1400–1700* (Oxford, 1994)

Hutton, R., *The Stations of the Sun, a History of the Ritual Year in Britain* (Oxford, 1996)

Hygin, *L'œuvre gromatique, Corpus agrimensorum Romanorum V Hyginus*, COST Action G2 (Luxembourg, 2000)

Jackson, J. K. H., *Studies in Early Celtic Nature Poetry* (Cambridge, 1935, repr. Philadelphia, 1977)

Jackson, J. K. H., *Language and History in Early Britain* (Edinburgh, 1953)

James, E., ed., *Gregory of Tours, Life of the Fathers* (Liverpool, 1985)

Jenkins, D., ed. and trans., *Hywel Dda, the Law* (Llandysul, Dyfed, 1990)

Johansson, C., *Old English Place-Names Containing lēah* (Stockholm, 1975)

Jolliffe, J. E. A., *Pre-feudal England: The Jutes* (London, 1933)

Jolly, K. L., *Popular Religion in Late Saxon England, Elf Charms in Context* (London and Chapel Hill, 1996)

Jones, A., ed., *The Jerusalem Bible* (London, 1966)

Jones, F., *The Holy Wells of Wales*, 2nd edn (Cardiff, 1954, repr. 1992)

Jones, G., 'Ghostly mentor, teacher of mysteries: Batholomew, Guthlac and the Apostle's cult in early medieval England', in *Medieval Monastic Education*, ed. G. Ferzoco and C. Muessig (Leicester, 2000), pp. 126–52

Joyce, P. W., *The Origin and History of Irish Names of Places*, 4th edn (Dublin, 1875)

Karamzin, N. M., *Istoriya gosudarstva rossiiskogo*, 12 vols, 5th edn (1842; repr. Moscow, 1989)

Katha Upanishad, VI: *The Upanishads. Translation from the Sanskrit with an Introduction by Juan Mascaró* (London/Harmondsworth, 1965)

Kelly, F., 'The Old English tree-list', *Celtica* 11 (1976), pp. 107–24

Kelly, S. E., ed., *Charters of St Augustine's Abbey Canterbury, and Minster-in-Thanet*, Anglo-Saxon Charters IV (Oxford, 1995)

Kelly, S. E., ed., *The Charters of Shaftesbury Abbey*, Anglo-Saxon Charters V (Oxford, 1996)

Kelly, S. E., ed., *The Charters of Selsey*, Anglo-Saxon Charters VI (Oxford, 1998)

Kelly, S. E., ed., *The Charters of Abingdon Abbey, Part 1*, Anglo-Saxon Charters VII (Oxford, 2000)

Kelly, S. E., *Charters of Abingdon Abbey, Part 2*, Anglo-Saxon Charters VIII (Oxford, 2001)

Kelly, S. E., *Charters of Malmesbury Abbey*, Anglo-Saxon Charters XI (Oxford, 2005)

Kelly, S. E., ed., *Charters of Bath and Wells*, Anglo-Saxon Charters XIII (Oxford, 2007)

Kemble, J. M.. *Codex diplomaticus aevi Saxonici*, 6 vols (London, 1839–48)

Kenward, H. K., and A. R. Hall, *The Archaeology of York, Volume 14: The Past Environment of York*, 14/7. Biological Evidence from Anglo-Scandinavian Deposits at 16–22 Coppergate (York 1995)

Ker, N. R., *A Catalogue of Manuscripts Containing Anglo-Saxon* (Oxford, 1957)

Kinsella, T., *The Tain* (Oxford, 1970)

Kitson, P. E., 'The root of the matter: OE *wyrt, wyrtwale, -a, wyrt(t)rum(a)* and cognates', in *Language, History and Linguistic Modelling: A Festschrift for Jacek Fisiak on his 60th birthday*, ed. R. Hickey and S. Puppel, vol. I (Berlin, 1997), pp. 127–41

Kozhanchikova, D. E., ed., *Stoglav, Council of Moscow* (1863, repr. St Petersburg, 1911)

Krapp, G. P., ed., *The Junius Manuscript*, Anglo-Saxon Poetic Records I (New York, 1931)

Krapp, G. P., ed., *The Paris Psalter and the Meters of Boethius*, Anglo-Saxon Poetic Records V (New York, 1932; London, 1933)

Krapp, G. P., ed., *The Vercelli Book*, Anglo-Saxon Poetic Records II (New York, 1932)

Krapp, G. P., and E. van K. Dobbie, eds, *The Exeter Book*, Anglo-Saxon Poetic Records III (New York, 1936)

Larrington, C., *The Poetic Edda, Translated with an Introduction and Notes* (Oxford, 1996)

Leather, E. M., *The Folk-Lore of Herefordshire* (Hereford and London, 1912, repr. Wakefield, 1973)

Lehmann, R. P. M., ed. and trans., *Early Irish Verse* (Austin, 1982)

Liebermann, F., ed., *Die Gesetze der Angelsächsen*, vol. I (Halle, 1903)

Logeman, H., ed., *The Rule of St Benet*, EETS, OS 90 (London, 1888)

Long, C. E., ed., *Diary of the Marches of the Royal Army during the Great Civil War Kept by Richard Symonds*, Camden Society 74 (London, 1859)

Loomis, C. G., *White Magic: An Introduction to the Folklore of Christian Legend* (Cambridge, Mass., 1948)

Losco-Bradley, P. M., and C. R. Salisbury, 'A medieval fish weir at Colwick, Nottinghamshire', *Transactions of the Thoroton Society of Nottinghamshire* 83 (1979), pp. 15–22

Love, R., ed. and trans., *Three Eleventh-Century Anglo-Latin Saints' Lives* (Oxford, 1996)

Loveday, R., *Inscribed across the Landscape. The Cursus Enigma* (Stroud, 2006)

Lowe, J., *Yew-trees of Great Britain and Ireland* (London, 1897)

Lucan, *Pharsalia*, trans. R. Graves (Harmondsworth, 1957)

Lucas, A. T., 'The sacred trees of Ireland', *Journal of the Cork Historical and Archaeological Society* 68 (1963), pp. 16–54

Mabey, R., *Flora Britannica. The Concise Edition* (London, 1998)

Mabillon, J., *Museum Italicum* (Paris, 1724)

Mackie, W. S., ed., *The Exeter Book, Part II*, poems IX–XXXII, EETS, OS 194 (London, 1934)

Maier, F., 'Das Kultbäumchen von Manching', *Germania* 68 (1990), pp. 129–65

Marshall, P., *Nature's Web, Rethinking our Place on Earth* (London, 1992)

Mawer, A., and F. M. Stenton, with F. T. S. Houghton, *The Place-Names of Worcestershire*, English Place-Name Society 4 (Cambridge, 1927)

Mawer, A., and F. M. Stenton, with J. E. B. Gover, *The Place-Names of Sussex, Part I*, English Place-Name Society 6 (Cambridge, 1929)

Mawer, A., and F. M. Stenton, with J. E. B. Gover, *The Place-Names of Sussex, Part II* (Cambridge, 1986), English Place-Name Society 8 (Cambridge, 1986)

McGurk, P., 'The labours of the months', in *An Eleventh-Century Anglo-Saxon Illustrated Miscellany: British Library Cotton Tiberius B. V, pt. 1*, ed. D. M. Dumville, M. R. Godden, and A. Knock, Early English Manuscripts in Facsimile, ed. G. Harlow, no. 21 (Copenhagen, 1983)

McIntyre, A., 'Tree culture', in A. Miles, *Silva. The Tree in Britain* (London, 1999), pp. 223–69

McManus, D., *A Guide to Ogam* (Maynooth, 1991)

Meaney, A. L., *Anglo-Saxon Amulets, Charms and Curing Stones* (Banbury, 1981)

Meaney, A. L., 'Ælfric and idolatry', *Journal of Religious History* 13 (1984), pp. 119–35

Menzies, W., *The History of Windsor Great Park and Windsor Forest* (London, 1864)

Metz, W., 'Das "gehagio regis" der Langobarden und die deutschen Hagenortsnamen', *Beiträge zur Namenforschung in Verbindung mit Ernst Dickenmann, herausgegeben von Hans Krahe* 5 (Heidelburg, 1954), pp. 39–51

Miller, S. ed., *Charters of the New Minster, Winchester*, Anglo-Saxon Charters IX (Oxford, 2001)

Miller, T., ed., *The Old English Version of Bede's Ecclesiastical History of the English People (Part 1)*, EETS, OS 95, 96 (London, 1891)

Millett, M., 'Excavations at Cowdery's Down, Basingstoke, 1978–1981', *Archaeological Journal* 140 (1983), pp. 151–279

Mills, A. D., *A Dictionary of English Place-Names* (Oxford, 1991)

Milner, J. E., *The Tree Book: The Indispensible Guide to Tree Facts, Crafts and Lore* (London, 1992)

Mitchell, A., *A Field Guide to the Trees of Britain* (London, 1978)

Mitchell, A., *Trees of Britain* (London, 1996)

Mitchell, B., *An Invitation to Old English and Anglo-Saxon England* (Oxford, 1995)

Mittuch, S., 'Medieval art of death and resurrection', *Current Archaeology* 209 (2007), pp. 34–40

Morris, C. A., *The Archaeology of York. Vol. 17, Fascicle 13, The Small Finds. Craft, Industry and Everyday Life; Wood and Woodworking in Anglo-Scandinavian and Medieval York* (York, 2000)

Morris, R., ed., *The Blickling Homilies*, EETS, OS 58, 63, 73 (1874, 1876, 1880; repr. as one vol. 1967)

Morris, R., *Churches in the Landscape* (London, 1989)

Morton, A., *The Trees of Shropshire* (Shrewsbury, 1986)

Morton, A., *Tree Heritage of Britain and Ireland* (Shrewsbury, 1998)

Muir, B. J., *The Exeter Anthology of Old English Poetry*, revised 2nd edn (Exeter, 2000)

Muir, R., *Ancient Trees, Living Landscapes* (Stroud, 2005)

Napier, A. S., and W. H. Stevenson, eds, *The Crawford Collection of Early Charters and Documents* (Oxford, 1895)

Nature Conservancy Council, *County Inventories of Ancient Woodlands* (Peterborough, various dates)

Neckel, G., *Edda: Die Lieder des Codex Regius nebst verwandten Denkmälern*, 4th edn (Heidelberg, 1962)

Nelson, P., 'An ancient box-wood casket', *Archaeologia* 86 (1937), pp. 91–100

Nennius, *British History and the Welsh Annals*, ed. and trans. J. Morris (London and Chichester, 1980)

Neville, J., *Representations of the Natural World in Old English Poetry* (Cambridge, 1999)

Nicholson, L. E., ed., *The Vercelli Book Homilies: Translations from the Anglo-Saxon* (London, 1991)

North, R., *Pagan Words and Christian Meanings* (Amsterdam and Atlanta, 1991)

O'Curry, E., *On the Manners and Customs of the Ancient Irish*: *A Series of Lectures Delivered by the Late Eugene O'Curry*, ed. W. K. Sullivan (London and Dublin, 1873)

O'Donovan, J., ed., *The Annals of the Kingdom of Ireland by the Four Masters*, 2nd edn (Dublin, 1856)

O'Donovan, M. A., ed., *The Charters of Sherborne*, Anglo-Saxon Charters III (Oxford, 1988)

Ó hÓgain, D., *The Sacred Isle. Belief and Religion in Pre-Christian Ireland* (Woodbridge, 1999)

O'Kelly, M. J., *Newgrange* (London, 1982)

Oliver, J., and J. Davies, 'Savernake Forest oaks', *Wiltshire Archaeological and Natural History Magazine* 94 (2001), p. 26

O'Loughlin, T., *St Patrick: The Man and his Works* (London, 1999)

Oppenheimer, S., *The Origins of the British. A Genetic Detective Story* (London, 2006)

Ordnance Survey, *Map of Dark Age Britain* (London, 1966)

Ordnance Survey Facsimiles, vol. II, ed. W. B. Sanders (Southampton, 1878–84)

Padel, O. J., *Cornish Place-Name Elements*, English Place-Name Society 56/57 (Cambridge, 1985)

Page, R. I., *Runes* (London, 1987)

Paterson, J. M., *Tree Wisdom* (London and San Francisco, 1996)

Payne, F. A., *King Alfred and Boethius* (Madison, Milwaukee and London, 1968)

Peterken, G. F., 'Development of vegetation in Staverton Park, Suffolk', *Field Studies* 3 (1969), pp. 1–39

Peterken, G. F., *Woodland Conservation and Management*, 2nd edn (London, 1993)

Philippson, E. A., *Germanisches Heidentum bei den Angelsachsen* (Leipzig, 1929)

Philpot, J. H., *The Sacred Tree in Religion and Myth* (London, 1897; Mineola, New York, 2004)

Pitts, M., 'Excavating the Sanctuary: new investigations on Overton Hill, Avebury', *Wiltshire Archaeological and Natural History Magazine* 94 (2001), pp. 1–23

Pliny, *Historia naturalis*, vol. V, book XVII, ed. H. Rackham (London, 1950)

Plummer, C., *Two of the Saxon Chronicles Parallel*, 2 vols (Oxford, 1892–9; reissued D. Whitelock, 1952)

Plummer, C., *Vitae sanctorum Hiberniae*, 2 vols (Oxford, 1910)

Pointereau, P., 'La diversité des systèmes arborés et des pratiques de gestion dans le sud de l'Europe: les dehesas ibériques et les hautains méditerranéens', 1er Colloque européen sur les trognes, Vendome 26–28 octobre 2006. Vendome: Maison Botanique, 2006: www.maisonbotanique.com

Pope, J. C., ed., *Homilies of Ælfric: A Supplementary Collection*, 2 vols, EETS, OS 259, 260 (London, 1967–8)

Prem, S. K., *The Yoga of the Kathopanishad* (Ahmedabad, 1982)

Price, E., 'East of Dean', *The Garden*, Journal of the Royal Horticultural Society 126, part 6 (2001), pp. 456–9

Pryor, F., *Seahenge. New Discoveries in Prehistoric Britain* (London, 2001)

Rackham, O., *Trees and Woodland in the British Landscape* (London, 1976)

Rackham, O., *Ancient Woodland, its History, Vegetation and Uses in England* (London, 1980)

Rackham, O., *The History of the Countryside* (London, 1986)

Rackham, O., *Trees and Woodland in the British Landscape*, revised edn (London, 1990, 1996)

Rackham, O., 'Savanna in Europe', in *The Ecological History of European Forests*, ed. K. Kirby and C. Watkins (Wallingford, 1998), pp. 1–24

Rackham, O., *Ancient Woodland, its History, Vegetation and Uses in England*, new edn (Dalbeattie, Kirkcudbrightshire, 2003)

Radford, E., and M. A. Radford, revised C. Hole, *Encyclopedia of Superstitions* (London, 1961)

Ramakrishnan, P. S., K. G. Saxena and U. M. Chandrashekara, eds, *Conserving the Sacred for Biodiversity Management* (Enfield, New Hampshire, 1998)

Rattue, J., *The Living Stream. Holy Wells in Historical Context* (Woodbridge, 1995)

Reader's Digest, *Field Guide to the Trees and Shrubs of Britain* (London, 1981)

Reed, M. *The Buckinghamshire Landscape* (London, 1979)

Rees, M., *Celtic Saints. Passionate Wanderers* (London, 2000)

Reichel-Dolmatoff, E., 'The landscape in the cosmoscape, and sacred sites and species among the Tanumuka and Yukuna Indiands (north-west Amazon)', in *Sacred Species and Sites, Advances in Biocultural Conservation*, ed. G. Pungetti, G. Oviedo and D. Hooke (Cambridge, forthcoming)

Reynolds, A., *Later Anglo-Saxon England, Life and Landscape* (Stroud, 1999)

Rhodin, A. L., L. Gren and V. Lindblom, 'Liljestenarna och Sveriges kristnande från Bysans', *Forvännen* 95 (2000), pp. 165–81

Richardson, K. M., 'Excavations in Hungsate, York', *Archaeological Journal* 116 (1959), pp. 51–114

Richens, R. H., *Elm* (Cambridge: 1983)

Ripper, S., and L. P. Cooper, *The Hemington Bridges: The Excavation of Three Medieval Bridges at Hemington Quarry, near Castle Donington, Leicestershire*, Leicester Archaeology Monograph 16 (Leicester, 2009)

Rivet, A. L. F., and C. Smith, *The Place-Names of Roman Britain* (London, 1979)

Roberts, B. K., and S. Wrathmell, 'Peoples of wood and plain: an exploration of national and local regional contrasts', in *Landscape, the Richest Historical Record*, ed. D. Hooke, Society for Landscape Studies (Birmingham, 2000), pp. 85–95

Roberts, B. K., and S. Wrathmell, *An Atlas of Rural Settlement in England* (London, 2000)

Roberts, B. K., and S. Wrathmell, *Region and Place. A Study of English Rural Settlement* (London, 2002)

Robertson, A. J., ed. and trans., *The Laws of the Kings of England from Edmund to Henry I* (Cambridge, 1925)

Robertson, A. J., *Anglo-Saxon Charters* (Cambridge, 1939)

Robinson, J. Armitage, *Gilbert Crispin, Abbot of Westminster* (Cambridge, 1911)

Rollason, D. W., 'The cults of murdered royal saints in Anglo-Saxon England', in *Anglo-Saxon England*, ed. P. Clemoes, 11 (Cambridge, 1983), pp. 1–22

Ross A., *Pagan Celtic Britain: Studies in Iconography and Tradition* (London, 1974)

Rumble, A. R., 'The Wheathampstead (Herts.) charter-bounds, A.D. 1060: a corrected text and notes on the boundary-points', *Journal of English Place-Name Studies* 9 (1977), pp. 6–11

Rutherford-Davis, K., *Britons and Saxons. The Chiltern Region 400–700* (Chichester, 1982)

Salway, P., *Roman Britain* (London, 1981)

Sandars, N. K., trans., *The Epic of Gilgamesh* (Harmondsworth, 1960)

Saraswati, B., 'The logos and the mythos of the sacred grove', in *Conserving the Sacred*, ed. Ramakrishnan, Saxena and Chandrashekara (1998), pp. 31–46

Sawyer, P. H., ed., *Charters of Burton Abbey*, Anglo-Saxon Charters II (Oxford, 1979)

Sawyer, P. H., *Anglo-Saxon Charters. An Annotated List and Bibliography* (London, 1968)

Schama, S., *Landscape and Memory* (London, 1995)

Schmeidler, B., ed., *Adam von Bremen, Hamburgische Kirchengeschichte* (Hanover, 1917)

Schneider, K., *Die germanischen Runennamen: Versuch einer Gesamtdeutung* (Meisenheim am Glan, 1956)

Scragg, D. G., ed., *The Vercelli Homilies and Related Texts*, EETS, OS 300 (Oxford, 1992)

Simek, R., *Dictionary of Northern Mythology* (English edn of *Lexicon der germanischen Mythologie*, 1984) (Cambridge, 1993)

Skeat, W. W., ed. *The Four Gospels in Anglo-Saxon, Northumbrian and Old Mercian Versions* (Cambridge, 1871–87; repr. Darmstadt, 1970)

Skeat, W. W., ed., *Ælfric's Lives of the Saints I, Vol. I*, EETS, OS 76 (London, 1881; repr. 2003)

Skeat, W. W., ed., *Ælfric's Lives of the Saints, Vol. II*, EETS, OS 94, 114 (London, 1890; repr. 2003)

Skinner, J., *The Confession of St Patrick and Letter to Coroticus* (New York, 1998)

Smith, A. H., *English Place-Name Elements, Part I*, English Place-Name Society 25 (Cambridge, 1956)

Smith, A. H., *English Place-Name Elements, Part II*, English Place-Name Society 26 (Cambridge, 1956)

Smith, A. H., *The Place-Names of the West Riding, Part II*, English Place-Name Society 31 (Cambridge, 1961)

Smith, A. H., *The Place-Names of the West Riding, Part III*, English Place-Name Society 32 (Cambridge, 1961)

Smith, A. H., *The Place-Names of the West Riding, Part IV*, English Place-Name Society 33 (Cambridge, 1961)

Smith, A. H., *The Place-Names of the West Riding, Part VI*, English Place-Name Society 35 (Cambridge, 1961)

Smith, A. H., *The Place-Names of Gloucestershire, Part I*, English Place-Name Society 38 (Cambridge, 1964)

Smith, A. H., *The Place-Names of Gloucestershire, Part II*, English Place-Name Society 39 (Cambridge, 1964)

Smith, A. H., *The Place-Names of Gloucestershire, Part IV*, English Place-Name Society 41 (Cambridge, 1965)

Smith, A. H., *The Place-Names of Westmorland, Part I*, English Place-Name Society 42 (Cambridge, 1967)

Smith, B., *A History of Malvern* (Leicester, 1964)

Smith, J. M. H., 'Oral and written; saints, miracles and relics in Brittany c.850–1250', *Speculum* 65 (1990), pp. 309–43

Smith, R., 2001. 'The Russian bear, and others', unpublished paper, University of Birmingham Institute for Advanced Research in Arts and Social Science

Stead, I. M., J. B. Bourke and D. Brothwell, eds, *Lindow Man: The Body in the Bog* (Ithaca, New York and London, 1986)

Stenton, F. M., *The Latin Charters of the Anglo-Saxon Period* (Oxford, 1955)

Stenton, F. M., *Anglo-Saxon England*, 3rd edn (Oxford, 1971)

Stevenson, W. H., ed., *Asser's Life of King Alfred (De rebus gestis Aelfredi)* (Oxford, 1904)

Stokes, J., and D. Rodger, *The Heritage Trees* (London, 2004)

Stokes, W., ed. and trans., 'The birth and life of St. Moling', *Revue celtique* 27 (1906)

Storms, G., *Anglo-Saxon Magic* (The Hague, 1948)

Stuart, D., *Dangerous Garden. The Quest for Plants to Change our Lives* (London, 2004)

Sundqvist, O., *Freyr's Offspring. Rulers and Religion in Ancient Svea Society*, Historia Religionum 21 (Uppsala, 2002)

Swanton, M., *Beowulf, Edited with an Introduction, Notes and a New Prose Translation* (Manchester, 1978)

Swanton, M., ed., *Anglo-Saxon Prose* (Letchworth, 1975)

Swanton, M. J., ed. and trans., *The Anglo-Saxon Chronicle* (London, 1996)

Sweet, H., ed., *King Alfred's West-Saxon Version of Gregory's Pastoral Care* I–II, EETS, OS 45 (London, 1871)

Sweet, H., *King Alfred's Orosius*, EETS, OS 79 (London, 1883, repr. 1959).

Szarmach, P. E., ed., *Vercelli Homilies, IX–XXIII* (Toronto, 1981)

Tacitus, Cornelius, *Dialogus, Agricola, Germania*, trans. W. Peterson and M. Hutton, Loeb Classical Library (London, 1914)

Tacitus, Cornelius, *The Agricola and the Germania*, trans. H. Mattingly; revised trans. S. A. Handford (London, 1970)

Tacitus, Cornelius, *Annals, Book I*, ed. N. P. Miller (London, 1959)

Talbot, C. H., ed. and trans., *The Anglo-Saxon Missionaries in Germany* (London and New York, 1954)

Talbot, C. H., 'Some notes on Anglo-Saxon medicine', *Medical History* 9 (1965), pp. 156–69

Talbot, C. H., *Medicine in Medieval England* (London, 1967)

Taylor, C. C., 'The Saxon boundaries of Frustfield', *Wiltshire Archaeological Magazine* 59 (1964), pp. 110–15

Taylor, L., 'The Old English Bede texts: negotiating the interface', in *Proceedings of Borderline Interdisciplinary Postgraduate Conference 2003*, ed. J. Nyhan, C. Griffin and K. Rooney, www.epu.ucc.ie/borderlines/taylor.

Tebbutt, C. F., 'A Middle Saxon iron-smelting site at Millbrook, Ashdown Forest, Sussex', *Sussex Archaeological Collections* 120 (1982), pp. 19–36

Tester, A., S. Anderson and R. A. Carr, 'A high status Middle Saxon settlement on the Fen Edge: excavations at Brandon 1979–88' (forthcoming)

Thacker, C., *The History of Gardens* (London, 1985)

Thorn, F., and C. Thorn, eds, *Domesday Book, 16, Worcestershire* (Chichester, 1982)

Thorpe, B., ed., *Ancient Laws and Institutes of England, Monumenta Ecclesiastica* (London, 1840)

Thorpe, B., ed., *The Sermones Catholici, or, Homilies of Ælfric: In the Original Anglo-Saxon with an English Version*, 2 vols (London, 1844, 1846)

Thorpe, B., *Diplomatarium Anglicum aevi Saxonici* (London, 1865)

Tille, A., *Yule and Christmas, Their Place in the Germanic Year* (1889; London, 1899)

Todd, M., *The Barbarians, Goths, Franks and Vandals* (London and New York, 1972, 1980)

Todd, M., *The South-West to AD 1000* (London, 1987)

Tolley, C., *Shamanism in Norse Myth and Magic*, Folklore Fellows' Communications 296–7, 2 vols (Helsinki, 2009)

Toulmin Smith, L., ed., *The Itinerary of John Leland in or about the Years 1535–1543, Part V* (London, 1964)

Tree Register: www.treeregister.org/pdf/Champion%20Trees

Tschan, F. J., trans., *Adam of Bremen: History of the Archbishops of Hamburg-Bremen*, Records of Civilization 53 (New York, 1959)

Turner, A. G. C. 'Some Old English passages relating to the episcopal manor of Taunton', *Proceedings of the Somerset and Natural History Society* 98 (1953), pp. 118–26

Turner, J., 'The *Tilia* decline: an anthropogenic interpretation', *New Phytologist* 61 (1962), pp. 328–41

Vannucci, M., 'Sacredness and sacred forests', in *Conserving the Sacred*, ed. Ramakrishnan, Saxena and Chandrashekara (1998), pp. 17–29

Vera, F. W. M., *Grazing Ecology and Forest History* (Wallingford and New York, 2000)

The Victoria History of the Counties of England. A History of Hampshire and the Isle of Wight, Volume III, ed. W. Page (London, 1908)

The Victoria History of the Counties of England. A History of the County of Worcester, Volume II, ed. J. W. Willis-Bund and W. Page (London, 1906)

Virgil, *Georgics, Edited with a Commentary*, ed. R. A. B. Mynors (Oxford, 1969)

Wade-Evans, A. W., *Welsh Medieval Law* (Oxford, 1909)

Wager, S. J., *Woods, Wolds and Groves. The Woodland of Medieval Warwickshire*, British Archaeological Reports, British Series 269 (Oxford, 1998)

Walker, M. F., and J. A. Taylor, 'Post-Neolithic vegetation changes in the western Rhinogau, Gwynedd, north-west Wales', *Transactions of the Institute of British Geographers*, new series 1 (1976), pp. 323–45

Wallenberg, J. K., *Kentish Place-Names*, Uppsala Universitets Årsskrift (Uppsala, 1931)

Warner, R. D-N., ed., *Early English Homilies from the Twelfth-Century MS. Vespasian D.XIV*, EETS, OS 152 (London, 1917)

Warner, R. D-N., ed., *Early English Homilies from the Twelfth Century MS. Vespasian D.xiv, Part 1*, EETS, OS 152 (London, 1962)

Watkins, C., *Woodland Management and Conservation (Britain's Ancient Woodland)*, Nature Conservancy Council (Newton Abbot and London, 1990)

Watson, A., 'The king, the poet and the sacred tree', *Études celtiques* 18 (1981), pp. 165–80

Watts, V., *The Cambridge Dictionary of English Place-Names* (Cambridge, 2004)

Weiss. P., *Kandinsky and Old Russia: The Artist as Ethnographer and Shaman* (New Haven and London, 1995)

Welldon-Finn, R., 'Hampshire', in *The Domesday Geography of South-East England*, ed. H. C. Darby and E. M. J. Campbell (Cambridge, 1971), pp. 287–363

West, S., *West Stow. The Anglo-Saxon Village*, 2 vols, East Anglian Archaeology 24 (Ipswich, 1985)

White, G., *The Natural History and Antiquities of Selborne* (London, 1789; repr. Menston, 1972)

Whitelock, D., *Anglo-Saxon Wills* (Cambridge, 1930)

Whitelock, D., *English Historical Documents, Vol. 1, c. 500–1042* (London, 1955, repr. 1979)

Whitelock, D., 'Wulfstan and the so-called Laws of Edward and Guthrum', *English Historical Review* 56 (London, 1941), pp. 1–21 (repr. in Whitelock, *History, Law and Literature*, 1981, XIV)

Whitelock, D., 'Wulfstan at York', in *Franciplegius, Medieval and Linguistic Studies in Honor of Francis Peabody Magoun, Jr*, ed. J. B. Bessinger Jr and R. P. Creed (New York, 1965), pp. 214–31 (repr. in Whitelock, *History, Law and Literature*, 1981, XV)

Whitelock, D., *History, Law and Literature in 10th–11th Century England* (London, 1981)

Whitelock, D., M. Brett and C. N. L. Brooke, eds, *Councils and Synods with other Documents Relating to the English Church, A.D. 871–1204, Part I, 871–1066* (Oxford, 1981)

Wightman, E. M., *Gallia Belgica* (London, 1985)

Wildhagen, K., *Der Cambridger Psalter* (Hamburg, 1910)

Wilks, J. H., *Trees of the British Isles in History and Legend* (London, 1972)

William of Malmesbury's Life of St. Wulfstan, Bishop of Worcester, ed. J. H. F. Peile (Oxford, 1934)

Williams, A., and G. H. Martin, eds, *Domeday Book. A Complete Translation* (London, 1992)

Wilson, D. M., 'Craft and industry', in *The Archaeology of Anglo-Saxon England*, ed. D. M. Wilson (Cambridge, 1976), pp. 253–81

Wirth, H., *Die heilige Urschrift der Menscheot*, Mutter Erde Verlang (Faruenberg, 1979)

Witney, K. P., *The Jutish Forest: A Study of the Weald of Kent from 450 to 1380 AD* (London, 1976)

Woodcock, A., *Liminal Images. Aspects of Medieval Architectural Sculpture in the South of England from the Eleventh to the Sixteenth Centuries*, British Archaeological Reports, British Series 386 (Oxford, 2005)

Woodward, A., and P. Leach, *The Uley Shrines: Excavation of a Ritual Complex on West Hill, Uley, Gloucestershire* (London, 1993)

Wormald, P., *The Making of English Law: King Alfred to the Twelfth Century, I: Legislation and its Limits* (Oxford, 1999)

Wright, T., ed., *A Volume of Vocabularies . . . from the Tenth Century to the Fifteenth* (London, 1857)

Yeates, S. J., *Religion, Community and Territory. Defining Religion in the Severn Valley and Adjacent Hills from the Iron Age to the Early Medieval Period, Vol I*, British Archaeological Reports, British Series 411(i) (Oxford, 2006)

INDEX

Page numbers in italics indicate tables or illustrations

ANGLO-SAXON STUDIES